CHURCHES TO VISIT IN SCOTLAND

HOLY TRINITY EPISCOPAL CHURCH, MELROSE

SCOTLAND'S CHURCHES SCHEME
gratefully acknowledges the sponsorship
provided by Sir Fraser and Lady Morrison
towards the production of this book

CHURCHES TO VISIT IN SCOTLAND

Illustrated by John R Hume

ST VINCENT STREET – MILTON FREE CHURCH, GLASGOW

Published on behalf of Scotland's Churches Scheme
by NMS Publishing Limited

Published on behalf of
SCOTLAND'S CHURCHES SCHEME
by
NMS PUBLISHING LIMITED
National Museums of Scotland, Chambers Street, Edinburgh EH1 1JF

Paperback ISBN 1 901663 78 7

British Library Cataloguing in Publication Data
A catalogue record for this book is available from the British Library.

Designed by Mark Blackadder.
Typeset in Ehrhardt and Gill Sans.

DIRECTOR
Dr Brian Fraser BA PhD FIPD

Office: Dunedin, Holehouse Road, Eaglesham, Glasgow G76 0JF
Telephone: 01355 302416 *Fax*: 01355 303181
E-mail: fraser@dunedin67.freeserve.co.uk
Website: http://churchnet.ucsm.ac.uk/scotchurch/
Registered Charity Number: SC 022868

FRONT COVER PHOTOGRAPH
Dalserf Parish Church, South Lanarkshire. Photograph © RCAHMS
BACK COVER PHOTOGRAPHS
Pluscarden Abbey, Elgin (left). Photograph © RCAHMS
St Michael's Parish Church, Linlithgow (right). Photograph © James Gardiner
SPINE PHOTOGRAPH
St Peter in Chains RC Church, Ardrossan. Photograph © George McGrattan

Printed in Scotland by Bell & Bain Ltd, Glasgow.

CONTENTS

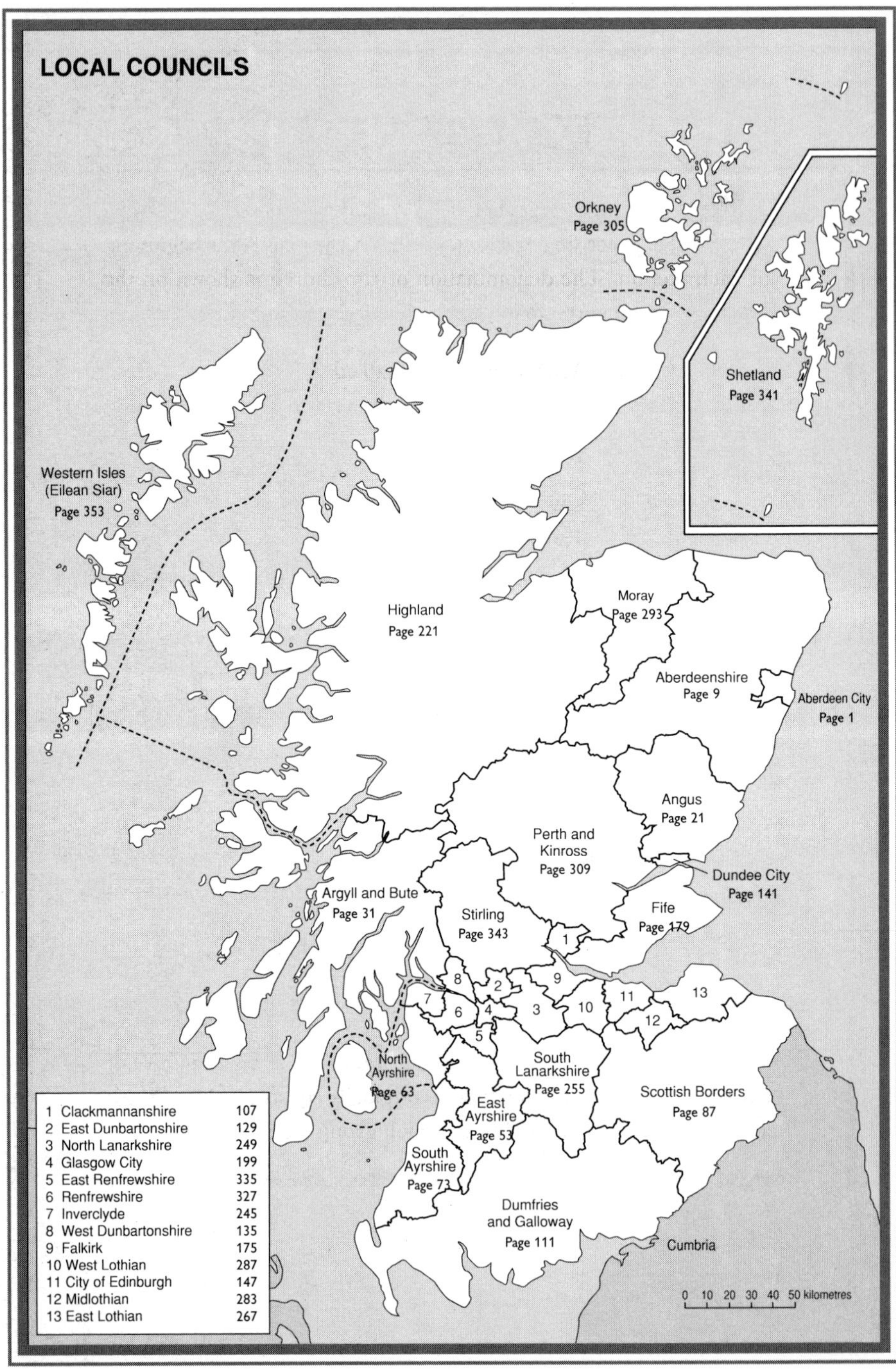

LOCAL COUNCILS
Orkney
Page 305
Shetland
Page 341
Western Isles
(Eilean Siar)
Page 353
Highland
Page 221
Moray
Page 293
Aberdeenshire
Page 9
Aberdeen City
Page 1
Angus
Page 21
Perth and
Kinross
Page 309
Dundee City
Page 141
Argyll and Bute
Page 31
Stirling
Page 343
Fife
Page 179
North
Ayrshire
Page 63
South
Lanarkshire
Page 255
East
Ayrshire
Page 53
Scottish Borders
Page 87
South
Ayrshire
Page 73
Dumfries
and Galloway
Page 111
Cumbria
0 10 20 30 40 50 kilometres
1 Clackmannanshire 107
2 East Dunbartonshire 129
3 North Lanarkshire 249
4 Glasgow City 199
5 East Renfrewshire 335
6 Renfrewshire 327
7 Inverclyde 245
8 West Dunbartonshire 135
9 Falkirk 175
10 West Lothian 287
11 City of Edinburgh 147
12 Midlothian 283
13 East Lothian 267

HOW TO USE THIS GUIDE

Entries are arranged alphabetically by council and then by locality. The number preceding each entry refers to the map at the beginning of each section. The denomination of the church is shown on the last line of each entry, followed by the relevant symbols:

- Access for partially abled
- Hearing induction loop for the deaf
- Welcomers and guides on duty
- Guidebooks and souvenirs
- Toilet for the disabled
- Features for children/link with schools
- Refreshments
- Toilets on premises
- **A** Category A Listing
- **B** Category B Listing
- **C** Category C Listing

Category A: Buildings of national or more than local importance, either architectural or historic, or fine little-altered examples of some particular period, style or type.
Category B: Buildings of regional or more than local importance, or major examples of some particular period, style or building type which may have been altered.
Category C: Buildings of local importance, or lesser examples of any period style, or building type, as originally constructed or altered; and simple traditional buildings which group well with others.

The information appearing in the gazetteer of this guidebook is supplied by the participating churches. While this is believed to be correct at the time of going to press, Scotland's Churches Scheme cannot accept any responsibility for its accuracy.

SCOTLAND'S CHURCHES SCHEME

Serving Churches of all denominations in Scotland

AIMS AND PURPOSES

1.

To promote spiritual understanding by enabling the public to appreciate all buildings designed for worship and active as living churches

2.

To advance the education of the public in history, architecture and other environmental subjects through the study of historic church buildings of all denominations in Scotland, their contents and environs

3.

To encourage co-operation among the churches themselves and between them and their local communities

4.

To publish details of churches open to visitors through a handbook *Churches to Visit in Scotland* as a guide for visitors, and to encourage support for the churches visited through donations, especially for specific appeals

5.

To receive donations for churches, in particular or in general, in order to provide when requested advice on the care and reception of visitors and the provision of historical and other information

6.

To promote the common purpose of mission through the ministry of welcome for visitors, tourists and pilgrims

FOREWORD

Scottish Stained Glass

It is a sad consequence of Humanity's restless search for knowledge and understanding that we leave in the wake of that journey so many broken artefacts of previous similar endeavours.

A walk amid the ruins of St Andrews Cathedral, and some meditation on the spot where once the famous shrine to our Patron Saint attracted pilgrims from every corner of Christendom, brings one to a realisation that, in 16th-century Scotland, a new order was achieved at a great price.

Other forces were equally disastrous to our art heritage. The 'rough wooing' laid waste our Borders Abbeys. The ambitions of the Wolf of Badenoch despoiled Pluscarden Priory and Elgin Cathedral – 'The Lantern of the North' – and our Union with England's crown in 1603 left James VI's Castillian Band with no one to sing to.

Under Scotland's Stuart Kings – especially James III, IV and V – late Medieval and Early Renaissance art flourished out of all proportion to our position on the periphery of Europe. Yet so much is lost. What other masterpieces came from Flanders at the time of Hugh van der Goes Trinity Alterpiece? How many precious breviaries and choir-books perished amid the flames of the Reformation?

It is only in the last 20 years that inspired scholarship has made us aware that in Robert Carver, Scotland had a musician the equal to any of his contemporaries in Tudor England, and whose harmonic daring put him with the best in the Courts of Flanders, Burgundy and Spain. Yet only one choir-book and a few motets by his contemporaries remain to tantalise our ears. 'The rest is silence'.

Of our Pre-Reformation stained glass, only the heraldic glass of c.1506 remains *in situ* in the Magdalen Chapel in Edinburgh's Cowgate. Yet it is no idle speculation to believe that St Andrews Cathedral must have glowed with glass from the 13th century –

The Golden Age. It was consecrated in 1317, perhaps in thanksgiving for Bannockburn! Its building must have coincided with the zeal of David de Bernam who, in the mid-13th century, founded over 150 churches. He had close links with France and would have known Chartres, St Denis, and the other great Cathedrals of the Isle de France. Chartres has one tragic, tangible link with Scotland that we know of. Its great South Transept Rose window was gifted by the Comte de Dreux – a town near Chartres. He is depicted along with his family on the window, one of whom was Yolande de Dreux, second wife of Alexander III of Scotland – the King who died riding to be with his young bride and with whose death 'oor Gawd wis changit into lead'.

Was that marriage perhaps commemorated in glass at St Andrews? It was one of Europe's largest cathedrals. It stood as a place of special pilgrimage along with Santiago de Compostela. French glaziers travelled the length and breadth of Europe – there is in York Minster a panel of a Jesse Tree window which is so similar to one in Chatrtres that one can only believe it to be the work of the same band of craftsmen who travelled across Europe throughout the Middle ages.

Although other countries in Europe contributed to the great dawning of stained glass as an art form in the 12th and 13th centuries, it is generally recognised that it was perfected in Norman France. One man especially, through the force of his personality and imagination, initiated the use of stained glass, not just as decoration in his cathedral of St Denis, but as a vehicle for his mystical search for God through the metaphysics of light.

Light for the Abbé Suget was the means by which Mankind moved out of his earthly existence into an awareness of external things. He was not alone in this and gathered around him a band of scholars – mainly Benedictine – who believed that the contemplation of exquisite carved objects (especially when showered in coloured light) led to an awareness of the Godhead. His contemporary, Bernard of Clairvaux, took a very different view, believing that Art distracted us from a close communion with God.

An echo of this argument must have resounded in the churches and abbeys of Scotland around the year 1560, and it still continues to a lesser extent this day.

Suget's Cathedral at St Denis became the prototype for the magnificent buildings which mushroomed across Europe in the 12th and 13th centuries. In their building, they inspired a unique synthesis of the Arts, the Sciences, Philosophy and Faith which today we loosely label 'Gothic'.

Suget himself was a mystic. He was fascinated by the power of light pouring through stained glass 'transforming that which is material into something immaterial'. He was not alone in this. Bishop Grossetete of Lincoln and Dante came to hold similar views on the metaphysics of light.

Stained glass windows to the medieval mind were therefore not merely illustrations of Biblical stories or depictions of Christ and His Saints. Their primary purpose was to transform a building into a kaleidoscope of coloured light – a vision of a 'new Heaven and a new Earth'. Windows were not openings in a wall, but a rainbow bridge of precious jewels unifying the entire building and leading one to a greater awareness of the Living God.

It is only in this present century that stained glass has regained some of that abstract power which transcends mere representation. From its pre-eminent position in the 13th century, stained glass went into a long decline as it was absorbed into the pursuits of Renaissance ideals. Experiments in perfecting an illusion of the Third Dimension punched great holes in the walls of religious buildings. Greek and Classical concepts replaced medieval mysticism until stained glass all but disappeared as a significant art form until the Gothic revival of the mid-19th century.

Even then there was little real understanding of the primary function of stained glass. A recent exhibition of a few of the Munich glass artists who in the mid-19th century were commissioned to reglaze Glasgow Cathedral underlines how far glaziers at that time were from an understanding of the ideals of Gothic Art and Philosophy. While one can only stand in awe at the consumate craftsmanship of Munich's cutters, painters and leaders, the final impression is that Glasgow's magnificent Cathedral lauded by Nicholas Pesvner as the supreme example of the first pointed 'English' Gothic – must have looked more like the interior of a Baroque palace.

Lead, which in the 13th century was regarded as every bit as essential as the glass itself, was in the mid-19th century relegated to a very minor role – a lonely thin black line skating its way around a white cloud in a blue sky – whereas the lead should be conceived as a dark black web which adds brilliance to the web-like quality of the glass.

By the beginning of the 20th century a new awareness of the essential qualities of stained glass was widespread in Scotland. The Arts and Crafts movement encouraged a new generation of innovative artists to rediscover the force and power of stained glass.

The most notable artist of this generation was Douglas Strachan and his work can be seen in many churches throughout the nation. This work inspired many artists to follow in his footsteps so that Scotland's churches, which 150 years ago were somewhat sombre and colourless places, are now ablaze with rich colours from fine artists and craftsmen and women too numerous to mention.

And what of stained glass in Scotland today? In every respect the future is one of optimism and a new sense of adventure. If, as I believe, Art is the '*speculum mundi*', then stained glass in Scotland now, along with the other Arts, reflects the new sense of confidence which is evolving out of Scotland's rediscovery of Nationhood.

It has been a long, slow journey born out of the traumas of the First World War. One has only to read Hugh McDiarmid, Edwin Muir and Lewis Grassic Gibbon to realise that Scotland mourned the loss of Empire with a voice far different from that of her southern neighbour. In the visual arts the Scottish Colourists found inspiration in France – shades of the 'Auld Alliance'. In glass, the Strachan brothers, Alf Webster and Herbert Hendrie, were all moved by the horrors of war to seek out a style in which colour was the dominant factor, in a highly emotional way reminiscent of the 13th-century masters.

The Second World War accelerated the move towards greater abstraction – for example, in the work of William Wilson. Sadie McLellan found her early inspiration in the work of Fernand Leger. She went on to produce the great Rose Window in Pluscarden Abbey in Dalles de Verre, a medium she also exploited with considerable success in Coia's post-modern churches. Her husband, Walter Pritchard, a muralist and stained-glass artist of great talent, became Head of that Department in the Glasgow School of Art – one of the most inspiring teachers, with interests ranging far beyond the visual arts.

So the future is bright – not just orange but in glass of all the colours of the rainbow – and provides an arch which spans the centuries and illumines our churches.

There is an index at the back of this excellent book. Let it be your passport on journeys of discovery. Seek out the names of those whose work excites you; let them lead you into Scotland's churches. Each building is a small Art Gallery and, as in all Art Galleries, works by other artists will demand attention and encourage further rewarding study. You will find other artists who, like me, fell victim to the wonder of God's light filtered through a web of lead and coloured glass.

Crear McCartney
STAINED GLASS ARTIST

SCOTLAND'S CHURCHES SCHEME

SCOTLAND'S CHURCHES SCHEME

LOCAL REPRESENTATIVES

Mrs Elizabeth Beaton, *Moray*
Mrs Margaret Beveridge, *Lothian*
Mrs Jane Boyd, *Glasgow*
Mrs Fiona Cameron, *Aberdeen/Press and Media*
Sheriff and Mrs Vincent Canavan, *North Lanarkshire*
Mr and Mrs Robert Cormack, *Orkney*
Mr Michael Dunlop, *Galloway*
Mrs Beatrice Fawkes, *Aberdeenshire*
Miss Joan Fish, *Ayrshire*
Mr Sandy Gilchrist, *Tweedale/Clydesdale*
Mr Michael Gossip, *Argyll & Bute*
Mrs Lyndall Leet, *North Highland*
Mr Norman McGilvray, *Renfrewshire*
Ms Atisha McGregor Auld, *West Highland/Western Isles*
Mr Ian Milne, *Inverclyde*
Mr Alan Naylor, *Falkirk*
Mrs Mary Reid, *Borders*
Mrs Marion Smith, *Dunbartonshire*
Mr Louis Stott, *Perthshire/Stirlingshire*
The Rev J W Scott, *Dumfriesshire*
The Rev Malcolm Trew, *Fife*
The Rev Peter Youngson, *Angus*

DIRECTOR

Dr Brian M Fraser

PREFACE

From the Chairman, Robin Blair LVO WS

Scotland's Churches Scheme was formed in 1994 as a charitable trust with the objective of improving the accessibility of Scotland's ecclesiastical heritage. This is the seventh edition of *Churches to Visit in Scotland*. It includes up to date details of all the churches who are members of the Scheme including 118 churches who have joined the Scheme since the publication of the last edition.

Scotland's Churches Scheme is unique. There is no other organisation in the world which provides information about the accessibility to visitors of religious buildings in any geographical area across such a range of denominations.

The Scheme has members from the Church of Scotland, the Roman Catholic Church, the Scottish Episcopal Church, the Free Church, the Baptist, Methodist and United Reformed Churches as well as the Greek Orthodox and Jewish Churches. We are also delighted to have a number of inter-denominational and ecumenical churches. We are proud to be able to provide a common bond to such a diverse range of interests.

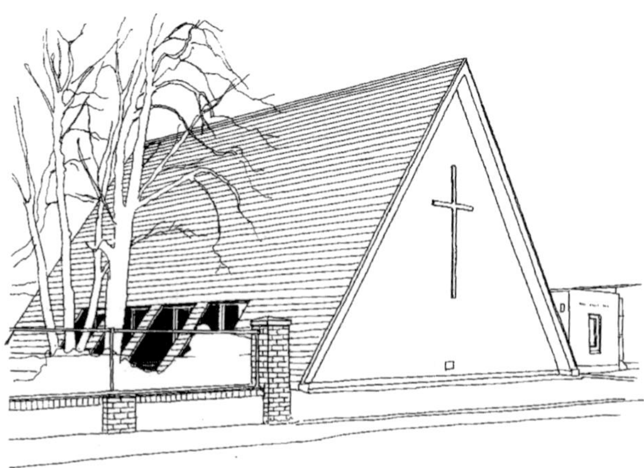

ROSYTH METHODIST CHURCH

THOMAS COATS MEMORIAL BAPTIST CHURCH, PAISLEY

Scotland's Churches Scheme does a great deal more than simply publish this Guide. We provide assistance in a number of ways to our member churches to help them in welcoming visitors. We have Local Representatives covering the whole of Scotland who work with the Director of the Scheme in providing advice on such topics as stewarding, promotion and interpretation, and historical research. The first 'how-to' booklets in a planned series have been well received – *How to Research your Church's History* and *How to Present your Church's Story*. In another area of activity, member churches are eligible to apply for grants from the Scheme towards costs incurred in having the organ played for specific events.

In each edition of this Guide we have highlighted some aspect of Scotland's ecclesiastical heritage. In this edition an excellent article by Crear McCartney appears on page ix in relation to stained glass.

I hope that you will enjoy the information and the illustrations in this Guide and that you will find it a useful companion wherever you happen to be in Scotland.

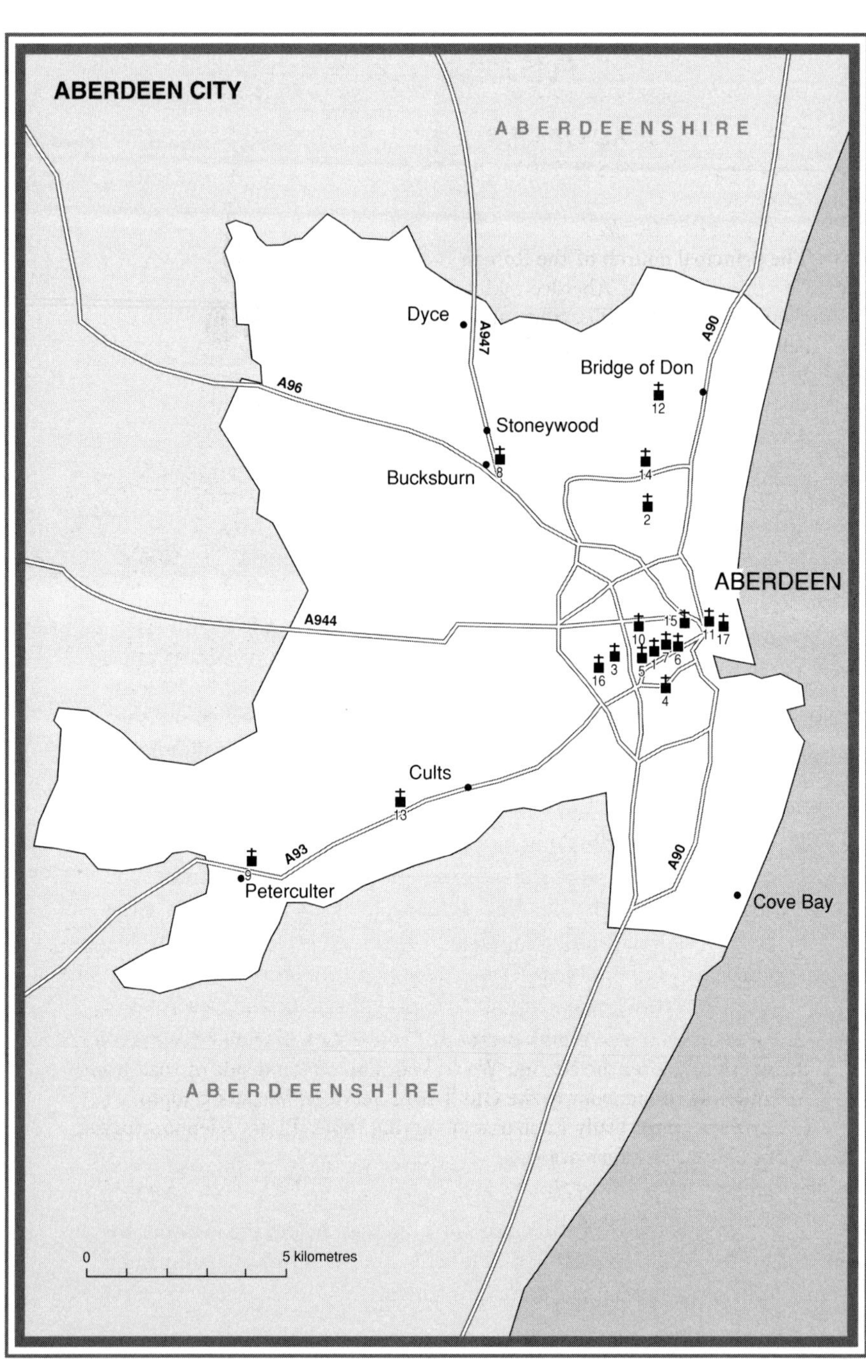
ABERDEEN CITY
ABERDEENSHIRE
Dyce
A947
A90
Bridge of Don
A96
12
Stoneywood
8
14
Bucksburn
2
ABERDEEN
A944
10
15
11
17
1
7
6
16
3
5
4
Cults
13
A93
9
Peterculter
A90
Cove Bay
ABERDEENSHIRE
0
5 kilometres

ABERDEEN

1 THE CATHEDRAL OF OUR LADY OF THE ASSUMPTION

NJ 937 061

Huntly Street, Aberdeen

The principal church of the Roman Catholic Diocese of Aberdeen, built in 1860 by Alexander Ellis. Spire and bells added in 1877, designed by R G Wilson. Contains religious artefacts by Charles Blakeman, Gabriel Loire, Ann Davidson, Felix McCullough, David Gulland and Alexander Brodie. The organ is a rare example of the work of James Conacher, Huddersfield, 1887. Off Union Street. Mass Times: Vigil Saturday 7pm; Sunday 8am, 11.15am, 6pm

Open daily, summer 8am-5pm, winter 8am-4pm Also Aberdeen Doors Open Day. Clergy House at 20 Huntly Street

ROMAN CATHOLIC WC **B**

THE CATHEDRAL OF OUR LADY OF THE ASSUMPTION

2 THE CHAPEL OF THE CONVENT OF ST MARGARET OF SCOTLAND

NJ 941 074

17 Spital, Aberdeen

The chapel, built in 1892, is one of the earliest works of Sir Ninian Comper, son of the Rev John Comper, Rector of St John's Church in Aberdeen, who in 1863 had invited sisters from St Margaret's Convent, East Grinstead, to work with him. The furnishings, fittings and windows were also designed by Sir Ninian, and executed in his workshop. The oak panelling over the stalls was a thank offering after the Second World War. On left hand side of road from Mounthooly roundabout to the Old Town. Services: Vespers 5.30pm (Thursdays 5pm); Daily Eucharist at varying times. Please telephone 01224 632648 for exact information

Open by arrangement. Apply at front door of convent. Chapel may be viewed through grille in west porch

SCOTTISH EPISCOPAL **A**

3 THE CHRISTIAN COMMUNITY

NJ 919 056

8 Spademill Road, Aberdeen

Situated in the west end of Aberdeen, this small church was built in 1991, by Camphill Architects, to house community facilities as well as priest's office and vestry. Simple interior in lilac wash lit by four flanking windows; the altar is lit only by candles. Oak candle holders, altar and pulpit. Altar painting by David Newbatt, a local artist. Sunday Service: Act of Consecration of Man (Communion) 10.30am

Open by arrangement with Mr William Milne, telephone 01224 647609

CHRISTIAN COMMUNITY ♿ WC

4 FERRYHILL PARISH CHURCH

NJ 939 054

Junction of Fonthill Road and Polmuir Road, Aberdeen

Designed by Duncan McMillan for the Free Church 1874. Early Gothic style with a tall square bell tower with octagonal spire. Side galleries added in 1896 were reduced in 1994. From 1929-90 the building was known as Ferryhill South Church. Contains several fine windows by James McLundie, A L Moore and others, including a number removed from the former Ferryhill North Church. The sanctuary was re-ordered 1994 by Oliver Humphries, and in 1994 the same architect was responsible for the creation of a fine new atrium and foyer. The memorial Chapel incorporates the 51st (Highland) Divisional Signals War Memorial, the Piper Alpha and Steele memorial windows, both by Jane Bayliss. Allen organ. Small historical museum in the basement. Sunday Service: 11am (10am in July and August); see notice boards for evening and weekday services and musical events

FERRYHILL PARISH CHURCH

Church website: www.ferryhillpc.org.uk

The Church and the Foyer Coffee Shop are open 9.30am to 11.30am, Monday to Saturday. Other times, telephone 01224 584176 or 01224 589465

CHURCH OF SCOTLAND ♿ WC **B**

5 GILCOMSTON SOUTH CHURCH

NJ 935 059

Union Street, Aberdeen

Sandstone and granite building by William Smith 1868. Spire added in 1875 and rebuilt in 1995. Stained glass by David Gauld, Douglas Strachan and Jane Bayliss. Oak screen and choir stalls. Binns pipe organ 1902. A hundred yards from west end of Union Street. Sunday Services: 11am and 6.30pm; Wednesday 7.30pm; Saturday Prayer Meeting 7pm

Open Aberdeen Doors Open Day. Other times, telephone Mr John Glibborn 01224 873919

CHURCH OF SCOTLAND C

GILCOMSTON SOUTH CHURCH

6 GREYFRIARS JOHN KNOX CHURCH

NJ 943 044

Broad Street, Aberdeen

Striking Gothic building, designed to complement the impressive granite front of Marischal College. Both designed by architect A Marshall Mackenzie. Light and airy interior. Great window from original 1532 Franciscan church, moved here 1903. Stained glass in this and six side windows by C E Kempe. Organ 1903 by Willis. Chancel panelled with pew ends c.1690. Sunday Service: 11am

Open 10.30am–12.30pm Thursday, Friday and Saturday, mid-June to mid-September

CHURCH OF SCOTLAND A

GREYFRIARS JOHN KNOX CHURCH

7 KIRK OF ST NICHOLAS

NJ 941 063

Back Wynd, Aberdeen

The 'Mither Kirk' of Aberdeen dates from the 12th century. The present building is largely 18th and 19th century. The west end 1755 by James Gibbs, the east end by Archibald Simpson 1837. The church contains the Chapel of the Oil Industry, and the 15th-century St Mary's Chapel. The carillon of 48 bells is the largest in Great Britain. Seventeenth-century embroidered wall hangings. Situated in Aberdeen city centre. Sunday Service: 11am, also July and August 9.30am; Daily Prayers: Monday to Friday 1.05pm.

Open 8 May to 29 September, Monday to Friday 12 noon–4pm, Saturday 1–3pm. Other times, on application to the Church Office 10am–1pm, telephone 01224 643494

CHURCH OF SCOTLAND **A**

8 NEWHILLS CHURCH

NJ 876 095

Bucksburn, Aberdeen

The present church was built in 1830 to a design by Archibald Simpson, near to the site of the original 17th-century church (now part of the graveyard). Painted coat of arms of the patron, Lord James Hay of Seaton, and the Earl of Fife and several modern banners add colour to the interior. Sunday Services 10.30am and 6pm (not July and August)

Open Monday to Friday 9am–1pm

CHURCH OF SCOTLAND

(by arrangement) **C**

NEWHILLS CHURCH

9 PETERCULTER PARISH CHURCH

NO 594 996

North Deeside Road, Peterculter, Aberdeen

Prominently sited on the main road, this church was built in 1895 and has a recent extension built in 1995 providing a meeting place. Extensively refurbished in 2001, it now offers a multi-purpose sanctuary which can be used by the local community. Sunday Service: 11.00am (10.00am in July/August)

Open Saturday mornings, or by arrangement with the church office, telephone 01224 735845 (mornings only)

CHURCH OF SCOTLAND

10 ROSEMOUNT CHURCH

NJ 933 069

120 Rosemount Place, Aberdeen

Traditional church 1870 converted to multi-purpose Celebration Centre in 1984. Ground floor accommodates Sunday worship, weekday activities and coffee lounge. Gallery houses 'Jonah's Journey' – children's museum. Situated close to two municipal parks. By road or by bus 22 from lower end of Union Street. Sunday Service: 11am

Open all year (not public holidays), Monday to Saturday 10am-12 noon, Sunday 2.30-4.30pm (except July)

CHURCH OF SCOTLAND WC **C**

11 ST ANDREW'S CATHEDRAL

NJ 945 065

King Street, Aberdeen

Built by Archibald Simpson 1817 and altered and enhanced by Sir Ninian Comper 1939-45. Gold burnished baldacchino over the high altar. National memorial to Samuel Seabury, first Bishop of America consecrated in Aberdeen in 1784. Interesting roof heraldry depicting American states and Jacobite supporters of the '45 rebellion. Stained glass. Sir John Betjeman described it as one of Aberdeen's best modern buildings. Three-manual organ by Hill, Norman & Beard, recently restored. Services: Holy Communion 8am; Sung Eucharist 10.15am; Evensong 6.30pm

ST ANDREW'S CATHEDRAL

Open May to September, Monday to Saturday 10am-4pm

SCOTTISH EPISCOPAL WC **A**

12 ST COLUMBA'S PARISH CHURCH

NJ 1094

Braehead Way, Bridge of Don

St Columba's Parish Church is shared with the local Roman Catholic congregation. The most notable feature is a steel cross at rear of the church. Sunday Services: 10am and 6.30pm

Open by arrangement, telephone Mr Thompson 01224 703753

CHURCH OF SCOTLAND

ST COLUMBA'S PARISH CHURCH

13 ST DEVENICK'S BIELDSIDE

NJ 882 025

North Deeside Road, Bieldside

Pink and grey granite church, designed by Arthur Clyne and opened in 1903. Organ (Wadsworth) installed in 1910; 'best specimen of its kind by Wadsworth ever placed in Aberdeen or for a considerable distance round about'. North transept completed in 1959 by building of Lady Chapel, which seats 24. West gallery and foyer added 2000. Sunday Services: 8.30 and 10.30am; Thursday 10.30

Church website: www.stdevenicks.org.uk

27 May 2002 centenary of laying of foundation stone. Open by arrangement, telephone the office 01224 863574

SCOTTISH EPISCOPAL B

ST DEVENICK'S BIELDSIDE

14 ST MACHAR'S CATHEDRAL

NJ 939 008

The Chanonry, Aberdeen

Fourteenth to 16th-century nave with unique heraldic ceiling and fortified west front. Interesting monuments, stained glass. Ruined transepts. Peal of eight bells. Sunday Services: 11am and 6pm

Church website: www.ifb.net/stmachar

Open daily 9am-5pm. Recitals programme information, telephone 01224 485988

CHURCH OF SCOTLAND A

ST MACHAR'S CATHEDRAL

15 ST MARGARET OF SCOTLAND

NJ 942 067

Gallowgate, Aberdeen

Completed in 1869, the spacious sanctuary includes many fine examples of the work of Sir Ninian Comper, including the chapel of St Nicholas, the first building he designed and with the original stained glass. His style is mainly Early English with elements of Byzantine and Renaissance. Memorial garden. Just north of Marischal College. Sunday Services: Parish Mass 10.30am, Evensong 6pm

Open Tuesday mornings. Other times, telephone Canon Nimmo 01224 644969, or A Allan 01224 872960. Gallowgate Festival Saturday in early August

SCOTTISH EPISCOPAL B

16 ST MARY'S CHURCH

NJ 929 060

Carden Place, Aberdeen

The variety of granites and patterned roof tiles earned it the nickname 'The Tartan Kirkie'. To a design by Alexander Ellis and the Rev F G Lee, dating from 1864. The east end sustained severe damage during an air raid in April 1943. Reconstructed 1952. Altar triptych by Westlake (c.1862) in the crypt. The church is home to a Samuel Green chamber organ, built in 1778. Display of historical photographs in the choir vestry (1905) adjoining church. On the left between Skene Street and Queen's Road. Sunday Services: 8am and 10.15am; Tuesday 7pm; Wednesday 11am; Thursday 7pm

Church website: www.beehive.thisisnorthscotland.co.uk/st-marys-aberdeen

Open by arrangement, telephone the Rector 01224 584123

SCOTTISH EPISCOPAL **A**

17 ST PETER'S CHURCH

NJ 942 065

Chapel Court, Justice Street (off the Castlegate)

By James Massie, 1803-4, gallery added 1815 and façade finished 1817, by Harry Leith. Within the courtyard is the residence occupied since 1774, including, in the 18th century, the Vicars Apostolic of the Lowland district: Bishop James Grant and Bishop John Geddes. Services: Saturday Vigil 6pm (5pm in winter); Sunday 11am; Weekdays as announced

Open Monday, Wednesday, Friday 10.30am-2pm, or by arrangement

ROMAN CATHOLIC **B**

ST PETER'S CHURCH

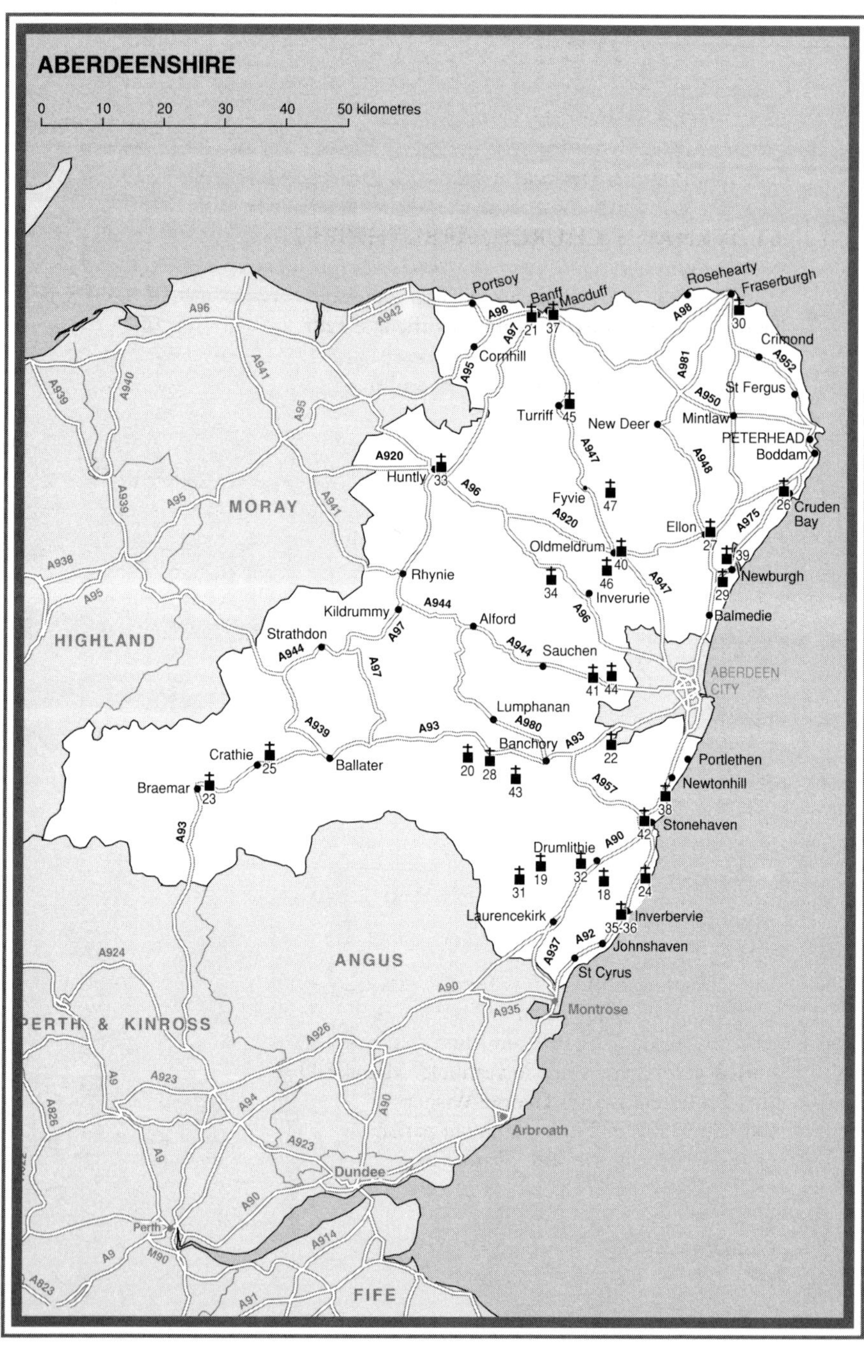
ABERDEENSHIRE
0 10 20 30 40 50 kilometres
Portsoy
Banff
Macduff
Rosehearty
Fraserburgh
Crimond
St Fergus
Cornhill
Turriff
New Deer
Mintlaw
PETERHEAD
Boddam
Huntly
Fyvie
Ellon
Cruden Bay
Oldmeldrum
Newburgh
Rhynie
Inverurie
Balmedie
Kildrummy
Alford
Strathdon
Sauchen
ABERDEEN CITY
Lumphanan
Banchory
Crathie
Ballater
Braemar
Portlethen
Newtonhill
Stonehaven
Drumlithie
Laurencekirk
Inverbervie
Johnshaven
St Cyrus
Montrose
Arbroath
Dundee
Perth
MORAY
HIGHLAND
ANGUS
PERTH & KINROSS
FIFE

ABERDEENSHIRE

Local Representatives: Mrs Beatrice Fawkes, 3 Northfield Gardens, Hatton, Peterhead (*telephone* 01779 841814); Mrs Fiona Cameron, The Newk, Monboddo Road, Torphins (*telephone* 013398 82405)

18 ST TERNAN'S CHURCH, ARBUTHNOTT

NO 801 746

Almost certainly a St Ternan cult church long before it became a parish church by the late 12th century. The chancel dates from the early 13th century, the Arbuthnott family aisle and the bell-tower from the late 15th century and the nave is medieval or earlier but has been much altered. The church was gutted by fire in 1889 and reopened in 1890 with the nave and chancel restored as at the time of consecration in 1242; the architect for the restoration was A Marshall Mackenzie. The unique Arbuthnott Missal, Psalter and Prayer Book (now in Paisley Museum) were transcribed and illuminated in the Priest's Room above the Arbuthnott Aisle between 1497 and 1500. On the B967, three miles from Inverbervie. For Services, see local paper and notice board

ST TERNAN'S CHURCH, ARBUTHNOTT

Open all year. Refreshments in Grassic Gibbon Centre in village

CHURCH OF SCOTLAND A

19 ST PALLADIUS or AUCHENBLAE PARISH CHURCH

NO 726 784

Auchenblae, nr Laurencekirk

Built by John Smith 1829 as Fordoun Parish Church on a site known as Kirkton of Fordoun. Religious site since 7th century. St Palladius died and reputedly buried here. Celtic stone in vestibule. Memorial to first Protestant martyr George Wishart (born at Mains of Pittarrow in old parish of Fordoun) in graveyard. Seating in nave replaced 1990. Stained glass rose window. Sunday Service: 11am, excluding first Sunday of month

Open by arrangement, telephone Rev David Jack 01561 340203

CHURCH OF SCOTLAND B

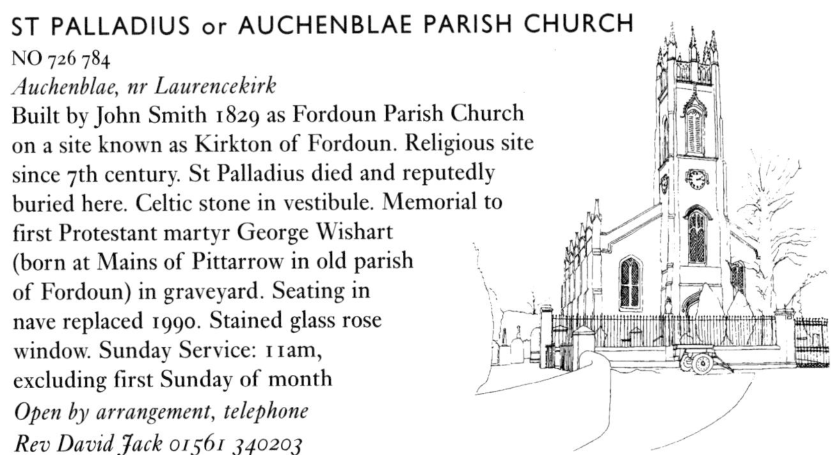

ST PALLADIUS or AUCHENBLAE PARISH CHURCH

20 BIRSE AND FEUGHSIDE PARISH CHURCH, BALLOGIE

NO 554 973

Ballogie, near Banchory

Dates from 12th century. Link with Crusades. Seventeenth-century graveyard. United with Finzean and Strachan. Sunday Service: 11am, July

Open May to September, Monday to Friday 10am-4pm

CHURCH OF SCOTLAND B

BIRSE AND FEUGHSIDE PARISH CHURCH, BALLOGIE

21 BANFF PARISH CHURCH

NJ 689 638

High Street, Banff

Built in 1789, Andrew Wilson architect and builder, with tower added in 1849, William Robertson. Chancel added and interior altered in 1929. Stained glass. Small chapel created at rear of church in 1994. Pulpit, font, communion table and stained glass in chancel all gifted in 1929. Other furnishings from Trinity & Alvah Church, united in 1994. Beside St Mary's car park. Sunday Services 11am and 6.30pm

Open mid-June to August, 2-4pm. Also Doors Open Day, September

CHURCH OF SCOTLAND A

22 ST MARY'S CHAPEL, BLAIRS

NJ 883 009

The building, designed by Richard Curran of Warrington, was opened in 1901 and follows the neo-Gothic style, while the unusual interior design is due to the fact that it is a former collegiate chapel. The walls originally had painted decoration, but in 1911 were lined with marble. At the same time were added the reredos and baldacchino in carved wood with its figures of the Scottish patron saints, Andrew and Margaret. The church also has fine stained glass windows. Four miles south of Aberdeen on B9077. Sunday Service: 9.00am. The Blairs Museum (adjacent to the chapel) is open from May to October (12-4pm)

Church website: www.blairs.net

Open Monday, Tuesday and Thursday 10.30am-2pm. Saturday/Sunday by arrangement, telephone 01224 869424

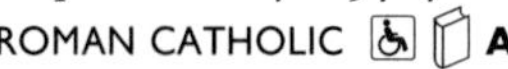

A

ST MARY'S CHAPEL, BLAIRS

23 BRAEMAR CHURCH

NO 1591

Behind the Braemar Mews

The inspiration for the building of this former Free Church in 1870 was the Rev Hugh Cobban. Unusually, he was buried in the church, behind the pulpit. Four lancet stained glass windows with lilies, a branch with fruit and a tree with palms. Some interesting tapestry banners, described as 'living pictures'. Sunday Service: 10am

Open 9am–9pm April to October

CHURCH OF SCOTLAND C

24 ST PHILIP'S, CATTERLINE

NO 869 789

St Ninian was reputed to have landed at Catterline. The present building, designed by Charles Brand, dates from 1848 and was built on the site of an earlier church, retaining its historic graveyard. The style is Early English. The interior has been recently refurbished. Off A9 between Montrose and Stonehaven and near Dunottar Castle. Sunday Services: 9.30am, Holy Communion second and last Sundays in month

ST PHILIP'S, CATTERLINE

Open by arrangement, telephone Mr Reid 01569 750360

SCOTTISH EPISCOPAL C

25 CRATHIE PARISH CHURCH

NO 265 949

On A93 Ballater–Braemar

Queen Victoria laid the foundation stone in 1893, the church opened 1895. Cruciform design by A Marshall Mackenzie. The church stands on a hill overlooking the ruins of the 14th-century church and the River Dee. Memorial stones, plaques and stained glass commemorate royalty and ministers. Fine Iona marble communion table and 17th-century oak reredos. Sunday Service: 11.30am

Open April to October, Monday to Saturday 9.30am–5pm; Sunday 12.45pm–5pm

CHURCH OF SCOTLAND B

CRATHIE PARISH CHURCH

26 ST JAMES'S CHURCH, CRUDEN BAY

NK 069 356

Chapel Hill, Cruden Bay

The tall spire of St James's can be seen from miles around. Designed by William Hay in 1842. The font is from the chantry chapel, built after the battle between the Scots and the Danes in 1012. One and a half miles from Cruden Bay. Sunday Service: Family Communion 9.30am

Church website:

www.saintmaryandsaintjames.net

Open daily 10am-dusk

SCOTTISH EPISCOPAL ♿ 👂 **B**

ST JAMES'S CHURCH, CRUDEN BAY

27 ST MARY ON THE ROCK, ELLON

NJ 958 301

Craighall, Ellon

A superb example of the work of George Edmund Street, built in 1871 to incorporate chancel, nave, narthex and spire. Floor tiles by Minton. Good glass, including windows by Clayton & Bell on the north side of the nave, Lavers & Barreau on the south side, all dating from the 1880s, and by Jane Bayliss 1996. On the A90/A948, at the south end of the town. Sunday Service: Eucharist 9.30am, Parish Eucharist 11.15am

Church website:

www.saintmaryandsaintjames.net

Open daily 10am-dusk

SCOTTISH EPISCOPAL ♿ 👂 **A**

ST MARY ON THE ROCK, ELLON

28 FINZEAN CHURCH

NO 617 924

Finzean, near Banchory

Small mission church. United with Birse and Strachan. Between Banchory and Aboyne on South Deeside Road. Sunday Service: 11am, June and September

Open May to September, Monday to Friday 10am-4pm

CHURCH OF SCOTLAND **B**

29 FOVERAN PARISH CHURCH

NJ 985 241

One mile south of Newburgh on A975

Built 1794, organ apse added 1900, interior refurbished 1934 with pews and fittings from the demolished Foveran United Free Church. Number of items from medieval church (since disappeared): early 15th-century Turin Stone, 17th-century bust of Sir John Turing, Queen Anne hour-glass attached to pulpit and font using carved medieval column. Various monuments including bronze plaque to painter and etcher James McBey, born nearby. Sunday Service: 11am (shared with Holyrood Chapel, Newburgh)

FOVERAN PARISH CHURCH

Open by arrangement, key available from the Manse, or from Newburgh Post Office during opening hours

CHURCH OF SCOTLAND B

30 FRASERBURGH OLD PARISH CHURCH

NJ 998 671

The Square, Fraserburgh

Present building dates from 1801, with a church on this site since 1572. The pulpit is one of the highest in Scotland and the superb memorial window designed by Douglas Strachan 1906 was gifted by Sir George Anderson, Treasurer of the Bank of Scotland, in memory of his parents. A front pew in the south gallery is marked as the place where Marconi, pioneer of wireless telegraphy, worshipped during his stay in Fraserburgh. Sunday Services: 11am and 6pm

Open daily June-September

CHURCH OF SCOTLAND WC C

FRASERBURGH OLD PARISH CHURCH

31 FETTERCAIRN PARISH CHURCH

No 651 735

Fettercairn nr Laurencekirk

Built in 1803 and with a steeple added in 1860, the building was completely refurbished and extended in 1926. The interior has interesting stained glass and locally made furnishings. Sunday Service: 9.30am

Open by arrangement, telephone the Minister 01561 340203

CHURCH OF SCOTLAND WC B

32 GLENBERVIE PARISH CHURCH

No 766 807

Glenbervie, nr Stonehaven

Built 1826 and preserving original design and features. Oil lamps electrified. Stones preserved and sheltered. Grandparents of Robert Burns buried in old kirkyard. Sunday Service: 11am, first Sunday of month

Open by arrangement, telephone

Rev David Jack 01561 340203

CHURCH OF SCOTLAND **B**

GLENBERVIE PARISH CHURCH

33 ST MARGARET'S CHURCH, HUNTLY

NJ 528 402

Chapel Street, Huntly

Octagonal church with impressive classical front façade built 1834. The architect was Bishop James Kyle in collaboration with William Robertson. Spire 80ft with fine toned bell. Altar piece and other paintings from the Gordon family of Xeres, Spain 1840. Restored 1990 by Doric Construction, Aberdeen.

Sunday Service: 9.45am

Open by arrangement, telephone

Mr W McKay 01466 792409

ROMAN CATHOLIC WC **A**

ST MARGARET'S CHURCH, HUNTLY

34 ST DROSTAN, INSCH

NJ 630 281

Commerce Street, Insch

Alexander Ross 1894. Agreeable rustic Gothic in red granite with sandstone dressings. Red-tiled roof with broach-spired wooden bellcote. Font 1892, and screen 1904. Church is on road from Insch railway station to town centre. B992 off A96. Service: second and fourth Sundays, Sung Eucharist 10am

Open by arrangement, telephone

Mrs Mitchell, Greenhaugh, Rannes Street, Insch 01464 820276

SCOTTISH EPISCOPAL **C**

ST DROSTAN, INSCH

35 BERVIE PARISH CHURCH, INVERBERVIE

NO 830 727

43 King Street, Inverbervie

Built in 1836 with elegant clock and bell tower. Two stained glass windows originally from United Free Church. Hammond organ 1904. In centre of town. Sunday Service: 11.30am

Open by arrangement, telephone Mr W Beattie, 39 King Street 01561 361256, or 9 Farquhar Street 01561 362728

CHURCH OF SCOTLAND  **B**

BERVIE PARISH CHURCH, INVERBERVIE

36 KING DAVID OF SCOTLAND EPISCOPAL CHURCH, INVERBERVIE

NO 828 733

Victoria Terrace, Inverbervie

Small, simple church with very pretty interior. Shared with the local Roman Catholic community. Sunday Service: 9.30am Holy Communion; Saturday: Roman Catholic Mass 6.30pm

Open daily 9am–4.30pm

SCOTTISH EPISCOPAL

37 MACDUFF PARISH CHURCH

NJ 701 643

Church Street, Macduff

Once used to guide boats to safe haven, this white box kirk of 1805 high on the bluff above the harbour was transformed in 1865 by architect James Matthews of Aberdeen into a magnificent Italianate landmark, with notable stained glass windows and a lovely three-storey tower with a lead-domed roof and cupola above. Galleried interior, most of the fittings dating from 1865. Magnificent views. Nearby stand the town cross and an anchor, symbolic of the message of the church. Sunday Services: 11am and 6pm

Church website: www.macduffparishchurch.fsnet.co.uk

Open by arrangement, telephone 01261 832316

CHURCH OF SCOTLAND **B**

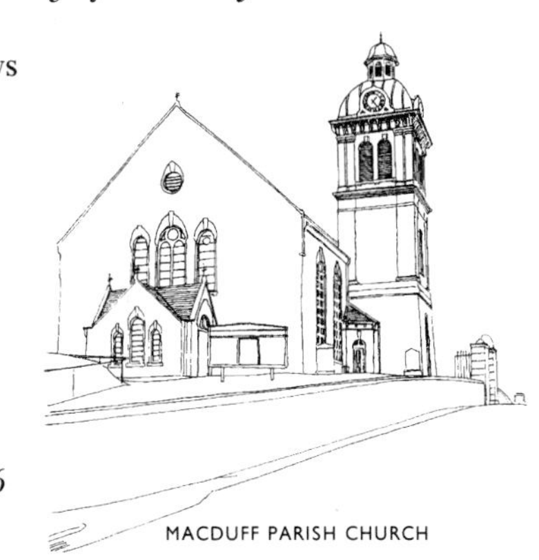

MACDUFF PARISH CHURCH

38 ST TERNAN'S, MUCHALLS

NO 891 921

Muchalls, by Stonehaven

Simple country church with attractive chancel. The oldest church building in the Diocese of Brechin, built 1831–70. Sunday Service: 10.30am Holy Communion

Open by arrangement, telephone 01569 730967

SCOTTISH EPISCOPAL

ST TERNAN'S, MUCHALLS

39 HOLYROOD CHAPEL, NEWBURGH

NJ 999 253

Main Street, Newburgh

Built in 1838 as the original Newburgh Mathers school; converted as Chapel of Ease for Foveran Parish Church 1882. Clock Tower added 1892, interior refurbished 1907, including pitch pine roof in imitation of St Laurence, Forres. Named in honour of the original medieval chapel of the Holy Rood and St Thomas the Martyr in Inch Road, Newburgh – all that remains of this is the Udny Family Mausoleum in the Holyrood Cemetery. Sunday Service: 11am (shared with Foveran Church)

Open by arrangement, key available from the Manse, or from Newburgh Post Office during opening hours

CHURCH OF SCOTLAND **B**

HOLYROOD CHAPEL, NEWBURGH

40 ST MATTHEW & ST GEORGE, OLDMELDRUM

NJ 812 279

Ross & Joass 1863. Pleasing granite Early Decorated with striking chequered voussoirs to west window. Octagonal spire alongside the simple nave and chancel. Tendril-like freestone tracery is carved with real freedom. Stained glass by Hardman records the Life of Our Lord. Intricate Arts & Crafts monument to Beauchamp Colclough Urquhart of Meldrum. Church is at the north end of the village on A947. Sung Eucharist 11.30am

Open by arrangement, telephone the Rector 01651 872208

SCOTTISH EPISCOPAL ♿ **B**

ST MATTHEW & ST GEORGE, OLDMELDRUM

41 SKENE PARISH CHURCH, KIRKTON OF SKENE

NJ 803 077

Quarter mile off A944 Aberdeen-Alford Road, 9 miles from Aberdeen city centre

The church was built in 1801 and contains stained glass by Blair & Blyth. Sunday Service: 11.15am

Open by arrangement, telephone the Minister 01224 743277 or the Beadle 01224 743534

CHURCH OF SCOTLAND ♿ WC **B**

SKENE PARISH CHURCH, KIRKTON OF SKENE

42 ST JAMES THE GREAT, STONEHAVEN

NO 873 857

Arbuthnott Street, Stonehaven

The nave was built by Sir Robert Rowand Anderson in 1877 in Norman/Early English style. The chancel was added in 1885 and the narthex and baptistry in 1906 by Arthur Clyne. Baptistry glass by Sir Ninian Comper 1929. Elaborately sculptured reredos by Gambier-Parry of London. Off south side of Market Square in Stonehaven. Sunday Services: 8.30 and 10.30am; Thursday 10.30am

Open Easter to end September, Monday to Friday 2-4pm

SCOTTISH EPISCOPAL ♿ WC **A**

ST JAMES THE GREAT, STONEHAVEN

43 STRACHAN CHURCH

NO 674 923

Strachan, near Banchory

Situated on old drove road. Ancient graveyard. United with Birse and Finzean. Between Banchory and Aboyne on South Deeside Road. Sunday Service: 11am, May and August

Open May to September, Monday to Friday 10am-4pm

CHURCH OF SCOTLAND **C**

44 TRINITY CHURCH, WESTHILL

NJ 8307

Westhill Drive, Westhill (off A944 Aberdeen-Alford Road)

Built 1981 by Stock Brothers. Ecumenical and multi-purpose. Plans for an extension of the building during 2002. Services: Roman Catholic 9am; Church of Scotland 10am; Scottish Episcopal 11.15am.

Open most of week, check with Minister, telephone 01224 743277

INTERDENOMINATIONAL ♿ WC

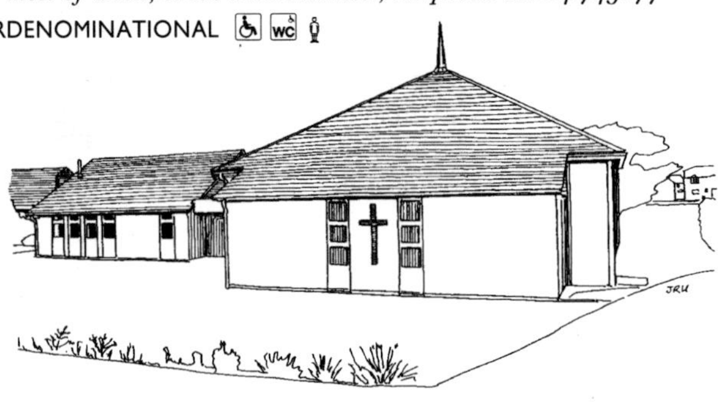

TRINITY CHURCH, WESTHILL

45 ST CONGAN'S, TURRIFF

NJ 722 498

Deveron Road, Turriff

Elegant church by William Ramage 1862 with a red, slender Gothic western tower. Mural tablet of Bishop Jolly who is depicted in the east window. Beautiful stained glass. Oak rood screen, pulpit and lectern are the important ornaments. A short distance away are the ruins of the medieval church whose elaborate bellcote of 1635 survives. Services: Sundays 11.00am (winter), 10.30am (Easter to end-October), Wednesdays 10.00am

Open weekend 12/13 October 2002, 135th anniversary of dedication. Open by arrangement with the Assistant Priest, telephone 01888 562530

SCOTTISH EPISCOPAL WC (at Hall) **B**

46 ALL SAINTS', WHITERASHES

NJ 855 235

Gothic style nave and chancel built by James Matthews in 1858. Windows by Sir Ninian Comper of saints chosen for the Christian names of the Irvines of Drum and Straloch. On A947, three miles south of Oldmeldrum. Service: first Sunday, Evensong 3pm

Open by arrangement, telephone the Rector 01651 872208

SCOTTISH EPISCOPAL (one step) **B**

ALL SAINTS, WHITERASHES

47 ALL SAINTS', WOODHEAD OF FETTERLETTER

NJ 790 385

Early English aisleless nave and chancel by John Henderson 1849. The fine tower with the slated broach spire was added in 1870. Described by Pratt in Buchan as 'one of the finest examples of a Scottish village church'. Crosses and a sheaf of arrows from Fyvie Priory are incorporated in the walls. The altar and reredos are from St Margaret's, Forgue. One and a half miles east of Fyvie. Sunday Service: 10.15am

Open by arrangement, telephone Mrs Cleaver, Gowanlea, Woodhead 01651 891513

SCOTTISH EPISCOPAL **B**

ALL SAINTS', WOODHEAD OF FETTERLETTER

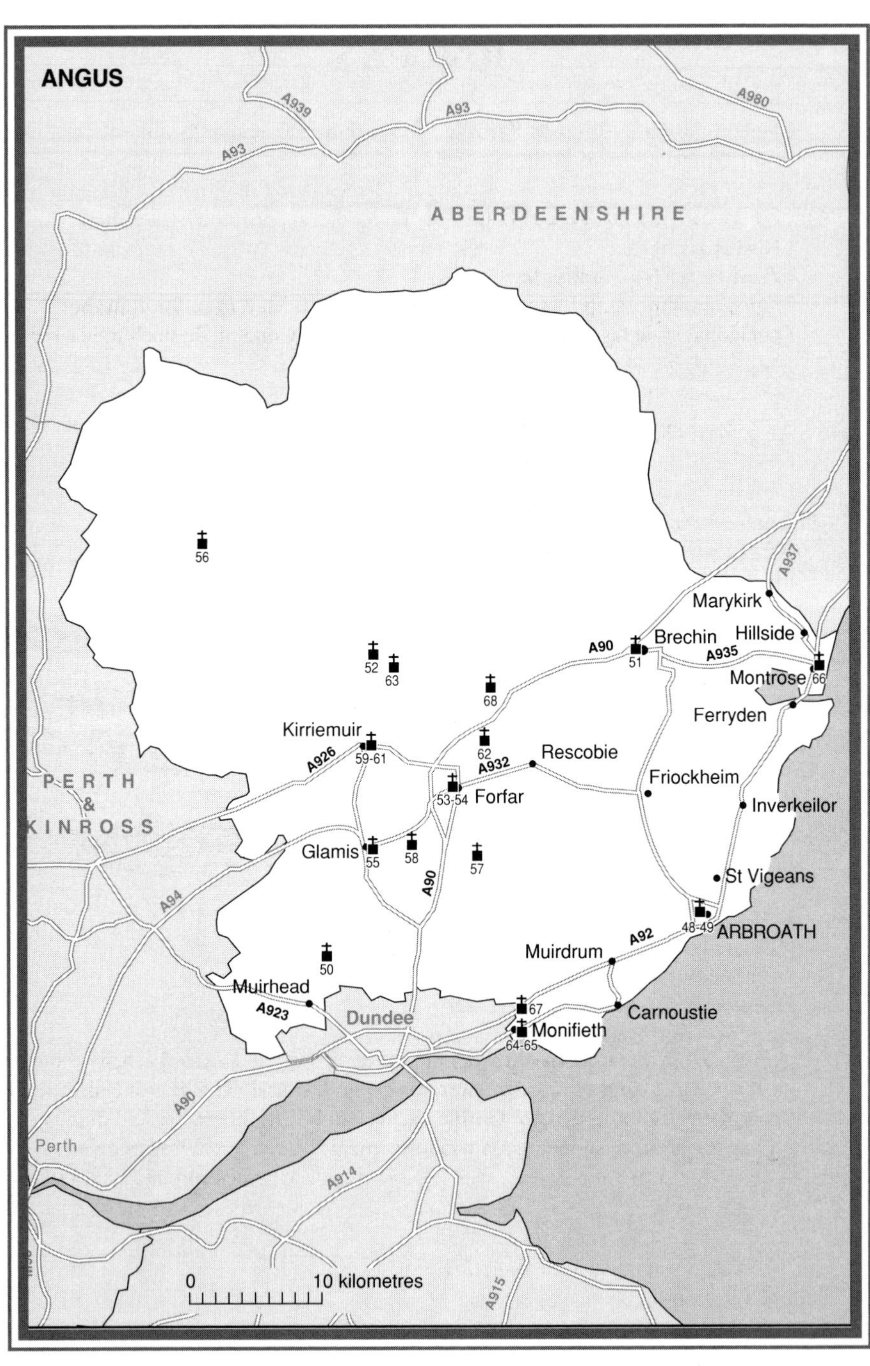
ANGUS
A939
A93
A980
A93
ABERDEENSHIRE
56
52
63
68
A937
Marykirk
Hillside
A90
Brechin
51
A935
Montrose
66
Ferryden
Kirriemuir
59-61
A926
62
Rescobie
A932
Friockheim
53-54
Forfar
PERTH
&
KINROSS
Inverkeilor
Glamis
55
58
57
A90
A94
St Vigeans
48-49
ARBROATH
Muirdrum
A92
50
Muirhead
A923
67
Dundee
Carnoustie
Monifieth
64-65
A90
Perth
A914
0
10 kilometres
A915

ANGUS

Local Representative: The Rev Peter Youngson, 'Correen', Northmuir, Kirriemuir (*telephone 01575 572832)*

48 ST JOHN'S, ARBROATH

NN 645 411

Ponderlaw Street, Arbroath

Opened for worship by the Rev John Wesley on 6 May 1772. Built in the octagonal style favoured by Wesley, this is the only one of these churches left in Scotland. Known as the 'Totum Kirkie'. Vestibule added 1883. The Lifeboat Window is a memorial to the loss of the Lifeboat *Robert L Lindsay* and six crew members in 1953. Old manse adjacent to church. Sunday Service: 11am

Open by arrangement, telephone Mr Nicoll 01241 875172

METHODIST

49 ST VIGEAN'S CHURCH, ARBROATH

NO 583 446

St Vigean's, Arbroath

Dedicated to St Vigean (or Fechin), Irish saint, died 664. Church rebuilt in 12th century, but not dedicated until 1242. Some 15th-century alterations; 19th-century restoration with lovely stained glass windows. Largely unaltered since. Sunday Service: 11.30am

Key available from house opposite church main gate. St Vigean's Museum also open

CHURCH OF SCOTLAND A

ST VIGEAN'S CHURCH, ARBROATH

50 AUCHTERHOUSE CHURCH

No 342 381

Kirkton of Auchterhouse

Built 1630 with stone from earlier churches of 1275 and 1426. Partially rebuilt 1775. Chancel and nave with tower at west end. Burial vault at east end. Interior completely renovated 1910. Gothic chancel arch lends character and dignity. Three impressive stained glass windows, medieval octagonal font, stool of repentance and 18th-century clock. Linked with Murroes and Tealing. Situated on south side of Sidlaw Hills one mile east of B954 Dundee to Meigle, six miles from Meigle. Sunday Service: 11.30am

Open by arrangement, telephone John Skea 01382 320257, or Elizabeth Adams 01382 320302

CHURCH OF SCOTLAND B

AUCHTERHOUSE CHURCH

51 BRECHIN CATHEDRAL

No 595 601

Church Lane, Brechin

Founded in the 11th century, the round tower of that date is of Irish inspiration. Thirteenth, 14th and 15th-century medieval architecture underwent major restoration in 1900-2 supervised by J Honeyman (Honeyman, Keppie & Mackintosh). Special features include the 12th-century font and a collection of Pictish sculptures. Stunning 20th-century stained glass by Henry Holliday, Gordon Webster, Douglas Strachan, Herbert Hendrie, William Gauld, Hugh Easton and the firm of William Morris. The cathedral also contains the largest group of William Wilson windows in Scotland. Sunday Service: 11am. Short Communion in Queen Isle after Service on fourth Sunday of the month.

Service to mark centenary of restoration on Sunday 28 April 2002 at 11am. Open most days all year 9am-4pm. With guides in summer months only (and by special arrangement outwith these times). Afternoon teas in church hall, alternate Thursdays 2pm. Brechin Caledonian Railway nearby. Historical artefacts in Brechin Library. Brechin Town Trail. Pictavia. Angus Pictish Trail

CHURCH OF SCOTLAND

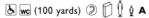

wc (100 yards) **A**

BRECHIN CATHEDRAL

52 CORTACHY CHURCH

NO 396 597

Cortachy Church was built by the 7th Earl of Airlie, the sole heritor, in 1828 on the site of a previous church. The architect was David Patterson. It has a magnificent setting overlooking the river South Esk. The gallery gives the church a seating capacity of 300. Inside there are memorials to the 9th and 12th Earls and against the east gable is the Burial Aisle of the Airlie family. Sunday Service: 10 am, excluding fifth Sunday of month

Church website: www.gkopc.co.uk

Open by arrangement with church office, telephone 01575 572819

CHURCH OF SCOTLAND **B**

53 LOWSON MEMORIAL CHURCH, FORFAR

NO 465 509

Jameson Street, Forfar

A gem of a church designed by A Marshall Mackenzie 1914. In the style of late Scots Gothic, cruciform in shape with five-bay nave, aisleless transepts and a one-bay chancel. Built of a ruddy-hued local stone. Low central tower and squat spire. Wooden wagon roof. Excellent stained glass, Douglas Strachan. At east end of Forfar off Montrose Road. Sunday Service: 11am

Church website: //lowson-memorial.org.uk

Open Monday to Friday 9.30am–4.30pm all year

CHURCH OF SCOTLAND **A**

LOWSON MEMORIAL CHURCH, FORFAR

54 ST JOHN THE EVANGELIST, FORFAR

No 458 507

71 East High Street, Forfar

Built on the site of an earlier church, the present building was designed in Early English style by Sir R Rowand Anderson and consecrated in 1881. The broach spire intended for the tower was never built. Panelling and redecoration of the roof by Sir Matthew Ochterlony, late 1940s. Altered in 1975 by Dr F R Stevenson to provide Lady Chapel and vestries. The font has traditionally been associated with St Margaret and Restenneth Priory. Three-manual pipe organ by Conacher of Huddersfield. Stained glass by Charles E Kempe and Septimus Waugh. Queen Elizabeth The Queen Mother was confirmed in the church. Historic graveyard predates present church. Sunday Services: 8.30 and 11am, weekdays as announced

Open daily, summer months 9am–4pm, winter months 9am–2pm

SCOTTISH EPISCOPAL (on request) **B**

ST JOHN THE EVANGELIST, FORFAR

55 ST FERGUS CHURCH, GLAMIS

No 386 469

Kirk Wynd, Glamis

Present church built 1792 on site of church dedicated to St Fergus 1242. Substantially altered and beautified 1933. Classic bell tower and spire. Seventh-century Celtic stone in manse garden and Well of St Fergus nearby. Category B kirkyard with interesting stones. Strathmore Aisle (category A) built in 1459 by Isabella Ogilvy on death of her husband Patrick Lyon, 1st Lord Glamis. United with Inverarity and Kinnettles. Sunday Service: 11.30am

Open daily

CHURCH OF SCOTLAND  **A/B**

ST FERGUS CHURCH, GLAMIS

56 GLEN PROSEN CHURCH

No 328 657

Glen Prosen, by Pitcarity, Kirriemuir

Present church built 1802, paid for by local inhabitants, ensuring continuous worship in the glen for nearly 400 years. Special features include wood carvings by Sir Robert Lorimer and war memorial porch with rare slated cross. Sunday Service: first and third Sundays 12 noon; summer months Holy Communion (Scottish Episcopal) fourth Sunday 8.30am; Songs of Praise for Guide Dogs for the Blind: April to September, first Sunday of month 6pm

Open daily, access via vestry door

CHURCH OF SCOTLAND **B**

57 INVERARITY CHURCH

No 460 440

Inverarity

Church built 1754 with recent impressive renovation. Kirk Bell by Peter van dem Heim dated 1614, cast in Holland. Gable porches added 1854. Modern church/community hall next to church. Situated at eastern boundary of village on triangle of ground at division of B9127.

Sunday Service: 10am

Open by arrangement, telephone Mr A L Ingram 01307 840223

CHURCH OF SCOTLAND B

INVERARITY CHURCH

58 KINNETTLES CHURCH

No 426 460

Kirkton, Kinnettles

Built 1812, architect Samuel Bell, in Gothic style with belfry. Late 19th-century additions. Typically rural and unspoiled. Said to be an excellent example of an 'auld Scottish kirk'. Beautiful stained glass and original precentor's box. United with Glamis and Inverarity. Sunday service: 6pm, second Sunday of month

Open by arrangement, telephone Norman Knight 01307 820348

CHURCH OF SCOTLAND B

KINNETTLES CHURCH

59 KIRRIEMUIR OLD PARISH CHURCH

No 386 539

Bank Street, Kirriemuir

Ninth-century stones were found when the church was rebuilt on this earlier Christian site in 1788 to a design by James Playfair, father of William Henry Playfair. The steeple was completed in 1790. Stained glass includes the triple window of The Last Supper, a Violet Jacobs window, and windows by William Wilson. Interesting kirkyard, the earliest stone dating from 1613. In centre of the town, behind Bank Street's shops. Sunday Services: 9am and 11.15am

Open Monday to Friday, 10am–12 noon and 1.30–3.30pm (call at office if door locked)

CHURCH OF SCOTLAND B

60 ST ANDREW'S CHURCH, KIRRIEMUIR

No 386 535

Glamis Road, Kirriemuir

Late Gothic style church (originally the South United Free Church) with a 60-ft tower by Patrick Thoms 1903. It replaced an earlier church (the South Free Church) built in 1843 for those who left the South Church (across the road) at the 'Disruption'. In the grounds are the headstones of the Rev Daniel Cormick, first minister of the South Free Church and of the Rev A Duff, minister of the South Church. Linked with Oathlaw and Tannadice. Sunday Service: 11.15am

Open daily 9am-5pm

CHURCH OF SCOTLAND

ST ANDREW'S CHURCH, KIRRIEMUIR

61 ST MARY'S CHURCH, KIRRIEMUIR

NO 383 544

West Hillbank, Kirriemuir

Gothic revival church by Sir Ninian Comper 1903 built to replace classical church of 1797 destroyed by fire. Stained glass by Comper and William Wilson. Two-manual tracker organ, Hamilton of Edinburgh 1906. Sanctus bell 1741. Conspicuous red sandstone bell-tower. Signposted to north side of the town. Sunday Services: first, second and third Sundays 10am Sung Eucharist; fourth Sunday 10am Matins, 11.30am Said Eucharist; fifth Sunday 10am Family Service: 11.30am Said Eucharist

Key at Rectory, 128 Glengate, or 91 Glengate, Kirriemuir

SCOTTISH EPISCOPAL **A**

ST MARY'S CHURCH, KIRRIEMUIR

62 ST MARGARET'S CHURCH, LUNANHEAD

No 476 522

Carsebarracks, Lunanhead

Built in the planned village of Carsebarracks on the site of an earlier chapel in 1907 by the builder/architect William L McLean of Forfar as a gift of Mrs Susan Helen Gray of Bankhead House in memory of her husband. Stained glass window of the Crucifixion (1913), by A D Fleming of London. Mural (1909) by Miss W M Watson of Edinburgh. On the B9134, one mile east of Forfar. Service: first and third Sundays, excluding July and August 2pm

Open by arrangement, telephone Mr Orrock 01307 468156

SCOTTISH EPISCOPAL

63 MEMUS CHURCH

NO 427 590

Memus Church was built as the Free Church of Tannadice in 1843 in an outlying part of the parish. It is a plain rectangular building free of external ornamentation apart from the bellcote. The internal furnishings are of very fine pitch pine. The church had only two ministers in 103 years. Sunday Service: 10.30am, first and third Sundays

Church website: www.gkopc.co.uk

Open by arrangement with church office, telephone 01575 572819

CHURCH OF SCOTLAND **B**

64 HOLY TRINITY CHURCH, MONIFIETH

NO 499 327

High Street, Monifieth

Black and white half-timbered style building by Mills & Shepherd 1909. Originally intended as church hall, adapted to church. Pleasant sheltered garden. Buses from Dundee to Monifieth, Carnoustie and Arbroath stop outside. Sunday Services: 8am, 10.30am

Open daily

SCOTTISH EPISCOPAL ♿ WC **B**

HOLY TRINITY CHURCH, MONIFIETH

65 ST BRIDE'S, MONIFIETH

NO 499 325

6-8 Brook Street, Monifieth

The original church was established in 1880 in a converted cottage, which became the hall when the new church was built in 1983. A light airy building, it was designed by Brocks Bros of Leeds. Stained glass by Australian Gail Donovan. Services: Monday, Wednesday, Friday in St Bride's 10am; Saturday 9.30am; Tuesday, Thursdays in St Mary's Home 10am; Saturday Vigil Mass 6.00pm; Sunday 10.30am and 6.00pm

Open daily 8.30am–7.30 pm

ROMAN CATHOLIC

66 MONTROSE OLD CHURCH

NO 715 778

High Street, Montrose

Built 1793 by John Gibson with a 'lovely flying-buttressed spire (J Gillespie Graham 1832) which is Montrose's town-mark' (Colin McWilliam, *Scottish Townscape*). By rail Intercity London to Aberdeen. Sunday Service: 11am, also last Sunday 6.30pm

Open June to August, Monday to Friday 2pm–4.30pm

CHURCH OF SCOTLAND **A**

67 MURROES AND TEALING CHURCH

No 461 351

Murroes, nr Broughty Ferry

T-plan church by William Smith 1848 on a site occupied by a church for 750 years. Church records from 1202. Interesting gravestones and coping on churchyard wall carved with texts in English, Latin and Greek. Interior is simple and relatively original. Pews with doors, four impressive stained glass windows in south wall and small pipe organ in gallery recently restored. Former coach house and stables restored to provide hall, chapel, kitchen and toilet facilities. Linked with Auchterhouse. Sunday Service: 10am

Open by arrangement, telephone Gordon Laird 01382 350242

CHURCH OF SCOTLAND

MURROES AND TEALING CHURCH

68 TANNADICE CHURCH

NO 475 581

Present church by John Carver built 1866 on site of previous buildings. Place of Christian worship since 7th century. Monastery recorded in 1187 and Kirk of Tanatheys consecrated by the Bishop of St Andrew's 1242. Union with Oathlaw 1982. St Columba and St Francis windows at west end of church 1976 in memory of 2nd Lord Forres of Glenogil. Former Oathlaw war memorial windows on north wall, by James Ballantine 1923 and Neil Hamilton 1949. Linked with St Andrew's, Kirriemuir four miles north of Forfar on B957, A90 from Dundee.

Sunday Service: 9.45am

Key available at Post Office 9.30-11.30am. Or by arrangement, telephone Mrs Davidson 01307 850345

CHURCH OF SCOTLAND

C

TANNADICE CHURCH

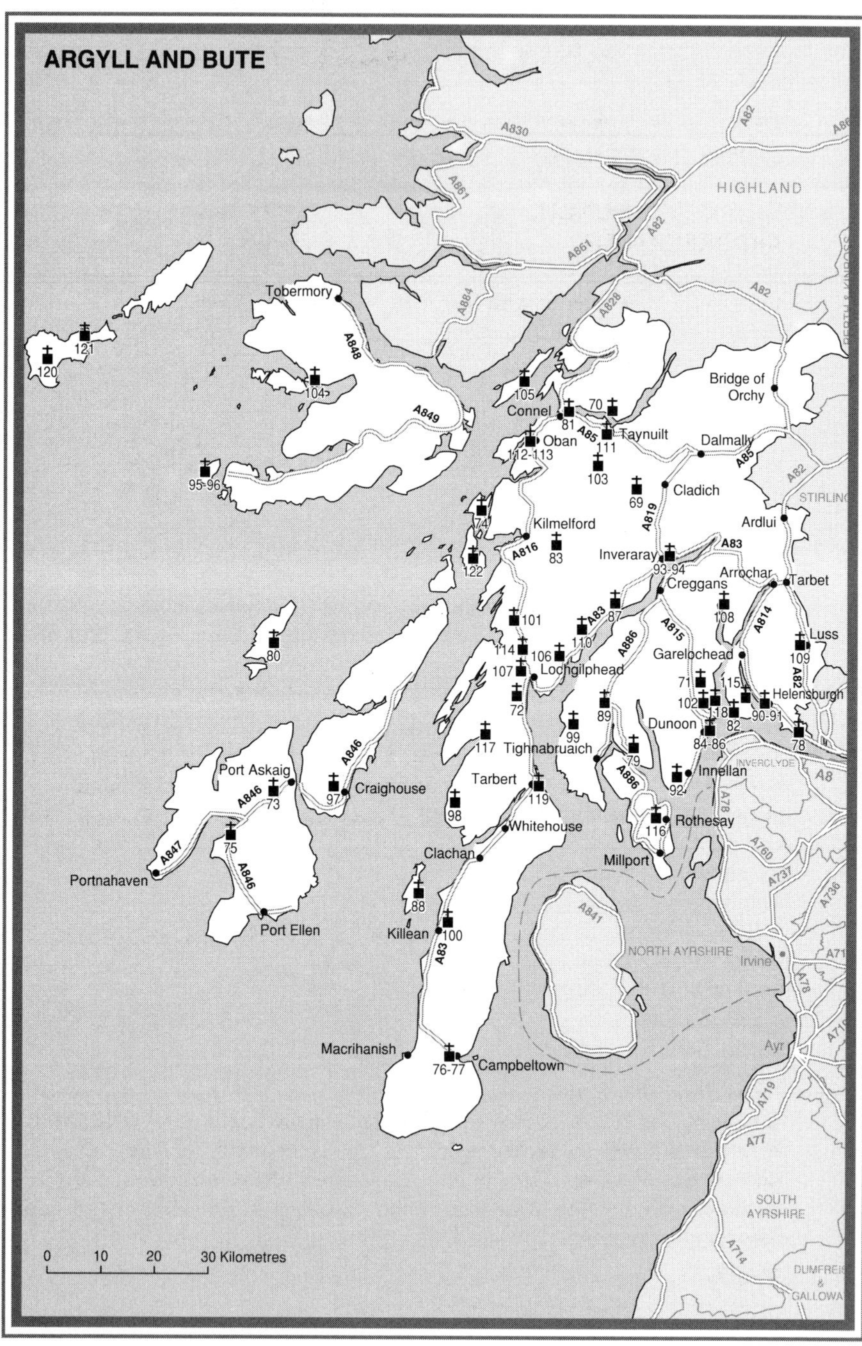
ARGYLL AND BUTE
HIGHLAND
STIRLING
INVERCLYDE
NORTH AYRSHIRE
SOUTH AYRSHIRE
Tobermory
Connel
Oban
Taynuilt
Dalmally
Bridge of Orchy
Cladich
Kilmelford
Inveraray
Ardlui
Arrochar
Tarbet
Creggans
Luss
Garelochead
Helensburgh
Lochgilphead
Dunoon
Tighnabruaich
Innellan
Tarbert
Whitehouse
Rothesay
Millport
Clachan
Port Askaig
Craighouse
Portnahaven
Port Ellen
Killean
Macrihanish
Campbeltown
Irvine
Ayr
0 10 20 30 Kilometres

ARGYLL & BUTE

Local Representative: Mr Michael Gossip, Tigh-na-Coille, Ardrishaig (*telephone 01546 603454)*

69 ST JAMES' CHURCH, ARDBRECKNISH

NN 072 212

Built 1891, stone interior with fine series of monuments and excellent windows. Bells rehung 1991. Grass churchyard overlooking Loch Awe. Sunday Service: in summer 11am, 3pm Eucharist on 3rd Sunday of the month (winter). Linked with St John's Cathedral, Oban

Church website: www.scotland.anglican.org/argyll

Open daylight hours in summer

SCOTTISH EPISCOPAL

ST JAMES' CHURCH, ARDBRECKNISH

70 CHURCH OF THE HOLY SPIRIT, ARDCHATTAN

NM 971 349

Built 1886. Fine First World War memorial incorporating the three banners of Scotland, England and Ireland. Ardchattan crucifix on south wall. Stone pedestal font and ancient stone stoup. One mile west of Bonawe Quarry, beside Loch Etive. Sunday Service: 2nd Sunday, 12.15pm. Linked with St John's Cathedral, Oban

Website: www.scotland.anglican.org/argyll

Open by arrangement, contact Mrs Colquhoun, The Ferry House, Ardchattan

SCOTTISH EPISCOPAL

71 ARDENTINNY

NS 188 876

Shore Road, Ardentinny

Simple oblong kirk of 1838-9 with three tall windows each side. Gabled front with gabled porch and arched bellcote at apex. Pulpit with sounding board decorated with finials. The church contains the memorials to the men of *HMS Armadillo*, the wartime Royal Navy Commando Unit who trained in Ardentinny. Sunday Service: 2.30pm

Open daily

CHURCH OF SCOTLAND WC **B**

72 ARDRISHAIG PARISH CHURCH

NR 854 852

Tarbert Road, Ardrishaig

Gothic tower-fronted nave church of 1860 with low semi-octagonal transpets and vestibule added 1904. The octagonal castellated stage of the tower and the sharp spire were added in 1868. Edwardian Art Nouveau patterned stained glass in all windows. Sunday Service: 11.00am

Open by arrangement with Mr Gossip, telephone 01546 603454 or the Minister, telephone 01546 603269

CHURCH OF SCOTLAND

ARDRISHAIG PARISH CHURCH

73 KILMENY PARISH CHURCH, BALLYGRANT, ISLE OF ISLAY

NR 353 636

Kilmeny Parish Church is situated in sheltered wooded grounds which are at the moment being developed. The present church was remodelled in 1828 to plans by Thomas Telford and stands about 400m NE of its medieval predecessor. There is evidence of a number of early Celtic Church foundations within the parish boundary, and nearby is the famous Finlaggan site, administrative centre of the Lords of the Isles. The church has been the recipient of some fine gifts, the most recent being an organ donated by the Caol Ila Distillery Company during their 125th anniversary in 1996. The interior has recently been upgraded with confortable seating both on pews and padded chairs. Linked with Kilarrow. Situated above the main Port Askaig/Bowmore road. Sunday Service: 12.30pm, 10am July and August

Open July to August, Thursday 10.30am–12.30pm and 2–4pm

CHURCH OF SCOTLAND **B**

74 KILBRANDON KIRK, BALVICAR, ISLE OF SEIL

NM 758 155

Kilbrandon Kirk was built in 1866 and contains a beautiful set of five stained glass windows – the work of Douglas Strachan. The windows were commissioned by Miss Mackinnon of Ardmaddy Castle in 1937 in memory of her friend the Marchioness of Breadalbane. On the B8003, one mile south of the Balvicar turn-off. Sunday Service: 10am, except last Sunday 11am

Open all year

CHURCH OF SCOTLAND

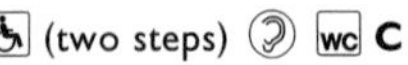

(two steps) **C**

KILBRANDON KIRK, BALVICAR
ISLE OF SEIL

75 KILARROW PARISH CHURCH, BOWMORE, ISLE OF ISLAY

NR 312 596

This 18th-century church, known as 'The Round Church', was built by Daniel Campbell of Shawfield and Islay in 1767. A year after the building commenced, the village of Bowmore came into being as a 'planned village' to rehouse those of the village of Kilarrow who were not directly involved in the work of Islay Estate, mainly agricultural workers and weavers. The two-storey circular body of the church has a main central pillar 19 inches in diameter, possibly of hemlock oak, harled and plastered. Above the coved ceiling is a radial king-post roof truss into which eight major beams are jointed. The gallery was added in 1830, increasing its capacity to 500. Extensive renovation has been carried out in recent years. At the top of Main Street. Linked with Kilmeny. Sunday Service: 11am

KILARROW PARISH CHURCH, BOWMORE, ISLE OF ISLAY

Open daily all year, 9am-6pm

CHURCH OF SCOTLAND (during summer months)  A

76 HIGHLAND PARISH CHURCH, CAMPBELTOWN

NR 720 201

New Quay Street, Campbeltown

'To be causewayed with whinstone and paved with hewn flags. The lock on the front door to be of 20/- value and the rest to have snecks and wooden bolts': the instruction of the architect George Dempster of Greenock, for a new church, built for the Highland, Gaelic-speaking, congregation of the area, and completed in 1807. Harled rubble with red sandstone dressings, an oblong with rectangular stair towers at each end of the front. Three galleries. The planned belfry was not large enough for the heritors, so a steeple was built; twice since it has been rebuilt, the casualty of lightning strikes. The pipe organ, Harrison & Harrison, Durham 1954, is a memorial to the fallen of the Second World War. Sunday Services: 11.15am and 6.30pm

Open daily

CHURCH OF SCOTLAND

B

HIGHLAND PARISH CHURCH, CAMPBELTOWN

77 LORNE AND LOWLAND CHURCH, CAMPBELTOWN

NR 718 206

Longrow, Campbeltown

Built in 1872 to the design of John Burnet, historically called The Longrow Church. Classical, influenced by Italian Renaissance style. Its bell-tower is a well known landmark. Two stairways lead from the entrance foyer to a horse-shoe gallery. Fine plaster ceiling. Pulpit 1895. Sunday Services: 11.15am, 7pm (fortnightly)

Open July to August, Monday to Friday 11am-4pm. Other times, telephone Mr J Gill 01586 552781

CHURCH OF SCOTLAND  C

LORNE AND LOWLAND CHURCH, CAMPBELTOWN

78 CARDROSS PARISH CHURCH

NS 345 775

Station Road, Cardross

Church founded 1225 on west bank of River Leven and rebuilt in village 1640. Present building 1872. Stained glass windows, Sadie McLellan 1972, embroidered panels, Hannah Frew Paterson 1981, woven silk hangings, Sarah Sumsion 1990, and engraved glass windows, John Lawrie 1992. Peal of six bells augmented to eight for the Millennium. A82 from Glasgow; half hourly train service from Glasgow Queen Street. Sunday Services: 9.30am and 10am; June, July, August 10am only; also September to Easter second Sunday 7pm

Open Monday, Wednesday, Thursday and Friday mornings, or by arrangement, telephone Mrs S McLatchie 01389 841509

CHURCH OF SCOTLAND WC B

CARDROSS PARISH CHURCH

79 COLINTRAIVE CHURCH

NS 045 735

Erected 1840 by Mrs Campbell of Southhall as a chapel of ease, part of Inverchaolain parish. Became a Free Church in 1843, United Free in 1900 and returned to the Church of Scotland in 1929. United with Kilmodan Church. Spectacular views over Kyles of Bute. Sunday Service: 10am or 11.30am, alternating monthly with Kilmodan

Open daily

CHURCH OF SCOTLAND 

80 COLONSAY PARISH CHURCH

NR 890 941

By Scalasaig ferry terminal

Built by Michael Carmichael, 1802, on a site of a medieval chapel and close to a Bronze Age burial site. Neighbouring former Parochial School is mentioned in John Buchan's *Island of Sheep*. The church originally had galleries at both ends, accessed by extramural staircases. Attractive wooden ceiling. Sunday Service: 11.00am

Normally open at all times. For assistance, telephone Kevin Byrne 01951 200320

CHURCH OF SCOTLAND **B**

81 ST ORAN'S CHURCH, CONNEL

NM 914 343

Gothic Revival cruciform church of 1888 with lancet and pointed traceried windows, gabled porch and a central tower with corbelled parapet. Good interior with open timbered ceiling. Fine collection of 20th-century glass by various artists. Beautiful views up Loch Etive from garden. On A85. Sunday Service: 10.30am

Open during daylight hours

CHURCH OF SCOTLAND **B**

ST ORAN'S CHURCH, CONNEL

82 CRAIGROWNIE CHURCH, COVE

NS 224 810

Church Road, Cove, near Helensburgh

Daughter Church of Rosneath, opened 1851. Architect David Cousin, enlarged by Honeyman & Keppie 1889. Organ by James J Binns of Leeds. Various examples of stained glass including J Benson, S Adam, Mayer & Co. Frescoes by the sisters Doris and Anna Zinkeisen of the four Evangelists. Nearby Church Hall in a former church designed by Hugh Barclay, 1858, with windows by F Hase-Hayden, A Webster, A McW Webster and others. Sunday Service: 11.30am, 10am in 2002

Open by arrangement with the Minister, telephone 01436 842274

CHURCH OF SCOTLAND

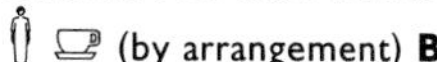 (by arrangement) **B**

CRAIGROWNIE CHURCH, COVE

DALAVICH CHURCH

83 DALAVICH CHURCH

NM 968 124

15 miles from Taynuilt

The building dates from about 1770. Linked with Muckairn and Kilchrenan. A small bell-tower built on the gable to celebrate the Millennium. Sunday Services: 10.00am, second and fourth Sundays of the month

Open by arrangement, telephone MacIntosh, 1 Dalavich, by Taynuilt

CHURCH OF SCOTLAND

84 DUNOON BAPTIST CHURCH CENTRE

NS 171 770

9 Alexandra Parade, Dunoon

Formerly the American servicemen's YMCA. The centre welcomes all visitors to the beautiful Cowal Peninsula. Browse in the well-stocked Christian book and gift shop. Sample excellent coffee and home baking with a splendid view of the Clyde estuary. Next to Tourist Information Centre and five minutes from the pier. Sunday Services: 11am and 6.30pm

Open Monday to Saturday 10am–4pm

BAPTIST A

85 DUNOON OLD AND ST CUTHBERT'S CHURCH

NS 173 769

Church Square, Dunoon

The present building probably stands on the site of a much earlier church which until 1688 was the Cathedral Church of both the Roman Catholic and Episcopalian Bishops of Argyll. Towards the end of the 18th century the building became dilapidated and was demolished, the stone being used to build Gillespie Graham's Late Decorated Gothic Revival church of 1816. The belfry tower was added in 1839 and the church was lengthened and widened by Andrew Balfour in 1909. Chancel window 1939 by Douglas Hamilton. Gravestones of the 13th and 17th century in the kirkyard. Sunday Service: October to May 11am, June to September 10.30am

1–3 August 2002, Flower Festival. June to September inclusive: exhibition (history and memorabilia), Monday to Saturday 10.30am–12.30pm and 2–4pm. Other times open by arrangement, telephone the Rev P Lang, 1 Royal Crescent, Dunoon 01369 701291

CHURCH OF SCOTLAND **B**

86 ST JOHN'S CHURCH, DUNOON

NS 172 769

Argyll Street, Dunoon

A magnificent nave and aisles kirk by R A Bryden 1877 built to supersede the original Free Church of 1843. Normandy Gothic spired tower. Galleried 'concert hall' interior. Raised choir behind central pulpit. Three-manual pipe organ by Brook & Co 1895. Interesting stained glass including windows by Stephen Adam and Gordon Webster, also Lauder Memorial. Sunday Services: 10.15am and 6.30pm (last Sunday of the month)

Open June, July, August and September: Monday to Friday 10am–12noon. September Sunday concerts at 3pm (last 3 Sundays in September), includes organ recitals, visiting choirs, etc 01369 830639

CHURCH OF SCOTLAND

 **A**

ST JOHN'S CHURCH, DUNOON

87 CUMLODDEN PARISH CHURCH, FURNACE

NS 014 994

Built in 1841 by local mason, David Crow, to a design by James Nairn of Balloch. Interior redesigned 1894. Contains an early Christian cross-shaft showing a bearded figure, 8th or 9th century, removed from Killevin Burial Ground. Stained glass, 1924, by William Meikle & Sons, Glasgow. Sunday Service: 10.30am, 4th Sunday 11.00am

Open by arrangement with the Minister, telephone 01499 500288

CHURCH OF SCOTLAND WC **C**

88 GIGHA AND CARA PARISH CHURCH, ISLE OF GIGHA

NR 643 481

Built 1923. Windows by Gordon Webster. First minister Dr Kenneth MacLeod author of 'The Road to the Isles'. Gigha Gardens and nine-hole golf course ten minutes walk from church. Ferry from Tayinloan/Kintyre 20 minutes. Sunday Service: 12 noon

Open daily

CHURCH OF SCOTLAND WC (at village shop)

89 KILMODAN CHURCH, GLENDARUEL

NR 995 842

Clachan of Glendaruel

A Georgian T-plan church of 1783 on site of an earlier church of 1610. Completely restored in 1983. Segmental-arched windows; lofts in the three arms. Two long narrow communion tables. Memorial to Rev John MacLaurin and his two famous sons (Colin, author of MacLaurin's Mathematical Theorem). Bus and post bus from Dunoon. On A886. United with Colintraive. Sunday Services: 10am or 11.30am, alternating monthly with Colintraive

Open daily

CHURCH OF SCOTLAND WC (nearby)

KILMODAN CHURCH, GLENDARUEL

90 ST MICHAEL AND ALL ANGELS, HELENSBURGH

NS 292 825

William Street, Helensburgh

ST MICHAEL AND ALL ANGELS, HELENSBURGH

Built by Robert Rowand Anderson in 1868 in French Gothic style. Tower with peal of eight bells added in 1930. Richly decorated interior with oak chancel screen, elaborately carved Austrian oak north porch screen. West porch screen (1996) of light oak and engraved glass by James Anderson. Alabaster and mosaic reredos against encaustic tiling. Organ by August Gern, foreman to Cavaille-Coll. Fine sculpted west portal nave and chancel capitals. Good stained glass; light by Clayton & Bell, Shrigley & Hunt, Adam & Small, and Barraud & Westlake, with five windows by C E Kempe including fine rose window in west façade. 800m west of Central railway station, off Clyde Street. Services: Sunday 8am, 10.15am and 6.30pm; Tuesdays 10.30am; Wednesdays 7.30pm

Open daily 9am-5pm

SCOTTISH EPISCOPAL A

91 THE WEST KIRK OF HELENSBURGH

NS 295 825

Colquhoun Square, Helensburgh

Victorian Gothic building of 1853, J, W H & J M Hay, restored after disastrous fire in 1924 by Robert Wemyss, with a porch by William Leiper. Impressive panelled interior, with fine woodwork and half-timbered ceiling. Exceptionally fine stained glass including memorial windows to Andrew Bonar Law, one time Prime Minister, and to John Logie Baird, inventor of television and son of the Manse in Helensburgh. Hill House (Charles Rennie Mackintosh) is one mile away. Sunday Service: 10am May to August, 11am September to April

Open daily all year 9am-5pm; and with guides June to August, Monday, Wednesday and Friday 2-4pm. Exhibition summer months

CHURCH OF SCOTLAND

B

THE WEST KIRK OF HELENSBURGH

92 INNELLAN PARISH CHURCH

NS 152 707

7 Matheson Lane, Innellan

Built of local whin rubble in 1852 and expanded in 1867 and again in 1887. Fine stone pulpit from 1887 re-ordering. The central stained glass window is a version of Holman Hunt's 'The Light of the World' which glows whatever the lighting conditions. The church is best known for its association with George Matheson who ministered for 18 years from 1869 during which time he wrote 'O Love that wilt not let me go'. Sunday Service: 11.30am

Open by arrangement with the Clerk to the Congregational Board, telephone 01369 830554

CHURCH OF SCOTLAND

93 ALL SAINTS CHURCH AND BELL-TOWER, INVERARAY

NN 095 085

The Avenue, Inveraray

Gothic-style church built 1885 in local red granite, designed by Wardrop and Anderson of Edinburgh. Many of the interior furnishings given by Niell Dairmid, 10th Duke of Argyll. Belltower, in Gothic revivial by Hoare & Wheeler, built 1923-31 as a memorial to Campbell dead of First World War and previous wars. Peal of 10 bells by John Taylor of Loughborough, 1926. Exhibition in entrance to ringing chamber. Sunday Service: 2nd Sunday 3.00pm

Church website: www.scotland.anglican.org/inveraray.htm

Open daily, early April to end September

SCOTTISH EPISCOPAL WC **B** (Church) **A** (bell-tower)

94 GLENARAY & INVERARAY PARISH CHURCH, INVERARAY

NN 096 084

Church Square, Inveraray

Designed by Robert Mylne in 1792 to house two congregations, English and Gaelic. A solid wall separated the two. Gaelic portion converted to church hall 1957. Sunday Service: June, July and August 10.45am (experiment for 2001), all other months 11.45am

Open July and August on request at Church exhibition and sale in Church Hall at rear of Church

CHURCH OF SCOTLAND **A**

GLENARAY & INVERARAY PARISH CHURCH, IN INVERARAY

95 IONA ABBEY

NM 287 245

Isle of Iona

On the original site of St Columba's monastery c.563. St Columba's Shrine dates from the 9th century, most of the present buildings from around 1200. The massive restoration of the Abbey Church was undertaken by the Iona Cathedral Trust, who own the buildings, and was completed in 1910. The Iona Community now occupy the monastic buildings which they restored under the leadership of the Rev Dr George MacLeod. Historic Scotland now have the resposibility to care for the Abbey and associated monuments. Beautiful Augustinian nunnery, 12th-century ruin, Reilig Odhrain (Royal burial ground), 'Street of the Dead', imposing standing crosses and one of the largest collections of early Christian carved stones in Europe. Ferry from Oban to Mull, by bus/car to Fionnphort, pedestrian ferry to Iona. Services: Sunday 10.30am and Monday to Saturday 2.00pm, March to October; also Monday to Saturday 9.00am all year

Open at all times

INTER-DENOMINATIONAL WC **A**

96 IONA PARISH CHURCH

NM 285 243

Isle of Iona

A Thomas Telford church of 1828. Pews, pulpit and communion table realigned in 1939. Former manse of same date now a heritage centre with picnic area adjacent. Ferry from Oban to Mull. Bus/car to Fionnphort for ferry to Iona. Sunday Service: 12 noon. Short Service: Tuesday 1pm and each weekday in high summer

Open daily

CHURCH OF SCOTLAND **B**

IONA PARISH CHURCH

97 JURA PARISH CHURCH

NR 527 677

Craighouse, Isle of Jura

The harled church was built in 1776. Pennant in his *Voyage to the Hebrides* (1776) says 'land in Jura, at a little village, and see to the right on the shore the church, and the minister's manse'. Alterations 1842 and 1922. Superb photographic exhibition of 'Old Jura' in gallery behind the church. Sunday Service: 11.30am

Open at all times

CHURCH OF SCOTLAND

98 KILBERRY PARISH CHURCH

NR 741 620

The church was built in 1821. A plain oblong building, galleries on three sides, later alterations provided an internal stair and removed the original external access. At Lergnahension, twelve miles from Tarbert on the B8024. Sunday Services: fortnightly, summer 10am, winter 2pm

Open all year during daylight hours

CHURCH OF SCOTLAND **B**

KILBERRY PARISH CHURCH

99 KILFINAN PARISH CHURCH

NR 934 789

A place of worship since 1235. Gothic 1759, including the earlier Lamont Vault of 1633. Stones of interest. B8000 from Tighnabruaich or Strachur. Sunday Service: 12 noon

Open all year

CHURCH OF SCOTLAND **B**

100 KILLEAN & KILCHENZIE KIRK, A'CHLEIT, KINTYRE

NR 681 418

A83, 1 mile north of Muasdale

The church, 1787-91 by Thomas Cairns, is set on a rocky promontory out to sea. White harled with round arched windows. Belfry added 1879 by Robert Weir. The pulpit, in the long west wall, is a First World War memorial with Celtic style carving and faces a large laird's loft. Beside the pulpit is a marble monument of 1818 to Col Norman Macalister. Sunday Service: 11.15am

Flower Festival mid-July 2002. Open daily

CHURCH OF SCOTLAND WC (on request) **A**

101 KILMARTIN PARISH CHURCH

NR 836 993

Kilmartin, by Lochgilphead

On the site of earlier churches, the present building opened in 1835. The architect was James Gordon Davis. Three interesting memorial panels from the 18th and 19th centuries to members of the family of Campbell of Duntroon. The church has two outstanding crosses, with explanatory panels provided by Historic Scotland. The kirkyard contains the mausoleum of Bishop Neil Campbell and medieval tomb slabs. Extensive views over Bronze Age burial cairns. Services: see local paper and notice board

Open April to October, 9.30am-6pm

CHURCH OF SCOTLAND B

KILMARTIN PARISH CHURCH

102 KILMUN PARISH CHURCH, ST MUNN'S

NS 166 821

Kilmun, by Dunoon

On the site of a Celtic monastery, overlooking Holy Loch. Tower of 15th-century collegiate church. Present building dates from 1841, by Thomas Burns with interior remodelled by P MacGregor Chalmers in 1899. Important stained glass by Stephen Adam and Alfred Webster. Water-powered organ. Ancient graveyard with fine 18th-century carved stones. Mausoleum of Dukes of Argyll, Douglas vault. Grave of Elizabeth Blackwell, first lady doctor. On A880, 6 miles from Dunoon. Sunday Service: 12 noon

Open May to end September, Tuesday to Thursday and holiday Mondays 1.30-4.30pm (last tour 4pm). Other times, including coach parties by arrangement, telephone Valerie Gilles 01369 840342. Younger Botanic Gardens, two miles, open April to October

CHURCH OF SCOTLAND WC B

KILMUN PARISH CHURCH, ST MUNN'S

KILCHRENAN PARISH CHURCH

103 KILCHRENAN PARISH CHURCH

NN 037 229

The building was built in 1770 on the site of an earlier church dating back to the 12th century. Some stones from that church have been incorporated into the present building. There are interesting tombstones in the graveyard including that of Cailean Mor in 1294. Linked with Muckairn and Dalavich.

Sunday Services: 10.00am on the first, third and fifth Sundays of the month

Open during daylight hours

CHURCH OF SCOTLAND

104 KILNINIAN PARISH CHURCH

NM 458 398

Kilninian, Isle of Mull

Built in 1755, this is the oldest church on Mull and once was the senior church on the island. A very simple rectangular building enhanced by Telford. The vestry contains eight very ancient burial stones originally thought to have been lifted from Iona to protect them from pillage by the Vikings. Communion table, 20ft, with benches, a rare example. Services: first Sunday, Morning Service 8.45am; all other Sundays, informal worship 10.00am

CHURCH OF SCOTLAND

KILNINIAN PARISH CHURCH

105 ST MOLUAG, ISLE OF LISMORE, KENTALLEN

NN 007 573

'The Cathedral of Argyll' was built in late 14th to early 15th-century and attributed locally to 'The Roman' or 'An Roimhanach'. Six stained glass windows, two modern by Mitton. Eight medieval carved slab-stones, said to be of the 'Loch Awe' school and recumbent carved stone within the building. Traditional Baptismal font is carved in a natural rock surface. Exhibition on 800 years of Christianity on Lismore

Open at all times

CHURCH OF SCOTLAND WC (by arrangement)

ST MOLUAG, ISLE OF LISMORE, KENTALLEN

106 LOCHGAIR PARISH CHURCH

NR 922 905

Originally Mission Church of Glassary Parish. Built 1867 to a simple oblong design. Half-octagon box pulpit centred between blind lancets. Services: first and third Sundays 3.00pm, second Sunday of the month; Gaelic Service: 3.00pm, fifth Sunday 6.30pm

Open during daylight hours

CHURCH OF SCOTLAND WC **C**

107 CHRIST CHURCH, LOCHGILPHEAD

NR 860 884

Bishopton Road, Lochgilphead

Church and adjoining rectory designed by John Henderson, 1850-51. Nave-and-chancel church with an arch-braced nave roof. Organ chamber built 1887-8 to house the organ by William Hill & Son, 1876. Sunday Services: 9.00am (except 1st Sunday) and 11.00am

Church website: www.scotland.anglican.org/lochgilphead.htm

Open during daylight hours

SCOTTISH EPISCOPAL (ramps available) **B**

108 LOCHGOILHEAD & KILMORICH PARISH CHURCH

NN 198 015

Lochgoilhead

Dedicated to the Three Holy Brethren, the church is first mentioned in papal letters of 1379. It was rebuilt in the 18th century incorporating the medieval walls. Many features of interest. A83 Arrochar–Inveraray, top of Rest and Be Thankful, B828 and B839 into village. Sunday Service: 10.30am

Open by arrangement, telephone Mr W Workman 013013 280.

Church Fair in August. Coffee mornings depending on local weather conditions

CHURCH OF SCOTLAND **B**

LOCHGOILHEAD & KILMORICH PARISH CHURCH

109 LUSS PARISH CHURCH

NS 361 929

This picturesque church, the third built on this site on the banks of Loch Lomond, with its beautiful stained glass windows and uniquely timbered roof, features frequently in 'Take the High Road'. The ancient graveyard has 15 listed ancient monuments. Luss Village, off A82. Sunday Service: 11.45am

Open daily from 10am

CHURCH OF SCOTLAND **B**

110 LOCHFYNESIDE PARISH CHURCH, MINARD

NR 978 962

Good example of a corrugated-iron church by Speirs & Co of Glasgow, 'Designers and Erectors of Iron and Wood Buildings'. Stained glass window by Sax Shaw, 1984. Pulpit of ancient ash from Crarae estate, designed by Ilay M Campbell. Service: 12 noon except fourth Sunday

Open by arrangement with the Minister, telephone 01499 500288

CHURCH OF SCOTLAND

LOCHFYNESIDE PARISH CHURCH, MINARD

MUCKAIRN PARISH CHURCH, TAYNUILT

111 MUCKAIRN PARISH CHURCH, TAYNUILT

NN 005 310

Built in 1829 the church stands adjacent to the ruins (1228) of Killespickerill, once the seat of the Bishop of Argyll. Two stones of antiquity are built into the walls of the present Church. Tombstones from the 14th century can be seen in the graveyard. Linked with Kilchrenan and Dalavich. Sunday Service: 11.45am

Open during daylight hours

CHURCH OF SCOTLAND WC

112 CATHEDRAL CHURCH OF ST JOHN THE DIVINE, OBAN

NM 859 304

George Street, Oban

The cathedral is a small part of the projected building, consisting of chancel, crossing, nave of one bay and one transept by James Chalmers, 1908, attached at right angles to existing church by Charles Wilson and David Thomson, giving an extraordinary building internally. Tall reredos on a Scottish theme with painting of Ascension set in the West Highlands by Norman Macdougall. Vast hovering bronze eagle. Choir stalls in form of Celtic graveyard. Much Iona marble and terrazzo. Sunday Services: 8am, 10.15am, Wednesdays 11am

Church website: www.scotland.anglican.org/argyll

Open daily

SCOTTISH EPISCOPAL  C

CATHEDRAL CHURCH OF ST JOHN THE DIVINE, OBAN

113 ST COLUMBA'S CATHEDRAL, OBAN

NM 855 307

Corran Esplanade, Oban

Built between 1932 and 1958, St Columba's Cathedral is the principal Church of the Roman Catholic Diocese of Argyll and the Isles. Designed by Giles Gilbert Scott in the neo-Gothic style, of highly distinctive, lofty, pink granite. The tower soars above the Esplanade. High timber reredos with intricate Gothic fretwork, designed by Scott and carved by Donald Gilbert. Services: Saturday, Vigil Mass 7 pm; Sunday, Mass 10.30am

Church website: www.stcolumbascathedral.co.uk

Open dawn to dusk

ROMAN CATHOLIC **A**

114 ST COLUMBA'S, POLTALLOCH

NR 816 965

Poltalloch Estate, by Kilmartin

In the gentle parkland of ruined Poltalloch House (William Burn 1849), St Columba's was conceived as a private chapel but built as a church with congregation and incumbent. Built 1852 to a design by William Cundy of London in Early English style with leafy carvings and pointed arches. Complete set of stained glass by William Wailes. Two Whitechapel Foundry bells. Three misericord seats. Sunday Services: first Sunday 9.00am, third Sunday 3.30pm

Church website: www.scotland.anglican.org/kilmartin.htm

Open Daily

SCOTTISH EPISCOPAL **B**

115 ST MODAN'S PARISH CHURCH, ROSNEATH

NS 2583

A814 to Garelochhead, then B833 to Rosneath

There has been a church at Rosneath since the time of St Modan c.AD 600–50, the present building, 1853, is by architect David Cousin. The bell from the earlier church, and now on display in the present building, was made by Ian Burgerhuis in 1610 and was rung as a summons to arms during the 1715 Jacobite rebellion. Two-manual organ by Hill, 1875. Reredos of ten commandments by W A Muirhead and The Last Supper by Meredith Williams, carved by Thomas Wood. Mural of St Modan by Mary Ainsworth, 1995. Stained glass by Clayton & Bell, Douglas Strachan, Stephen Adam & Co, Gordon Webster, Crear McCartney. Sunday Service: 10.30am (11.30am in 2002)

Open by arrangement, telephone the Minister 01436 842274

CHURCH OF SCOTLAND WC (by arrangement) **A**

ST MODAN'S PARISH CHURCH, ROSNEATH

116 TRINITY PARISH CHURCH, ROTHESAY

NS 089 645

Castle Street, Rothesay

Opened as the Free Church in 1845. Designed by Archibald Simpson in severe Gothic with a square tower surmounted with a slender spire. The interior, in contrast, is softened by the warmth of the hammer-beam roof and colourful stained glass windows, a triple lancet First World War memorial by Oscar Paterson and, adjacent to the pulpit, the Second World War memorial by Gordon Webster. Only Church of Scotland church in the centre of Rothesay. Sunday Services: 11am and 6.30pm, first Sunday of the month

Open by arrangement with Miss A A Montgomery, telephone 01700 502248

CHURCH OF SCOTLAND **B**

117 SOUTH KNAPDALE PARISH CHURCH

NR 781 775

Achahoish, by Lochgilphead

Parish of South Knapdale was formed in 1734 and churches were built at Achahoish and Inverneill (now a ruin). Achahoish was completed 1775, rectangular in plan with a square castellated tower added in the 19th century. Ancient font basin from St Columba's Cave. Sunday Services: May to September 9.45am, October to March 12.30pm

Open by arrangement with Mr and Mrs Brown, Inn Cottage, Achahoish, telephone 01880 770269

CHURCH OF SCOTLAND **C**

SOUTH KNAPDALE PARISH CHURCH

118 STRONE (ST COLUMBA'S)

NS 193 806

Shore Road, Strone

The square, battlemented tower and spire survive of the original 1858 church and are used as a navigation aid for shipping. The rest of the building 1907-8 by Peter MacGregor Chalmers using material from the old church. Stained glass by Stephen Adam and Gordon Webster. United with Ardentinny in 1932. Sunday Service: 10.30am

Open daily

CHURCH OF SCOTLAND (after Service) **B**

119 TARBERT PARISH CHURCH

NR 863 686

Campbeltown Road, Tarbert

Built in 1886 on the site of an earlier mission church dating from 1775 and granted *quoad sacra* status in 1864. Architects J McKissack and W G Rowan of Glasgow. The building features an imposing square tower rising over 100ft, surmounted by a crown and lantern. Stained glass windows and unusual roof decoration. Eighteenth-century graveyard within walking distance. Sunday Service: 11.30am

Open April to September, 10am–5.30pm

CHURCH OF SCOTLAND **B**

TARBERT PARISH CHURCH

120 HEYLIPOL CHURCH, TIREE

NM 964 432

Barrapol, Tiree

The distinctiveness of Heylipol church or Eaglais na Mointeach – the Church of the Moss – is enhanced by its location at a crossroads in a stretch of open country. Built 1902 by architect William MacKenzie of Oban, in cruciform Gothic with a bell-tower over the porch. Sunday Services: 11.30pm and 6.00pm (alternating with Kirkapol Church)

Open at all times. Information on a Tiree pilgrimage route linking ancient and modern ecclesiastical sites can be obtained from the Tiree Heritage Society, c/o Miss Fiona MacKinnon, Lodge Farm, Kirkapol, Tiree PA77 6TW

CHURCH OF SCOTLAND WC

121 KIRKAPOL CHURCH, TIREE

NM 041 468

Kirkapol, Gott Bay, Tiree

The current church of Kirkapol (Norse for 'Church Town') is a continuing witness to the Christian faith that stretches back to Columban times. Built in 1842 by architect-contractor Peter MacNab as a simple square box with galleries on three sides focused on a central pulpit. Some of the granite came from the same quarry as that for the Skerryvore lighthouse. Inside, the focus is the box pulpit of 1893 at the centre of the north wall. Sunday Services: 11.30pm and 6.00pm (alternating with Heylipol Church)

Open at all times

CHURCH OF SCOTLAND WC **B**

122 KILCHATTAN KIRK, TOBERONOCHY, ISLE OF LUING

NM 743 104

Toberonochy, Isle of Luing

Kilchattan Kirk was built in 1936 and houses a beautifully carved, floor-standing, wooden lectern and two wooden offering plates donated by Latvian ship owners to mark the rescue efforts of the islanders when one of their ships foundered in a storm on the island of Belnahua in 1938. Just beyond the school on the road to Toberonochy. Sunday Service: 11.30am, except last Sunday in month 3.15pm

Open all year

CHURCH OF SCOTLAND WC

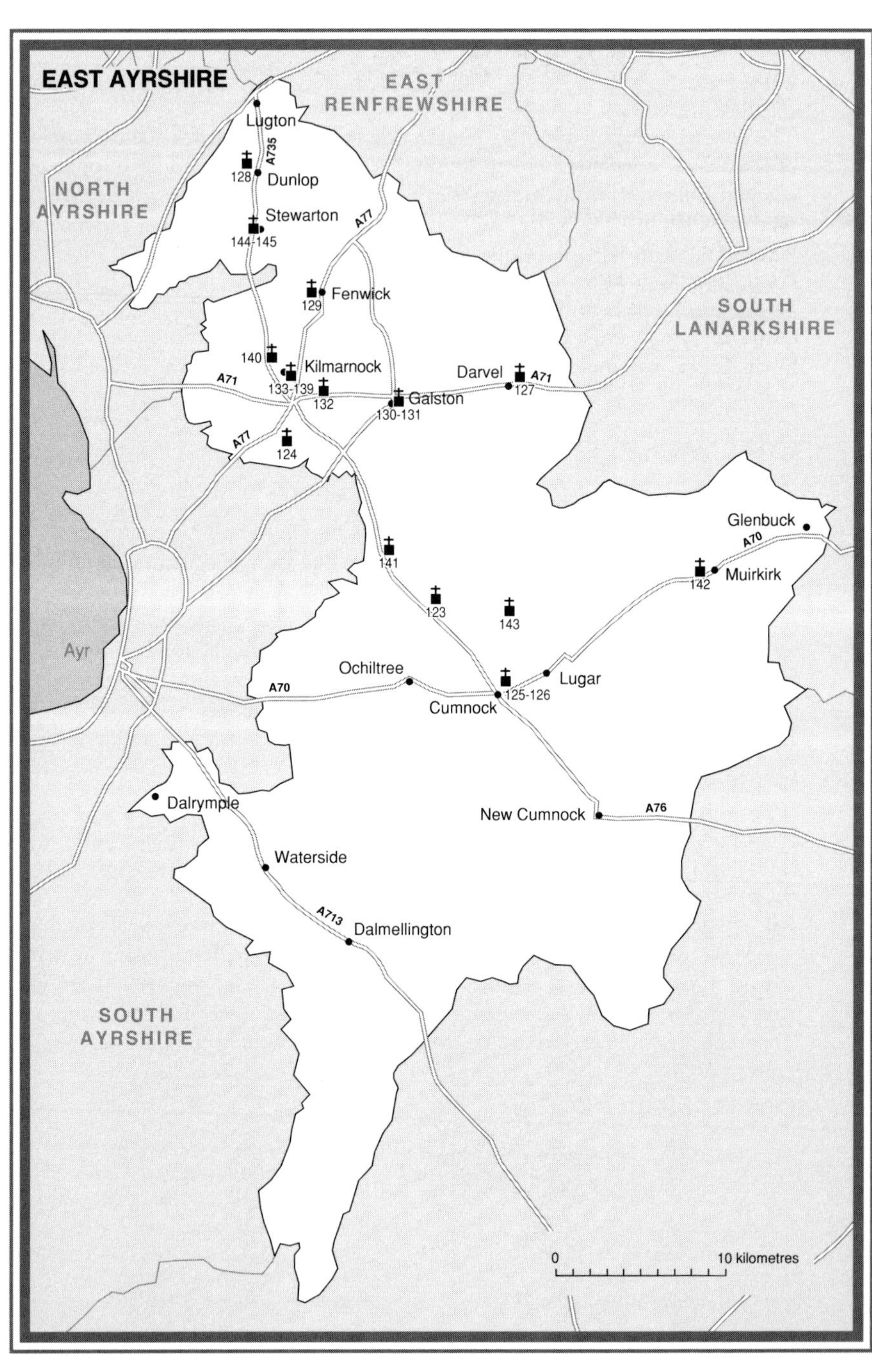
EAST AYRSHIRE
EAST RENFREWSHIRE
NORTH AYRSHIRE
SOUTH LANARKSHIRE
SOUTH AYRSHIRE
Ayr
Lugton
A735
128
Dunlop
Stewarton
144-145
A77
129
Fenwick
140
Kilmarnock
133-139
132
A71
Darvel
127
Galston
130-131
124
Glenbuck
A70
142
Muirkirk
141
123
143
Ochiltree
A70
Cumnock
125-126
Lugar
Dalrymple
New Cumnock
A76
Waterside
A713
Dalmellington
0
10 kilometres

EAST AYRSHIRE

Local Representative: Miss Joan Fish, 31 Oaklands Avenue, Irvine (*telephone* 01294 272654)

123 CATRINE PARISH CHURCH

NS 528 260

Chapel Brae, Catrine

Charming church, built as a chapel of ease in 1792, financed by Sir Claud Alexander of Ballochmyle. It was established as a parish church when Catrine was made a *quoad sacra* parish in 1871. Major renovations in 1874, 1960 and 1992. Stained glass. Harrison & Harrison pipe organ 1883. Overlooking Catrine in the river Ayr valley. B713, off A76 Dumfries–Kilmarnock, between Mauchline and Auchinleck. Sunday Service: 12 noon

CATRINE PARISH CHURCH

Open by arrangement, telephone Mr Holland 01290 551718

CHURCH OF SCOTLAND ♿ 👂 WC **A**

124 CRAIGIE PARISH CHURCH

NS 427 323

Pleasant traditional country kirk built 1776. Remains of previous church c.1580, but the site was occupied by a church from medieval times. Three miles from Prestwick Airport off A77 (two miles along Tarbolton Road).

Sunday Service: 12 noon first and third Sundays

Open by arrangement, telephone Mrs J Morris 01563 860283

CHURCH OF SCOTLAND ♿

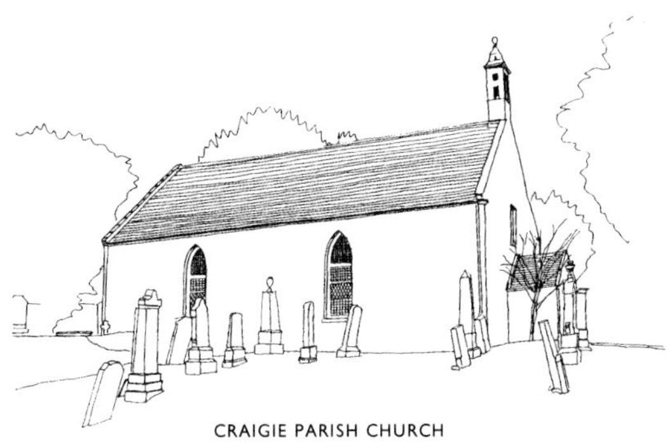

CRAIGIE PARISH CHURCH

125 OLD CUMNOCK OLD CHURCH

NS 508 202

The Square, Cumnock

OLD CUMNOCK OLD CHURCH

Commanding a prominent position in the square of this old market town, the church was built in 1866 through the patronage of the Marquess of Bute and the Bute family seats remain in the Memorial Chapel. Organ 1966. Mosaic of Jesus walking on the water by James Harrigan. Bell in vestibule was cast in 1697 by Quinus de Vesscher of Rotterdam, and was used in the two churches which preceded the present building. Services: Sunday 11.30am; on days of opening 12.30pm; plus Tuesday and Friday 12.30pm

Open July and August Tuesday and Fridays 12noon-4pm, Thursdays 11am-2pm

CHURCH OF SCOTLAND (at Words of Wisdom opposite church) **B**

126 ST JOHN THE EVANGELIST, CUMNOCK

NS 572 196

92 Glaisnock Road, Cumnock

Rare Scottish example of the work of William Burges, 1882, for the Marquess of Bute, and the first ecclesiactical building in Scotland to be lit by electricity. Lush feast of painted surfaces, rich furniture, glorious stained glass and an altarpiece by J F Bentley and N J Westlake. Services: Saturday 6.00pm, Sunday 11.45am

Open by arrangement with Parish Priest, telephone 01290 421031

ROMAN CATHOLIC **B**

127 OUR LADY OF THE VALLEY, DARVEL

NS 5637

4 West Donington Street, Darvel

Church built by seceders in 1874 and closed in 1927. Various users of the building, *eg* Girl Guides, until early 1950s when it again lay empty. Purchased in mid-1960s by Darvel Parish Church and used as a Church Hall before being sold to the Catholic community and opened by Bishop Maurice Taylor on 25 November 1984. Sunday Service: 10am

Church website: www.saintsophias.fsnet.co.uk

Open by arrangement, contact Mr A Dougherty telephone 01560 320346

ROMAN CATHOLIC

128 DUNLOP PARISH CHURCH

NS 405 494

Main Street, Dunlop

A Christian site since the 13th century, the present church dates from 1835, though the sculptured stonework of the Dunlop Aisle, 1641, was preserved. Magnificent collection of stained glass by Gordon Webster. Beside the church is Clandeboyes Hall, 1641, built as a school. Built on to the back of Clandeboyes is the early 17th-century monumental tomb of Hans Hamilton, first Protestant minister of Dunlop. Sunday Service: 11am

Open Sunday 2-4 pm, June-September

CHURCH OF SCOTLAND WC **B** (church)
A (tomb and hall)

DUNLOP PARISH CHURCH

129 FENWICK PARISH CHURCH

NS 465 435

Kirkton Road, Fenwick

Built, 1643, in the shape of a Greek cross, with four arms of equal length. Features of note include outside stairs to Rowallan loft with the coat of arms of the Mures of Rowallan above the door, crowstepped gables and 'the jougs' on the south wall. Several Covenanting artefacts, including the battleflag of the Fenwick Covenanters. Walled graveyard contains several notable graves and monuments. Sunday Service: 11am September to May, 10am June to August

Open for half an hour after morning worship or by arrangement with the Minster, telephone 01560 600217

CHURCH OF SCOTLAND WC (in Hall) WC **A**

130 GALSTON PARISH CHURCH

NS 500 367

Cross Street, Galston

Present church, designed by John Brash of Glasgow, erected 1809 on site of Christian worship since 1252. Third church since Reformation. Spire 120ft. Chancel added 1912 and three-manual pipe organ by J J Binns 1913. Stained glass windows the work of Oscar Paterson, a contemporary of Charles Rennie Macintosh. Full restoration of church building completed in 1999. Floodlit since 2000. Ministers include Dr George Smith, great-grandfather of Robert Louis Stevenson and mentioned by Robert Burns in 'The Holy Fair' (grave on north side of church). Also Rev Robert Stirling, inventor of the Stirling Engine. Gravestone of Andrew Richmond, killed by Graham of Claverhouse, on south porch door along with a memorial to five Covenanters. Sunday Service: 11am

Church website: www. galstonparish.org.uk

Open by arrangement, telephone Mrs May McHoull 01563 820890

CHURCH OF SCOTLAND **B**

131 ST SOPHIA, GALSTON

NS 504 365

Bentinck Street, Galston

Constructed 1885-86, architect Sir R Rowand Anderson, the church is a distinctive building freely based on Haghia Sophia in Istanbul. At the behest of Lord Bute, who commissioned the church, Anderson, and possibly Weir Schultz, brought to Galston this dark brick echo of the Byzantine Empire. Currently closed for restoration. Services: Saturday 6.00pm, Sunday 11.30am; Daily Mass as announced

Church website: www.saintsophias.fsnet.co.uk

Open by arrangement, telephone Mr T Heggan 01563 821587

ROMAN CATHOLIC (disabled access available on request)

132 ST PAUL'S ROMAN CATHOLIC, HURLFORD

NS 458 370

Galston Road, Hurlford

The church is a yellow brick building dating from the 1850s. Gothic arches feature in the light and bright interior. Services: Saturday 6.30pm, Sunday 10.30am

Open by arrangement, telephone 01563 525963

ROMAN CATHOLIC A

133 HENDERSON PARISH CHURCH, KILMARNOCK

NS 431 380

London Road, Kilmarnock

Brilliantly individual Arts & Crafts treatment of Gothic motifs by Thomas Smellie, Kilmarnock, completed in 1907. Very tall tower above tall church built on rising ground, with halls below. Carillon of bells 1950. Fine Norman & Beard three-manual organ restored in 1987. Stained glass windows by Gordon Webster 1907, and, in side chapel, by Wendy Robertson 1987. On Burns Heritage Trail, leading to Dean Castle Country Park (open all year). Church in town centre, adjacent to Grand Hall, Palace Theatre and bus station. Sunday Services: 9.45am and 11am

Open by arrangement, telephone Mr J Neil 01563 528212

B

HENDERSON PARISH CHURCH, KILMARNOCK

HOLY TRINITY CHURCH, KILMARNOCK

134 HOLY TRINITY CHURCH, KILMARNOCK

NS 426 377

Portland Road, Kilmarnock

The nave to a design by James Wallace 1857, with chancel and sanctuary by Sir George Gilbert Scott 1876. Wall and ceiling murals in the chancel; stained glass. At the junction of Portland Road with Dundonald Road, 200 yards from King Street. Sunday Services: 9.15am Holy Communion, 11am Sung Eucharist, 6pm Evensong; Matins 11am, first Sunday if not a festival

Church website: www.copinger.org.uk/htk/

Open daily (except when Rector is on holiday)

SCOTTISH EPISCOPAL **B**

135 LAIGH WEST HIGH KIRK, KILMARNOCK

NS 428 379

John Dickie Street, Kilmarnock

Body of the church by Robert Johnstone 1802. Enlarged 1831 with later 19th-century session room. Major refurbishment 1996 by W I Munro Architects, winning 1997 Civic Trust Award for part of town centre regeneration. Interesting monuments and stained glass. Covenanters' graves in adjacent kirkyard. Close to bus and rail stations. Sunday Services: 11am, also 9.30am June to August

Bi-centenary year celebrations 2002-3 programme of events throughout the year. Flower Festival 27-28 September 2002. Open Tuesday, Thursday and Friday mornings. Other times, telephone 01563 528051

CHURCH OF SCOTLAND   **A**

LAIGH WEST HIGH KIRK, KILMARNOCK

136 OLD HIGH KIRK, KILMARNOCK

NS 430 382

Soulis Street, Kilmarnock

Kilmarnock's oldest church, built 1732 of local stone by the Hunter Brothers to a design adapted from St Martin's-in-the-Fields London. Austere exterior contrasts with pleasing interior enhanced by unique set of 23 stained glass windows by W & J J Keir, glaziers to Glasgow Cathedral. Graveyard with tombs including John Wilson, publisher of Robert Burns' first book of poems. Sunday Service: 11am

Open by arrangement, telephone Mr G Thomson 01563 526064

CHURCH OF SCOTLAND WC **A**

OLD HIGH KIRK, KILMARNOCK

137 OUR LADY OF MOUNT CARMEL, KILMARNOCK

NS 428 401

Kirkton Road, Onthank, Kilmarnock

Opened in 1963, Our Lady of Mount Carmel serves the areas of Onthank, Altonhill and Wardneuk in Kilmarnock as well as the villages of Kilmaurs and Fenwick. A large church, possibly its most distinctive features are its stained glass windows and the figure of Christ Crucified. Services: Saturday 6.30pm; Sunday 10am

Open by arrangement with the Parish Priest, telephone 01563 523822

ROMAN CATHOLIC WC

138 ST MARNOCK'S PARISH CHURCH, KILMARNOCK

NS 427 377

St Marnock's Street, Kilmarnock

Perpendicular Gothic, rectangular plan 6-bay church with centrally placed tower on north gable end, by John Ingram 1836. Fine carillon of bells. Three-manual pipe organ 1872, painted organ screen. Extensive restoration programme completed in 1997. In centre of town with easy access from bus and railway station. Sunday Service: 11am (and 9.30am June to mid-August)

Open first Sunday in September each year 12 noon–4pm. Or by arrangement, telephone the Session Clerk 01563 520210. E-mail: jwrca@globalnet.co.uk

CHURCH OF SCOTLAND (free) WC **B**

ST MARNOCK'S PARISH CHURCH, KILMARNOCK

139 ST MATTHEW'S, KILMARNOCK

NS 442 388

Glassyards Road, Kilmarnock

Modern building built in 1977 to have a dual purpose of both hall and church combined. Services: Saturday 6.30pm; Sunday 9.30 and 11am; Monday, Tuesday, Friday and Saturday 10am; Wednesday 8.15am

Open for services

ROMAN CATHOLIC

140 ST MAUR'S GLENCAIRN PARISH CHURCH, KILMAURS

NS 415 408

The church at Kilmaurs was in the possession of Kelso Abbey as early as 1170. In 1413 the present foundation was endowed by Sir William Cunninghame as a collegiate church. Rebuilt by Robert S Ingram 1888 in a cruciform shape. Stained glass, 20th-century, including a window by Roland Mitton of Livingston, and three rose windows. The clock tower holds the original bell inscribed 'Michael Burgerhuys Me Fecit 1618'. Glencairn Aisle adjacent to the church with sculptured mural 1600 commissioned by James seventh Earl of Glencairn, in memory of the Earl and Countess of Glencairn, and worked by David Scougal, mason and burgess. On A735. Sunday Service: 11am

Open by arrangement, telephone the Rev John Urquhart 01563 538289

CHURCH OF SCOTLAND **B**

ST MAUR'S GLENCAIRN PARISH CHURCH, KILMAURS

141 MAUCHLINE PARISH CHURCH

NS 498 272

Loudoun Street, Mauchline

Present church by William Alexander 1829 stands on site of St Michael's Church founded in 13th century. Single bell cast in 1742. Willis pipe organ 1888 rebuilt in 1980. Associations with Covenanters and Robert Burns, many contemporaries of whom are buried here. At junction of B743 with A76. Sunday Service: 11am

Open June to August, Tuesday and Wednesday 2–4pm.

Also Ayrshire Doors Open Day (date to be announced)

CHURCH OF SCOTLAND WC **B**

142 ST THOMAS THE APOSTLE, MUIRKIRK

NS 699 278

Wellwood Street, Muirkirk

The material for this church, built in 1906, was transported from Belgium. Sunday Service: 10.00am

Open by arrangement with Parish Priest, telephone 01290 421031

ROMAN CATHOLIC

143 SORN PARISH CHURCH

NS 550 268

Main Street, Sorn

A rather splendid edifice, quietly assured, built in 1656 and much reconstructed in 1826. Outside stairs to three galleries. Jougs on the west wall. East wall memorial to George Wood, last Covenanter to die 1688. Sunday Service: 10.30am

Open by arrangement, telephone Miss McKerrow 01290 551256

CHURCH OF SCOTLAND WC **B**

SORN PARISH CHURCH

144 OUR LADY AND ST JOHN'S, STEWARTON

NS417 457

69 Lainshaw Street, Stewarton

Our Lady and St John was built in 1974 and functions as church and hall. Modern stations of the Cross by a local arts teacher. Services: Monday, Wednesday, Friday 11am; Tuesday, Thursday 10 am; Saturday Vigil 5pm; Sunday 11.45am

Open by arrangement with the Sisters, telephone 0156 483322

ROMAN CATHOLIC

145 ST COLUMBA'S PARISH CHURCH, STEWARTON

NS 419 457

1 Kirk Glebe, Stewarton

Built in 1696, renovated in 1775, and widened in 1825 with later additions. Bell-tower. Lainshaw Loft used for smaller services. New and restored windows installed for tercentenary in 1996. Beside the mini-roundabout at the south end of Stewarton. Sunday Service: 11am

Open by arrangement, telephone the Minister 01560 482453

CHURCH OF SCOTLAND **B**

ST COLUMBA'S PARISH CHURCH, STEWARTON

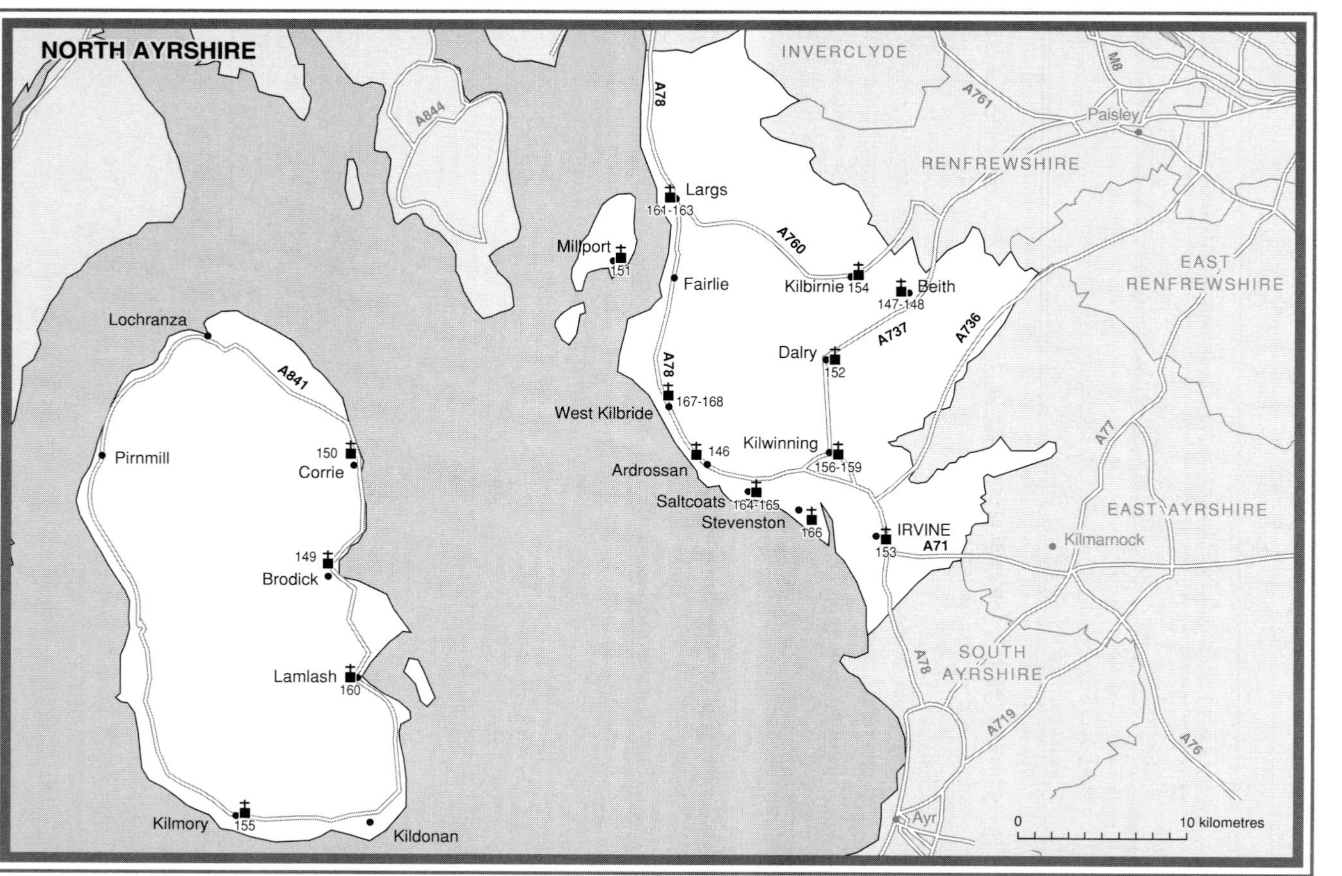
NORTH AYRSHIRE
INVERCLYDE
RENFREWSHIRE
EAST RENFREWSHIRE
EAST AYRSHIRE
SOUTH AYRSHIRE
Paisley
Kilmarnock
Ayr
M8
A761
A844
A78
A760
A737
A736
A77
A71
A719
A76
A841
Largs
161-163
Millport
151
Fairlie
Kilbirnie
154
Beith
147-148
Dalry
152
167-168
West Kilbride
146
Ardrossan
Kilwinning
156-159
Saltcoats
164-165
Stevenston
166
IRVINE
153
Lochranza
Pirnmill
150
Corrie
149
Brodick
Lamlash
160
Kilmory
155
Kildonan
0
10 kilometres

NORTH AYRSHIRE

Local Representative: Miss Joan Fish, 31 Oaklands Avenue, Irvine (*telephone* 01294 272654)

146 ST PETER IN CHAINS, ARDROSSAN

NS 233 421
1 South Crescent, Ardrossan
Designed by Jack Coia and opened in 1938, St Peter in Chains is probably the most academic of this period. The church, in reddish facing brick, has a high west gable as at St Columba, Hopehill Road, Glasgow and a tower to the right reminiscent of Stockholm Town Hall. Striking brick main doorway with stone keystone; the door feature continues to the gable roof and ends in a small well-detailed cross. Services: Monday to Saturday Mass 9.30am, 7pm; Saturday Vigil Mass 6.30pm; Sunday 10am, 12noon and 6.30pm
Open daily 9am–7.30pm
ROMAN CATHOLIC **A**

ST PETER IN CHAINS, ARDROSSAN

147 BEITH HIGH CHURCH

NS 350 539
Kirk Road, Beith
Built in 1807 and extended in 1885. Gothic T-plan kirk dominated by the tall five-stage tower. Stained glass by Gordon Webster. Harrison & Harrison pipe organ 1885. From Beith bypass along Barrmill Road to Kirk Road. Sunday Service: 10.30am. Joint service with Beith Trinity during the month of August
Open by arrangement, telephone the Rev Andrew Black 01505 502686
CHURCH OF SCOTLAND
WC **B**

BEITH HIGH CHURCH

148 BEITH TRINITY CHURCH

NS 351 544

Wilson Street, Beith

Built 1883, architect Robert Baldie. The chief external feature is a graceful octagonal tower. Interior destroyed by fire 1917, rebuilt 1926. Gothic style, with rectangular nave, Gothic arched chancel and one transept on the east side. Stained glass by John C Hall & Co. Organ 1937 by Hill, Norman & Beard. Sunday Service: 11.00am. Joint service with Beith High during the month of July

Opening by arrangement telephone 01505 502131

CHURCH OF SCOTLAND WC

BEITH TRINITY CHURCH

149 BRODICK CHURCH, ISLE OF ARRAN

NS 012 359

Knowe Road, Brodick (1 mile north of pier, turn left at sports park)

The present church was built in 1910 from local red sandstone. The pulpit, built by local craftsmen, is an exact replica of John Knox's pulpit. Two stained glass windows are in memory of church member Bethia Torrance who died in 1958. Sunday Service: 10.45am

Open by arrangement, telephone Mr Hannah 01770 302248.

Flower Festival Easter 2000

CHURCH OF SCOTLAND WC **B**

150 CORRIE CHURCH, ISLE OF ARRAN

NS 024 437

6 miles north of Brodick

Designed by J J Burnet 1887 as 'one of a family of long, low friendly churches'. Constructed in red sandstone in an early Gothic style with a simple stone belfry and wooden porch. An unusual baptismal font is set into the arch and church wall and rush-bottomed chairs take the place of pews. Lit by circular candelabra. Two tapestries by Mrs Sandeman and two recently installed stained glass windows designed by Richard Leclerc. Sunday Service: 12noon

Open by arrangement, telephone the Session Clerk 01770 810675 or Mr McConnachie 01770 810246 or Mrs Pringle 01770 810210

CHURCH OF SCOTLAND WC **B**

CORRIE CHURCH, ISLE OF ARRAN

151 THE CATHEDRAL OF THE ISLES, CUMBRAE

NS 165 561

College Street, Millport, Isle of Cumbrae

Cathedral, college and cloister by William Butterfield 1851. A Tractarian church built by 6th Earl of Glasgow. Peal of bells, organ, stained glass by William Wailes and Hardman. Visitors welcome to picnic in the grounds. Ferry from Largs and bus to Millport. Sunday Service: 11am Sung Eucharist; other times see notice board in porch

Church website: www.scotland.anglican.org/argyll

Open daily

SCOTTISH EPISCOPAL WC **A**

152 ST MARGARET'S PARISH CHURCH, DALRY

NS 291 496

The Cross, Dalry

David Thomson was the architect of this landmark Victorian Gothic building (1871-73) on an earlier site. Inventive 159ft broach spire 'worthy of the many tasks thrust upon it'; the whole building is a 'powerful, carefully handled composition'. The restored interior (with good acoustics) of the early 1950s presents 'a space of deep solemnity enhanced' by Beith-made pulpit, table, lecturn and stained glass by Guthrie & Wells, Charles Payne, C L Davidson, plus the only decent amount of Munich glass and only Francis Hemony bell (1661) in a UK church. Three-manual Blackett & Howden organ (1899). Communion silver of 1618. Bronze sundial and some interesting stones in Kirkyard. Kirk bears the name of the original medieval dedication: St Margaret of Antioch (see modern Rona Moody window) the only such in Scotland. In the vicinity – Blair House may be viewed from outside; Cleeves Cove (interesting limestone cave system). Sunday Services: 11.30am all year; 6.30pm September to April (except first of month); 10.30am May to August, and 1 November to April

Open by arrangement, telephone 01294 833135/832234.

Also Ayrshire Doors Open Day

CHURCH OF SCOTLAND WC **B**

ST MARGARET'S PARISH CHURCH, DALRY

ST ANDREW'S PARISH CHURCH (FERGUSON MEMORIAL), IRVINE

153 ST ANDREW'S PARISH CHURCH (FERGUSON MEMORIAL), IRVINE

NS 3239

Caldon Road x Oaklands Avenue, Irvine

St Andrew's was gifted in 1957 to commemorate the centenary of the death of John Ferguson, founder of the Ferguson bequest. Architect Rennie & Bramble of Saltcoats. Stained glass windows by Mary Wood 1957, Ann Marie Docherty 1998 and stained glass designers of Milngavie 2000. The congregation has shared the church with the local Scottish Episcopalian congregation who built on a chapel/meeting room, containing tapestry by Vampboulles, and coffee lounge in 1981. Architect R L Dunlop of Troon. Sunday Services: Scottish Episcopal 9.30am; Church of Scotland 11.15am

Open Tuesdays 10-10.45am. Tuesday Morning Club for Senior Citizens, with tea and coffee in coffee lounge, October to May

CHURCH OF SCOTLAND

154 THE AULD KIRK OF KILBIRNIE

NS 315 536

Dalry Road, Kilbirnie

A pre-Reformation church on the site of 6th century cell dedicated to St Brendan of Clonfert. The nave dates from 1470 and the bell-tower from 1490. Glengarnock aisle added 1597. Crawfurd aisle added in 1642 with unique Renaissance-style carving. Pulpit c.1620. At junction of B780 and B777. Bus to Kilbirnie, rail to Glengarnock. Sunday Services: 9.30am and 11am

Church website: www//members.tripod.co.uk/auldkirk/

Open July to August, weekdays 2-4pm except Mondays; Ayrshire Doors Open Day, September. Other times, telephone Mr J Lauchland 01505 683459

CHURCH OF SCOTLAND **A**

THE AULD KIRK OF KILBIRNIE

155 KILMORY PARISH CHURCH, ISLE OF ARRAN

NR 700 449

Present church built 1880 over previous building 1765. Small, delightful church with plain windows surrounded by red-coloured stained glass, providing a warm ambience. Linked with Lamlash. Situated in village of Kilmory, turn right after Creamery on road from Whiting Bay. Sunday Service: 10am

Open by arrangement, telephone Mrs Mairi Duff 01770 870305

CHURCH OF SCOTLAND **B**

156 THE ABBEY CHURCH, KILWINNING

NS 303 433

Main Street, Kilwinning

Built in 1774 by John Garland and John Wright. The church is on the site of the ruined Abbey, founded in 1188, and replaced a second church of 1590. Sunday Services: 9.15am and 11am September to May; 10am June and August

Or by arrangement, telephone Mr J Muir, 30 Underwood, Kilwinning 01294 552929

CHURCH OF SCOTLAND

THE ABBEY CHURCH, KILWINNING

157 ERSKINE CHURCH, KILWINNING

NS 303 434

Main Street, Kilwinning

Simple UP-style building, 1838, down a lane from Main Street. Pedimented open bellcote flanked by acones. Gable finials. Pleasant restored interior with gallery. Sunday Service: 11.30am

Open by arrangement, telephone Mr Welsh 01294 554376

CHURCH OF SCOTLAND [wheelchair] [WC] [hearing loop] C

158 FERGUSHILL CHURCH, KILWINNING

NS 337 430

Benslie Village, Kilwinning

Church extension for the mining community from Kilwinning Parish Church in 1879 to a plan prepared by William Railton of Kilmarnock. Attractive church with bell-tower. Fine views to Arran. Sunday Service: 10am

Open by arrangement, telephone Mrs Borland 01294 850257

CHURCH OF SCOTLAND [WC]

FERGUSHILL CHURCH, KILWINNING

159 ST WININ'S, KILWINNING

NS 300 432

St Winning's Lane, Kilwinning

Modern functional building with basic decoration. Seats 400 and is well-used by the 700 or 800 congregation who attend weekend masses. Services: Saturday 6.30pm, Sunday 10.00am and 12 noon

Church website: www.st-winins.org.uk

Open by arrangement with Parish House, telephone 01294 552276

ROMAN CATHOLIC [wheelchair] (side entrance) [hearing loop] [accessible WC] (in Hall) [WC]

160 LAMLASH PARISH CHURCH, ISLE OF ARRAN

NS 026 309

Shore Road, Lamlash, Isle of Arran

A massive campanile tower over 90ft high sits above this Gothic-style, red sandstone building by H & D Barclay 1886. The church was built by 12th Duke of Hamilton to replace an earlier building of 1773. Boarded, barrel-vaulted ceiling and carved, wooden tripartite Gothic sedilia. The tower hosts a peal of nine bells played every Sunday before service, largest peal still existing, cast for a Scottish church in a Scottish foundry. Seven stained glass windows by Anning Bell, Meiklejohn, Gordon Webster and Christian Shaw; all other windows are hand painted, German cathedral glass. Pipe organ, William Hill,

Norman and Beard 1934. In the front grounds are an ancient cross and baptismal font from the old monastery on Holy Isle in Lamlash Bay. Major restoration programme begun 1997. Sunday Service: 11.30am

Open by arrangement. See Church notice board for information, or contact Captain J L Davidson, Rock Cottage, Cordon, Lamlash, telephone 01770 600787

CHURCH OF SCOTLAND **A**

161 CLARK MEMORIAL CHURCH, LARGS

NS 202 593

Bath Street, Largs

Gifted by John Clark of the Anchor Thread Mills, Paisley, and designed by William Kerr of T G Abercrombie, Paisley 1892. Red sandstone from Locharbriggs and Corsehill in Early English Gothic style. Superb stained glass, all manufactured in Glasgow at height of Arts and Crafts movement. Hammer-beam roof. Views of the Clyde and Cumbraes. Sunday Service: 10am, Thursday 10.30am

Open daily 10am-4pm (except Tuesdays). Viking Festival one week each September

CHURCH OF SCOTLAND **A**

CLARK MEMORIAL CHURCH, LARGS

162 ST COLUMBA'S PARISH CHURCH, LARGS

NS 203 596

Gallowgate, Largs

The old parish church was replaced by the present building in 1892. It is a handsome structure, architects Henry Steele and Andrew Balfour, of red stone with a three-stage tower with spire and clock. Interesting carved octagonal oak pulpit and notable windows. 'Father' Willis organ. Memorial to General Sir Thomas MacDougall Brisbane, astronomer, soldier and Governor of New South Wales. Sunday Service: 11am

Church website: www.btinternet.com /~jfultonmurdoch/columba.htm

Open 10am-noon, Monday to Friday

CHURCH OF SCOTLAND (by arrangement)

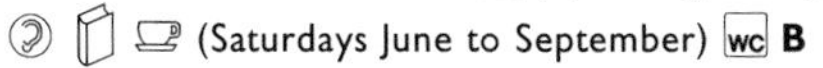

(Saturdays June to September) **B**

ST COLUMBA'S PARISH CHURCH, LARGS

163 ST MARY'S STAR OF THE SEA, LARGS

NS 201 603

28 Greenock Road, Largs

A bright modern building opened in 1962. The architect was Mr A R Conlon of Reginald Fairlie & Sons. Features include a tapestry at the High Altar depicting Jesus and two disciples at Emmaus, eight stained glass panels above the main door, and a statue outside the main door of Our Lady, Star of the Sea, by eminent Scottish sculptor, Hew Lorimer. Services: Saturday Vigil 6.30pm, Sunday 9.00 and 11.30am

Open 8.30am-8pm in summer, 8.30am-3.30pm in winter

ROMAN CATHOLIC

164 ST BRENDAN'S, SALTCOATS

NS 247 430

63 Corrie Crescent, Ayr

St Brendan's has a magnificent contemporary stained glass window depicting the life of St Brendan and a unique crucifix, designed locally and fabricated in steel. Services: Saturday 6.30pm, Sunday 11am

Open by arrangement, telephone 01294 463483

ROMAN CATHOLIC

165 ST CUTHBERT'S PARISH CHURCH, SALTCOATS

NS 244 418

Caledonia Road, Saltcoats

Designed by Peter MacGregor Chalmers and dedicated in 1908, the fourth building of the congregation of Ardrossan Parish. The chancel displays a marble reredos of the Last Supper. Sixteen stained glass windows on the Life of Christ by William Wilson 1947; two windows by Gordon Webster 1976. Model of a French frigate of 1804, by a sailor William Dunlop, hangs in the church. He made it as a thanksgiving for his surviving the Napoleonic wars when a canonball narrowly missed his hammock! Sunday Service: 11.15am

Open by arrangement, telephone Mrs Hanlon 01294 466636

CHURCH OF SCOTLAND **B**

166 ST JOHN, STEVENSTON

NS 272 425

Hayocks Road, Stevenston

Built 1963 to designs by Mr Houston Jr. Features laminated trusses suporting the roof and beautiful stained glass by M Gabriel Loire of Chartres representing biblical scenes and St John the Evangelist. Brass baptismal font depicting a half tree trunk sheltering a fawn: 'As the deer longs for streams of water, so my soul yearns for you, my God.' Services: Saturday Vigil 6.30pm, Sunday 9.30 and 11.30am, weekdays 10am (subject to change)

Church website: www.stjohnsre.force9.co.uk

Open by arrangement with Parish Priest, telephone 01294 463225

ROMAN CATHOLIC

OVERTON CHURCH, WEST KILBRIDE

167 OVERTON CHURCH, WEST KILBRIDE

NS 203 481

Ritchie Street, West Kilbride

Just over 100 years old, designed by Mr Le Blanc (of Glasgow Baths fame). Very good stained glass with two recent modern additions. Two manual Binns Organ – tubular pneumatic. Unusual hipped wooden ceiling to nave. Sunday Service: 11am all year, 6.30pm during autumn and winter.

Open Thursday 10am–12noon, or by arrangement, telephone Mr Leary 01294 823140

CHURCH OF SCOTLAND (by arrangement) (Thursday mornings)

168 ST BRIDE'S, WEST KILBRIDE

NS 206 484

9 Hunterston Road

The church was built and opened in 1908. The Marian shrine in the grounds was erected in 1958 for the Golden Jubilee. Services: Saturday Vigil 6.30pm, Sunday 10.30am, weekdays (including Saturdays) 9.30am

Open daily 9am-6pm

ROMAN CATHOLIC

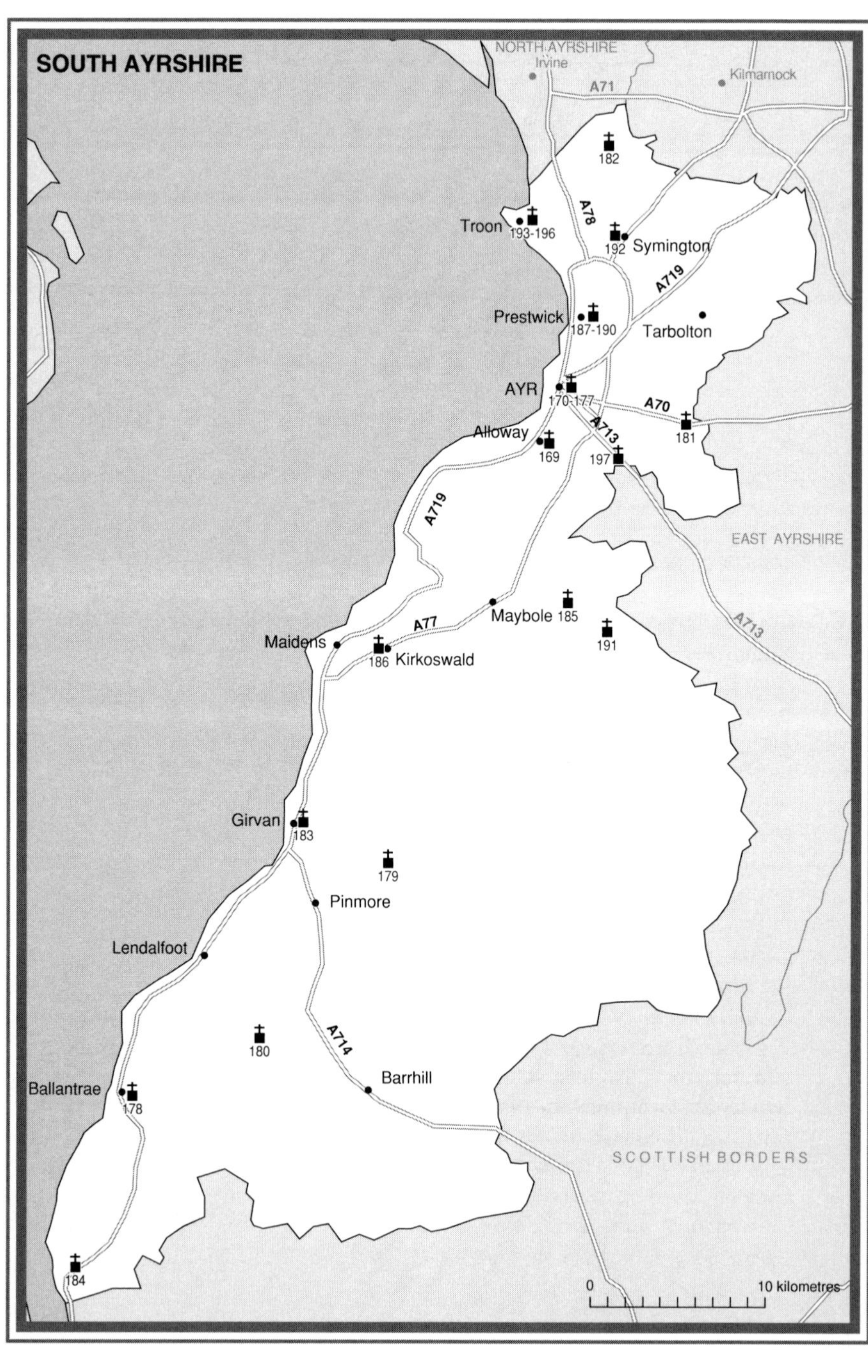
SOUTH AYRSHIRE
NORTH AYRSHIRE
Irvine
Kilmarnock
A71
182
A78
Troon
193-196
192
Symington
A719
Prestwick
187-190
Tarbolton
AYR
170-177
A70
181
Alloway
169
A713
197
A719
EAST AYRSHIRE
Maybole
185
191
A77
A713
Maidens
186
Kirkoswald
Girvan
183
179
Pinmore
Lendalfoot
180
A714
Barrhill
Ballantrae
178
SCOTTISH BORDERS
184
0
10 kilometres

SOUTH AYRSHIRE

Local Representative: Miss Joan Fish, 31 Oaklands Avenue, Irvine (*telephone* 01294 272654)

169 ALLOWAY PARISH CHURCH

NS 332 181

Built in 1858, architect Campbell Douglas. South transept added in 1877, chancel built and nave extended in 1890. Excellent stained glass including Stephen Adam, Clayton & Bell, Gordon Webster, W & J J Keir. Douglas McLundie's memorial window to D F McIntyre, pilot on first flight over Mount Everest in 1933. Two windows by Susan Bradbury were installed in 1996, one depicting the four seasons, the other in memory of Robert Burns. Three further Bradbury windows were added in 2001, enhancing the porch and santuary area throughout with stained glass. B7024 south of Burns' cottage. Sunday Services 9.45am and 11.15am

ALLOWAY PARISH CHURCH

Open June to September, Monday to Friday 10am–4pm.
Conducted tours, contact local tourist office

CHURCH OF SCOTLAND B

170 THE AULD KIRK OF AYR (ST JOHN THE BAPTIST)

NS 339 219

Off High Street, Ayr

The approach to the Auld Kirk is through Kirkport and the 1656 Lynchgate into the kirkyard. The Commonwealth Government paid for the 1654 T-plan kirk after Cromwell's troops had occupied the old Church of St John on the sands. Respectful alterations by David Bryce of 1836. High quality interior with three lofts on Corinthian columns and a splendid double-decker pulpit. One of the few remaining 'Obit' boards records money donated to the poor. This church is not a museum, but living and active. Sunday Service: 11am (10am July and August)

Church website: www.auldkirk.org

Open Saturday mornings by arrangement, telephone the church office 01292 262938

CHURCH OF SCOTLAND A

HOLY TRINITY CHURCH, AYR

171 ST QUIVOX, AUCHINCRUIVE, AYR

NS 375 241

Christian presence on the site dates back to the 13th century. The medieval building was restored 1595 and extended 1767 to create a T-plan church. Interior fittings date largely from the late 18th century, including a good pulpit. In the kirkyard, mausoleum of the Campbells of Craigie, by W H Playfair 1822. Sunday Service: 11.30am

Open by arrangement, contact Mrs A C Taylor telephone 01292 269746

CHURCH OF SCOTLAND ♿ WC **A**

ST QUIVOX, AUCHINCRUIVE, AYR

172 HOLY TRINITY CHURCH, AYR

NS 336 218

Fullarton Street, Ayr

Dedicated in 1888. Scotland's major example of the work of J L Pearson, designer of Truro Cathedral. Pulpit of Caen stone and very fine stained glass windows by, among others, Clayton & Bell. Next to Ayr bus station, walking distance from railway station. Sunday Services: 8am, 10.30am and 6.30pm; Wednesday Eucharist 11am

Church website: //website.lineone.net/~holytrinitychurch/southayrshire/indexx.html

Open mornings in summer. Concert series

SCOTTISH EPISCOPAL ♿ (for visiting groups by arrangement) WC **A**

173 ST ANDREW'S, AYR

NS 338 222

39 Park Circus, Ayr

St Andrew's, identified by its tall red sandstone spire, was opened in 1893. The worshipping congregation came from the Wallacetown Free Church disruption. The design, by John B Wilson, is Perpendicular Gothic. The beautiful stained glass includes work by John Blyth. The church is on the south side of the town between the railway and the sea front. Sunday Service: 11am

Church website: wwwstandewsayr.cwc.net

Open last Wednesday of the month, May to September 2–4 pm

CHURCH OF SCOTLAND ♿ WC **B**

ST COLUMBA, AYR

174 ST COLUMBA, AYR

NS 337 201

Midton Road/Carrick Park

Originally known as Trinity Church, St Columba's was dedicated in 1902. Built of red sandstone to designs by John B Wilson of Glasgow. Fine pipe organ 1904 by J J Binns, restored by Harrison & Harrison 1985. Stained glass by Sidney Holmes, C C Baillie and Susan Bradbury. Cultured octagonal pencil tower with carillon of bells. Special events and services to mark the centenary are planned. Sunday Services: 9.30 and 11.15am, 1st Sunday of month 6.30pm

Church website: www.ayrstcolumba.co.uk

Open 9am-12 noon, Monday, Tuesday, Thursday, Friday

CHURCH OF SCOTLAND WC **B**

175 ST JAMES'S PARISH CHURCH, AYR

NS 342 232

Prestwick Road/Falkland Park Road, Ayr

St James's Church was built as a chapel of ease in 1885 to designs by John Murdoch. John Murdoch, an engineer before he became an architect, was the most ambitious of the architects of Ayr in the late 19th century and received many important commissions. There is a rose window above the pulpit. Sunday Service: 11am

Open by arrangement with the Minister, telephone 01292 262420

CHURCH OF SCOTLAND WC **B**

176 ST LEONARD'S, AYR

NS 338 204

St Leonard's Road/Monument Road, Ayr

Built in 1886, several hundred yards from the site of the ancient chapel of St Leonard, the patron saint of prisoners. The architect was John Murdoch and the style belongs to the geometric period of decorated Gothic. The building comprises a nave with aisles, transepts and chancel (added in 1911). Two-manual pipe organ by Harrison & Harrison, rebuilt 1992. Many beautiful stained glass windows. Sunday Service: 10am

Open by arrangement, telephone Mr William Bruce on 01292 263694

CHURCH OF SCOTLAND **B**

177 ST PAUL'S ROMAN CATHOLIC, AYR

NS 348 200

Peggieshill Road, Ayr

The dedication stone was laid in 1966 and the church was opened 1967. Wall hanging by members of the parish of St Paul's meeting on the road to Damascus. Altar, lectern and ambo in Creetown granite. Services: Saturday Vigil 6.30pm, Sunday 10.00am and 12 noon, daily usually at 10am

Open by arrangement with Parish Priest, telephone 01292 260197

ROMAN CATHOLIC

178 BALLANTRAE PARISH CHURCH

NX 084 825

Main Street, Ballantrae

Built in 1819. Memorial to Lord Ballantrae. Regency pulpit. Nephew of Robert Burns was minister 1826-30. Kennedy tomb beside church. Ruins of Ardstinchar Castle. A77. Railway station at Girvan, 13 miles. Buses from Glasgow. United with Glenapp. Sunday Service: 11am

Open daily, May to September 10am-sunset

CHURCH OF SCOTLAND (in village) **B**

BALLANTRAE PARISH CHURCH

179 BARR PARISH CHURCH

NX 275 941

Main Street, Barr, by Girvan

Dating from 1878, built to a design by A Stevenson. Early Gothic gabled chapel. Slate roof, skew gables, rubble walls, freestone dressings. Picturesque south east bellcote. Fine wooden ceiling. Restored 1978 P J Lorimer, London. B734 from Girvan. Occasional buses from Girvan. Sunday Service: 12 noon

Open all year, 9am-7pm. Teas in July and August: Monday, Friday and Saturday 2.30-5pm

CHURCH OF SCOTLAND **C**

BARR PARISH CHURCH

180 COLMONELL CHURCH

NX 145 858

Built 1849 and renovated when the organ was installed. Organ screen and chancel by Robert Lorimer. Exceptional stained glass, including windows by Louis Davis and Douglas Strachan. Martyr's stone in graveyard from the time of the Covenanters, and Kennedy vault dating from 1620. Local lore gives a Christian presence here from AD c.600 when St Colman of Ella built his cell. Sunday Service: 10.30am

Open daily

CHURCH OF SCOTLAND **B**

181 ST CLARE'S, DRONGAN

NS 441 185

Watson Terrace, Drongan (1 mile south of A70, 7 miles east of Ayr)

Unassuming church building opened in 1967. Sunday Service: 9.45am

Open only for Sunday Service

ROMAN CATHOLIC WC

182 DUNDONALD PARISH CHURCH

NS 366 343

Main Street, Dundonald

Tranquil setting for this traditional stone church of 1804, built on the site of an earlier building. The clock tower was added 1841, and the chancel 1906. Some fine stained glass, particularly Henry Dearle's unique 'Last Supper'. Pipe organ, Norman & Beard 1906. Interesting grave stones in the tidy graveyard. Sunday Service: 11am

Open from 2-4pm every weekday, April to September, and by arrangement, telephone Rev Robert Mayes 01563 850243

CHURCH OF SCOTLAND WC **B**

183 SACRED HEARTS OF JESUS AND MARY, GIRVAN

NS 183 979

Harbour Lane, Girvan

A plain Gothic structure of 1860 with a huge prow-like porch added in 1959 by Stevenson & Ferguson. Stained glass windows of 1860. Services: 7pm Saturday, 9am and 11am Sunday

Open during daylight hours

ROMAN CATHOLIC

SACRED HEARTS OF JESUS AND MARY, GIRVAN

184 GLENAPP CHURCH

NX 075 746

This church has a Memorial window to Elsie Mackay, third daughter of Earl of Inchcape. She was killed in 1928 attempting to fly the Atlantic. Modern stained glass window above door, 'The Stilling of the Tempest', in memory of first Earl. Graveyard contains tombs of the three Earls of Inchcape. Seven miles south of Ballantrae on A77, ten miles north of Stranraer. United with Ballantrae. Sunday Service: occasional

Open summer and autumn

CHURCH OF SCOTLAND

GLENAPP CHURCH

185 KIRKMICHAEL PARISH CHURCH

NY 005 884

80 Patna Road, Kirkmichael, near Maybole

Believed to stand on the site of a 13th-century church under the care of the monks of Whithorn, the present church was built 1787 by Hugh Cairncross, and the belfry rebuilt 1887. Stone pulpit of 1919 depicting St Michael, St George, St Andrew and St Patrick incorporates the war memorial. Two large stained glass windows on either side of the pulpit, one by Christopher Whitworth Whall. The oldest building is the lychgate, the bell inside is dated 1702 and is still rung when a bride leaves the church after her wedding. Interesting stones in surrounding graveyard, including Covenanter's memorial, open every day. Two miles east of Maybole. Sunday Service: 10.30am

Open by arrangement, telephone the Minister 01655 750286

CHURCH OF SCOTLAND ♿ ☕ (in village) WC **B**

KIRKMICHAEL PARISH CHURCH

186 KIRKOSWALD PARISH CHURCH

NS 240 074

Robert Adam 1777, contemporary with Culzean Castle. It is suggested that while working with Lord Cassillis, his client at Culzean, Robert Adam came across the church during construction and recommended some changes, giving the building fine Palladian details. The church was visited by Robert Burns and more recently by President Eisenhower. Following a fire, the church was fully restored in 1997 and the opportunity was taken to research original Adam colour scheme. Burns' characters, Tam o' Shanter, Souter Johnnie and Kirkton Jean, are buried in the old graveyard, where also can be seen the baptismal font used to baptise Robert the Bruce. The church is situated just off the A77, in Kirkoswald 5 miles south of Maybole, and 7 miles north of Girvan.
Sunday Service: 11am

Open on the last Sunday of June, July, August and September, and on Ayrshire Open Doors Day. Can also be open at other times by arrangement, telephone 01655 760201 or 01566 760295 or 01655 760238

CHURCH OF SCOTLAND A

187 MONKTON & PRESTWICK NORTH

NS 350 263

10 Monkton Road, Prestwick

The church was built as a Free Church in 1874, architect James Salmon & Son, and the bell-tower was added 1890, architect John Keppie. The congregation, united with the Church of Scotland in 1900, now uses a computerised communication system for hymn singing and visual aids. The pulpit, from St Cuthbert's, Monkton, is mobile. The original St Cuthbert's Communion Table has been fixed as a panel between two stained glass windows. Sunday Service: 11am

Open by arrangement, telephone the Rev A Christie 01292 477499

CHURCH OF SCOTLAND

KINGCASE PARISH CHURCH, PRESTWICK

188 KINGCASE PARISH CHURCH, PRESTWICK

NS 348 244

Waterloo Road, Prestwick (behind Safeway store)

The church was built in 1912, extended 1956, in attractive red sandstone with three small but beautiful stained glass windows. Fairly small building in excellent state of repair. Sunday Services: 9.45am and 11.15am, 7pm (9pm in July and August). Large-print hymn books available

Church website: www.kincase.freeserve.co.uk

Open by arrangement with Church Office, telephone 01292 470755

CHURCH OF SCOTLAND

189 PRESTWICK SOUTH PARISH CHURCH

NS 352 260

Main Street, Prestwick

First church commission 1879 for James A Morris, a contemporary of Charles Rennie Mackintosh. Adept, light handling of Gothic forms, enlivened by Glasgow style carving. Carefully chosen interior fittings include glass by Oscar Paterson. Sunday Service: 11am

Open by arrangement with the Minister, telephone 01292 478788

CHURCH OF SCOTLAND

190 ST QUIVOX, PRESTWICK

NS 352 257

St Quivox Road, Prestwick

The building was completed in 1933 and is built of Accrington brick in Romanesque style. The church was extended in 1969 and incorporates the old building to form a rectangular shaped church. Inside are a sanctuary mosaic panel and the Stations of the Cross. Jubilee 2000 window. Sunday Services: 10am, 11.30am and 6pm

Open daily 10am–5pm

ROMAN CATHOLIC 

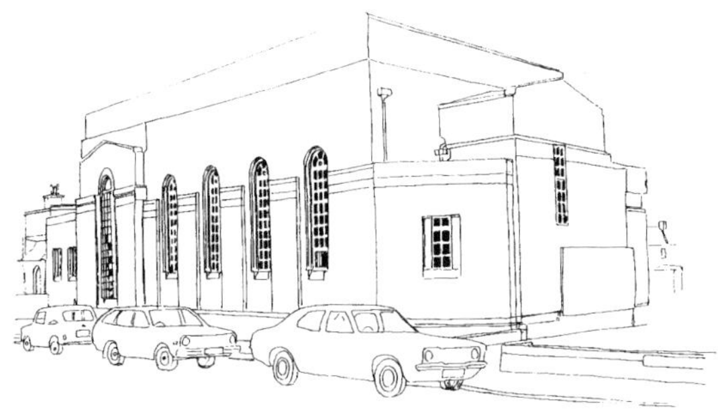

ST QUIVOX, PRESTWICK

191 STRAITON PARISH CHURCH (ST CUTHBERT'S)

NS 380 049

The main part of the church dates from 1758. The piscina of the original church is still visible on the east wall. Chantry chapel of late 15th century containing various memorial plaques to members of the Hunter Blair family. In 1901 the church was renovated by John Kinross and the bell-tower was added to the design of John Murdoch. The interior is noted for its beautiful carvings, especially on the ceiling and pulpit. Striking 'Millennium Banner' mounted on a pedestal made from a former pew. Tapestry cushions 1993 depict themes from the life and work of the community. The stone font is the gift of the Fergusson family. Splendid stained glass. Covenanter's memorial in graveyard, open every day. Of special interest is the artwork undertaken by the ladies of the local Sewing Guild to commemorate 1997 as 'The Year of Faith'; 1998 as 'The Year of Hope'; and 1999 as 'The Year of Love'. Straiton is four miles east of Kirkmichael. Sunday Service: noon

Open by arrangement, telephone the Minister 01655 750286

CHURCH OF SCOTLAND ♿ WC (nearby) **A**

STRAITON PARISH CHURCH (ST CUTHBERT'S)

SYMINGTON CHURCH

192 SYMINGTON CHURCH

NS 999 352

Known as Ayrshire's Norman church, the rectangular building with three feet thick walls was founded c.1160 by Symon de Loccard whose own story in itself makes a visit worthwhile. Restored 1919 by P MacGregor Chalmers. Norman arched windows, piscina and ancient oak-beamed ceiling. The stained glass, much of it by Douglas Strachan, is glorious in creation and colour. Though small in size, its stones breathe the atmosphere of prayer and praise of all the saints over 800 years. Two miles from Prestwick Airport on A77. Sunday Service: 10.30am

Open by arrangement, telephone Mrs Margaret Kerr 01563 830289, or Jim Knox 01563 830043

CHURCH OF SCOTLAND **A**

193 TROON OLD CHURCH

NS 321 309

Ayr Street, Troon

Neo-Gothic building in red sandstone by Hippolyte Blanc and dedicated in 1895. The stained glass of the Ascension window is by the Morris Studio; other windows by Gordon Webster. Alabaster reredos depicting Moses, St Paul and the Last Supper has a finely carved canopy and stands above a mosaic pavement of the Paschal Lamb. Richly carved pulpit, communion table and font. Various memorials. Sunday Service: 10.30am; Wednesday 11.15am

Open Tuesday to Sunday 10am–12 noon

CHURCH OF SCOTLAND WC (by arrangement), (Saturday and Sunday) **B**

TROON OLD CHURCH

194 OUR LADY AND ST MEDDAN CHURCH, TROON

NS 327 311

4 Cessnock Road, Troon

Built to a design by Reginald Fairlie 1910, this church is a mixture of architectural styles and also copies the rear view of Holy Rude Church in Stirling. The church has undergone major restoration funded by Historic Scotland. Two minutes from railway station, Glasgow–Ayr, half hourly train service. Sunday Mass 9am and 11.15am; Saturday Vigil Mass 6pm

Open daily until 4pm, and Ayrshire Doors Open Day, September

ROMAN CATHOLIC WC **A**

OUR LADY AND ST MEDDAN CHURCH, TROON

PORTLAND PARISH CHURCH, TROON

195 PORTLAND PARISH CHURCH, TROON

NS 323 309

South Beach/St Meddan's Street, Troon

Opened in 1914 as a United Free Church by H E Clifford & Lunan. Perpendicular Gothic in white sandstone with fine tracery in the great north window which is repeated in the nave windows. Interior has exposed stone with blonde Austrian oak pews and fittings. The stained glass chancel window was donated in 1920 as a war memorial by Mr A F Steven. Harrison & Harrison two-manual organ, rebuilt 1970. Halls extension added 1964. Two minutes walk from railway station. Sunday Service: 10.30am

Open July and August, Sunday and Thursday 2–4.30pm, and Ayrshire Doors Open Day, September

CHURCH OF SCOTLAND **B**

196 ST MEDDAN'S, TROON

NS 323 309

Corner of Church Street and St Meddan's Street, Troon

Built 1888-9 for the United Presbyterian Church, architect J B Wilson, St Meddan's has many noteworthy features. The tall and stately spire houses a clock which was originally part of the University of Glasgow's Old College in High Street, Glasgow. Many beautiful stained glass windows; the largest, opposite the pulpit, depicts the healing of Jairus's daughter. Sunday Services: 9.30am and 11.15am

Church website: www.troonstmeddanschurch.org

Open Monday, Tuesday and Thursday 9am–2pm

CHURCH OF SCOTLAND **B**

ST MEDDAN'S, TROON

197 ST FRANCIS XAVIER, WATERSIDE

NS 445 080

On A713, 10 miles south-east of Ayr

Brick-built church with red sandstone dressings. The church was opened 1895 to cater for the workers of Waterside ironworks. At its peak, the ironworks was one of the largest in Ayrshire and is now being developed as an interpretative centre for the industrial heritage of Ayrshire. Saturday: Vigil Mass 6pm.

Open only for Services

ROMAN CATHOLIC ♿ WC

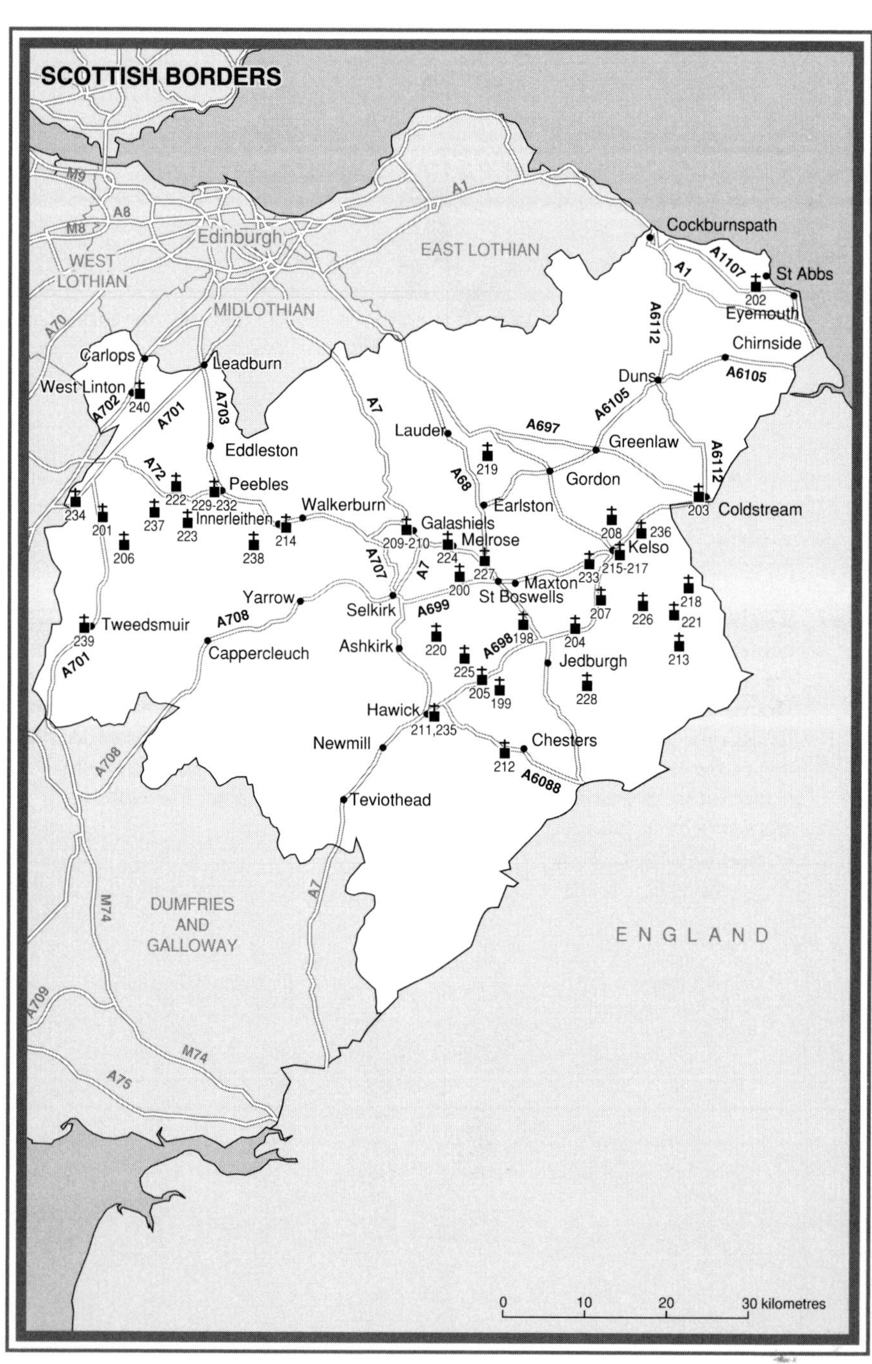
SCOTTISH BORDERS
M9
A8
M8
Edinburgh
WEST
LOTHIAN
MIDLOTHIAN
EAST LOTHIAN
A70
A1
Cockburnspath
A1107
St Abbs
A1
202
Eyemouth
A6112
Chirnside
Carlops
Leadburn
West Linton
240
A702
A701
A703
Duns
A6105
A6105
A7
Lauder
A697
Greenlaw
A6112
Eddleston
219
A68
Gordon
A72
222
Peebles
229-232
203
Coldstream
234
201
237
223
Innerleithen
214
Walkerburn
Galashiels
209-210
Earlston
208
236
Kelso
206
238
224
Melrose
215-217
A707
A7
227
233
200
Maxton
St Boswells
Yarrow
Selkirk
A699
207
218
226
221
239
Tweedsmuir
A708
198
204
213
A701
Cappercleuch
Ashkirk
220
A698
225
Jedburgh
205
199
228
Hawick
211,235
Newmill
212
Chesters
A6088
A708
Teviothead
M74
DUMFRIES
AND
GALLOWAY
A7
ENGLAND
A709
M74
A75
0
10
20
30 kilometres

BORDERS

Local Representatives: Mrs Mary Reid, 2 Crookhaugh, by Biggar (*telephone* 01899 880258) and Mr Sandy Gilchrist, 11 Mercat Loan, Biggar (*telephone* 01899 221350) – Tweedale

198 ANCRUM KIRK

NT 627 246

The present church, built of red sandstone, was opened in 1890 to replace an 18th-century building, the remains of which may be seen in the kirkyard, approximately one mile west of the present church. Four stained glass memorial windows. Sunday Service: 10.00am

Open by arrangement with keyholder Mr Rogerson, telephone 01835 830321

CHURCH OF SCOTLAND WC

199 BEDRULE CHURCH

NT 599 179

Bedrule, by Jedburgh

Beautifully rebuilt in 1914 by T Greenshields Leadbetter, the church has a plaque commemorating Bishop Turnbull, founder of Glasgow University in 1451. Stained glass, including Guild centenary window 1992 and windows by Douglas Strachan 1922. Memorial with interesting link to war-time 'Enigma' decoding project. Fine views over Rule Valley to Ruberslaw. Linked with Denholm and Minto. Time of fortnightly Sunday Service, which alternates with Minto, changes every four months: 11.30am February to May; 10am June to September; 11.30am October to January

Open during daylight hours.

CHURCH OF SCOTLAND (free) **B**

BEDRULE CHURCH

200 BOWDEN KIRK

NT 554 301

BOWDEN KIRK

Sitting by St Cuthbert's Way, the pilgrim route from Melrose to Lindisfarne, the church has a wealth of architectural history. It was founded in 1128, part of the north wall is possibly 15th century, east end from 1644, cross aisle from 1661, west gable and doorway at west end of north wall 17th century. Repaired in 1794 and with major alterations in 1909 by P MacGregor Chalmers. Carved wooden 17th-century laird's loft for Riddell-Carre family. Burial vaults of Riddell-Carre of Cavers-Carre and Dukes of Roxburghe. Memorials, including one to Lady Grizell Baillie, first Deaconess of the Church of Scotland. Many notable tombstones in graveyard. Sunday Service: 11am

Open during daylight hours

CHURCH OF SCOTLAND (from Post Office) **A**

201 BROUGHTON, GLENHOLM AND KILBUCHO PARISH CHURCH

NT 111 368

Broughton, Biggar

Built in 1804 and extended by Robert Bryden of Broughton and Glasgow 1886 to whom there is a memorial stained glass window in the north wall. Roof lights above the communion table are based on originals in Copenhagen Museum. Linked with Tweedsmuir, Skirling and Stobo with Drumelzier.

Sunday Service: 10am

Open by arrangement, telephone Mr Ian Brown 01899 830365

CHURCH OF SCOTLAND

202 THE PRIORY CHURCH, COLDINGHAM

NT 904 659

Coldingham, Berwickshire

Influential centre of Christian witness in Scottish Borders since 7th century. Present church formed from the choir and sanctuary area which comprised the eastern arm of the early 13th-century cruciform-plan Priory Church of St Mary. Splendid free-standing arch of original church to the east of the main building. South and west walls rebuilt 1662 and extensive renovation in 1850s. Interior renovation 1950 providing present chancel and its furnishings. Nine modern stained glass windows. Detailed scale model of the Priory on exhibition.

Sunday Service: 12 noon

Open Wednesdays, May to September 2-4pm, and by arrangement, telephone Mr A M Scott 018907 71280

CHURCH OF SCOTLAND **A**

THE PRIORY CHURCH, COLDINGHAM

203 COLDSTREAM PARISH CHURCH

NT 844 400

High Street, Coldstream

The square church tower with its four stages, clocks and octagonal stone roofed bell-tower and weathervane is a distinctive feature of the outline of Coldstream. It and the west entrance are part of the original church built in 1718. The rest of the church was rebuilt in 1905 to a design by J M Dick Peddie. A classical nave and aisles church with barrel-vaulted roof supported by eight Tuscan columns. A fine stone pulpit sits in front of the semi-circular arch which leads into the chancel. The church contains many reminders of its close association, along with the town, with the Coldstream Guards. The King's and Regimental Colours hang in the chancel. Plaque to the Rev Adam Thomson who formed the Coldstream Free Bible Press in 1845, thus breaking the monopoly held by Oxford and Cambridge Universities and the King's printers in Scotland.
Sunday Service: 11.15am

Open June to August, Thursday 2-4.30pm. Other times by arrangement, telephone Dr B J Sproule 01890 882271

CHURCH OF SCOTLAND WC **B**

204 CRAILING KIRK

NT 682 250

Built c.1775 on an ancient site of worship; the bell is dated 1702. Aisle added in the early 19th-century and further alterations and additions 1892. Restoration by P Macgregor Chalmers 1907. On A698 Jedburgh–Kelso. Services: second and fourth Sunday 10.30am, first Sunday of winter months 6.30pm. See local press for more details

Open by arrangement, telephone Mrs Rose, The Braeheids, Crailing 01835 850268

CHURCH OF SCOTLAND **B**

CRAILING KIRK

205 DENHOLM CHURCH

NT 569 186

Denholm, by Hawick

Dates from 1845. Interior much altered 1957. 150th anniversary wall hangings. Situated in a beautiful conservation village. Best small village in 'Beautiful Scotland in Bloom' 1999 and 2000. A698 Jedburgh–Hawick. Time of weekly Sunday Service changes every four months: see notice boards for details

DENHOLM CHURCH

Key from the Manse in Leyden's Road, or Robert L Brown, Marybank, Douglas Drive, Denholm 01450 870218

CHURCH OF SCOTLAND (free) **C**

206 DRUMELZIER KIRK

NT 135 343

Drumelzier, by Broughton

A simple rectangular building of pre-reformation origins. The original date is uncertain, but it owes its present appearance largely to major alterations carried out in 1872. Bellcote, 17th-century, on the west gable. Burial vault 1617 for the Tweedies of Drumelzier. United with Stobo and linked with Broughton, Tweedsmuir, Skirling. One hundred yards off B712 in Drumelzier village. Sunday Service: first and third of the month 6.30pm (except July and August)

For information on access, telephone the Rev Rachel Dobie 01899 830331, or Mr and Mrs Julian Birchall 01899 830319

CHURCH OF SCOTLAND **B**

DRUMELZIER KIRK

207 ECKFORD KIRK

NT 706 270

Eckford, by Kelso

Built 1771 on an ancient site of worship, incorporating fragments of the 1668 building and the north aisle of 1724. Very sweet interior with rich turn-of-the-century furnishings in the sanctuary. Jougs 1718, mort bell and 19th-century watch-tower. Many fine 17th-century gravestones. On A698 Jedburgh–Kelso. Service: first Sunday of summer months at 6.30pm, see local press for details

Open by arrangement, telephone Mrs Jean Dyet 01573 850308

CHURCH OF SCOTLAND **B**

ECKFORD KIRK

208 EDNAM PARISH CHURCH

NT 737 372

Ednam, by Kelso

Church built 1800 and recast 1902. Situated in the village of Ednam where hymnwriter Henry Francis Lyte was born. In union with Kelso North. Sunday Service: 10am

Open daily 10am-4pm, July and August

CHURCH OF SCOTLAND WC

209 GALASHIELS OLD PARISH CHURCH & ST PAUL'S

NT 490 362

Scott Crescent, Galashiels

Built in 1881 to plans in the Gothic Revival style by George Henderson, the main feature is the 190ft spire. Front porch added 1922. Good glass, including some by Douglas Strachan. Stone carvings by John Rhind and wood carving by Francis Lynn. Willis organ. Sunday Services: 11am and 6.30pm

Open by arrangement, telephone Dr Borthwick 01896 752221

CHURCH OF SCOTLAND

♿ (via hall) 👂 WC **B**

GALASHIELS OLD PARISH CHURCH & ST PAUL'S

210 ST PETER'S CHURCH, GALASHIELS

NT 496 356

Abbotsford Road, Galashiels

Gothic Revival style Hay & Henderson 1853. Reredos Sir Robert Lorimer 1914. Stained glass, memorial brasses. Setting of church with lawns, graveyard, hall and rectory encapsulated the Tractarian ideal. Quarter mile south of town centre on Selkirk road. Sunday Services: Holy Communion 8am, Sung Eucharist 10.30am

Open by arrangement. Key from the Rectory, Parsonage Road, Galashiels, telephone 01896 753118, or contact Mr R Brown, 52 Croft Street, Galashiels, telephone 01896 754657

SCOTTISH EPISCOPAL ♿ 📖 WC **C**

ST PETER'S CHURCH, GALASHIELS

211 ST CUTHBERT'S CHURCH, HAWICK

NT 491 361

Slitrig Crescent, Hawick

A Sir George Gilbert Scott building of 1858. Reredos J Oldrid Scott 1905. Chancel screen Robert Lorimer. Some fine stained glass including two contemporary windows of 1995. Sunday Services: Holy Communion 9.30am, Family Eucharist 10.30am, Friday 12 noon Holy Hour

Open Monday and Tuesday, 10am–12 noon, Wednesday 7am–12 noon, Thursday and Friday 2–4pm

SCOTTISH EPISCOPAL WC B

ST CUTHBERT'S CHURCH, HAWICK

212 HOBKIRK PARISH CHURCH

NT 587 109

Hobkirk, Bonchester Bridge, by Hawick

A Christian site for over 900 years. The present church was built in 1862. Stones from the earlier churches are incorporated in the font. The bell is inscribed 'I was made for Hobkirk in 1745'. One mile west of Bonchester Bridge on the A6088 Hawick–Newcastle (off A68). United with Southdean. Sunday Service: 11am

Open daily all year

CHURCH OF SCOTLAND

HOBKIRK PARISH CHURCH

213 HOWNAM PARISH CHURCH

NT 778 193

Hownam, Morebattle, Kelso

In an idyllic situation on the haugh by the Kale Water. The original building appears to have been cruciform, but was remodelled in 1752 as a rectangle, and substantially modernised in 1844. The interior was refurbished in 1986. From the original church there remains a round-headed doorway in the south wall, dating from the turn of the 15th and 16th centuries. Linked with Linton, Morebattle and Yetholm. Sunday Service: second and fourth of every month 12.30pm

Open all year during daylight hours

CHURCH OF SCOTLAND B

214 ST JAMES CHURCH, INNERLEITHEN

NT 329 366

High Street, Innerleithen

Built in 1881 to a design by John Biggar, a church with some interesting works of art including a large icon of Our Lady of Czestochowa, Poland. This is by K Kryska 1944, the captain of Polish Forces based in Peebleshire. Other monuments include ones dating from 1861 and a copy of the bust of John Ogilvie. The sanctuary has been brought back into use, and a narthex has been built inside the church to provide toilet and kitchen facilities. A rood screen division within the church provides a gathering and social space towards the rear of the nave. Sunday Service: 11.30am; Holy Days 7pm

ST JAMES CHURCH, INNERLEITHEN

Open summer 10am-4pm, and by arrangement, telephone Mrs Helen Garrett 01896 830025, or Mrs Anne Tait 01896 831184

ROMAN CATHOLIC **B**

215 KELSO NORTH PARISH CHURCH

NT 727 341

Roxburgh Street, Kelso

Erected 1866 for the congregation of Kelso North Free Church, architect Frederick T Pilkington. The front of the church is very ornate, being designed in the Gothic style, with the tower and spire rising to some 180ft. Extensively renovated in 1934 and 1984-9. Although the exterior is quite massive, in contrast the interior is fairly neat and compact. Sunday Services: 11.30am; Evening Worship 6.30pm first Sunday October to June

Open July and August, Monday to Friday 10am-4pm. Also Saturdays all year for coffee mornings

CHURCH OF SCOTLAND

 **A**

KELSO NORTH PARISH CHURCH

216 KELSO OLD PARISH CHURCH

NT 729 339

The Butts, Kelso

Octagonal plan church, James Nisbet, dating from 1773, and altered by William Elliot in 1823. Built to continue worship begun in Kelso Abbey in 1128. Recently extensively restored. Banners of Blues & Royals, presented to the church by the Duke of Roxburghe 1927. Off Market Square, by Knowes car park and adjacent to Kelso Abbey. Sunday Service: 11.30am

Open Easter to September, Monday to Friday 10am–4pm

CHURCH OF SCOTLAND WC A

KELSO OLD PARISH CHURCH

217 ST ANDREW'S CHURCH, KELSO

NT 728 337

Belmont Place, Kelso

Situated close to the banks of the River Tweed, built 1868 by Sir Robert Rowand Anderson. Altar, reredos, font and Robertson memorial sculpted in marble and Caen stone. Decorative wooden chancel roof and decorated pulpit. Stained glass. Small garden to rear (including Garden Room for meetings and Junior Church). Opposite Kelso Abbey on B6089. Sunday Services: 8.30am and 10.30am; Wednesday Eucharist 10.30am; Thursday Eucharist 7.00pm

Open daily 8.30am–5pm

SCOTTISH EPISCOPAL WC B

ST ANDREW'S CHURCH, KELSO

218 THE KIRK OF YETHOLM, KIRK YETHOLM

NT 826 281

The church for the delightful twin villages and parish of Yetholm stands on a site in use since David I's apportionment of parishes. Built by Robert Brown 1837 to replace a small dank thatched affair, it is a rectangular plan Gothic church of local whinstone with cream sandstone dressings, and a tower to the south. A remodelling in 1935, and the creation of an upper room out of the gallery in the 1970s, gives the interior a lightness belied by the sombre imposing exterior. Stained glass by Ballantine & Son, Edinburgh. The medieval bell is still in use. As the nearest burial ground to Flodden, the graveyard is believed to have interred officers fallen in that battle (1513). Gravestones 17th-century. Linked with Linton, Morebattle and Hownam. Sunday Service: 10am

THE KIRK OF YETHOLM, KIRK YETHOLM

Open daily during daylight hours

CHURCH OF SCOTLAND ♿ **B**

219 LEGERWOOD PARISH CHURCH

NT 594 434

Legerwood, Berwickshire

The church dates from 1127. Repaired in 1717 and 1804. Its chancel has a fine Norman arch. Sunday Service: 11.45am, first Sunday of each month

Open daily

CHURCH OF SCOTLAND ♿ **B**

LEGERWOOD PARISH CHURCH

220 LILLIESLEAF KIRK

NT 539 253

East of Lilliesleaf village

The church of 1771 was extended in 1883 and transformed by the addition of west part of nave and belltower in 1910. Good stained glass by William Wilson, 1966. Medieval font and ancient child's stone coffin. Sunday Service: 11.30am

Open during daylight hours

CHURCH OF SCOTLAND 

221 LINTON KIRK & HOSELAW CHAPEL

NT 773 262 and NT 802 318

Near Morebattle, Kelso

On a sandy knoll, a 12th-century church much altered in 1616, 1774, 1813 and finally restored to an approximation of its Romanesque appearance in 1912 by P MacGregor Chalmers. It retains its Norman feel and today the visitor enters under a unique stone tympanum to discover an attractive nave and substantial chancel, the arch richly carved (1912). A Norman font and chancel stalls are of particular interest. Linton Kirk is most noted for the stone above the porch said to depict a knight on horseback lancing two creatures – the stone is Norman and unique in Scotland, and legend suggests that this is the first known Somerville killing a worm. The Leishman father and son ministries completed most of the present improvements; the son Thomas also had a small chapel built in the district of Hoselaw (seven miles away) to serve the cottagers; architect P MacGregor Chalmers. Linked with Morebattle, Hownam and Yetholm. Sunday Service: first, third and fifth of every month; and fifth Sunday at Hoselaw Chapel (except December and January) 12.15pm

Open daily during daylight hours

CHURCH OF SCOTLAND **B**

222 LYNE KIRK

NT 192 405

On A72 from Peebles

Located on the site of a 12th-century church, the present church was built between 1640 and 1645 by John Hay of Yester (later 1st Earl of Tweeddale). The porch was added in the 19th century. The church interior remains substantially unaltered; of particular interest are the Dutch pulpit and canopied pews dated 1644. Pre-Reformation font. The earliest stone in the graveyard is dated 1707; the Adam and Eve stone dated 1712 is uncommon. Roman fort of Lyne immediately to the west. Service: 11am, first Sunday of each month

Open daily

CHURCH OF SCOTLAND **B**

223 MANOR KIRK

NT 220 380

Kirkton Manor, by Peebles

First referred to in 1186 as 'the chapel of Maineure'. Tradition speaks of an earlier chapel of the 4th century dedicated to St Gordian, a martyred Roman soldier. The present building was completed in 1874. The bell, rung before every service, is inscribed *In honore Santi Gordiani MCCCCLXXVIII* and is one of the oldest bells in use in Scotland. Pewter baptismal basin, inscribed *Manner Kirk 1703*. Services: second, third and fourth Sundays of each month 11am, fifth Sunday 6.30pm

Open daily

CHURCH OF SCOTLAND ♿ (ramp) 🗍

MANOR KIRK

224 HOLY TRINITY, MELROSE

NT 540 342

High Cross Avenue, Melrose

HOLY TRINITY, MELROSE

Built in the Early English style by Benjamin Ferrey 1846-50. Decorated chancel and transepts by Hay & Henderson 1900. The chancel floor is mosaic. Open timber roof carried on mask corbels. Stained glass windows in transept 1900, by Kempe, other commemorative glass by Mayer & Co and W Wilson 1963. Quarter mile from Melrose centre, on road to Darnick. Services: Sunday 8.30 and 11am; Wednesday 10.30am; Evensong first Sunday of month 6.30pm

Open by arrangement, telephone the Rector 01896 822626. Occasional concerts

SCOTTISH EPISCOPAL ♿ ⓔ WC **B**

225 MINTO CHURCH

NT 557 201

Minto, by Hawick

Designed by William Playfair, the church dates from 1830, the interior recast in 1934. Fine external war memorial. Panoramic views of Teviotdale and Minto Hill. Linked with Bedrule and Denholm. Time of fortnightly Sunday Service: alternates with Bedrule, changes every four months: February to May 11.30am, June to September 10am, October to January 11.30am, and so on

Key from Mrs Marjorie Walton, Kirk View, Minto, Hawick 01450 870351

CHURCH OF SCOTLAND ⓔ **C**

226 MOREBATTLE PARISH CHURCH

NT 772 250

Morebattle, Kelso

MOREBATTLE PARISH CHURCH

The church of 'Mereboda' is recorded as belonging to the Diocese of Glasgow from about 1116. The building was burnt down in 1544 and rebuilt; the present structure dates substantially from 1757, extensions having been made in 1899 and 1903. It is oblong in plan, with chancel, porch and vestry which seem to be additions. The bellcote at the west end is currently being rebuilt. Look for the plan in the porch which shows the archaeological work carried out in the early 1900s, and inscriptions painted on fabric on the west wall. Linked with Hownam, Yetholm and Linton. Sunday Service: 11.15am

Open all year during daylight hours

CHURCH OF SCOTLAND [wheelchair access] [hearing loop] B

227 NEWTOWN CHURCH

NT 315 693

St Boswells Road, Newtown St Boswells

Church opened in 1868. Contains memorials to past ministers. On bus routes between Jedburgh to Edinburgh and Galashiels. Sunday Service: 9.45am

Open by arrangement, telephone the Minister 01835 822106

CHURCH OF SCOTLAND WC

NEWTOWN CHURCH

228 OXNAM KIRK

NT 701 190

Oxnam, by Jedburgh

On the site of a medieval church dating from before 1153. The present church was built in 1738 and enlarged to form a T-plan in 1874. A characteristic Scottish 18th-century church with plain glass and white-washed walls. Many fine 17th and 18th-century gravestones. Continuo pipe organ by Lammermuir Pipe Organs 1990. Signposted from A68 at Jedburgh. Services: first and third Sundays, Christmas and Easter 10.30am

Open by arrangement, telephone Patrick Wood, Ladfield 01835 840358. Pennymuir Fair, ancient Border hill sheep fair, first Saturday in September

CHURCH OF SCOTLAND [hearing loop] B

OXNAM KIRK

229 LECKIE MEMORIAL CHURCH

NT 253 404

Eastgate, Peebles

Handsome Gothic style church with a fine terraced situation, built 1875-7, to designs by Peddie & Kinnear, in memory of Thomas Leckie, the first pastor of the Associate Burgher Congregation from 1794-1821. Gifted in trust, by the surviving members of his family. Following union in 1976 with St Andrews Church, now home of the St Andrews Leckie congregation. The pews have been removed and replaced with removable seating so the building is now multi-functional. Sunday Services: 10.30am and 6.00pm

Open by arrangement with the Minister, telephone 01721 721749

CHURCH OF SCOTLAND

230 PEEBLES OLD PARISH CHURCH

NT 246 406

High Street, Peebles

1887 by William Young of London in Gothic style containing features from earlier church. Fine crown spire dominates the High Street. An inviting flight of steps leads up to the entrance. The chancel was reconstructed by J D Cairns 1937. Entrance screen of 1965, woodwork by Messrs Scott Morton, metalwork by Charles Henshaw & Son, glass by Helen Turner. Pulpit 1913 by P MacGregor Chalmers. Part of pre-Reformation font incorporated in table in crossing, by Mitchall Design 1998. Pipe organ by August Gern 1887, rebuilt by Henry Willis 1937. Stained glass by Cottier of London and McCartney of Wiston. Sunday Service: 10am; Holy Communion 10am on last Sunday of month, January, April and October

Open 10am-4pm, mid-April to mid-October

CHURCH OF SCOTLAND WC **B**

231 ST JOSEPH'S CHURCH, PEEBLES

ST JOSEPH'S CHURCH, PEEBLES

NT 248 407

Rosetta Road, Peebles

The present building was opened in 1858. The couthy interior was reordered in 1971. The church includes various stained glass windows and statues. The most significant is the recently restored 14 Stations of the Cross by the Alinari Brothers of Florence.

Services: Saturday Vigil 6pm, Sunday 9.30am

Open daily 9am-6pm

ROMAN CATHOLIC B

232 ST PETER'S EPISCOPAL, PEEBLES

NT 253 405

Eastgate, Peebles

Built 1836-7 in finely hewn ashlar with an open timber roof. The floor is paved with mosaic tiles as is the reredos, beautifully executed with devices in gold and colour. Choir seats and altar of oak. Piscina on the south side with stone shelf and foliated basin. Fine stained glass. The organ, Harrison & Harrison, is one of the smallest three-manual instruments ever built and has been praised for its compactness and excellence of tone. Sunday Services: Holy Communion 8.30am, Eucharist 10.30am; Thursday: Holy Communion 10am

Open 9am-5pm, or daylight hours

SCOTTISH EPISCOPAL

233 ROXBURGH PARISH CHURCH

NT 700 307

Built in 1752, repaired in 1828, with additions of 1865. Fine painted heraldic panels. Stained glass 1947 by W Wilson. The exterior has a pair of cubical sundials. In the graveyard the (roofless) burial-vault of the Kers of Chatto. Fine modern continuo pipe organ, Lammermuir Pipe Organs 1990. Signposted two and a half miles west of Kelso on A699. Services: second and fourth Sundays 11.30am

Open by arrangement, telephone Mrs Palmer, North Cliff Cottages, Roxburgh 01573 450263

CHURCH OF SCOTLAND B

ROXBURGH PARISH CHURCH

234 SKIRLING PARISH CHURCH

NT 075 390

By Biggar

The earliest reference to a church in Skirling is in 1275. It was probably situated near to the present war memorial. It is not known when a church was built on the present site. However, records show that the church was virtually rebuilt in 1720. Further significant alterations were made in 1891. The bellcote is of particular interest, as is the sundial on the tower. The floral design of the stained glass east window forms a backdrop to the communion table and matching chairs presented by the artist, Sir D Y Cameron, in 1948. Round churchyard enclosed by a ha-ha and entered through fine wrought-iron gates. Two miles east of Biggar on A72, approached from opposite village green by a steep metalled access road.
Sunday Service: 11.30am

SKIRLING PARISH CHURCH

Open by arrangement, telephone A S Goodere 01899 860251

CHURCH OF SCOTLAND

235 SOUTHDEAN PARISH CHURCH

NT 631 092

Southdean, by Hawick

Built in 1876 to a design by George Grant of Glasgow on a site near to the ruins of two previous churches of 12th and 17th centuries. Font, 12th-century. Super-altar set into the communion table, one of only two known in Scotland. Good stained glass. Memorial to James Thomson (1700-48), author of 'Rule Britannia' and 'The Seasons', whose father was parish minister. Prior to the Battle of Otterburn 1388, the Earl of Douglas and his army met at the 12th-century church, whence the survivors returned to bury their dead. United with Hobkirk. Special Services only

Open daily all year

CHURCH OF SCOTLAND

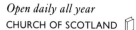

SOUTHDEAN PARISH CHURCH

236 SPROUSTON KIRK

NT 757 353

There has been a church in Sprouston since the 17th century. The present building was built 1781, though the bellcote bears the date 1703 and a 12th-century piscina is built into the chancel. The Minister in 1911 won first and third prize out of 36,000 entries in the *Daily Mail* National Sweet Pea Competition, enabling the new chancel to be built with the £1500 prize money. Douglas Strachan window of 'The Fall of Lucifer'. Pulpit falls of sweet peas embroidered by Mrs Doreen West. Sunday Service: 10am

Key available from Mr Tom Walker, telephone 01573 228172

CHURCH OF SCOTLAND **B**

237 STOBO KIRK

NT 183 377

Stobo, by Peebles

One of the oldest churches in the Borders, and of historical importance. Much of the present building dates from 12th century. It stands on the site of a 6th-century church reputedly founded by St Kentigern (St Mungo). The 12th-century building comprised nave, sanctuary and tower, the latter rebuilt from first floor level, probably 16th century. Major restoration in 1863, John Lessels. North aisle chapel restored in 1929, James Grieve. A new stone floor laid and a meeting room formed at first floor level of the tower in 1991. Linked with Broughton, Tweedsmuir and Skirling and united with Drumelzier. Stands 100 yards from B712, off A72, four miles west of Peebles or off A701, one and a half miles south of Broughton. Sunday Service: 11.30am

For information on access, telephone Mrs Rosemary Hall 01721 740229, or Rev Rachel Dobie 01899 830331

CHURCH OF SCOTLAND **B**

STOBO KIRK

238 TRAQUAIR HOUSE CHAPEL

NT 331 355

Traquair House, near Innerleithen

The chapel, formerly the billiard room above the brewhouse, replaced the 'secret chapel' in the main house used in penal times. Related memorabilia on view in house, which also contains a priest's hole and secret stairway. Chapel has carved oak panels said to have come from the chapel of Mary of Guise in Leith, and to be of Flemish origin. Service: Mass, 7pm last Wednesday April to October

Easter Egg Extravaganza (April). Traquair Fair first weekend in August. Christmas opening last weekend in November. Open April to end-October 12.30pm–5.30pm, except June, July and August 10.30am–5.30pm. Access to Chapel is included in admission to grounds

ROMAN CATHOLIC WC A

239 TWEEDSMUIR KIRK

NT 101 245

Tweedsmuir, by Broughton

The present building was erected in 1874 by John Lessels, to replace a much earlier church of 1643. Bell of 1773 still in use. Two high circular windows in the north and south transepts and some interesting stained glass. Oak for the panelling in the porch is from a tree planted at Abbotsford by Sir Walter Scott. First and Second World War memorials. The churchyard dates back to the first church and contains table-stone graves of the 18th century and several other stones of interest, including a Covenanter's grave and one, near the gate, to the many men who died in the construction of the Talla reservoir. Linked with Broughton, Skirling and Stobo with Drumelzier. Village six miles south west of Broughton on A701. Sunday Service: 10am

Open daily all year

CHURCH OF SCOTLAND B

TWEEDSMUIR KIRK

240 ST MUNGO'S CHURCH, WEST LINTON

NT 148 519

Main Street, West Linton

A 'Gladstone Church' built in 1851 when it served as both church and school. Unusually, the church runs from north to south instead of east to west. Fine stained glass by C E Kempe. Services: every Sunday 11am; second Sunday Choral Evensong 5.30pm

Open by arrangement, telephone the Rector 01968 672862

SCOTTISH EPISCOPAL WC

ST MUNGO'S CHURCH, WEST LINTON

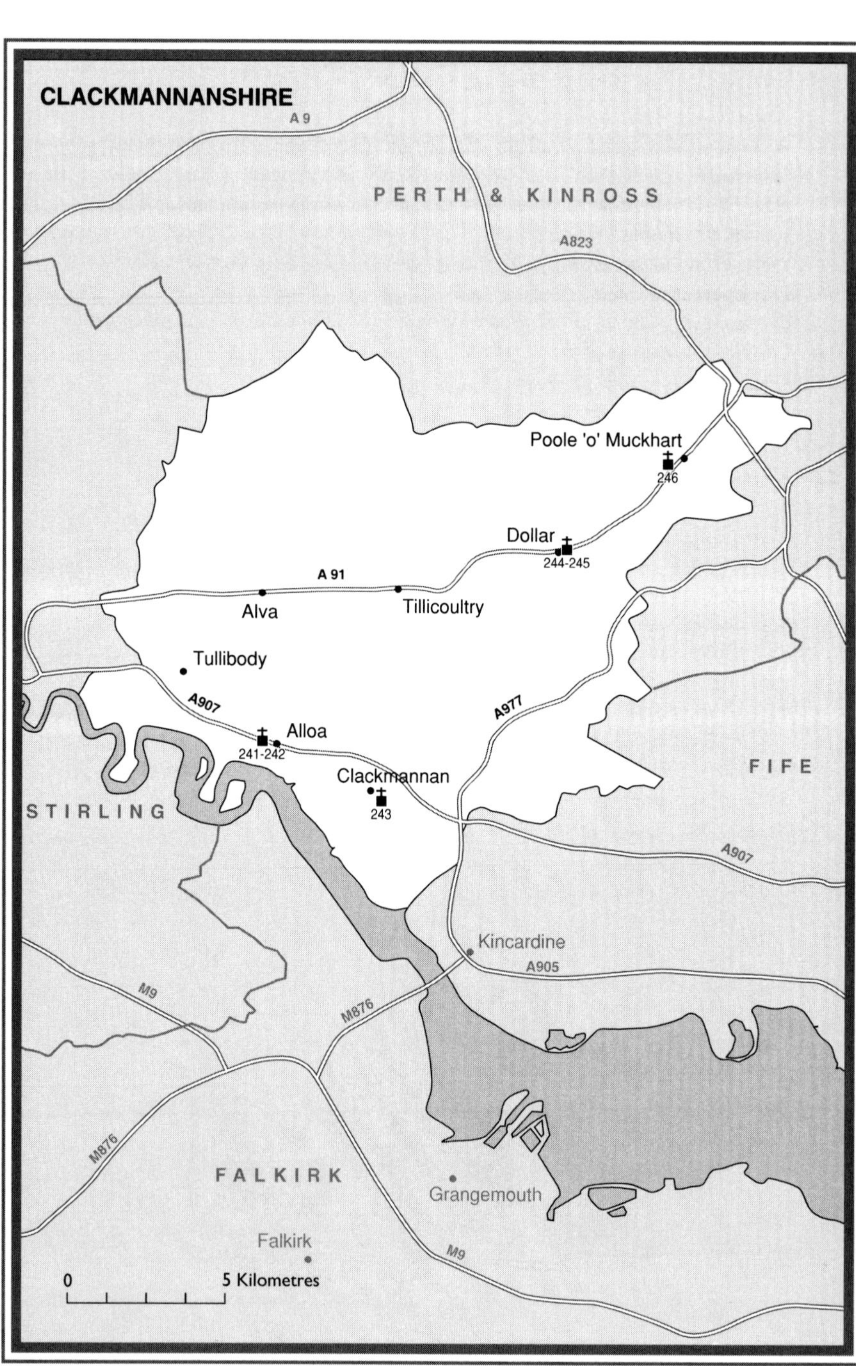
CLACKMANNANSHIRE
A 9
PERTH & KINROSS
A823
Poole 'o' Muckhart
246
Dollar
244-245
A 91
Alva
Tillicoultry
Tullibody
A907
Alloa
241-242
A977
FIFE
Clackmannan
243
STIRLING
A907
Kincardine
A905
M9
M876
M876
FALKIRK
Grangemouth
Falkirk
M9
0
5 Kilometres

CLACKMANNANSHIRE

241 ALLOA PARISH CHURCH (ST MUNGO'S)

NS 886 929

Bedford Place, Alloa

Delicate and picturesque Gothic Revival church by James Gillespie Graham 1819. Usual symmetry in plan, but greater felicity than normal in lacy Perpendicular. The 207ft spire with flying buttresses is visible from most parts of the town. Interior is by Leslie Grahame MacDougall in Lorimer-derived Gothic. Sunday Service: 11.15am

Open by arrangement, telephone 01259 721553. Close to Alloa Tower

CHURCH OF SCOTLAND **B**

242 ST JOHN'S CHURCH, ALLOA

NS 886 923

Broad Street, Alloa

Sir Robert Rowand Anderson designed St John's which was opened in 1869 and enlarged in 1873. Described by Thomas Bradshaw then as the 'most elegant place of worship in the County'. Early Geometric Gothic with a notable broach spire. The rich interior includes glass by Kempe, and a reredos with a mosaic of the Last Supper by the Italian Salviatti. The chancel was refurbished in 1913, its roof bearing 106 carved bosses. These, together with the woodwork of the choirstalls 1902, organ screen and war memorial, are all by Lorimer. The tower contains a ring of eight bells, six hung in 1871 and a further two in 1925. Sunday Service: Family Eucharist 11am

Open usually Wednesday and Friday 10am–12.30pm.
Other times, telephone 01259 212836

SCOTTISH EPISCOPAL **B**

ST JOHN'S CHURCH, ALLOA

243 CLACKMANNAN PARISH CHURCH

NS 910 918

High Street, Clackmannan

There has been a church at Clackmannan since St Serf visited from Culross in the eighth century. The present church was built in 1815 by James Gillespie Graham to replace a 13th-century church. Perpendicular Gothic with buttressed tower at the west end. Stained glass by Herbert Hendrie, Gordon Webster, Sadie Pritchard and Douglas Hamilton. Modern Makin Tocatta digital computerised organ. Graveyard has stones dating from the 17th century with several Bruce family memorials. Views over Carse of Forth. Sunday Services: 11am

CLACKMANNAN PARISH CHURCH

Open weekdays 2-4pm, third Monday in June to second Friday in September. Other times, telephone 01259 214238 or 01259 211255

CHURCH OF SCOTLAND **B**

244 DOLLAR PARISH CHURCH

NS 964 980

East end of Dollar, north side of A91, Bridge Street

Built 1842/3 to replace 18th-century church (ruin to north), designed by architect Tite of London. Chancel added 1926, porch added 1963. Triple stained glass window in memory of Rev Angus Gunn 1910. Three stained glass windows by Adam Robson and Jennifer Campbell, Union window 1979 by Douglas Hogg. Rushworth and Dreaper organ 1926. Reredos tapestry based on Ardchattan Cross designed by Adam Robson 1963. Sunday Service: 11.15am

Open by arrangement with Rev John Purves, telephone 01259 743432

CHURCH OF SCOTLAND **B**

DOLLAR PARISH CHURCH

ST JAMES THE GREAT, DOLLAR

245 ST JAMES THE GREAT, DOLLAR

NS 958 980

Harviestoun Road, Dollar

A small country church with a prayerful atmosphere, set in a well-kept garden. Consecrated in 1882, the building designed by Thomas Frame & Son, Alloa. The font is a memorial to Archbishop Archibald Campbell Tait of Canterbury (1868-83). Sunday Services: 8.30am and 10.30am, Thursday 9.45am

Open daily all year

SCOTTISH EPISCOPAL C

246 MUCKHART PARISH CHURCH

NO 001 010

North side of A91 at west end of Pool of Muckhart

Church 18th century. Stained Glass windows removed to Fossoway Church, Crook of Devon. Various plaques. Large gravestone on east wall of the church for the Christie family, Cowden. Nearby stone to Matsui, Japanese gardener to Miss Ella Christie. Sunday Service: 9.45am

Open at all times

CHURCH OF SCOTLAND

 B

MUCKHART PARISH CHURCH

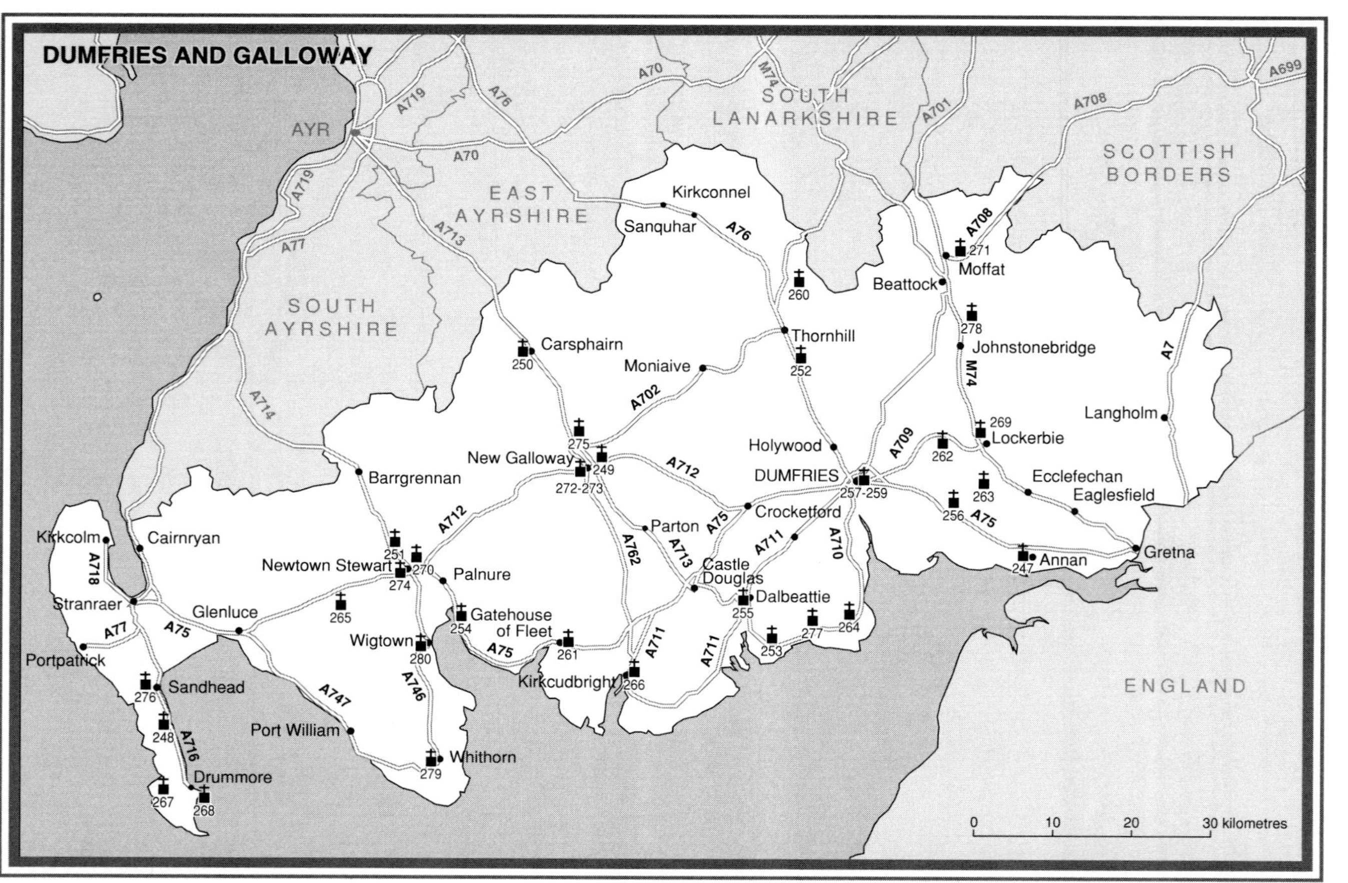
DUMFRIES AND GALLOWAY
AYR
SOUTH LANARKSHIRE
EAST AYRSHIRE
SOUTH AYRSHIRE
SCOTTISH BORDERS
ENGLAND
Kirkconnel
Sanquhar
Moffat
Beattock
Carsphairn
Thornhill
Moniaive
Johnstonebridge
Langholm
Lockerbie
Holywood
New Galloway
Barrgrennan
DUMFRIES
Ecclefechan
Eaglesfield
Crocketford
Parton
Kirkcolm
Cairnryan
Newtown Stewart
Palnure
Castle Douglas
Dalbeattie
Gretna
Annan
Stranraer
Glenluce
Gatehouse of Fleet
Wigtown
Portpatrick
Sandhead
Kirkcudbright
Port William
Whithorn
Drummore
A70
A76
A719
A77
A713
A714
M74
A701
A708
A699
A702
A712
A709
A7
A710
A711
A75
A762
A718
A747
A746
A716
250
251
270
274
275
249
272-273
260
252
271
278
269
262
263
256
257-259
247
265
254
280
261
266
255
253
277
264
276
248
267
268
279
0
10
20
30 kilometres

DUMFRIES & GALLOWAY

Local Representatives: The Rev J W Scott, The Manse of Durisdeer, Thornhill (*telephone* 01848 500231); Mr Michael Dunlop, Baltersan, Newton Stewart (*telephone* 01671 402543)

247 ST COLUMBA'S CHURCH, ANNAN

NY 199 665

Scott's Street, Annan

Built as a Congregational Church in 1794 on the site of a Secession Meeting House and re-opened as Catholic Church in 1839. Extended at both ends in 1904 by Charles Walker of Newcastle as the gift of the parish priest the Rev Lord Archibald Douglas. Stations of the Cross by Brendan Ellis 1984. Painted panels in sanctuary, Joe Burns 1997. The parish priest also serves St Francis' Church, Drove Road, Langholm (1960) and St Ninian's Church, Victory Avenue, Gretna (1925, 1918). Services: Saturday Vigil Mass 6pm, Sunday Mass 11am

Open daily 9am–6pm. When closed, key from adjacent presbytery or at 32 Scott's Street

ROMAN CATHOLIC WC **B**

248 ARDWELL

NX 100 457

One kilometre west of Ardwell village

Surrounded by trees and shrubs and fronted with grass and flowerbeds, Gothic cruciform church by P MacGregor Chalmers 1901. Tower with octagonal spire and corner pinnacles. Notable inside are the inscriptions in the masonry. Pulpit, reredos, screen and communion table in oak, elaborately carved. Stained glass window of the calming of the storm. Sunday Service: every two weeks (normally) 10am

The Church's centenary year will be celebrated in 2002. Open by arrangement with Mrs H McCreadie, Laundry Cottage, Ardwell Mains

CHURCH OF SCOTLAND WC **B**

249 BALMACLELLAN CHURCH, CASTLE DOUGLAS

NX 651 791

A harled, 'T plan' kirk, the body was built in 1753, with the north aisle added in 1833 by William McCandlish. The stained glass west window is dated 1928 and is by Gordon Webster. The graveyard has an early 18th-century table-stone commemorating the Covenanting martyr Robert Grierson. Plaque in churchyard commemorating Sir Walter Scott's 'Old Mortality', who came from Balmaclellan. Sunday Service: first Sunday of every month at noon

Open by arrangement, telephone the Minister 01644 430380

CHURCH OF SCOTLAND

BALMACLELLAN CHURCH

250 CARSPHAIRN PARISH CHURCH

NX 563 932

Carsphairn, Castle Douglas

Built in 1815 to replace church of 1636 destroyed by fire. Central communion table. Memorials including John Semple, Covenanting minister, and John Loudon MacAdam, roads pioneer. Covenanter's grave. A713 Ayr–Castle Douglas. Linked with Balmaclellan, Kells and Dalry. Sunday Service: 10.30am

Open by arrangement, telephone Mrs Campbell 01644 460208

Carsphairn Pastoral & Horticultural Show, first Saturday in June

CHURCH OF SCOTLAND WC **B**

CARSPHAIRN PARISH CHURCH

251 ALL SAINTS CHURCH, CHALLOCH

NX 385 675

Challoch, by Newton Stewart

Built as private chapel of Edward James Stopford-Blair of Penninghame House and consecrated 1872. Designed by W G Habershon & Pite of London and an excellent example of a small Victorian church. Ten stained glass windows, 17 memorial plaques, pine altar and wrought iron and brass rood screen. Fine Harston two-tracker organ 1881, restored 1993, and the only example of Harston's work still in use. Located two miles north of Newton Stewart on road to Girvan, A714. Sunday Services: 9am Holy Eucharist, 10.30am Sung Eucharist, first in month 10.30am Choral Matins. Daily 8am Morning Prayer, 5.30pm Evening Prayer. Feast days 7pm Holy Eucharist

Open daily, or telephone 01671 402101

SCOTTISH EPISCOPAL WC **A**

252 CLOSEBURN PARISH CHURCH

NX 904 923

Closeburn, by Thornhill

Built by James Barbour 1878 alongside former (1741) church. In Gothic style with a three-stage tower. Spacious interior with an elaborate hammerbeam roof supported on foliaged corbels. Pipe organ by Henry Willis & Sons 1887. Window in the north transept by the St Enoch Glass Studios 1948. Font originally from Dalgarnock. In the graveyard is the smart mausoleum built by Thomas Kirkpatrick of Closeburn in 1742. Sunday Service: 10.30am

Open by arrangement. Keys from either Mrs Lorimer, Lakehead Farm Cottages, or Mr Menzies, Closeburn Village

CHURCH OF SCOTLAND

WC **B**

CLOSEBURN PARISH CHURCH

COLVEND PARISH CHURCH

253 COLVEND PARISH CHURCH

NX 862 541

Rockcliffe, by Dalbeattie

A chaste Early Christian church by P MacGregor Chalmers 1911 of granite with red sandstone dressings, set on a rise overlooking the Solway Firth. Its bell-tower is topped by a steep pyramid roof. A pretty interior with nave, aisle and transept and a timbered roof. Plain plastered walls are a foil for the sandstone columns which support round-headed arches springing from cushion capitals to form arcades into the aisle and transept. In the chancel, the deep colour of the stained glass window, the Ascension by Stephen Adam & Co 1918, forms a lovely backdrop to the High Presbyterian arrangement of furnishings. Other windows by Adam & Co and by Margaret Chilton and Marjorie Kemp 1926. A710 from Dalbeattie, turn right onto unclassified road signposted Rockcliffe. Quarter mile on the right. Linked with Southwick and Kirkbean. Sunday Service: 11.30am

Open daily 10am–6pm

CHURCH OF SCOTLAND

254 KIRKMABRECK PARISH CHURCH, CREETOWN

NX 493 565

Large and tall with a tower above the front gable, built in 1834 by John Henderson. Panelling 1645 with Muir family coat of arms. In spring churchyard and graveyard carpeted with crocuses. On A75, six miles from Newton Stewart, signposted in village. Sunday Service: 11.30am

Open by arrangement, telephone Mr J Cutland, 5 Chain Road, Creetown 01671 820228

CHURCH OF SCOTLAND

KIRKMABRECK PARISH CHURCH, CREETOWN

255 ST PETER'S CHURCH, DALBEATTIE

NX 831 613

Craignair Street, Dalbeattie

Hall church 1814 of pinky granite with red sandstone dressings. Grey granite tower was added c.1850. Sunday Mass 9am and 11am

Open daily 9am–5pm

ROMAN CATHOLIC ♿ **B**

256 DALTON KIRK

NY 114 740

Dalton, by Lockerbie

Close by the roofless shell of the 1704 parish church stands J M Dick Peddie's 1895 sturdy Romanesque church. Unusually colourful kingpost-truss roof over the nave and scissors roof in the chancel. Three-light stained glass window of the Ascension by A Ballantine and Gardiner 1896. The graveyard contains a late Georgian burial enclosure and the suave classical monument to the Carruthers of Whitecroft. B725, signposted off A75 Annan–Dumfries. Sunday Services: 9.45am, 11.15am by rotation with Hightae and St Mungo

Open by arrangement, telephone the Manse, Hightae, Lockerbie 01387 811499

CHURCH OF SCOTLAND WC **B**

DALTON KIRK

257 CRICHTON MEMORIAL CHURCH, THE CRICHTON, DUMFRIES

CRICHTON MEMORIAL CHURCH, THE CRICHTON, DUMFRIES

NY 983 742
The Crighton, Bankend Road, The Crichton, Dumfries
Designed by architect Sydney Mitchell, Crighton Memorial Church was completed in 1897. The cathedral-style church is richly detailed and has a square tower 123ft high. The exterior is of red sandstone from Locharbriggs, Dumfries, whilst the elegant interior features pink sandstone from nearby Thornhill. Ornate oak roof. Stone carving by William Vickers of Glasgow. The boldly-designed floor is of Irish and Sicilian marble. Impressive stained glass by Oscar Paterson of Glasgow 1896 features throughout. Pulpit and choir stalls date from 1897. The magnificent organ (1902) has richly carved screens. Brass angel lectern 1910. Inter-denominational. Services: Sunday, Church of Scotland 10am; Thursday, Scottish Episcopal Eucharist 11am. Popular venue for weddings, concerts and other special events
Church website: www.crighton.org.uk
Open by arrangement, telephone Crichton Development Company 01387 247544
NON-DENOMINATIONAL WC **A**

258 GREYFRIARS CHURCH, DUMFRIES

NX 971 763
Church Crescent, Dumfries
A richly ornamented Gothic edifice by John Starforth 1868 with plenty of crisply carved detail, all in red sandstone snecked rubble. The steeple dominates both the building and the townscape. The interior is a huge, almost square space, richly decorated. Clustered shafts with leafy capitals support collar-braced and kingpost-truss roofs over the nave and transepts. Stained glass by James Ballantine & Son, Powell Bros, Camm Bros and L C Levetts. Pipe organ 1921 by Ingram. Sunday Services: 11am and 9.30am during summer; Evening Services: fortnightly
Details of opening on notice board
CHURCH OF SCOTLAND WC **A**

GREYFRIARS CHURCH, DUMFRIES

ST GEORGE'S, DUMFRIES

259 ST GEORGE'S, DUMFRIES

NX 971 764

George Street, Dumfries

Built as a Free Church in 1844 by William McGowan, and remodelled in 1893 by James Halliday who added the Italianate front of red sandstone. Almost square interior with north and south aisles marked off by superimposed Corinthian columns. Compartmented and coved main ceiling. Sunday Service: 11am, additionally July and August 9.30am (Family Service)

Church website: www.saint-georges.org.uk

Open by arrangement, telephone Dr Balfour 01387 253696

CHURCH OF SCOTLAND ♿ WC **B**

260 DURISDEER PARISH CHURCH

NS 894 038

Unspoilt, peaceful, Georgian country parish church, rebuilt 1716, topped by a belfry tower. X-plan, one arm of the cross is taller and more sophisticated, built for the Duke of Queensberry and remaining from the earlier church. Inside is the most amazing monument over the Queensberry burial vault, a baroque baldacchino carved in 1695 by John van Nost to the design of James Smith who was also architect of the later church. 'There are few buildings in which baroque magnificence and presbyterian decency are so happily combined' (George Hay, *Architecture of Scottish Post-Reformation Churches*). Martyr's Grave 1685. One mile east of A702 (signed). Sunday Service: 11.45am

Open during daylight hours. Drumlanrig Castle nearby

CHURCH OF SCOTLAND

♿ 📖 ☕ (afternoon teas, Sundays, July, August, September) WC **A**

DURISDEER PARISH CHURCH

261 ST MARY'S CHURCH, GATEHOUSE OF FLEET

NX 597 562

Dromore Road

Episcopalians in the area worshipped in the private chapel of Cally house until the present building of 1840 was purchased from the United Presbyterian Church and dedicated to St Mary in 1909. It is probably unique among Scottish Episcopal Churches in having a stained glass window commemorating John Knox! Sunday Service: Holy Communion 9.45am; Wednesday: Holy Communion 9.30am

Open by arrangement, telephone P Taylor 0557 330146

SCOTTISH EPISCOPAL ♿ 🦻 **B**

ST MARY'S CHURCH, GATEHOUSE OF FLEET

262 HIGHTAE KIRK

NY 090 793

Built as a Relief meeting house in 1796 and remodelled for the Reformed Presbyterians in 1865, when the windows were enlarged and the gableted west bellcote and small porch were added. On the B7020, two and a half miles south of Lochmaben. Sunday Services: 9.45am, 11.15am by rotation with Dalton and St Mungo

Open by arrangement, telephone the Manse, Hightae, Lockerbie 01387 811499

CHURCH OF SCOTLAND ♿ WC (adjoining manse)

263 ST MUNGO PARISH CHURCH, KETTLEHOLM

NY 143 771

Built under the patronage of the Rt Hon Robert Jardine MP of Castlemilk. Late Scots Gothic by David Bryce 1877 with a pinnacled-buttressed porch decorated with grotesque carved heads. Inside, a magnificently elaborate open roof. Organ 1905 by Abbot & Smith. Stained glass by James Ballantine & Son 1876. First World War memorial by F M Taubman. On the B723, three miles south of Lockerbie. Sunday Services: 9.45am, 11.15am by rotation with Dalton and Hightae

Open by arrangement, telephone the Manse, Hightae, Lockerbie 01387 811499

CHURCH OF SCOTLAND ♿ WC **B**

264 KIRKBEAN PARISH CHURCH

NX 980 592

Harled T-plan kirk said to have been designed by William Craik, sometime Laird of Arbigland. The tower on the west wall is of two lower stages 1776 with a Diocletian window in its second stage, and two upper stages added in 1836 by Walter Newall, the first with a clock and the top a big octagonal belfry cupola of polished ashlar under a lantern. A Venetian window in the east gable of the tail of the church. Inside, plain furnishings of 1883. A memorial font, presented by the United States Navy, in memory of John Paul Jones, a gardener's son from Arbigland, who founded it; designed and sculpted by George Henry Paulin 1946. In the village, turn left at the road junction to Carsethorn. Adjacent to the school on left. Linked with Colvend and Southwick. Sunday Service: 10am

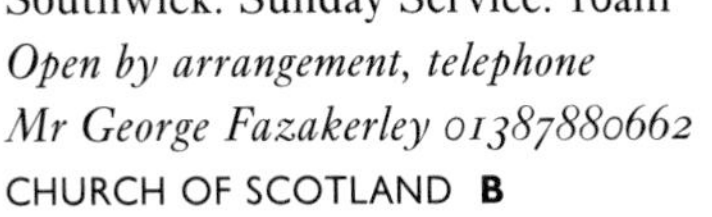

Open by arrangement, telephone Mr George Fazakerley 01387880662

CHURCH OF SCOTLAND **B**

KIRKBEAN PARISH CHURCH

265 KIRKCOWAN PARISH CHURCH

NX 327 610

Main Street, Kirkcowan

At the west end of the village, built in 1834 to replace a former church, of which only an ivy-clad east gable remains in its kirkyard (east end of village). The present church is a harled T-plan building with external stairs at the east and west gables leading to two galleries. A tower at the north side. Inside, three galleries in all, supported by marbled cast iron columns. Tall pulpit of 1834 and a late 19th-century chamber organ by J & A Mirrlees, brought here in 1966. Linked with Wigtown. Sunday Service: 10am

Open by arrangement, telephone Mr J Adair 01671 830214

CHURCH OF SCOTLAND **A**

266 GREYFRIARS (ST FRANCIS OF ASSISI), KIRKCUDBRIGHT

NX 682 511

Mote Brae, Kirkcudbright

The sanctuary of Greyfriars Church is the last remaining fragment of a Franciscan friary. Dating from either the 13th or 15th centuries, it has undergone many changes in both design and use over the years. The MacClellan Monument, erected in 1597, is one of the most interesting features of the church. On the left of the High Altar is an ancient piscina. There are also three fine modern stained glass windows including work by Gordon Webster. The cross and candlesticks are the work of Mabel Brunton, a distinguished member of the artists' colony which flourished in the town in the 1920s. Other interesting furnishings are the 17-century dower chest and the medieval holy water stoup. Sunday Services: Holy Communion 11.30am all year, and 8.15am end May to August; Friday: Holy Communion 10am

Open Easter week, July to August, and by arrangement,
telephone the Rector 01557 330146

SCOTTISH EPISCOPAL **A**

267 KIRKMAIDEN OLD KIRK

NX 139 324

Kirkmaiden, Drummore

Built 1638 to replace St Catherine's at Mull of Galloway in the most southerly parish in Scotland. T-shaped church with vaults of the McDouall family of Logan underneath balcony. 'Treacle' Bible on display. Bell from Clanyard Castle, a gift from the Earl of Dalhousie 1532. Sunday Service: 11.30am last Sunday May to September

Open daily Easter to October, or by arrangement with Mrs Symonds, telephone 01776 840601

CHURCH OF SCOTLAND

KIRKMAIDEN OLD KIRK

268 ST MEDAN'S, DRUMMORE

NX 135 367

Stair Street, Drummore

Built 1903 in red Dumfries sandstone with an attractive roof of red and yellow pine. Hymnus IV electronic organ. Morrison memorial window behind choir 1951. John McGuffog memorial window above pulpit, designed and made by Arthur C Speirs DA of Greenock 1996. Sunday Services: 11.30am, except last Sunday in month in May when service is in Kirkmaiden Old Church

Open by arrangement, contact Mrs Beck, telephone 01776 840210

CHURCH OF SCOTLAND ♿ WC **B**

269 HOLY TRINITY, LOCKERBIE

NY 136 815

Arthurs Place, Lockerbie

Built as Trinity Church 1874 for the United Presbyterian Church, became Church of Scotland 1929 and acquired in 1973 by the Catholic Church and renamed Holy Trinity. Designed by Ford Mackenzie, built in Corncockle sandstone in Gothic style with a large rose window and steeple. The organ, Ingram of Edinburgh, is a prominent feature. Plaque in vestibule commemorates 1000 years of Christianity in the Ukraine. Copy of Lockerbie Book of Remembrance. Services: Saturday Vigil 7pm; Sunday Mass 11.15am; other days as announced

Open daily 9am-5pm

ROMAN CATHOLIC **B**

270 MONIGAFF PARISH CHURCH, MINNIGAFF

NX 410 666

Minnigaff, Newton Stewart

Church completed in 1836 to a design by William Burn. Stained glass by William Wailes of Newcastle 1868 and Ballantine, Edinburgh 1910. Font from Earl of Galloway's private chapel. Organ built in 1873, Bryceson Brothers, London. Ruins of pre-Reformation church on medieval foundations. East gable 12th or early 13th-century. Motte and ditch. Eighth-century stone slab of Irish missionary influence. Grave stones including B-listed Heron monument. Yew tree 900 years old. Sunday Service: 10am, first Sunday of month Holy Communion 9.25am

Open July and August, Monday and Friday 2-4.30pm. Or by arrangement, telephone Mrs Shankland 01671 402164. Historical display June to September

CHURCH OF SCOTLAND (free) **B**

271 ST ANDREW'S, MOFFAT

NT 075 051

Churchgate, Moffat

Impressive church in Early English style by John Starforth 1884, with a central tower flanked by bowed stair towers. Richly-carved entrance leads to a wide interior with galleries on slender iron columns. Profusion of stained glass including rose window above the pulpit by Starforth. Other windows by James Ballantine & Son, Ballantine & Gardiner, and William Meikle & Sons. Pipe organ by Eustace Ingram 1894. Sunday Service: 11.00am; first Sunday of summer months 9.30am

Open June to September 10.30am-12.30pm and 2pm-4pm

CHURCH OF SCOTLAND (rear door) WC **B**

272 KELLS PARISH CHURCH, NEW GALLOWAY

NX 632 784

Kirk Road, New Galloway

Built in 1822 to a design by William McCandlish. A granite T-plan church with three-stage square tower at the centre of south wall. Interior mainly reconstructed in 1911 following original layout. Galleries on three sides with pulpit on long south wall. Notable churchyard with three 'Adam and Eve' stones of 1706-7, and a delightful upright for Captain Gordon's gamekeeper, John Murray. Linked with Carsphairn, Balmaclellan and Dalry. Sunday Service: 10.30am, not first Sunday

Open by arrangement 01644 430380

CHURCH OF SCOTLAND **B**

KELLS PARISH CHURCH, NEW GALLOWAY

ST MARGARET'S NEW GALLOWAY

273 ST MARGARET'S NEW GALLOWAY

NX 636 778

On edge of New Galloway on Ken Bridge road

Built 1904, chancel added 1908. The walls of the church are harled and the roofs are red tiled. The wooden panelling and furnishings are a mixture of Oregon pine and oak and the windows are variously by Kempe, Clayton & Bell, and James Powell & Sons. Services: 10.30am every Sunday and Wednesday

Key at Rectory next door, The Rev John Redpath 01644 420235

SCOTTISH EPISCOPAL

274 PENNINGHAME ST JOHN'S CHURCH, NEWTON STEWART

NX 410 654

Church Street, Newton Stewart

Church completed in 1840 to a design by William Burn. Groome's *Gazetteer* describes it as 'a handsome Gothic edifice'. Major restoration work on tower and steeple carried out in 2000. Organ built by J F Harston of Newark in 1878, and is believed to be the largest and most intact of all organs built by him. Renovated by Hill, Norman and Beard 1962. Spire 151ft. All glass replaced 1996. Interesting display of Communion silver including two chalices dated 1711. Church Street is parallel to town's main street. Sunday Service: 10.30am

Open Tuesday 12.30–2pm for lunchtime prayer meeting, or by arrangement, telephone Mr M C Dunlop 01671 402543

CHURCH OF SCOTLAND WC **A**

DALRY PARISH CHURCH, ST JOHN'S TOWN OF DALRY

275 DALRY PARISH CHURCH, ST JOHN'S TOWN OF DALRY

NX 618 813

Main Street, St John's Town of Dalry

Completed in 1831 to a design by William McCandlish to replace a ruined building of 1771, it is probably the third church to occupy the site. Early records are scarce, but a church, a dilapidated one at that, existed in 1427. Traditional T-shaped interior, plainly furnished. Pulpit with carved wooden canopy. Galleries on three sides. Stands near the Water of Ken with wide views of the Rhinns of Kells. Avenue of lime trees. Interesting old kirkyard with Covenanters' stone and Gordon Aisle, burial place of the Gordons of Lochinvar. Robert Burns fashioned his poem 'Tam o' Shanter' on a local tale. On A713 Castle Douglas–Ayr. Linked with Balmaclellan and Kells and Carsphairn. Sunday Service: 12 noon

Open by arrangement, telephone Mr L A Young 01644 430472

CHURCH OF SCOTLAND WC **B**

276 SANDHEAD

NX 097 500

Main Street, Sandhead

Substantial timber construction with steeply pitched tiled roof and cedar-board clad walls by architects Goudie & Hill 1962. The unusual structure uses laminated timber portal frames with obscured glass between the frames in both side walls. Flat-roofed porch with masonry bell-tower. Internally, much varnished wood. Inverted-pyramid shaped pulpit. Sunday Services: 10am

Open by arrangement, contact Mrs C McKay, 25 Main Street or Mr Cowan, Dorlin, Main Street

CHURCH OF SCOTLAND WC (Wednesdays and Sundays, 2-4pm in summer)

SANDHEAD

277 SOUTHWICK PARISH CHURCH

NX 906 569

Caulkerbush, by Dumfries

Standing by woodland just outside the policies of Southwick House, a stone church of local grey granite with dressings of red sandstone. By Peddie & Kinnear 1891, a mixture of Early Christian and Norman. Its crossing tower was derived from the 14th-century tower of St Monans Parish Church. A wagon roof over the nave, the chancel arch enriched with chevron decoration. On either side of the chancel arch, a neo-Norman font by Cox & Buckley 1898 and a neo-Jacobean pulpit. Wrought iron Arts and Crafts light fittings, once for oil lamps. Late 19th-century stained glass. Organ replaced in May 1999 with Ahlborn SL100. A710 from Dumfries, turn right immediately over Southwick Bridge onto B793 Dalbeattie. Linked with Colvend and Kirkbean. Sunday Service: 10am

Open daily 10am-6pm

CHURCH OF SCOTLAND WC

SOUTHWICK PARISH CHURCH

278 WAMPHRAY PARISH CHURCH

NY 131 965

Neat rectangle by William McGowan 1834, with a slender tower and bellcote. Notable 18th-century headstones in the graveyard and a monument to the Rt Rev A H Charteris, Founder of The Woman's Guild and Moderator of the General Assembly in 1892. Sunday Service: 12.30pm

Open by arrangement with Mrs Braid, telephone 01576 470275

CHURCH OF SCOTLAND

279 ST NINIAN'S PRIORY CHURCH, WHITHORN

NX 444 403

Bruce Street, Whithorn

Built 1822 with later 19th-century tower. Simple rectangular hall church. Carved oak pulpit. Stained glass east windows gifted by the daughter of Gemmell Hutcheson RSA in memory of her father. Located on the site of Whithorn 'dig' in the former precincts of Whithorn Priory. First Scottish Christian community founded here by St Ninian, pre-dates Iona. From A75 turn south at Newton Stewart on A714 then A746. Sunday Services: 10.30am and 7pm

Open Easter to end of October, 10am–5pm

CHURCH OF SCOTLAND ♿ 🦻 📖 A

ST NINIAN'S PRIORY CHURCH, WHITHORN

280 WIGTOWN PARISH CHURCH

NX 436 555

Bank Street, Wigtown

The parish church on an ancient ecclesiastical site, largely rebuilt in 1730, was by the middle of the next century thought to be 'an old mean-looking edifice'. A new church, by the London architect Henry Roberts, was built nearby in 1851, still using the Georgian T-plan with a French pavilion roof on the tower. Built of granite, it encloses a broad nave and east transept. P MacGregor Chalmers added a communion table and font, an organ chamber, and rearranged the seating in 1914. In the transept are three carved stones, one a Celtic cross shaft decorated on both faces with interlaced rings, similar to those of the same period at Whithorn. Stained glass in the east transept window by James Ballantine & Son 1867. Linked with Kirkcowan. Sunday Services: 11.30am and 6.30pm (in church hall)

Open Easter to September, Monday to Friday 2-4pm

CHURCH OF SCOTLAND WC **B**

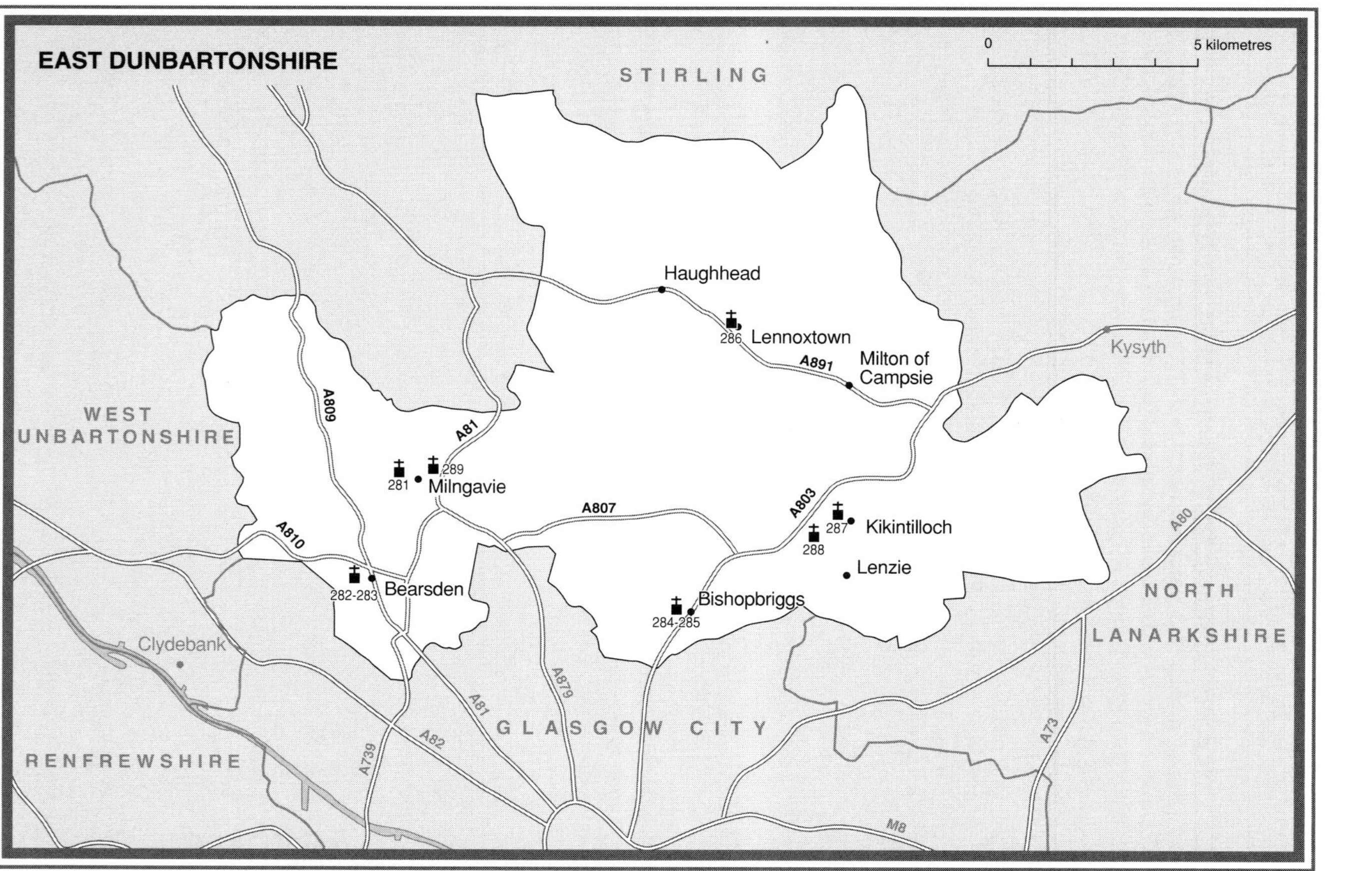
EAST DUNBARTONSHIRE
0
5 kilometres
STIRLING
WEST
UNBARTONSHIRE
RENFREWSHIRE
GLASGOW CITY
NORTH
LANARKSHIRE
Haughhead
286
Lennoxtown
A891
Milton of
Campsie
Kysyth
A809
A81
281
289
Milngavie
A807
A803
287
Kikintilloch
288
Lenzie
A810
282-283
Bearsden
284-285
Bishopbriggs
Clydebank
A81
A879
A82
A739
A80
A73
M8

EAST DUNBARTONSHIRE

Local Representative: Mrs Marion Smith, 30 Roman Court, Roman Road, Bearsden (*telephone* 0141 942 1236)

BALDERNOCK PARISH CHURCH

281 BALDERNOCK PARISH CHURCH

NS 577 751

near Milngavie

The religious history of the site goes back to the 13th century. The present church was built in 1795 on the site of an earlier church. The bell-tower contains a curious panel which may have come from the nearby Roman wall. The octagonal gatehouse and stone stile feature in Moffat's play 'Bunty Pulls the Strings'. Interesting gravestones, including Archibald Bulloch from whom President Theodore Roosevelt and Eleanor Roosevelt descended. The church stands at the end of a lovely one mile walk from Milngavie.

Sunday Service: 11am

Open Sunday 2-4pm, June to August

CHURCH OF SCOTLAND WC B

282 BLESSED JOHN DUNS SCOTUS CHAPEL, BEARSDEN

NS 535 720

2 Chesters Road, Bearsden, Glasgow

The Chapel of Scotus College was designed by J F Stephen and dedicated in 1997. The main internal features are its barrel-vaulted ceiling and glass walls. The 14 stained glass panels representing the Stations of the Cross are by Shona McInnes and are full of rich symbolism. A number of other items were specially commissioned for the Chapel, including processional cross, presidential Chair, candlesticks and a Christ-figure. A pamphlet is available giving excellent details

Open during term time 7am-9pm. Also telephone 0141 942 8384

ROMAN CATHOLIC WC

NEW KILPATRICK PARISH CHURCH, BEARSDEN

283 NEW KILPATRICK PARISH CHURCH, BEARSDEN

NS 543 723

Manse Road, Bearsden

Building began in 1807 on the site of an earlier church 1649, and within the original settlement established by Paisley Abbey in 1232. Very fine collection of stained glass including windows by Stephen Adam, Alfred and Gordon Webster, Norman M Macdougall, C E Stewart, James Ballantine and Eilidh Keith. By rail to Bearsden, by Kelvin Bus 118 to Bearsden Cross. Services: Sunday 10.30am and 6.30pm; Wednesday 12 noon

Open June to August, Wednesday 12.30-4pm, Sunday 2pm-5pm. Other times by arrangement, telephone M L Smith 0141 942 1236. Close to Roman Bath House east of Bearsden Cross

CHURCH OF SCOTLAND WC **B**

284 ST JAMES THE LESS, BISHOPRIGGS

NS 612 712

Hilton Road, Bishopriggs

Built 1980 when the congregation moved from Springburn, this church by Glasgow architects Weddell and Thomson preserves the most striking features of the 1881 Springburn building and contains many items from other Glasgow churches: stained glass by Edward Burne-Jones and Stephen Adam and part of the old High Altar of Iona Abbey. Pipe organ by J W Walker & Sons 1964. Sunday Services: 9am Eucharist, 10.30am Sung Eucharist; Thursday 10.10am Morning Prayer, 10.30am Eucharist

Open Sundays and Thursdays 10am-12noon, or by arrangement with the Rector, telephone 0141 772 4514

SCOTTISH EPISCOPAL WC

285 CADDER PARISH CHURCH

NS 616 723

Cadder Road, Bishopriggs

A simple country church in a delightful and peaceful setting, built 1825 to designs by David Hamilton. The Chancel was added in 1908 and the gallery altered 1914. Finely carved screen at the front of the gallery of Austrian oak. Very fine stained glass windows by Steven Adam, Gordon Webster, Sadie McLellan and Crear McCartney. Pipe organ by Norman & Beard. Watch-house and cast-iron mort safe in the graveyard. Sunday Service: 11.15am (plus 9.30am in summer)

Church website: www.greyfriars@webartz.com

Open by arrangement with the Minister, telephone 0141 772 1363

CHURCH OF SCOTLAND WC **A**

286 CAMPSIE PARISH CHURCH, LENNOXTOWN

NS 629 777

Main Street, Lennoxtown

Modern church with interesting wood carving and stained glass. Craft centre and old church with fascinating graveyard at Campsie Glen, two miles. Bus 175 Campsie Glen via Kirkintilloch. Sunday Service: 11am

Open by arrangement, telephone Mrs M Tindall 01360 310 911

CHURCH OF SCOTLAND WC **A**

CAMPSIE PARISH CHURCH, LENNOXTOWN

ST DAVID'S MEMORIAL
PARK CHURCH, KIRKINTILLOCH

287 ST DAVID'S MEMORIAL PARK CHURCH, KIRKINTILLOCH

NS 654 737

Alexandra Street, Kirkintilloch

The present church by P MacGregor Chalmers 1926, adjacent to site of the original building (1843), was dedicated as a gift of Mrs Paton Thomson in memory of her parents. Two-manual pipe organ, a significant Anneessens 1899 rebuilt and enlarged. Off A803. Sunday Services: 11am and (most Sundays) 6.30pm

Open every Wednesday 11am–2pm for meditation and prayer

CHURCH OF SCOTLAND

288 ST CYPRIAN'S CHURCH, LENZIE

NS 653 727

Beech Road, Lenzie

Built in 1873 by Alexander Ross of Inverness in Gothic style with a three-stage tower at the east end and a gabled porch at the west end. The use of contrasting materials gives a colourful interior. Painting of the Last Supper on the reredos. Memorial choir screen made in local iron foundry. Half-mile north from Lenzie Cross. Sunday Services: 8.30am, 11am and 6.30pm (not July and August)

Open by arrangement, telephone the Rector 0141 776 4149

SCOTTISH EPISCOPALIAN  **B**

289 CAIRNS CHURCH, MILNGAVIE

NS 556 748

Buchanan Street, Milngavie

The oldest congregation in Milngavie, services were first held on Barloch Moor before the first building was erected in 1799. The present church was built to the design of J B Wilson in a late decorated Gothic style, and was opened in 1903. The red tiled spire rises above the surrounding roofs. New halls and rooms by Page & Park, 2000, provide a new dimension to the presentation of the church – intimate, welcoming and friendly – a partnership with history. Interior features a range of banners. Sunday Services: 10.45am and 7pm (summer 10am only)

Access by arrangement with church office, telephone 0141 956 4868

Tuesday to Friday 09.30am-12.30pm

CHURCH OF SCOTLAND **B**

CAIRNS CHURCH, MILNGAVIE

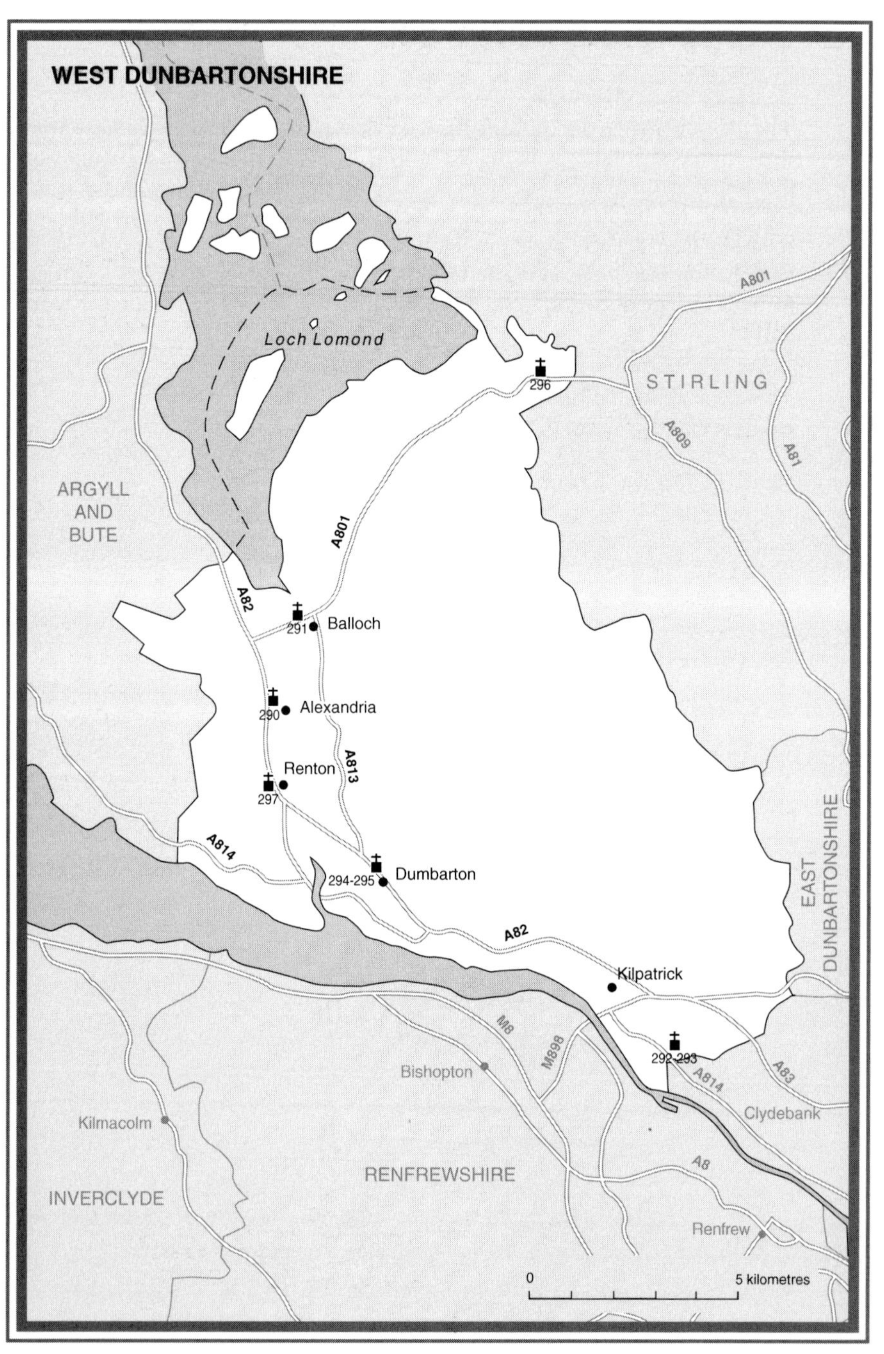
WEST DUNBARTONSHIRE
Loch Lomond
A801
296
STIRLING
A809
A81
ARGYLL
AND
BUTE
A801
A82
291
Balloch
290
Alexandria
A813
Renton
297
A814
294-295
Dumbarton
EAST
DUNBARTONSHIRE
A82
Kilpatrick
M8
M898
292-293
A814
A83
Bishopton
Clydebank
Kilmacolm
A8
RENFREWSHIRE
INVERCLYDE
Renfrew
0
5 kilometres

WEST DUNBARTONSHIRE

290 ST MUNGO'S CHURCH, ALEXANDRIA

NS 389 796

Main Street, Alexandria

Dedicated 1894, J M Crawford, architect, in pointed Gothic style. Early 20th-century addition of side aisle. Simple interior with simple altar furniture. Open timber roof with curved brace supported on stone corbels. Three-light stained glass window in memory of Agnes J Burham of New York featuring Christ in Majesty, St Michael the Archangel, St Agnes and St Agatha. Sunday Services: Eucharist 9am, Sung Eucharist 11am; Wednesday: Eucharist 10am

Church website: //dspace.dial.pipex.com/town/plaza/aaj50/

Open by arrangement, telephone the Priest-in-charge, St Mungo's Rectory 01389 752633

SCOTTISH EPISCOPAL WC **B**

291 ALEXANDRIA PARISH CHURCH, BALLOCH

NS 389 798

Lomond Road, Balloch

Building refurbished and upgraded 1995-6. Digital organ by Allen. A number of items produced by the congregational Sewing Group include the Heritage Tapestry 30 by 27 inches, finely embroidered pulpit falls and communion table cords, four hand sewn banners (two on local themes) crafted in 1998 and 1999 for the Millennium. Several noteworthy items of stained glass by Gordon Webster. Contemporary Noah's Ark mural in main hall. In the grounds, a War Memorial commemorating members of the congregation killed in action 1914-18 and 1939-45. Off A82. Five to ten minutes walk from Balloch railway station. Sunday Service: 11am; and Jazz Praise services at 7pm usually on last Sunday of February and following alternate months

Open by arrangement lunches/afternoon teas for groups by arrangement, Miss E McCreadie 01389 752370

CHURCH OF SCOTLAND WC

ALEXANDRIA PARISH CHURCH, BALLOCH

KILBOWIE ST ANDREW'S CHURCH, CLYDEBANK

292 KILBOWIE ST ANDREW'S PARISH CHURCH, CLYDEBANK

NS 497 702

Kilbowie Road, Clydebank

For the congregation founded as St John's on the Hill 1897, the present church was built in 1904 on land gifted by William Black of Auchentoshen. In simple Perpendicular style, a low cruciform church of red sandstone. The battlemented belfry added 1933. Recent refurbishment. Memorial side chapel with tapestry and stained glass window by Eilidh Keith 1997, dedicated to the victims of the Clydebank blitz. The bell 1933 is one of few remaining in this former industrial community of Scotland. M8 Junction 19, A82 to A8014 turn off. Five minutes walk from railway station. Sunday Service: 11am, except July and August

Open 13 March each year 10am-4pm (Blitz Memorial Day), Commemorative Service 12noon. Other times by arrangement, and Doors Open Day, telephone Rev R Grahame 0141 951 2455

CHURCH OF SCOTLAND

ST JOSEPH'S CHURCH, CLYDEBANK

293 ST JOSEPH'S CHURCH, CLYDEBANK

NS 510 733

Faifley Road, Clydebank

Replacing a Coia church which was burned down, the building is one of the newest in the country, being opened in 1997. The award-winning design by Jacobsen & French utilises tall windows to provide light while natural wood is featured extensively. Sunday Services: 9 and 11.30am; Saturday Vigil 6pm; Daily Mass 9.30am

Open Wednesday 9-11am, Saturday 5-7pm, Sunday 9-12.30

ROMAN CATHOLIC

294 RIVERSIDE PARISH CHURCH, DUMBARTON

NS 398 752

High Street, Dumbarton

Built in 1811 to a design by John Brash on the site of earlier 13/14th-century and 17th-century churches. The steeple and pedimented gable command the westward curve of the High Street. Urns perch on the belfry and adorn the gatepiers. The interior was refurbished 1886. Stained glass includes the Queen Margaret window by the Abbey Studio of Glasgow and Ascension window by C E Stewart. Eleventh/12th-century Crusader stone now housed in gallery. Sunday Service: 11.15am

Open weekdays 9.30am-12.30pm

CHURCH OF SCOTLAND WC **A**

ST AUGUSTINE'S CHURCH, DUMBARTON

295 ST AUGUSTINE'S CHURCH, DUMBARTON

NS 397 752

High Street, Dumbarton

Built in 1873, the architect Sir Robert Rowand Anderson designed the building in the Gothic Revival Style. Stained glass at baptismal font by Stephen Adam with others to a design by Carl Alnquist. The organ was designed and built for the church by Smith and Brock. Sunday Services: 9 and 11am

Open Saturday mornings, and by arrangement, telephone church office 01389 734514

SCOTTISH EPISCOPAL ♿ **A**

296 THE CHURCH OF KILMARONOCK

NS 452 875

By Drymen

The present church building dates from 1813 and has a stout classical dignity. Parish long-established when documented records began; the screen at the entrance to the nave lists incumbents since 1325. Memorial wall plaques. Ancient stones in graveyard. North side of A811, three miles west of Drymen. Sunday Service: 11am, May to September

Open by arrangement, telephone the Rev Andrew Mitchell 01360 660295. Occasional events by the Friends of Kilmaronock

CHURCH OF SCOTLAND ♿ **B**

THE CHURCH OF KILMARONOCK

297 RENTON TRINITY PARISH CHURCH

NS 390 780

Building originally constructed as Renton Old Parish Church 1892, architects H & D Bradlay. United with Renton Union Church and Renton Millburn Church 1969. Building has since been refurbished and upgraded. Five stained glass windows by Oscar Paterson, Glasgow 1912–22. Sunday Services: 11am and at 6.30pm second Sunday of March, June, September, December

Open Thursdays 10.30am–1.30pm. or by arrangement, telephone Rev Cameron Langlands 01389 752017

CHURCH OF SCOTLAND A

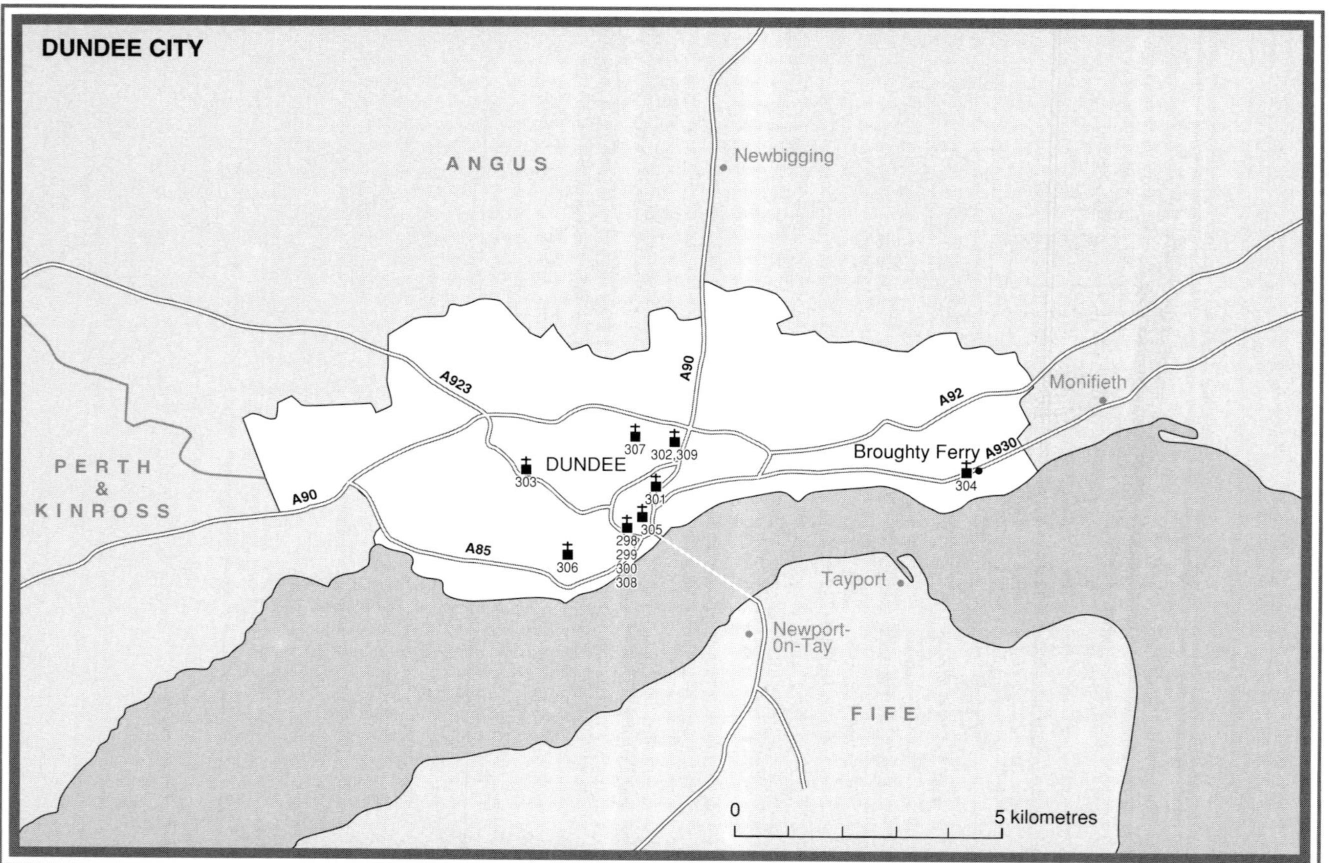
DUNDEE CITY
ANGUS
Newbigging
PERTH & KINROSS
A923
A90
A92
Monifieth
DUNDEE
307
302,309
303
Broughty Ferry
A930
304
301
305
298
299
300
308
A85
306
Tayport
Newport-On-Tay
FIFE
0
5 kilometres

DUNDEE

298 DUNDEE PARISH CHURCH (ST MARY'S)

NO 401 301

Nethergate, Dundee

Founded in 1190 by Earl of Huntingdon. Rebuilt 1844 by William Burn. Beautiful 19th and 20th-century stained glass windows. War memorial 1914-18. Impressive organ installed in 1865. Reading desk with interesting history. North of Discovery Point and railway station. Sunday Service: 11am; Holy Communion last Sunday of month

Open May to September, Monday, Tuesday, Thursday, Friday 10am-12 noon

CHURCH OF SCOTLAND WC **B**

299 MEADOWSIDE ST PAUL'S CHURCH

NO 401 300

114-116 Nethergate, Dundee

Built in 1852, replacing the Mariners' Church, to a design by Charles Wilson. It 'boasts a fine spire terminating the elevation of Nethergate before it is disrupted by the ring road'. Hammer beam roof. Organ by Walker & Co 1902, overhauled by Rushworth & Dreaper 1971. Stained glass, some by Jones & Willis, and by Alexander Russell. A hall complex, M J Rodgers 1988. A feature of the garden is an artistic stone wall by David Wilson. Sunday Service: 11am

Open Wednesday 12 noon-1.30pm for prayer and meditation

CHURCH OF SCOTLAND (Cornerstone Coffee House adjoining) WC **B**

300 ST ANDREW'S CATHEDRAL

NO 400 299

150 Nethergate, Dundee

Designed by George Mathewson in 1835, impressive arcaded interior. Outstanding 19th and 20th-century stained glass by Mayer of Munich. Sunday Mass: 10.30am, 7pm. Weekday Mass: 10am

Open Monday to Saturday 9am-3pm

ROMAN CATHOLIC

GLASITE KIRK NOW PART OF THE CHURCH HALLS OF THE ST ANDREW'S PARISH CHURCH

301 ST ANDREW'S PARISH CHURCH

NO 404 307

King Street, Dundee

Trades Kirk with interesting history, dating from 1774, Samuel Bell with plans by James Craig, Edinburgh. Beautiful stained glass. Includes Glasite kirk 1777 now part of church hall complex. Handsome spire with peal of fine musical bells. Lovely gardens. Teas on Saturdays. Next to Wellgate Shopping Centre. Sunday Service: 11am all year; also 9.30am June, July and August

Church website: www.standrewschurch.co.uk

Open Tuesday, Thursday, Saturday 10am–12 noon all year. Also Doors Open Day

CHURCH OF SCOTLAND (Saturdays) WC **A**

ST ANDREW'S PARISH CHURCH

302 ST JOHN THE BAPTIST CHURCH

NO 411 314

116 Albert Street, Dundee

The present building was consecrated in 1886. Designed with a French style roof by the Rev Edward Sugden 1885. The sanctuary and chancel are panelled in late Gothic style, the details suggested by the woodwork in King's College Chapel, Aberdeen. Open wood roof and pillars give this interior a Scandinavian feel. Reredos by William Hole. The font cover is a splendid carved wooden spire

Open Thursday 9-11am. Other times by arrangement, telephone Rev James Forbes 01382 461640

SCOTTISH EPISCOPAL WC **B**

303 ST MARGARET'S, LOCHEE

NO 382 312

17/19 Ancrum Road, Dundee

The roof of this church, 1888, designed by the Rev E Sugden, has attracted the attention of the Architecture Department of Duncan of Jordanstone College. The font, in the form of an angel holding a large shell, is thought to be a copy of a font by Danish artist Bertel Thorvaldsen in Copenhagen Cathedral. Services: Sunday: Holy Communion 8.00am, Sung Eucharist 11.00am; Thursday: Holy Communion 10.00am

Open by arrangement with the Treasurer, Dr Urquhart, telephone 01382 322928

SCOTTISH EPISCOPAL WC (after Sunday Sung Eucharist)

304 ST MARY'S CHURCH, BROUGHTY FERRY

NO 461 310

Queen Street, Broughty Ferry

Designed by Sir George Gilbert Scott 1858 and added to 1870. Sir Robert Lorimer extended the chancel 1911. The pulpit, screen, choir stalls and reredos are all by Lorimer. Garden of Remembrance. On the main road from Carnoustie and Monifieth to Dundee. Frequent bus service. Sunday Services: 8.30am, 11am, 6.30pm; Weekdays: Matins 7am, Evensong 6pm

Open daily all year

SCOTTISH EPISCOPAL **A**

305 ST PAUL'S CATHEDRAL

NO 404 303

Castlehill, 1 High Street, Dundee

Designed by Sir George Gilbert Scott, the Cathedral stands on the site of Dundee's ancient Castle. Gothic in style, but Gothic with a difference. Tall, graceful columns give an impression of lightness and airiness. East end of High Street at junction with Commercial Street. Walking distance from rail and bus stations. Sunday Services: 8am, 9.40am, 11am, 6.30pm

Open Monday to Saturday 11am-5pm

SCOTTISH EPISCOPAL WC **A**

306 ST PETER'S FREE CHURCH

NO 390 298

St Peter Street, Dundee

1836, by Hean Brothers. Remarkably douce for a revivalist kirk; yet this was the seat of the Rev Robert McCheyne (1813-43) a major player in the Evangelical revival, who made these sober rafters ring. An elegant, classical church with a gallery carried on cast-iron columns. Original pulpit. The plain simplicity of the building is ennobled by the tower and stone spire against its east gable. The church has served different denominations since its opening: Free, United Free, and Church of Scotland. It became a Free Church again in 1987. From city centre, west for one mile along High Street, Nethergate and Perth Road. Turn right into St Peter Street. Sunday Services: 11am and 6.30pm; Wednesday: Prayer Meeting 7.30pm

Open by arrangement, telephone Rev D Robertson 01382 861401

FREE CHURCH OF SCOTLAND **B**

307 ST SALVADOR'S CHURCH

NO 403 313

Church Street, Dundee

Glorious painted interior with stencilled wall decoration and open roof, built in 1868 in early Arts & Crafts Gothic by G F Bodley. Carnegie Street end of Church Street, off Hilltown. Buses 20 and 22. Daily Services: Tuesday 9.30am, Wednesday 10am, Thursday 12.30pm, Friday/Saturday 8am. Evensong daily 5.30pm except Sunday 5pm. Sunday Services: 9am, 11am, 5pm

Open most mornings. Also Doors Open Day, September

SCOTTISH EPISCOPAL **B**

308 THE STEEPLE CHURCH

NO 402 301

Nethergate, Dundee

Church building dates from 1788, Samuel Bell. Entry through 15th-century St Mary's Tower. A landmark, known as Old Steeple. City centre. Sunday Services: 11am and 6.30pm (July and August 7pm)

Open July to August, Tuesday 10am-1pm, Saturday 12 noon-3pm. Also Doors Open Day and other summer activities. Mary Slessor Exhibition, July to August (details in Church)

CHURCH OF SCOTLAND **B**

THE STEEPLE CHURCH

309 STOBSWELL PARISH CHURCH

NO 411 315

Albert Street, Dundee

On a prominent site, by Charles Edward and Thomas S Robertson 1874. The buildings have recently undergone extensive refurbishment. L-shaped church. Fine stained glass windows by William Wilson. From city centre buses 15, 17, 32, 33, 35 and 36. Sunday Service: 11am (July and August 10.30am)

Open Dundee Doors Open Day, September

CHURCH OF SCOTLAND ♿ 👂 WC (for disabled) **B**

STOBSWELL PARISH CHURCH

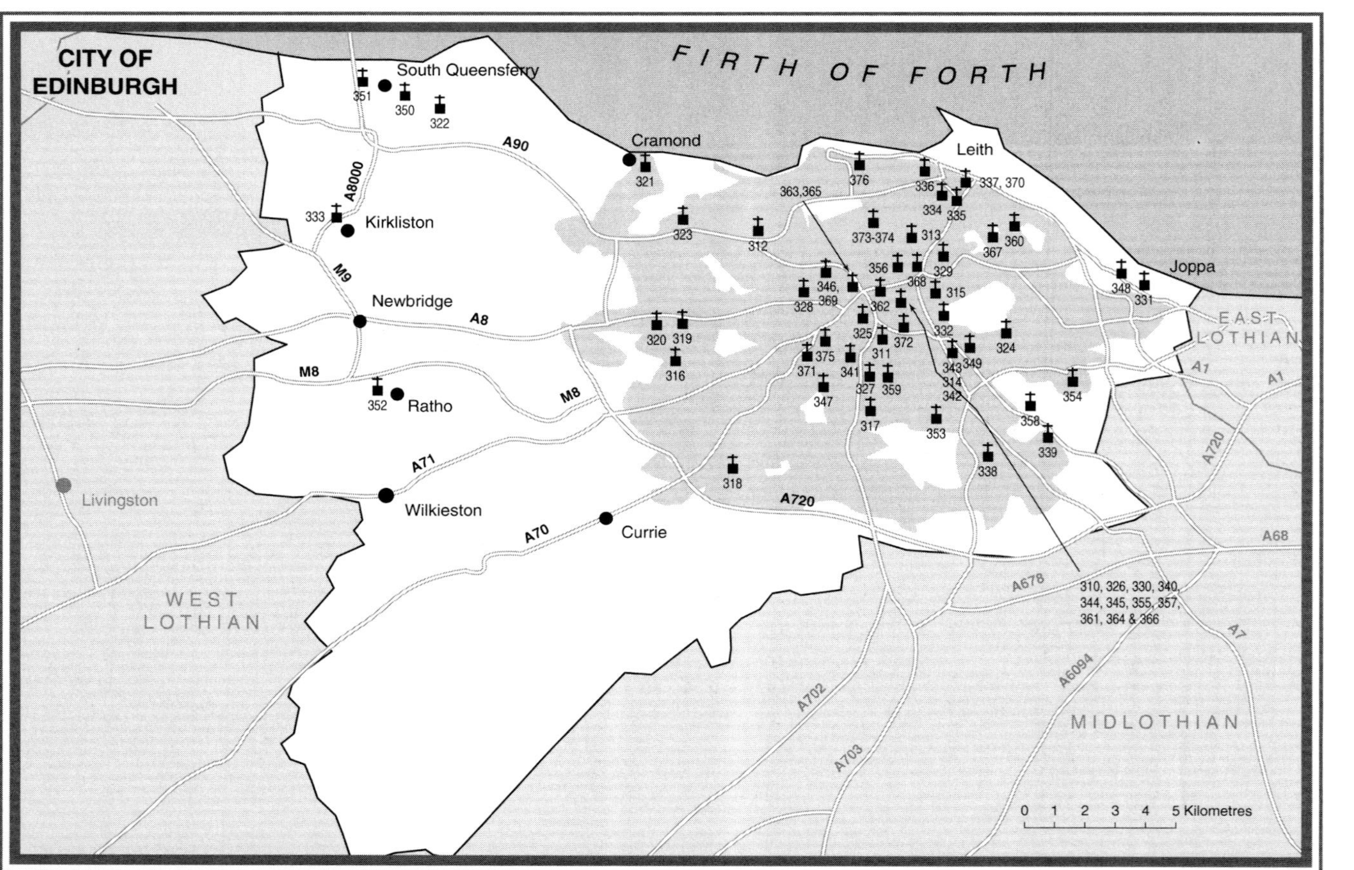
CITY OF
EDINBURGH
FIRTH OF FORTH
South Queensferry
351
350
322
A90
Cramond
321
Leith
376
336
337, 370
363,365
334
335
333
Kirkliston
A8000
323
312
373-374
313
367
360
356
329
M9
346,
369
368
315
348
331
Joppa
Newbridge
A8
328
362
320
319
325
372
332
324
EAST
LOTHIAN
375
311
343
349
316
371
341
314
A1
M8
327
359
342
354
352
Ratho
347
M8
317
353
358
339
338
A71
318
Livingston
Wilkieston
A720
A720
A70
Currie
A68
A678
310, 326, 330, 340,
344, 345, 355, 357,
361, 364 & 366
WEST
LOTHIAN
A7
A6094
A702
MIDLOTHIAN
A703
0 1 2 3 4 5 Kilometres

EDINBURGH

310 AUGUSTINE UNITED CHURCH

NT 257 734

41 George IV Bridge, Edinburgh

AUGUSTINE UNITED CHURCH

Built 1857-61 by J J M & W H Hay with Romanesque, Renaissance and Classical elements for the congregation of the second Scottish Congregational Church in Edinburgh. The projecting centre of the gable front is carried up as the 'bride's-cake' tower which is topped by a spire of three diminishing octagonal stages. Composite hammerbeam and kingpost roof. The Bradford computer organ 1994 uses the pipes and case of the former Ingram organ 1929. Major alterations to interior, to plans by Stewart Tod and Partners 1995. Two stained glass windows by Robert Burns, formerly in the gallery, now at ground floor level. Now, with the meger of several congregations, a member of the United Reformed Church. Sunday Service: 11am; Holy Communion first and third Sundays

Church website: www.augustine.org.uk

Normally open Monday to Friday 12noon-2pm, during the summer (except August)

UNITED REFORMED **B**

311 BARCLAY CHURCH

NT 249 726

Bruntsfield Place, Tollcross, Edinburgh

1864 in powerful Ruskinian Gothic, this is Frederick T Pilkington's greatest achievement. Spire 230ft is well known landmark. Spectacular theatrical space within with double gallery. Painted ceiling. Removal of centre and other pews in sanctuary with other minor alterations and the installation of spiral staircases to the first gallery, 1999, by Gray, Marshall Associates of Edinburgh. One hundred metres south of King's Theatre. Sunday Services: 11am and 6.30pm

Open July and August, Tuesday and Thursday 2-4pm. Other times and details of special events, telephone Rev Graham Leitch 0131 447 8702

CHURCH OF SCOTLAND  **A**

312 BLACKHALL UNITED FREE CHURCH

NT 216 750

1 House o' Hill Road, Edinburgh

Modern church completed in 1968. A90 at the junction between Telford Road and Queensferry Road. LRT buses 32, 52 and 41a, SMT 43.

Sunday Service: 11am

UNITED FREE CHURCH OF SCOTLAND

BLACKHALL UNITED FREE CHURCH

313 BROUGHTON ST MARY'S PARISH CHURCH

NT 256 748

12 Bellevue Crescent, Edinburgh

A burgh church, built to serve Edinburgh's spreading New Town. Designed in 1824 by Thomas Brown as centrepiece of Bellevue Crescent. Neo-classical style, graceful interior with fluted Corinthian columns supporting gallery. Original pulpit. Nathaniel Bryson's stained glass 'Annunciation' is of particular note. Robert Stevenson, lighthouse builder and grandfather of Robert Louis Stevenson, elder 1828-43. Ten to fifteen minutes walk from east end of Princes Street. City buses 8, 9, 19, 39 to Bellevue Crescent. Sunday Service: 10.30am

Open May to September, Wednesday 10am-12 noon, and Monday to Saturday during the first week of the Edinburgh Festival in August 10-4pm

CHURCH OF SCOTLAND 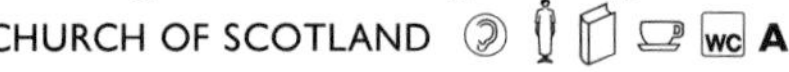 A

BROUGHTON ST MARY'S PARISH CHURCH

314 BUCCLEUCH & GREYFRIARS FREE CHURCH

NT 261 728

West Crosscauseway (off Nicolson Street)

Built 1857 by Hays of Liverpool in Gothic style for the Free Buccleuch congregation established at the 1843 Disruption. The congregation has sought to remain true to the original Free Church vision of reformed theology and evangelical outreach. One of the largest hammerbeam roofs in the country and an impressive spire. Services: Sunday 11.00am and 6.30pm; Wednesday 7.30pm

Open by arrangement with the Minister, telephone 0131 664 6306

FREE CHURCH OF SCOTLAND A

315 CANONGATE KIRK

NT 265 738

Canongate, Royal Mile, Edinburgh

This interesting and recently restored 17th-century church was opened in 1691, its plan by James Smith being unique among 17th-century Scottish churches. Restored in 1991, Stewart Tod Partnership. The churchyard contains the remains of many famous Scots, including economist Adam Smith. 'Open Kirk' information sheets in several languages. New Frobenius organ Opus 1000, first in Scotland, now installed. On the Royal Mile, opposite Huntly House Museum. LRT bus 1 from Castle. Sunday Services: Family Service 10am, Parish Worship 11.15am

Open mid-June to mid-September, Monday to Saturday, 10.30am–4.30pm.

Churchyard open all year

CHURCH OF SCOTLAND A

CANONGATE KIRK

316 CARRICK KNOWE PARISH CHURCH

NT 203 721

Saughton Road North, Edinburgh

Built in 1953, and described as of Norman design with a strong Scottish character. The last post war church to be built of stone – the external walls of Blaxter dressed stone, and Darney rubble, both from Northumberland Quarries. Furnishings in Scottish Border oak, commissioned by the Church of Scotland as part of their exhibit for the Empire Exhibition in Glasgow of 1938 – beautiful examples of ecclesiastical craftsmanship. Baptismal bowl gifted by Her Majesty Queen Elizabeth The Queen Mother. Tapestry, Dovecot Studios, Edinburgh. Opposite Union Park.

Buses 1 and 6.

Sunday Service: 11am

Open every morning except Wednesday 9.30am–12 noon

CHURCH OF SCOTLAND

 A

CARRICK KNOWE PARISH CHURCH

317 CLUNY PARISH CHURCH

NT 246 707

Cluny Drive, Morningside, Edinburgh

Built as St Matthew's 1890 by Hippolyte Blanc, inspired by late 13th-century Gothic. United with South Morningside 1974 which building now forms the Church Centre. Chancel with Italian marble floor added 1900. Thirteen stained glass windows on side aisles of nave and St Andrew Window in North Transept. East Window: 'Four Apostles', Sir Edward Burne-Jones 1900; West Window: four scenes from the ministry of Jesus, Percy Bacon & Co 1905. Last 'Father Willis' organ in Scotland, installed 1901. Sunday Services: summer 9.30am and 11am; autumn, winter, spring 11am and 6.30pm

Open during Edinburgh Festival, Tuesdays, Wednesdays and Thursdays, with organ recitals at 1pm; or by arrangement, telephone 0131 447 6745 (church office, Tuesday to Friday, 9am-12noon)

CHURCH OF SCOTLAND

318 COLINTON PARISH CHURCH (ST CUTHBERT'S)

NT 216 692

Dell Road, Edinburgh, at foot of Colinton village, beside Water of Leith. The church of 1650 was rebuilt in 1771 and enlarged by David Bryce in 1837. Sydney Mitchell transformed the building in a neo-Byzantine style between 1907 and 1908. The angel decorated, barrel-vaulted nave is supported on sandstone columns. Mitchell adorned the semi-circular apse with murals and fine woodwork including the pulpit, communion table and rood-screen. Both the latter and the marble font are beautifully inscribed. To the south of the church, Page and Park have built new rooms which, through their contemporary design, embrace the wonderful woodland setting. The Offertory House of 1807 heralds this most interesting of buildings with its ancient graveyard set within a bend of the Water of Leith. Sunday Services: 9.30 and 11am

Church website: www.colintonparish.org

Open Monday to Thursday 9am-4pm, Friday 9am-12.30pm. Swing Cafe – open for morning coffee and light lunches, Monday to Friday 10am-2pm. Contact the church office, telephone 0131 441 2232

CHURCH OF SCOTLAND

B

COLINTON PARISH CHURCH (ST CUTHBERT'S)

319 CORSTORPHINE OLD PARISH CHURCH

NT 201 728

Kirk Loan, Corstorphine, Edinburgh

Interesting 15th-century church with tower, pre-Reformation relics, Scottish heraldic panels and fine medieval tombs, including those of the founders Sir Adam Forrester, Lord Provost of Edinburgh (died 1405) and Sir John Forrester, Lord Chamberlain of Scotland in the reign of James I. Fine Victorian stained glass. Interesting gravestones in churchyard. Sunday Services: 10am and 11.30am

Open Wednesdays 10.30am–12 noon, except December and January. Coincides with opening of Dower House (Corstorphine Trust) during summer

CHURCH OF SCOTLAND (partial) **A**

CORSTORPHINE OLD PARISH CHURCH

320 CORSTORPHINE UNITED FREE CHURCH

NT 199 727

Glebe Terrace, Corstorphine (off St John's Road, opposite Harp Hotel)

Intimate, secluded, friendly little church. Various ante-rooms and large hall, with new modern kitchen. Good grassed area for barbecues. Sunday Service: 10.30am

Open by appointment, telephone Pastor George Banks 0131 552 3666

UNITED FREE CHURCH OF SCOTLAND WC

321 CRAMOND KIRK

NT 190 768

Cramond Glebe Road, Edinburgh

A cruciform kirk of 1656 with 15th-century tower. Interior altered 1701, 1811, large reconstruction 1911 by Donald McArthy and James Mather. Pitch pine hammerbeam roof, oak furnishings, white marble font. Burgerhuys bell 1619. Jock Howieson mosaic. Plan of kirkyard available. Roman settlement remains. Off Whitehouse Road. City buses 40 and 41/41A. Sunday Services: 9.30 and 11am, July and August 10am

Church website: www.cramondkirk.org.uk

Open daily during Edinburgh Festival 2–5pm. Cramond Village exhibition at the Maltings

CHURCH OF SCOTLAND WC **B**

322 DALMENY PARISH CHURCH (ST CUTHBERT'S)

NT 144 775

Main Street, Dalmeny, nr South Queensferry

The most complete example of Romanesque architecture in Scotland. Dates from c.1130. Superb medieval south doorway, arch stones elaborately carved with animals, figures and grotesque heads. Historic graveyard. Off A90, follow signs for Dalmeny and South Queensferry.

Sunday Service: 11.30am

DALMENY PARISH CHURCH (ST CUTHBERT'S)

Open April to September, Sunday 2–4.30pm. Other times, key from the Post Office or Manse, or 5 Main Street. Parties please telephone Mr W Ross in advance 0131 331 1479

CHURCH OF SCOTLAND 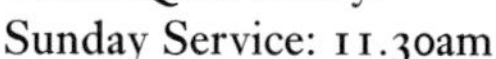

323 DAVIDSON'S MAINS PARISH CHURCH

NT 207 752

1 Quality Street off Queensferry Road

Originally Cramond Free Church. A small T-plan kirk with flat Gothic windows by David Cousin 1843. The timber bellcote with a prickly slated hat was added to the centre gable in 1866. Interior enlarged to the north in 1970. Major refurbishment to the chancel area in 1999. To the east the little school and house by Robert R Raeburn 1846 were extended with a hall by Auldjo Jamieson & Arnott 1933 maintaining the domestic scale by means of a dormered roof. Fully refurbished in 1995. Essentially a village church.

Sunday Services: 10.30am and 6.30pm

Church website: www.davidsonsmainsparishchurch.org.uk

Open Tuesday to Thursday 10am–2pm. At other times telephone the Beadle, Mr John Brown 0131 336 2065

CHURCH OF SCOTLAND

DAVIDSON'S MAINS PARISH CHURCH

324 DUDDINGSTON KIRK

NT 284 726

Old Church Lane, Duddingston Village, Edinburgh

Attractive 12th-century church, situated beside Duddingston Loch bird sanctuary, south of Arthur's Seat. Dr Neil's garden lies adjacent in the church glebe land. During the ministry of the Rev John Thomson 1804-1840 (himself a noted landscape painter), the English painter Turner, and the Scottish writer Sir Walter Scott, both visited the manse. City bus 42/46 to Duddingston Road. Sunday Services: 10am and 11.30am

Open June to September, Saturday 11am-5pm, Sunday 2-5pm

CHURCH OF SCOTLAND WC **A**

325 EDINBURGH METHODIST MISSION

NT 248 730

Central Hall, West Tollcross, Edinburgh

1901 by Dunn & Findlay, Edinburgh. Several alterations have been made to suit the changing needs of the congregation. Main hall has a curved and ribbed ceiling on arches rising from Ionic columns. Leaded windows of clear 'cathedral' glass embellished in the style of Glasgow Art Nouveau. Lower landings are decorated with mosaic tiles. A well-known venue for concerts, conferences and meetings. Half-mile south of Princes Street west end, via Lothian Road. LRT buses 10, 11, 15-18, 23, 24, 27, 45, 47. Sunday Services: 11am

Open Monday to Friday 9am-10pm, Saturday 9am-12.30pm.

Venue for the National Association of Youth Orchestras during Edinburgh Festival, daily performances

METHODIST (lift access via Dunbar Street) WC **B**

326 EDINBURGH SEVENTH-DAY ADVENTIST CHURCH

NT 258 732

3 Bristo Place, Edinburgh

A red sandstone building, by Sydney Mitchell & Wilson 1900, this church is unusual in having its sanctuary on the first floor. The rather handsome staircase is flanked by a tiled wall. The sanctuary interior is well lit by four large windows looking onto the street. Pulpit and furnishings in pine; two galleries, one of which houses a pipe organ by Gray & Davison. Services: Saturday 10am (Bible Study) and 11.15am (Worship Service)

Open by arrangement, telephone Pastor Dr Claude Lombart 01883 729432, mobile 07939 263660. Secretary: Ms Audrey Ogilvie 01383 822343, mobile 07909 573557

Edinburgh Fringe Festival Venue, August

SEVENTH-DAY ADVENTIST

EDINBURGH SEVENTH-DAY ADVENTIST CHURCH

327 ERIC LIDDELL CENTRE

NT 246 719

15 Morningside Road, Holy Corner

Former North Morningside Church of Scotland in neo-Norman by David Robertson 1879-81. Dramatic intervention by Nicholas Groves-Raines 1992 and 1999 for conversion to Eric Liddell Centre which provides community services and accommodation for organisations of Christian witness. Galleries provide viewing of impressive collection of stained glass, including windows by William Wilson and John Duncan. Chinese Evangelical Church Services in Mandarin and English 1.00 pm every Sunday

Church website: www.eric-liddell.org

Open daily 10am-5pm, or in evenings by arrangement with Reception, telephone 0131 447 4520

CHINESE EVANGELICAL CHURCH (on request) (Sycomore Coffee House) **B**

328 CHURCH OF THE GOOD SHEPHERD

NT 228 734

Murrayfield Avenue, Edinburgh

Designed by Sir Robert Lorimer and dedicated in 1899, the building contains some fine examples of stained glass, including a modern window depicting The Good Shepherd. There is a fine Willis organ which was rebuilt in 1967. Sunday Services: Holy Communion 8.30am, Sung Communion 10am, fourth Sundays Matins; Wednesday Holy Communion 11am

Open Edinburgh and Scottish Churches Doors Open Days. Or by arrangement, telephone James Young 0131337 7615

SCOTTISH EPISCOPAL **B**

CHURCH OF THE GOOD SHEPHERD

329 GREENSIDE PARISH CHURCH

NT 263 745

Royal Terrace, Edinburgh

T-plan design by Gillespie Graham 1839 with tower added in 1851, set amidst Playfair's great terraces. Connections with Robert Louis Stevenson who knew it as 'the church on the hill'. Off London Road. Sunday Services: 11am and 6.30pm (no evening service July and August)

Open by arrangement, telephone the Session Clerk 0131 669 5324

CHURCH OF SCOTLAND **B**

GREENSIDE PARISH CHURCH

GREYFRIARS TOLBOOTH & HIGHLAND KIRK

330 GREYFRIARS TOLBOOTH & HIGHLAND KIRK

NT 256 734

Greyfriars Place, Edinburgh

The first post-Reformation church built in Edinburgh 1620, altered 1722, 1858, 1938 and 1990. The National Covenant signed here in 1638. Fine 19th-century coloured glass by Ballantine, and Peter Collins organ 1990. Historic kirkyard, former Franciscan Friary garden, has fine examples of 17th-century monuments, the Martyrs' Monument, Covenanters' Prison and memorial to Greyfriars Bobby. South end of George IV Bridge. City buses 2, 12, 23, 24, 27, 28, 29, 40, 42, 45, 47. Sunday Services: 11am and 12.30pm (Gaelic), first Sunday of month Holy Communion 9.15am; Thursdays all year Lunchtime Service with organ music 1.10-1.30pm

Open April to October, Monday to Friday 10.30am-4.30pm, Saturday 10.30am-2.30pm, November to March Thursday 1.30-3.30pm. Churchyard open all year Monday to Friday 8am-6pm, Saturday and Sunday 10am-4pm.

Special events: year round programme of concerts and lectures (programme available). Tours for groups, telephone Visitors Officer 0131 226 5429

CHURCH OF SCOTLAND WC (by arrangement) A

331 ST PHILIP'S, JOPPA

NT 313 736

Abercorn Terrace, Joppa, Edinburgh

A really striking edifice in the Early Decorated style by J Honeyman 1877. Broach spire 170ft over a lofty belfry. Aisled nave with entry in the south gable. Inside, a remarkably complete interior. Clustered piers with leafy capitals support the nave arcade, foliated corbels on the clerestorey support the wood-lined tunnel-roof. Fine stained glass windows to aisles. Sunday Service: 11am

Open by arrangement, telephone Mr Mitchell 0131 669 3641

CHURCH OF SCOTLAND WC **B**

332 KIRK O' FIELD PARISH CHURCH

NT 264 732

146 Pleasance, Edinburgh

Built as Charteris Memorial Church in 1912. Late Scots Gothic by James B Dunn. Lorimerian vine enrichment on the vestibule ceiling. Wagon-roofed nave with west gallery. Memorial to the Rev A H Charteris 1908. Mission Hall 1891 dedicated to St Ninian. City buses 2, 21. Sunday Service: 11am

Open the first Saturday in September, 10am–1pm

CHURCH OF SCOTLAND

333 KIRKLISTON PARISH CHURCH

NT 125 744

The Square, Kirkliston

Mainly 12th-century church. Has two Norman archways, the largest of which was blocked up in the 19th century. Two beautiful modern stained glass windows. In the 19th century a small watchtower was built in the graveyard where the earliest identifiable stone is dated 1529. Sunday Service: 11am

Open by arrangement, telephone Mrs Keating 0131 333 3298, or Mrs Brechin 0131 333 3252

CHURCH OF SCOTLAND A

KIRKLISTON PARISH CHURCH

334 EBENEZER UNITED FREE CHURCH, LEITH

NT 266 764

31 Bangor Road, Leith

The Ebenezer congregation was founded in 1891. The original church building in Great Junction Street was demolished in 1979 to make way for new housing. The present building, by Sir Frank Mears & Partners, was opened in 1984. Bangor Road runs south from Great Junction Street in Leith. Sunday Services: 11am and 6.30pm

Open first Saturday of each month, 10am–12 noon

UNITED FREE CHURCH OF SCOTLAND

335 LEITH METHODIST CHURCH

NT 268 761

1 Junction Place, Leith

Built 1932 by Maclennan & Cunningham as 600-seater Central Hall in artificial stone and harl on site of former Secession Church. In Methodist use from 1868. Horizontally subdivided in 1987 with flexible worship area upstairs and community centre downstairs. Off Great Junction Street, behind McKenzie-Millar. Sunday Service: 11am

Open weekdays, except Wednesday 10am–2pm, Saturday 10am–12 noon

METHODIST A

336 NORTH LEITH PARISH CHURCH

NT 263 765

Madeira Street, Leith

Georgian building designed by William Burn 1816. Renovated 1950 Ian G Lindsay & Partners, and 1993 Stewart Tod & Partners. Impressive two-storey 'country house' front. Light interior with galleries supported by Ionic columns. Stained glass James Ballantine. Three-manual pipe organ, built by Wadsworth of Manchester 1880. Small graveyard and garden. Off Ferry Road, close to Leith Library. Sunday Services: 11am all year, 6.30pm (excluding July and August)

Open by arrangement, telephone the church office 0131 553 7378

CHURCH OF SCOTLAND WC A

NORTH LEITH PARISH CHURCH

337 SOUTH LEITH PARISH CHURCH

NT 271 761

Kirkgate or Constitution Street, Leith

A church was erected in 1483 as a chapel attached to the collegiate Church of Restalrig. The present building dates from 1847, built to a design by Thomas Hamilton. Tower and porch incorporate coats of arms of four successive Scottish monarchs. Fine hammerbeam roof. Italian marble pulpit. Stained glass and emblems of the Trade Guilds. Set in ancient graveyard with interesting monuments. At the foot of Leith Walk. Sunday Services: 11am, also 6.30pm October to May, and 9.30am June to July

Church website: www.slpc.co.uk

Open June to August, third Sunday 2-4pm. Also Mondays to Fridays 12 noon-2pm during August

CHURCH OF SCOTLAND WC A

338 LIBERTON KIRK

NT 275 700

Kirkgate, Liberton, Edinburgh

Sitting in a commanding position overlooking the city, a church was founded here in 1143 by David I, although there is evidence of an earlier church dating from AD 800. The present building was erected in 1815 to replace a former church destroyed by fire. Designed by James Gillespie Graham, it is a rectangular semi-Gothic building with corbelled parapet tower and thin pinnacles. A memorial stained glass window depicting Cornelius, by Ballantine 1905. Three striking contemporary pulpit falls and four outstanding wall hangings by D Morrison.

The kirkyard contains many stones of special interest, including a table-top tomb to a local farmer, its ends carved in relief with agricultural scenes. Sunday Services: 9.30am and 11am (10.30am, July and August)

Church website: www.libertonkirk.freeserve.co.uk

Open Monday to Friday 9am–5pm by arrangement, telephone Mrs W Munro 0131 664 3795

CHURCH OF SCOTLAND WC **A**

339 LIBERTON NORTHFIELD PARISH CHURCH

NT 280 699

280 Gilmerton Road, Edinburgh

Built 1869 as a Free Church to designs by J W Smith. North-east tower and broach spire added by Peddie & Kinnear 1873. Interior with raked floor and an ornate arch-braced timber roof springing from short ashlar colonnettes with a variety of leafy capitals. Transepts entered by triple arches expressed on the exterior by triple gables. Virtually unaltered organ by E F Walcker 1903. Sunday Services: 11am and 6.30pm

Open by arrangement, telephone Rev John McPake 0131 658 1754.

Flower Festival weekend, late September

CHURCH OF SCOTLAND WC **B**

340 MAGDALEN CHAPEL

NT 256 734

41 Cowgate, Edinburgh

The chapel was built in 1541 by Michael McQuhane and his wife Janet Rhynd. Its main features are the medieval stained glass roundels. The panelling records gifts from members of the Incorporation of Hammermen who were patrons of the chapel until 1862. The chapel is now owned by the Scottish Reformation Society and serves as its headquarters

Open Monday to Friday 9.30am–4pm. Other times by arrangement.

Parties welcome, telephone Rev A S Horne 0131 220 1450

INTER-DENOMINATIONAL **A**

341 CHRIST CHURCH, MORNINGSIDE

NT 245 719

Holy Corner, Bruntsfield, Edinburgh

French Gothic by Hippolyte Blanc, a member of the congregation, 1876. Gables and flying buttresses face on to the road; the main entrance is beneath the tower. Original murals in chancel and nave roof. Extensive stained glass by Ballantine. Sunday Services: Holy Communion 8am, Sung Eucharist 10am, Evensong (winter) 6.30pm, Compline (summer) 9pm; Monday to Friday: Morning Prayer and Eucharist 8am, Thursday Holy Communion 11am

Church website: www.christchurchedinburgh.org.uk

Open 11am–3pm Wednesday and Friday

SCOTTISH EPISCOPAL WC **B**

342 MAYFIELD SALISBURY CHURCH

NT 266 717

West Mayfield

Originally built as Mayfield Free Kirk, 1897, this is a fine example of the French Gothic style of Hippolyte Blanc. Spire 48-feet added 1894. Magnificent collection of stained glass by Ballantine & Gardiner, Charles L Davidson, Henry Dearl of Morris & Co, Guthrie & Wells and William Meikle. Church House, orginally the manse, houses the Mayfield Radio Unit which broadcasts to hospitals in the Edinburgh area. Sunday Services: 10.30am and 6.30pm September to June; 9.30am, 10.30am and 8.00pm July to August

Open weekdays 9.00am-4.00pm, except Wednesdays, Saturday 9am-12 noon (coffee)

CHURCH OF SCOTLAND **B**

343 ST COLUMBA'S CHURCH, NEWINGTON

NT 265 721

9 Upper Gray Street, Edinburgh

A free treatment of the classic Renaissance style by R M Cameron, 1888. West façade has a large semicircular window and pedimented gable finished with a plain Latin cross. Oblong interior with open timber roof and semi-circular end forming a chancel and apse. The chancel arch is a later addition. Notable features include a collection of statues in the window niches. Extensive natural lighting from roof lights and west window. Two-manual pipe organ by Matthew Copley, 1997. Masses: Monday-Friday 9.30am, Saturday 11am, Sunday 11am and 6.30pm

Open after Masses, or by arrangement with the Parish Priest, telephone 0131 667 1605

ROMAN CATHOLIC WC WC (toilet adapted in church hall) **B**

344 NICOLSON SQUARE METHODIST CHURCH

NT 261 732

Nicolson Square, Edinburgh

By Thomas Brown 1815 set diagonally across the corner of the square behind a forecourt. Classical two-storey front based on Adam's design for the west block of the University. Inside, fluted cast-iron columns support the U-plan gallery. Substantial moderisation 1972. Organ by Forster & Andrews of Hull. Interesting modern chapel in basement created in 1989 by Nira Ponniah. Small public garden at rear. Sunday Services: 11am and 6.30pm

Church website: www.nicsquare.freeserve.co.uk

Open Monday to Friday 9.30am-3.30pm. Fringe performances during Edinburgh Festival, and concerts at other times

METHODIST (cafe in basement) WC **A**

NICOLSON SQUARE METHODIST CHURCH

345 OLD ST PAUL'S

NT 260 737

Jeffrey Street, Edinburgh

The hidden gem of the Old Town. Dating from 1884, Hay & Henderson. Entrances in Carrubber's Close and Jeffrey Street give little clue to the splendour within. Historic Episcopal church with Jacobite past has magnificent furnishings. A living church with daily worship and a prayerful atmosphere. Off Royal Mile. Sunday Services: Holy Eucharist 8am, 10.30am, 5pm, Evensong 6.30pm; Daily Worship 12.20pm

Open daily, 9am-6pm

SCOTTISH EPISCOPAL WC **B**

346 PALMERSTON PLACE CHURCH

NT 241 734

Palmerston Place, Edinburgh

Inspiration for Peddie & Kinnear's design of 1875 came from the 17th-century St Sulpice in Paris. A notable feature is the central ceiling motif of a dove within a sunburst. Wells Kennedy organ, 1991, incorporates the oak case of the earlier 1902 organ. Meeting place for the Presbytery of Edinburgh and the Synod of the Scottish Episcopal Church. Sunday Services: 11am, 6.30pm (except July and August)

Open by arrangement, telephone 0131 220 1690

CHURCH OF SCOTLAND WC **B**

PALMERSTON PLACE CHURCH

347 POLWARTH PARISH CHURCH

NT 750 495

36-38 Polwarth Terrace, Edinburgh

Splendid example of late 10th and early 20th-century architecture by Sydney Mitchell and Wilson, 1901, with the tower by James Jerdan & Sons, 1913. The architecture shows pre-Reformation influences, including stone carvings of the face of Mary, the mother of Christ, and several 'Green men'. Marble chancel augmented by one of the finest pulpits in the country, sculpted by William Beveridge in 1903. Ascension window at the east end of the chance by Clayton & Bell Pipe organ by Forster & Andrews. On local bus routes Nos 10, 27, 38. Sunday Service: 11am

Church website: www.polwarth.org.uk

Open by arrangement with the Minister, telephone 0131 667 4055. Church office open 4.30-7.30pm Thursdays

CHURCH OF SCOTLAND B

348 PORTOBELLO OLD PARISH CHURCH

NT 309 738

Bellfield Street, off Portobello High Street

The oldest church in Portobello, built 1809 by William Sibbald, in classical style with a pediment. The clock tower was added in 1839. Organ by Peter Conacher, 1873, rebuilt by Henry Willis, 1984. Furniture of Austrian oak. Mort safe and interesting memorials in graveyard. Public swimming baths and safe, sandy beach at end of the street. Good bus service (no 26) from city centre. Sunday Service: 11am

Open 10am-2pm Monday to Friday all year

CHURCH OF SCOTLAND B

349 PRIESTFIELD PARISH CHURCH

NT 271 721

Dalkeith Road, Edinburgh

Built in 1877, Sutherland & Walker, in the Italian Lombardic style. Beautiful stained glass windows designed by three young artists in 1921. Other features of note are the handsome pulpit and organ gallery and a most unusual baptismal font. On Dalkeith Road, A68. City buses 2, 14, 21, 33, 2a, c3, c11, 85, 86. Sunday Service: 11am

Open by arrangement, contact Minister 0131 667 5644

CHURCH OF SCOTLAND A

QUEENSFERRY PARISH CHURCH, SOUTH QUEENSFERRY

350 QUEENSFERRY PARISH CHURCH, SOUTH QUEENSFERRY

NT 130 782

The Loan, South Queensferry, Edinburgh

Well-used and well-loved Burgh Church, built in 1894 and extended in 1993. Of special interest is the display of banners and the wrought iron railings which incorporate a burning bush motif. Centre of village. Sunday Services: 10am and 11.30am

Church website: www.qpc.freeuk.com

Open all year, Monday to Friday 10-11.30am. Access to historic graveyard (1635-early 1900s) can be arranged in advance, telephone 0131 331 1100

CHURCH OF SCOTLAND **A**

351 PRIORY CHURCH OF ST MARY OF MT CARMEL, SOUTH QUEENSFERRY

NT 129 784

Hopetoun Road, South Queensferry, Edinburgh

Orginally a Carmelite Friary founded in 1330, the church fell into disrepair during the 16th century. It was restored for the use of the Episcopal church in 1890, the work being begun by John Kinross. Later work was carried out in the 1960s by Ian Lindsay. Church extensively refurbished in 2000, new floor (with underfloor heating), and a glass engraved screen to side chapel. Font cover designed by Lorimer. Fourteenth-century aumbry. Mass dial on outside south wall. Sunday Services: 9.30 and 11am; Thursday: 10am

Open by arrangement, telephone the church office 0131 331 5540. Also open during Ferry Fair Week in August

SCOTTISH EPISCOPAL WC **A**

PRIORY CHURCH OF ST MARY OF MT CARMEL, SOUTH QUEENSFERRY

352 RATHO PARISH CHURCH

NT 138 710

Baird Road, Ratho, Edinburgh

An interesting medieval cruciform church, with later aisles. The east aisle dated 1683, the south 1830. To the west of the south aisle is a 12th-century doorway, partially visible, with scalloped capitals and decorated hoodmould. Twentieth-century refurbishment revealed a Celtic cross stone which might suggest early worship on this site. In the south porch a 13th-century tomb slab belonging to one of the Knights Templar who owned Ratho in the Middle Ages. In the graveyard are several interesting headstones and a panelled coffin formed of a single stone. Sunday Service: 11am

Church website: www.rathoparishchurch.org.uk

Open by arrangement, telephone Mrs Watson 0131 333 1732

CHURCH OF SCOTLAND WC A

353 REID MEMORIAL CHURCH

NT 261 710

West Savile Terrace, Edinburgh

Church, hall and church officer's house by Leslie G Thomson 1933 form an architectural oasis. A lofty, cruciform church with meticulous neo-Perpendicular detail. Stained glass windows by James Ballantine, pipe organ Rushworth & Dreaper, painting on reredos of Last Supper by William R Lawson. Cloister court to rear with carved panel of Christ at the well of Samaria by Alexander Carrick. On local bus routes 24, 38, 38a, 40 and 41. Sunday Services: 10.30am and first Sunday of month 6.30pm

Open 11am-5pm Wednesdays and Fridays during Edinburgh Festival

REID MEMORIAL CHURCH

354 THE ROBIN CHAPEL

NT 295 715

Thistle Foundation, Niddrie Mains Road

Memorial to Robin Tudsbery, killed in the last days of the Second World War, built by Architect John F Matthew, 1950, at the centre of a housing complex for physically disabled people and their families. Peaceful and secluded interior enhanced by stone capitals carved by Maxwell Adam, wood carvings by Thomas Good, wrought-iron work by James Finnegan and stained glass by Sadie McLellan. Sunday Service: 4.30pm

Open by arrangement with the Chaplain, telephone 0131 661 3366

NON-DENOMINATIONAL

355 SACRED HEART CHURCH

NT 252 730

28 Lauriston Place, Edinburgh

Stone fronted building designed by Father Richard Vaughan SJ 1860, altered by Archibald Macpherson 1884. Holyrood Madonna of carved wood, probably late 16th century. Stations of the Cross by Peter Rauth 1874. Conservators presently working on these works of art in stages. Organ from Roseburn Free Church in 1907. Designed by C P S Covell (who also designed the pulpit). Rebuilt in 1963 by Rushworth and Dreaper. It was improved again in 1974. A gift of fine oak panelling from St Margaret's Convent (now Gilles Centre) has enabled the Choir Loft to be greatly enhanced. Buses to Tollcross. Masses: Saturday Vigil 6.30pm; Sunday 7.45am, 10am and 11.15am, and 8pm

Church website: www.rc.net/standed/sacredheart

Open every day

ROMAN CATHOLIC **B**

356 ST ANDREW'S AND ST GEORGE'S PARISH CHURCH

NT 255 741

George Street, Edinburgh

This beautiful elliptical church with its delicate spire and Adam style plaster ceiling has been described as the architectural gem of the New Town. Built in 1784, designed by Major Andrew Frazer. Two fine 20th-century stained glass windows, one by Douglas Strachan (1875-1950), the other by Alfred Webster (1884-1915). Light lunches in undercroft. At the east end of George Street and one block north of Princes Street. Sunday Services: 9am (Communion), 9.45am, 11am. Weekday Prayers; 1pm (Communion Service: Tuesday)

Open all year, Monday to Friday 10am-3pm. Undercroft open 12-2pm, telephone 0131 225 3847/fax 0131 225 5921. Special Edinburgh Festival programme of events. Week-long Christian Aid book sale in May

CHURCH OF SCOTLAND **A**

357 ST ANDREW'S ORTHODOX CHAPEL

NT 257 728

23a George Square, Edinburgh

Built in 1779 as a one-storey and basement villa across the centre lane on the west side of George Square. Large Venetian window faces onto George Square. Orthodox furnishings and icons. Services: Saturday 6.30pm, Sunday and Feasts 9.00am Matins, and Liturgy 10.30am

Open by arrangement, telephone Archimandrite John Maitland-Moir 0131 667 0372

ORTHODOX WC **A**

ST ANDREW'S ORTHODOX CHAPEL

358 ST BARNABAS EPISCOPAL CHURCH

NT 290 693

4 Moredun Park View, Edinburgh

Small modern church in housing scheme 1950. Altered in 1969. St Barnabas tapestry. Moredun Scheme is between A7 and A772 on south side of city. Sunday Service: Eucharist 10.30am; Tuesday: Prayer Group 6.30pm

Open Wednesday mornings

SCOTTISH EPISCOPAL **A**

359 ST BENNET'S

NT 248 717

42 Greenhill Gardens, Church Hill, Edinburgh

The chapel attached to the home of the Archbishops of St Andrews and Edinburgh. A charming Byzantine church built by R Weir Schultz 1907, under the will of the third Marquess of Bute, to take the outstanding Italianate classical interior designed by William Frame in 1889 for the chapel at House of Falkland. Porch by Reginald Fairlie 1934. There are examples of stained glass windows by Gabriel Loire of Chartres dating from the 1970s; other windows were installed in 1999 commemorating the 1600th anniversary of St Ninian and the 1400th anniversary of St Columba, as well as a millennium window. The chapel contains memorabilia of the Archbishops since the restoration of the hierarchy. Buses 11, 15, 16, 17 and 23 to Church Hill. Church Service times as announced

Open weekdays 9am–5pm

ROMAN CATHOLIC WC **A**

ST BENNET'S

ST CHRISTOPHER'S

360 ST CHRISTOPHER'S

NT 292 748

Craigentinny Road, Edinburgh

Built by James McLachlan in 1934-8, the foundation stone was laid by John Buchan, author of *The Thirty Nine Steps*. The exterior is of variegated red brick with round arched windows and tiled roof. The interior is a darker plum-coloured brick with a low wagon roof and segmental arches. The organ came from St Catherine's Grange church and was rebuilt with all speaking pipes in 1975. There are two stained glass windows by Sax Shaw and one by George Reid. Sunday Service: 10.30am; Communion on last Sunday in January, March and June to October

Open Saturday 10am-12 noon Tuesdays and Saturdays, and by arrangement, telephone Mr R Mutch 0131 669 6735

CHURCH OF SCOTLAND

361 ST COLUMBA'S BY THE CASTLE

NT 254 735

Johnston Terrace, Edinburgh

By John Henderson, 1847, a single-nave building of six bays under a pitch-slated roof with a battlemented tower. Four-bay aisleless nave and one-bay chancel; the sixth bay forms the entrance and vestibule to the west end. Triple arcading at the west wall, originally supporting a gallery, now subsumed into a suite of rooms served by a new staircase. Stone altar, font and pulpit. Gifted oak panelling on lower east wall c.1914. The blocked east window has been filled with a mural 'Christ Enthroned' by John Busby 1962. Pipe organ, James Conacher & Sons 1880, rebuilt in 1965 by N P Mander and relocated in 1998 by Lightoller. Church hall, originally a school, below the church. Redevelopment and refurbishment, Simpson & Brown 1998. Sunday Service: Eucharist 10am, and at other times as announced

Open by arrangement, telephone the Rector 0131 228 6470

SCOTTISH EPISCOPAL **B**

362 THE PARISH CHURCH OF ST CUTHBERT

NT 248 736

Lothian Road, Edinburgh

The present church, the seventh on the site, is over 100 years old, 1894 by Hippolyte Blanc, retaining the 1790 spire. Altered in 1990, Stewart Tod. Tradition has it that St Cuthbert had a cell church here. If so, Christian worship has taken place here for 1300 years. Furnishings include scroll-topped and Renaissance style stalls, marble communion table, murals and stained glass window by Tiffany. One of the finest romantic organs in Scotland, rebuilt 1997. Display of life of St Cuthbert in vestibule. Interesting graveyard, with many famous names, is an oasis in the centre of the city. Buses to Princes Street and Lothian Road. Sunday Services: 9.30am, 11am, 6.30pm (Service of Healing)

Open mid-May to mid-September, Monday to Friday 10am-4pm, Saturday 10am-12 noon, 10am-4pm July and August

CHURCH OF SCOTLAND WC **A**

363 ST GEORGE'S WEST CHURCH

NT 245 736

Shandwick Place, Edinburgh

Designed by David Bryce 1869 with campanile by Sir R Rowand Anderson 1881. Special features are the rose window and the pulpit. Woodwork excellent, mainly original. The organ by Thomas Lewis 1897. The first organist was Alfred Hollins, famous blind organist and composer (1897-1942). City Centre West End. Sunday Services: 11am and 7pm; Prayers: Monday to Friday 1pm

Busy Church Centre and cafe open Monday to Friday 10am-3.30pm; Saturday 10.30am-12.30pm, all year

CHURCH OF SCOTLAND WC **B**

ST GEORGE'S WEST CHURCH

364 ST GILES' CATHEDRAL

NT 257 736

High Street, Edinburgh

The Cathedral was founded in the 1100s and mostly rebuilt during the 15th and 16th centuries. It was the church of John Knox during the Reformation and played an important part in the history of that time. The church contains fine examples of late medieval architecture and a wide range of traditional and modern stained glass and memorials. The magnificent Rieger organ was installed in 1992. The Thistle Chapel, designed by Robert Lorimer for the Order of the Thistle, was added in 1911. Sunday Services: 8am, 10am, 11.30am and 6pm, 8pm

Church website: www.stgiles.net

Open Easter to mid-September, Monday to Friday 9am-7pm, Saturday 9am-5pm, Sunday 1pm-5pm. Mid-September to Easter, Monday to Saturday 9am-5pm, Sunday 1pm-5pm

CHURCH OF SCOTLAND WC **A**

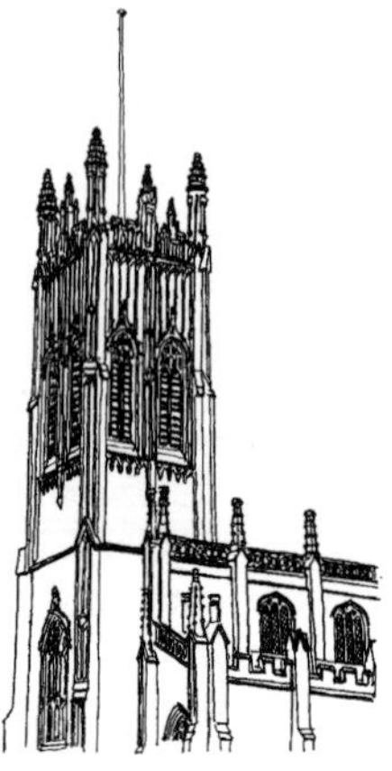

ST JOHN THE EVANGELIST

365 ST JOHN THE EVANGELIST

NT 247 736

Princes Street, Edinburgh

Designed by William Burn 1817. Recently cleaned and restored. Notably good stained glass. Sir Walter Scott's mother, Anne Rutherford and Sir Henry Raeburn RA are buried in Dormitory Garden. Undercroft includes a cafe restaurant, Christian bookshop (multi-denominational), One World Shop, and Peace and Justice Centre. At the foot of Lothian Road and opposite the Caledonian Hotel. Sunday Services: Holy Communion 8am, Sung Eucharist 9.45am, Choral Matins 11.15am, Choral Evensong 6pm, Eucharist with music from Taizé 8pm. Further details on telephone answering machine (0131 229 7565). Weekday Service: 1pm; Communion Service: Wednesday 11am

Church website: www.thechoir.co.uk

Open daily in working hours

SCOTTISH EPISCOPAL (Cornerstone Cafe) **A**

366 ST MARGARET'S CHAPEL

NT 253 735

Edinburgh Castle, Edinburgh

The oldest surviving structure in the castle built by King David I (1124-53). Interior divided into two by a fine arch decorated with chevron ornament. Semi-circular east chancel. Copy of the Gospel Book owned by St Margaret to whom the chapel was dedicated by her son, David I. Stained glass windows depicting St Andrew, St Ninian, St Columba and St Margaret by Douglas Strachan c.1930. Magnificent views from castle ramparts. Other attractions within the castle (Historic Scotland) include 'Honours of the Kingdom' exhibition, now with the Stone of Destiny

Open summer 9.30am-6pm, winter 9.30am-5pm (last ticket sold 45 minutes before closing)

NON-DENOMINATIONAL **A**

367 ST MARGARET'S PARISH CHURCH

NT 284 745

27 Restalrig Road South, Edinburgh

ST MARGARET'S PARISH CHURCH

Rebuilt by William Burn 1836 on the foundations of the previous 15th-century church. The flowing window tracery follows the original design, stained glass by William Wilson 1966. Attached to the south-west corner is the hexagonal St Triduana's Chapel, once the lower storey of a two-tier chapel built for James III about 1477. The vault springs from a central pier, its six shafts topped by capitals with crinkly foliage. Notable 17th and 18th-century monuments in the graveyard. Sunday Service: 10.30am

Church website: www.st-margarets.freeserve.co.uk

Open Monday to Friday 11am–1pm, or by arrangement, contact Mr Skakle 0131 661 2510, or the church office 0131 554 7400

CHURCH OF SCOTLAND **A**

368 ST MARY'S CATHEDRAL

NT 259 743

Broughton Street, Edinburgh

There has been a church on the site since 1814. However, all that remains of the original, designed by James Gillespie Graham, is the neo-Gothic façade. Following a fire in 1892 it was decided to enlarge the church. This led to the addition of the present sanctuary and side aisles. In 1932 it was decided to heighten the roof by 20 feet. The interior contains the superb baldacchino designed in 1928 by Reginald Fairlie. It stands over the High Altar whose tabernacle was designed by Betty Koster and cast by George Mancini. Sunday Services: 7.30am, 9.30am and 11.30am; Saturday 10am, 12.45pm and 6pm Vigil; Monday to Friday 7.30am and 10am, 12.45pm. Mass on Sunday 7.30pm

Church website: www.btinternet.com/~stmaryscathedral/st_marys

Open daily 7am–6pm (later on Saturday/Sunday)

ROMAN CATHOLIC **A**

ST MARY'S CATHEDRAL, EDINBURGH

369 ST MARY'S EPISCOPAL CATHEDRAL

NT 242 735

Palmerston Place, Edinburgh

Built in 1879 to the award-winning design of Sir Gilbert Scott, this neo-Gothic building reflects the spirit of that age: it is massive, its three spines lend distinction to the Edinburgh skyline and it rejoices in a wealth of ornate and symbolic detail, the evidence of a flourishing craftsmanship. Of particular note are the pelican lectern, Lorimer's rood and the J Oldrid Scott's reredos of the high altar, featuring the Scottish saints Columba and Margaret. In the grounds stand the 17-century Old Coates House (now the Theological Institute of the Scottish Episcopal Church) and the Song School, famous for its recently restored murals, painted by Phoebe Anna Traquair 1888-92 on the theme of '*Benedicite omnia opera*'. The Cathedral maintains an internationally renowned choir, which sings on Sundays and for Evensong on weekdays. During holiday periods the Cathedral welcomes visiting choirs. The Cathedral is open daily; the Song School may be viewed by appointment. Services: for full details contact the Cathedral answering machine on 0131 225 6293

Church website: www.cathedral.net

Open daily 7.30am-6pm (5pm Saturday)

SCOTTISH EPISCOPAL WC **A**

370 ST MARY, STAR OF THE SEA, LEITH

NT 272 762

106 Constitution Street, Edinburgh

E W Pugin and Joseph A Hansom's church 1854 had no chancel, no north aisle and was orientated to the west. The north aisle was added in 1900 and the chancel in 1912 when the church was turned round and the present west entrance made. Inside the church has simple pointed arcades and a high braced collar roof. Access from Constitution Street or New Kirkgate. Services: Monday to Friday 10am; Saturday 10am and Vigil Mass 6pm; Sunday 10am and 11.30am

Open Monday to Friday 9am-11am, Saturday 9am-11.30am, Sunday 9am-12.30pm

ROMAN CATHOLIC WC **B**

ST MARY, STAR OF THE SEA, LEITH

371 ST MICHAEL'S CHURCH

NT 234 722

1 Slateford Road, Edinburgh

ST MICHAEL'S CHURCH

One of architect John Honeyman's most notable buildings, completed 1883. Square 41-metre tower and longest aisle in the city. Sanctuary illuminated by clerestoried nave beneath dark-timbered roof. Unusual reredos bearing Ten Commandments, Beatitudes and the Creed. Pulpit and lectern decorated with biblical fruits by Gertrude Hope. Communion table, fall and Bible markers by Hannah Frew Paterson, dedicated in April 2001. Organ by Brindley and Foster 1895. Stained glass, including work by Douglas Strachan (1895-1925). The building was extensively restored in 1998 and provides for a variety of worship, cultural and outreach activities. Bus routes 4, 28, 34 and 44. Sunday Services: 11am; June to August 10am and 11am. Occasional Evening Services

Church website: www.stmichaels-kirk.co.uk

Open Edinburgh Doors Open Day, and by arrangement, telephone 0131 337 5646

CHURCH OF SCOTLAND

372 ST MICHAEL'S AND ALL SAINTS' CHURCH

NT 251 729

Brougham Street, Edinburgh

A shrine of the Anglo-Catholic movement in Scotland. The church was mostly built in 1867 but the west end not completed until 1876 and the Lady Chapel added in 1897, all to designs by R Rowand Anderson. Austere Gothic externally but the interior is a magnificently spacious setting for a sumptuous display of furnishings, including an elaborate Spanish pulpit of c.1600, carved and painted altarpieces by William Burges (1867) and Hamilton More-Nisbet (1901), and a huge high altar reredos, again carved and painted, by C E Kempe (1889). Extensive collection of stained glass with windows by Wailes, Clayton & Bell, Kempe, and Sir Ninian Comper. Sunday Services: Low Mass 8am, High Mass 11am, Choral Evensong and Benediction 6.30pm; Tuesday: Low Mass 8am; Wednesday: Low Mass 12.30pm; Thursday: Low Mass 6pm; Friday: Low Mass 10.30am; Saturday: Low Mass 12.30pm

Open all year Wednesday 12 noon-2.30pm, Friday 10am-2pm, Saturdays during Edinburgh Festival, and by arrangement, telephone the Rector 0131 229 6368

SCOTTISH EPISCOPAL (Saturdays during Edinburgh Festival) **A**

373 ST STEPHEN'S CENTRE

NT 250 746

St Vincent Street, Edinburgh

Built 1828 as St Stephen's Church, this is the ecclesiastical masterpiece of W H Playfair. Severe Greek detail but Baroque in spirit, with a large tower dominating the vista from Queen Street downhill through the Northern New Town. Interior recast in 1956 when a floor was inserted at the level of the former gallery whose cast iron Egyptian columns were retained. No Services

Open Monday to Friday 9am–9pm, telephone Development Officer, David Nicholson 0131 556 2661

CHURCH OF SCOTLAND

374 STOCKBRIDGE PARISH CHURCH

NT 247 748

Saxe Coburg Street, Edinburgh

Classical church by James Milne 1823 with an Ionic pilastered and pedimented front and a small domed steeple. The interior contains the original U-plan gallery. In 1888 Hardy & Wight added the apse which was decorated in 1987 with war memorial murals by the German artist Reinhardt Behrens depicting the Lothian coastline 'at the going down of the sun and in the morning …'. Historic two-manual organ by August Gern installed 1995. Sunday Service: 11am; Wednesday Service: 1pm

Telephone the Administrator, Christopher Barr 0131 332 0122

CHURCH OF SCOTLAND WC **A/B**

STOCKBRIDGE PARISH CHURCH

375 VIEWFORTH ST DAVID AND ST OSWALD

NT 244 725

104 Gilmour Place, Edinburgh

Originally a Free Church. Built by Pilkington and Bell 1871 to an orthodox four-square plan with restrained detail. The massive upward growth contrasts with the fragile shafted geometric window in the central gable. Octagonal belfry, truncated in 1976. Powerful interior, rebuilt after a fire in 1898, with very thin cast-iron columns supporting huge transverse beams over the side galleries. Organ reconstructed 1976 from two instruments by Blackett & Howden 1899 and Forster & Andrews 1904. Sunday Service: 10.30am. Shared by Associated Presbyterian congregation. Sunday Services: 12 noon; Wednesday: 7pm

Church website: www.viewforth.org

Telephone the Church Administrator 0131 229 1917

CHURCH OF SCOTLAND WC **B**

376 WARDIE PARISH CHURCH

NT 246 768

Primrose Bank Road, Trinity

A jolly Gothic church with Francophile detail, by John McLachlan 1892. Distinctive silhouette with central lantern and conical pinnacles. Inside, a clear-span tunnel roof. A complete and perfect set of Gothic oak furnishings by Scott Morton & Co 1935 including the organ case (organ by Rushworth & Dreaper). Sunday Services: 11am, 10.30am, July and August

Open Tuesday, Thursday and Friday 9am–12 noon, telephone the church office 0131 551 3847

CHURCH OF SCOTLAND WC

WARDIE PARISH CHURCH

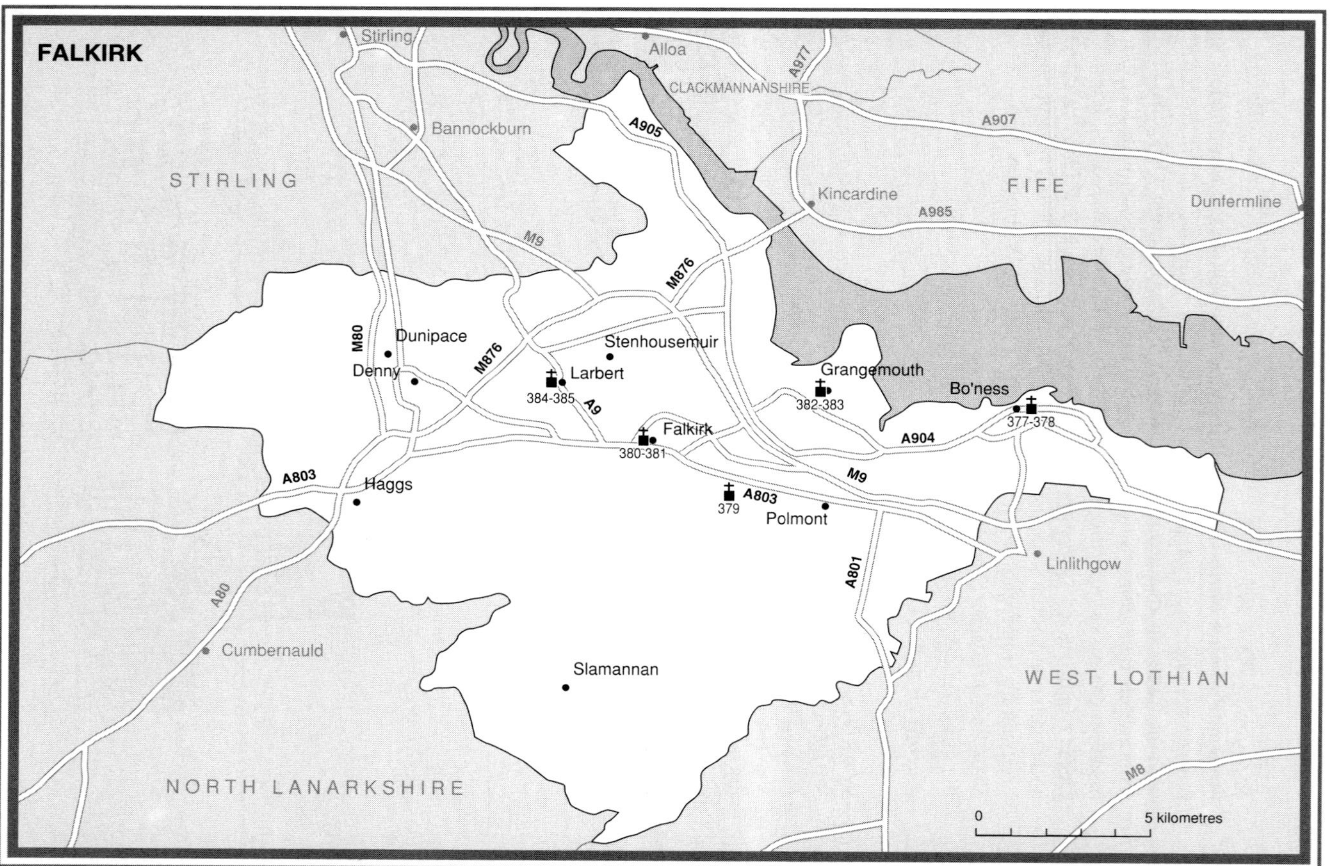
FALKIRK
Stirling
Alloa
A977
CLACKMANNANSHIRE
A907
A905
Bannockburn
STIRLING
FIFE
Kincardine
A985
Dunfermline
M9
M876
M80
Dunipace
Stenhousemuir
Denny
M876
Larbert
384-385
A9
Grangemouth
382-383
Bo'ness
377-378
Falkirk
380-381
A904
A803
Haggs
M9
A803
379
Polmont
Linlithgow
A801
A80
Cumbernauld
Slamannan
WEST LOTHIAN
NORTH LANARKSHIRE
M8
0
5 kilometres

FALKIRK

Local Representative: Mr Alan Naylor, Candiehill, Candie, Avonbridge, Falkirk (*telephone* 01324 861583)

377 ST CATHERINE'S CHURCH, BO'NESS

NS 999 812

Cadzow Crescent, Bo'ness

The congregation was formed in 1888 and moved to the present building in 1921. The hall was added in 1928. The sanctuary windows depict the children of the Bible. Organ by Miller of Dundee. Off Dean Road, adjacent to Douglas Park. Services: Sunday: Sung Eucharist 11.30am; Wednesday: Said Eucharist 10.15

Open by arrangement, telephone the Rector 01324 482438

SCOTTISH EPISCOPAL ♿ WC

378 CARRIDEN PARISH CHURCH, BO'NESS

NT 019 812

Carriden Brae, Carriden, Bo'ness

The first church of Carriden was consecrated in 1243 by Bishop David de Bernam, although it is believed that the parish goes back to the time of St Ninian, AD c.396. The present church is the third. Designed by P MacGregor Chalmers, 1909, in simple Romanesque style with a west tower and stone spire. The bell was cast in Rotterdam, Peter Oostens 1674. Inside a wooden sailing ship 'The Ranger' hangs from the barrel shaped pitch pine roof. Six-bay nave. Baptistry chapel with a wall painting thought to be of the Scottish School. Sounding board on north wall, 1655. A fine stone arcaded baptismal font, two-manual pipe organ moved from the John Knox Church, Gorbals after the blitz of 1941. Sunday Service: 11.15am

Open Tuesday 9am–12 noon, and Wednesday 12 noon–1pm

CHURCH OF SCOTLAND ♿ 🦻 WC **B**

379 BRIGHTONS PARISH CHURCH

NS 928 778

Main Street, Brightons

Built in 1847. Local quarry owner Alexander Lawrie gifted the stone to build the church to a design by Brown & Carrick of Glasgow. T-plan church with small steeple with bell. Side galleries added in 1893. Chancel area modernised 1935. Windows 1993 by Ruth Golliwaws of New Orleans, USA. B805, four miles south of Falkirk; or B810, half-mile from Polmont Station. Sunday Services: 11am and 1st Sunday; September to May 6pm

Church website: www.brightonsparishchurch.org.uk

Open for prayer September to June, Thursday 10am–12 noon

CHURCH OF SCOTLAND ♿ 🦻 WC

380 FALKIRK FREE CHURCH

Beaumont Drive, Newcarron, Falkirk

The present congregation began in 1991 and moved into its new building in 1998. The building reflects modern architecture but maintains a spiritual and practical ambience. Sunday Services: 11am and 6.30pm; Prayers: Wednesday and Saturday 7.30pm, Saturday 7pm. Other activities contact the Minister

Open by arrangement, telephone the Rev R MacLeod 01324 631008

FREE CHURCH OF SCOTLAND

381 FALKIRK OLD AND ST MODAN'S PARISH CHURCH

NS 887 800

Manse Place, off High Street, Falkirk

Dating from 1811, although 12th-century pillars remain in the vestibule. There has been a Christian church on this site for 1200; local legend links the earliest foundation with the Celtic St Modan in the 6th century. The square tower dates from the 16th century, and the gable marks of the earlier nave and chancel are visible. Above the tower an 18th-century bell-tower with 13 bells. Two late 19th-century stained glass windows; pipe organ of same period. Twelfth-century sanctuary cross. Major refurbishment in the 1960s. Sunday Services: winter 11.15am and 6.30pm, summer 9.30 and 11.15am

Open Monday to Friday 12 noon–2pm. Lunches served

CHURCH OF SCOTLAND **B**

382 ST MARY'S CHURCH, GRANGEMOUTH

NS 932 818

Ronaldshay Crescent, Grangemouth

The present church was built in 1938 to replace a 'tin kirk' of 1901; the architect was Maxton Craig of Edinburgh. A small hall was added in 1978. The west window, 1962, depicts the industries of Grangemouth. Altar cross, candlesticks and vases by Edward Spencer, the Artificers' Guild, his last work. Adjacent to Zetland Park in the centre of the town. Services: Sunday: Said Eucharist 8.30am, Sung Eucharist 10am; Tuesday: Said Eucharist 10am

Open first Saturday of month, 12 noon–2pm. Or by arrangement, telephone the Rector 01324 482438

SCOTTISH EPISCOPAL

383 GRANGEMOUTH: ZETLAND CHURCH, GRANGEMOUTH

NS 931 818

Ronaldshay Crescent, Grangemouth

Building by Wilson & Tait completed 1911. Cruciform in plan with a south aisle and north and south transepts. Four arches support a timber barrel roof and there is a small gallery at the end of the nave. Second World War memorial stained glass window by Douglas Hamilton, Glasgow, with four lights depicting Peace, Victory,

Willingness to Lay Down Life and The Glory of the King of Heaven. Willis organ of 1890 installed 1983 and Memorial Chapel furnished in the south transept 1990 used for private prayer and small services. Grounds have won Falkirk Council's Church Gardens award for past eight years. Sunday Service: 11.15am

Open Wednesday mornings, 9.30-11.30am, March to October

CHURCH OF SCOTLAND **B**

384 LARBERT OLD CHURCH

NS 856 822

Denny Road, Larbert

Near site of earlier chapel – 12th-century dependency of Eccles Kirkton of St Ninian's and Cambuskenneth Abbey. The present church was built in 1820, architect David Hamilton, replacing a pre-Reformation church which was located within the adjacent churchyard. The chancel was added in 1911. The fine oak panelling dates from 1887. There are good memorial windows including Gordon Webster and Stephen Adam. The apsidal triptych of the Transfiguration is believed to be the only example of Frank Howard's work (1805-66) in Scotland and was executed by Edmundson of Manchester. There are some interesting memorial plaques. The graveyard includes the burial place of James Bruce, Abyssinian explorer, and Master Robert Bruce, the post-Reformation divine, as well as the early partners of the Carron Company. The bell-tower has a carillon of chimes dateing from 1985. Sunday Services: 11.30am and 6.30pm

LARBERT OLD CHURCH

Open by arrangement, telephone 01324 562955

CHURCH OF SCOTLAND

385 OUR LADY OF LOURDES AND ST BERNADETTE, LARBERT

NS 865 829

323 Main Street, Larbert

The present building designed by Reginald Fairlie, dating from 1930s, was intended to be a hall but used for worship until a permanent church could be built. When this plan was abandoned in the 1950s the building was adapted to become exclusively the place of worship. Entrance porch by Sam Sweeney added 1995. Marian Grotto in grounds 1983 to mark the Golden Jubilee, recently embellished and decorated by local talent from within the church community. Sunday Services: 11.30am and 6.30pm Mass

Open 9am-dusk, or apply to Presbytery adjacent to Church

ROMAN CATHOLIC

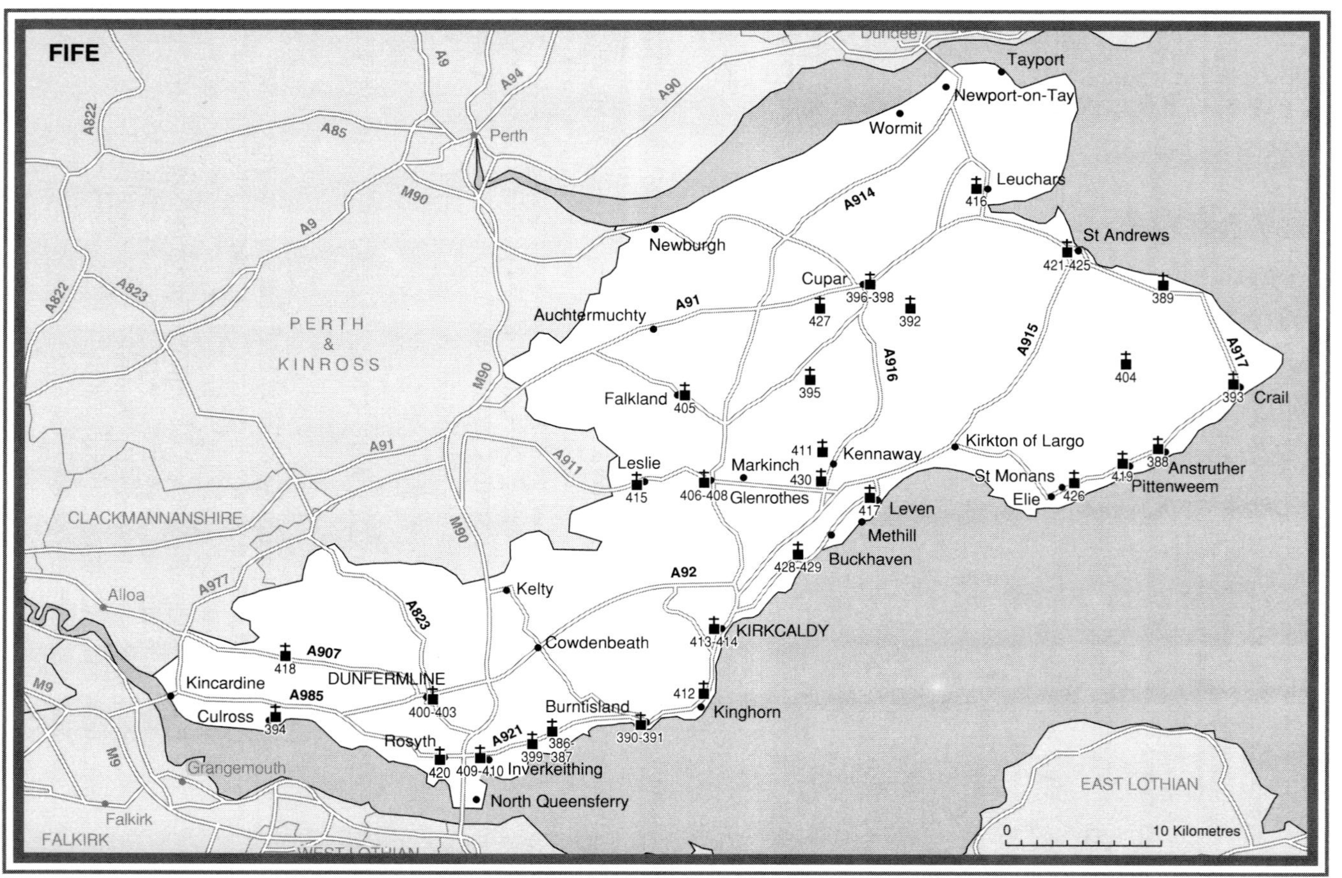
FIFE
Dundee
Tayport
Newport-on-Tay
Wormit
Perth
Leuchars
416
A914
St Andrews
421-425
Newburgh
Cupar
396-398
427
392
389
A91
Auchtermuchty
A915
A916
A917
404
PERTH
&
KINROSS
395
Falkland
405
393
Crail
Kirkton of Largo
411
Kennaway
Markinch
430
Leslie
415
406-408
Glenrothes
St Monans
Elie
426
419
Pittenweem
388
Anstruther
417
Leven
Methill
428-429
Buckhaven
CLACKMANNANSHIRE
A92
Kelty
Alloa
A823
413-414
KIRKCALDY
Cowdenbeath
418
A907
DUNFERMLINE
Kincardine
A985
400-403
412
Kinghorn
Burntisland
Culross
394
390-391
Rosyth
A921
399
386-
387
420
409-410
Inverkeithing
Grangemouth
North Queensferry
Falkirk
FALKIRK
WEST LOTHIAN
EAST LOTHIAN
0
10 Kilometres
A9
A94
A90
A85
A822
M90
A823
M90
A91
A911
A977
M9

FIFE

Local Representative: The Rev Malcolm Trew, 155 Park Road West, Rosyth
e-mail: malcolm.trew@virgin.net

386 ST COLUMBA'S CHURCH, ABERDOUR

NT 186 851

Inverkeithing Road, Aberdour

Built in 1843 for the Earl of Moray as a private chapel for his employees in Aberdour. It was transferred to the Scottish Episcopal Church in 1918. A cruciform plan, tall and light with lancet windows. The west window blocked off by the addition of a balcony, which has recently been enclosed. A921 from Dalgety Bay, in the village on the right. Linked with St Peter's, Inverkeithing and St Serf's, Burntisland. Sunday Service: 11am

Flower Festival 1-4 August 2002. Open by arrangement, telephone Mrs Clifford 01383 860521, or Mrs Wallington 01383 860795

SCOTTISH EPISCOPAL WC

387 ST FILLAN'S, ABERDOUR

NT 193 855

Hawkcraig Road, Aberdour

One of the finest examples of Norman architecture in Scotland, this 'miniature Cathedral' sits in its own graveyard overlooking Aberdour harbour. The early church, standing in 1123, consisted of the nave and chancel, lit by deep splayed windows which still exist. The church was enlarged in the 15th century by the addition of a side aisle, and in the 17th by the small transeptual aisle, now used by the choir. The church fell into disrepair in the 18th century and was restored in 1925. 'Even to enter St Fillan's is to worship.' Sunday Service: September to May 10.30am, June to August 10am

Flower Festival 27-30 July 2002. Open every day

CHURCH OF SCOTLAND

ST FILLAN'S, ABERDOUR

388 ANSTRUTHER PARISH CHURCH

NO 567 037

Burial Brae (off Crail Road), Anstruther

James Melville (brother of Andrew, the leading Covenanter) inspired the purchase of land in 1590 for a new church, but he was exiled by James VI and the church was not built until 1634. Described in 1837 as 'one of the most elegant country churches anywhere to be seen'. Tahitian Princess buried outside the south wall. Many interesting features. Anstruther is the birthplace of Thomas Chalmers. A917 Crail, 400 yards east of St Andrews cross road. Bus services: Fife Scottish 95 and 57, Minibus M1 and M611, Stagecoach X23. Sunday Service: 11am; Healing Service second Sunday of month 2pm

Open April to September, Tuesday 2-3pm, Thursday 11am-12 noon. All year coffee morning, Tuesday 10am-12 noon in Hew Scott Hall (converted 13th-century West Anstruther Church)

CHURCH OF SCOTLAND ♿ **B**

389 BOARHILLS CHURCH

NO 562 137

On A917 west of Boarhills

Church built 1866/7, although there has been a burial ground here considerably longer. The architect was George Rae. Original oil lamps, now converted to electricity. Sunday Service: 10am in February, April, June, August, October and December

Open by arrangement with the Minister, telephone 01334 472948

CHURCH OF SCOTLAND ♿ (back door) **C**

390 BURNTISLAND PARISH CHURCH

NT 234 857

East Leven Street, Burntisland

Built in 1592 to an unusual square plan. One of the first post-Reformation churches built in Scotland, still in use. The General Assembly of the Church of Scotland met in Burntisland in May 1601 in the presence of James VI when a new translation of the Bible was approved. Information available on the churchyard. Extensive refurbishment completed in 1999. Sunday Services: 11am and 6.30pm

Open June to August, 10am-12 noon and 2-4pm. Other times key from Curator, telephone 01592 873275

CHURCH OF SCOTLAND ♿

 **A**

BURNTISLAND PARISH CHURCH

391 ST SERF'S CHURCH, BURNTISLAND

NT 230 864

Ferguson Place x Cromwell Road, Burntisland

Built in 1905 to a design by Truro Cathedral architect J L Pearson, the stone is from the local Grange quarry. The chancel is divided from the nave by a fine Gothic arch. The east end of the chancel is semi-octagonal behind a tri-form arch springing from slender columns, surmounted by a Gothic arch. Linked with St Peter's, Inverkeithing and St Columba's, Aberdour. Sunday Service: 9.30am; Tuesday: 11am

Open by arrangement, telephone Mrs M McQuarrie 01592 873117

SCOTTISH EPISCOPAL WC **B**

392 CERES CHURCH

NO 399 117

Kirk Brae, Ceres

Built 1806 to a design by Alexander Leslie, with a battlemented tower, its spire added in 1852, the building has the original box pews and long communion tables running the full length of the church. Crenellated tower with obelisk corner pinnacles. The 17th-century stone-slated Lindsay vault in the kirkyard was possibly attached to the medieval church. Linked with Springfield Church. Sunday Service: 11.00am

Open on Doors Open Day, September, and by arrangement, telephone the Minister 01334 828233

CHURCH OF SCOTLAND  **B**

CERES CHURCH

393 CRAIL PARISH CHURCH

NO 613 080

Marketgate, Crail

Consecrated in 1243 with alterations 1526, 1796. Restored 1963. Judith Campbell windows (1970 and 1975). Pictish cross slab. Seventeenth-century carving. Pipe organ 1936, Harrison & Harrison (1936). Graveyard (with dead house). Hourly bus service, Leven–St Andrews (some to Dundee). Sunday Service: 11.15am; also 17 June to 2 September at 9.30am (informal)

Open 2-4pm, 18 June to 1 September

CHURCH OF SCOTLAND WC **A**

394 CULROSS ABBEY

NS 989 863

Kirk Street, Culross

Built on the site of a Celtic Christian Culdee church. Abbey founded in 1217 by Malcolm, seventh Earl of Fife; dedicated to St Mary and St Serf. Much of the original building remains, although a great deal of it is in ruins. The monks' choir forms the present parish church, in continuous use since 1633. Modernised in 1824 and restored in 1905 by Sir R Rowand Anderson. Many features of interest. Situated in 16th-century small town of Culross. Seven and a half miles west of Dunfermline. Sunday Service: 11.30am

Open daily, summer 10am-dusk, winter 10am-4pm

CHURCH OF SCOTLAND WC **A**

395 CULTS KIRK

NO 347 099

Kirkton of Cults, south side of A914, Half-mile from Pitlessie, four miles SW of Cupar

A place of worship since the 12th century, the present kirk built 1793. Bell inscribed 'John Meikle, Edinburg, fecit for the Kirk of Cults, 1699'. Lepers window, Laird's Pew, Memorials, one by Chantry of Sir David Wilkie RA, the most famous son of the manse, one by Samuel Joseph of his father and mother. Wilkie Hall, Pitlessie village, collection of etchings and engravings by Wilkie, viewing by appointment 01337 830491. Sunday Service: 11.30am until July 2002, then 10am

Open 8am-8pm

CHURCH OF SCOTLAND **B**

CULTS KIRK

396 CUPAR OLD AND ST MICHAEL OF TARVIT PARISH CHURCH

NO 380 146

Kirkgate, Cupar

The tower dates from 1415; its spire and belfry (containing two bells 1485 and 1689) were added in 1620 and the four-face clock in 1910. The church itself was rebuilt in 1785. Inside are war memorials on the east and south walls and the guidon of the Fife and Forfar Yeomanry. A recess in the west wall contains the 15th-century recumbent figure of a knight ('Muckle Fernie'). Adjacent graveyard contains hand of David Hackston, a Covenanter from Rathillet. Sunday Service: 11am, and September to April 6.30pm

Open Saturdays 10am-12pm, June to August, or by appointment 01334 653036

CHURCH OF SCOTLAND WC **A**

CUPAR OLD AND ST MICHAEL OF TARVIT PARISH CHURCH

397 ST JAMES THE GREAT CHURCH, CUPAR

NO 376 146

St Catherine Street, Cupar

Built in 1866 to a design by Sir R Rowand Anderson. Fine choir screen, reredos and panelling, Lorimer 1920. Town centre, A91 Stirling to St Andrews. By rail from Edinburgh and Dundee. By coach from Kirkcaldy, Dundee, St Andrews and Stirling. Services: Sunday 8am and 11am; Wednesday 10am

Open weekdays, 10am–3pm

SCOTTISH EPISCOPAL WC **B**

398 ST JOHN'S PARISH CHURCH, CUPAR

NO 373 147

Bonnygate, Cupar

The 150ft spire with belfry dominates the view of Cupar from the many approaches. Built 1878, Campbell Douglas & Sellars, Glasgow, when first Cupar Free Church became too small. Galleried interior. Set on a raised area in stepped gardens. The inside of the church was re-decorated in February 2001. Sunday Service: 11am. Mid-week half hour service every Wednesday 9.30am

Church website:
www.churchofscotland/congregations/stjohn's

Open all year, Wednesday 9.30am–11.30am. Other times by arrangement 01334 655851

CHURCH OF SCOTLAND WC **B**

ST JOHN'S PARISH CHURCH, CUPAR

399 DALGETY PARISH CHURCH, DALGETY BAY

NT 155 836

Regents Way, Dalgety Bay

A hall church designed by Marcus Johnston, built in 1981. Worship area and suite of halls which are used by congregation and local community groups. War memorial in grounds. Sunday Services: 9.30am and 11.30am, all year; also second Sunday 6.30pm, October to March

Open by arrangement, telephone Mr W Wood, 13 Doune Park, Dalgety Bay 0138 822 529

CHURCH OF SCOTLAND

DALGETY PARISH CHURCH, DALGETY BAY

400 DUNFERMLINE ABBEY

NT 090 873

St Margaret Street, Dunfermline

Founded in 1072. Consists today of the nave of medieval monastic church (1150) and the modern parish church (1821) erected over foundations of original Choir. Burial place of King Robert the Bruce and numerous other Scottish royals including Malcolm III (Canmore) and his Queen St Margaret of Scotland. Exquisitely carved pulpit by William Paterson, Edinburgh 1890. Fine pipe organ of 1882, rebuilt Walker in 1986. Signposted from outskirts of city. Sunday Services: 9.30am and 11am

Open April to October, Monday to Saturday 10am–4.30pm, and Sunday 2–4.30pm. Abbey shop also open as above. Groups by arrangement, telephone Mr F Tait 01383 872242

CHURCH OF SCOTLAND

DUNFERMLINE ABBEY

401 ST LEONARD'S, DUNFERMLINE

NT 096 869

Brucefield Avenue

The most striking feature of the church, P McGregor Chalmers, 1904, is a round Celtic tower. Inside, the semi-circular apse has a dramatic painting of the Risen Christ surrounded by Gospel characters, designed by the architect and painted by Mr A Samuel 1927. Heraldic gallery dedicated to the Scottish Wars of Independence led by Wallace and Bruce. Sunday Service: June to August 10am; September to May 9.30am and 11am

Open Tuesday and Thursday mornings (church office)

CHURCH OF SCOTLAND ♿ WC 🦻 B

ST LEONARD'S, DUNFERMLINE

402 ST MARGARET'S MEMORIAL CHURCH, DUNFERMLINE

NY 096 876

Holyrood Place, Dunfermline

A commanding building forming part of the ancient gateway to the town at the East Port. Built in 1896 to a design by Sir R Rowand Anderson in 12th-century Transitional style. Stained glass circular window by John Blyth, stone reredos by Hew Lorimer, wood carving by Steven Foster and historical prints by Jurek Pütter. Three new stained glass windows by Douglas Hogg.

Services: Saturday 6.30pm; Sunday 9am and 11am; Weekdays 10am

Open by arrangement, telephone Father Barr 01383 625611

ROMAN CATHOLIC ♿ 🦻 📖 WC B

403 VIEWFIELD BAPTIST CHURCH, DUNFERMLINE

NT 095 875

East Port, Dunfermline

Gothic design by Peter L Henderson, 1882-84. Front façade skewed giving a vestibule narrower at one side than the other and making necessary the cylindrical addition for the east gallery staircase. Wood vaulted ceiling upheld by laminated wood arches, supported internally by six cast-iron pillars. Pipe organ. Sunday Services: 11am and 6.30pm

Church website: www.viewfield.org.uk

Church office open 9.30am-2.30pm every weekday, telephone 01383 620465

BAPTIST WC 🦻 ☕ (open 10am-2pm Monday-Friday, in adjacent Viewfield Centre)

VIEWFIELD BAPTIST CHURCH, DUNFERMLINE

404 DUNINO CHURCH

NO 541 109

In woods up farm road off B9131

There has been a church at Dunino since 1240. The present building is 1827 by James Gillespie Graham with the chancel and porch 1928 by J Jeffrey Waddell & Young. Font by Sir Robert Lorimer, stained glass by J Jennings of London and W Wilson. Early Celtic carved stone in the churchyard. Sunday Service: 10am in January, March, May, July, September and November

Open daily

CHURCH OF SCOTLAND B

405 FALKLAND PARISH CHURCH

NO 252 074

The Square, Falkland

On the site of an earlier building, the present church was completed in 1850 to a design by David Bryce and gifted to the people of Falkland by Onesiphorus Tyndall Bruce, of the family of Bruce of Earlshall. The style is Victorian Gothic. Centre pews convert to long communion tables. Stained glass 1897. A912 Perth–Kirkcaldy. Bus service: 36 from Perth. Sunday Service: 2002 – 10am, 2003 – 11.30am

Open 1 June to 2 September 2002, Tuesday and Wednesday 2pm-4pm. 10 June to 3 September 2003, Tuesday and Wednesday 2pm-4pm

FALKLAND PARISH CHURCH

CHURCH OF SCOTLAND B

406 ST COLUMBA'S PARISH CHURCH, GLENROTHES

NO 270 009

Rothes Road, Glenrothes

Built in 1960 and designed in conjunction with the theologians at St Mary's College of St Andrews University with the emphasis on how the Scottish Reformation could be best expressed in a church building. The sanctuary features seating around three sides, with the Lord's table in the centre. Mural of Alberto Morocco measuring 59 feet by 9 feet of scene from the last days of Christ. Iron bell-tower is a landmark in the centre of the town. Sunday Service: 11am September to May, July to August 10am

Open 10am-12.30pm Monday, Wednesday and Friday

CHURCH OF SCOTLAND

407 ST LUKE THE EVANGELIST, GLENROTHES

NO 273 008

Ninian Quadrant, Glenrothes

By J Cassells 1960 the church is in a Perpendicular style, set alongside a playpark in the earliest and most central part of the new town of Glenrothes. Furnished with the warmth of pine, its interior is light and airy with an unusual layout, and houses several items of interest. Sunday Services: 9.15 and 10.45am

Open Monday and Thursday 10am-1pm, Tuesday 9am-10.30am, Sunday 9am-12.30pm

SCOTTISH EPISCOPAL A

408 ST PAUL'S CHURCH, GLENROTHES

NO 281 005

Warout Road, Glenrothes

Completed 1957 from design by Isi Metzstein and Andy McMillan of Gillespie, Kidd & Coia. Described by *The Scotsman* as 'the most significant piece of architecture north of the English Channel' and in *The Twentieth Century Church* as 'a homage to architecture's liberating function'. Interior contains the 'Catalonian' altar crucifix 1957 and 'The Madonna' or 'Lady Piece' by Benno Schotz 1960. Carved Stations of the Cross and figure of St Paul by Harry Bain 1983. Follow Woodside Road from town centre, corner of Woodside Road/Warout Road. Sunday Services: 11.30am and 6.30pm

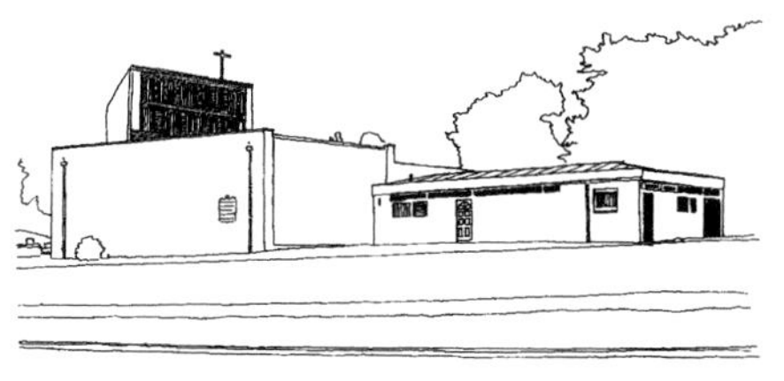

ST PAUL'S CHURCH, GLENROTHES

Open first Saturday of the month, 11am-6pm

ROMAN CATHOLIC B

409 ST PETER'S PARISH CHURCH, INVERKEITHING

NT 131 830

Church Street, Inverkeithing

A Norman foundation, church dedicated to St Peter 1244. The present building is a nave and aisles church by Gillespie Graham 1827 attached to a 14th-century tower. Refurbished 1900, P MacGregor Chalmers. Fourteenth-century stone font, one of the finest in Scotland, thought to have been gifted by King Robert III for the baptism of his son the Duke of Rothesay. Sunday Service: 11.15am

Open July to August, Friday 2-4pm, Saturday 10am-12noon, 2pm-4pm

CHURCH OF SCOTLAND

ST PETER'S PARISH CHURCH, INVERKEITHING

410 ST PETER'S EPISCOPAL CHURCH, INVERKEITHING

NT 128 827

Hope Street, Inverkeithing

ST PETER'S EPISCOPAL CHURCH, INVERKEITHING

The church was built to serve the Scottish Episcopal community in Jamestown, at one time outside the Royal Burgh of Inverkeithing. The nave was built in 1903 to a design by Henry F Kerr and the chancel added in 1910. The interior was altered in 1980 to form a worship area and hall. Set in well-kept gardens on the southern approach to the town from the Forth Road Bridge. Linked with St Columba's, Aberdour and St Serf's, Burntisland.
Sunday Service: Holy Communion 11am

Open by arrangement, telephone D Macdonald 01383 414194

SCOTTISH EPISCOPAL WC

411 ST KENNETH'S PARISH CHURCH, KENNOWAY

No 350 023

Cupar Road, Kennoway

ST KENNETH'S PARISH CHURCH, KENNOWAY

The church in Kennoway dates back to St Kenneth, who preached in the 6th century. The present Romanesque church was built in 1850 and was designed by Thomas Hamilton. Six stained glass windows by Marjorie Kemp, 1950. Monuments to past ministers. Sunday Services: 11.15am and, during term time, 7.00pm

Church website: www.st-kenneths.freeserve.co.uk

Open Monday to Friday 9.30am-12.30pm, plus Tuesday 1.00-3.00pm and Thursday 5.00-7.00pm

CHURCH OF SCOTLAND WC B

412 KINGHORN PARISH CHURCH

NT 272 869

St James Place, Kinghorn

KINGHORN PARISH CHURCH

The Kirk by the Sea for over 750 years has an unrivalled view across the beach to the Firth of Forth and Edinburgh. It has a historic bell-tower and a 'Sailors' Aisle' built in 1609 celebrating the naval connection and a model of the first Unicorn.
Sunday Services: 9.30am and 11am (except first Sunday of month: 10.30am in church hall)

Open every Tuesday 6pm-8 pm

CHURCH OF SCOTLAND

413 ST BRYCE KIRK (formerly Kirkcaldy Old Parish Church), KIRKCALDY

NT 280 917

Kirk Wynd, Kirkcaldy

Consecrated in 1244 by the Bishop of St Andrews, the ancient tower offers excellent views of Kirkcaldy. The body of the church is by James Elliot 1808. Good stained glass windows, some by Morris & Co from Burne-Jones designs of 1886. United with St Brycedale. Historic graveyard. Sunday Service: 11am

Church website: www.stbrycekirk.fsnet.co.uk

Open during August, Friday and Saturday 10am-4pm

CHURCH OF SCOTLAND **B**

ST BRYCE KIRK (FORMERLY KIRKCALDY OLD PARISH CHURCH), KIRKCALDY

414 ST BRYCE KIRK (formerly St Brycedale), KIRKCALDY

NT 279 917

St Brycedale Avenue, Kirkcaldy

Built as a Free Church 1877-81 by James Matthews of Aberdeen. A 60-metre tower and spire and associated pyramid-roofed twin towers lift the church out of the ordinary. In 1988, a transformed church at first-floor level was created above a multi-purpose ground-floor. Organ by Brindley & Foster 1893. Stained glass includes windows by Adam & Small 1881, Douglas Strachan 1923, and Edward Burne-Jones (executed by William Morris & Co) 1889. Now united with Kirkcaldy Old. On junction of Kirk Wynd and St Brycedale Avenue. Sunday Service: 11am

Church website: www.stbrycekirk.fsnet.co.uk

Open Monday to Thursday 9am-10pm, Friday 9am-3pm, Saturday 9am-1pm. Coffee Bar open Monday to Thursday 10am-9pm, Friday 10am-3pm, Saturday 10am-1pm

CHURCH OF SCOTLAND

ST BRYCE KIRK (FORMERLY ST BRYCEDALE), KIRKCALDY

415 ST MARY, MOTHER OF GOD, LESLIE

NO 251 018

High Street, Leslie

Originally Leslie Free Church by R Thornton Shiells 1879. In 1900 it was renamed the Logan United Free Church after the Minister at that time. Closed as a Free Church in 1956 and opened as Roman Catholic in 1959. Tower 120ft and spire. Stained glass by John Blyth, painting of the Crucifixion by Geoffrey Houghton-Brown. Sunday Service: 9.30am

Open first Saturday of each month 11am-6pm

ROMAN CATHOLIC ♿ 𝄢 WC **B**

ST MARY, MOTHER OF GOD, LESLIE

416 ST ATHERNASE CHURCH, LEUCHARS

NO 455 214

Main Street, Leuchars

Twelfth-century Norman church in a historic conservation setting. The belfry was added c.1700, and nave restored in 1858. Chancel and apse of outstanding architectural interest. Sunday Service: 11am

Open March to October daily 9.30am-6pm. Teas, Tuesdays 10am-4pm. Tours for groups, telephone Church Officer, 18 Schoolhill, Leuchars 01334 838884

CHURCH OF SCOTLAND 𝄢 WC **A**

ST ATHERNASE CHURCH, LEUCHARS

417 LEVEN PARISH CHURCH (formerly Scoonie Kirk)

NO 383 017

Durie Street, Leven

Scoonie Kirk is the original Parish Church of Leven with its roots going back over 16 centuries. The church moved to its present site in 1775. In 1904 the building was extended following a design by the eminent church architect P MacGregor Chalmers which incorporated some of the earlier building. The unique pipe organ was built by the French organ builder August Gern 1884 and was restored 1992. The building also has some very striking stained glass windows. Sunday Services: 9.30am (all age worship), 11.00am (traditional worship)

Church website: www.scooniekirk.freeserve.co.uk

Open Easter to September, Tuesdays 11am-1pm

CHURCH OF SCOTLAND ♿ 𝄢 WC **B**

LEVEN PARISH CHURCH

418 CHURCH OF THE HOLY NAME, OAKLEY

NT 025 885

Station Road, Oakley

Built by the Smith-Sligo family of Inzievar House to a design by Charles Gray. Consecrated October 1965. Outstanding features include stained glass windows by Gabriel Loire of Chartres. Carved Stations of the Cross also by Gabriel Loire. Services: Vigil Mass Saturday 6.30pm; Sunday Mass 10.15am

Open by arrangement, telephone the Parish Priest at Priest's House (adjacent via grass path to right of church)

ROMAN CATHOLIC

CHURCH OF THE HOLY NAME, OAKLEY

419 PITTENWEEM PARISH CHURCH

NO 549 026

Kirkgate, Pittenweem

This ancient monument has developed over a long time. The earliest work is around 1200. The Church was extended in 1532 with an entrance from Cove Wynd and the addition of the Tolbooth Tower with Bailies Loft. The interior was refurbished in 1883 in Victorian style with new entrance, galleries and stairs. The bell dates from 1662, while the clock in the tower is a fine example by John Smith. Stained glass by William Wilson and John Blyth of the 1950s and 1960s.

PITTENWEEM PARISH CHURCH

Sunday Service: 11.30am

Open weekdays 8am-6pm. Keys from the Post Office (C & A Campbell's) in Market Place

CHURCH OF SCOTLAND A

420 ROSYTH METHODIST CHURCH

NT 114 842

Queensferry Road x Woodside Avenue, Rosyth

Founded in 1916, the present building was opened in 1970. A sanctuary of A-frame design with single storey hall and ancillary rooms adjoining by Alan Mercer, architect. Striking 30ft-high mural, painted in Byzantine style by Derek Seymour. Sunday Services: 9.30am (Scottish Episcopal), 11am (Methodist)

Open by arrangement, telephone Mr Martin Rogers 01383 415458

METHODIST

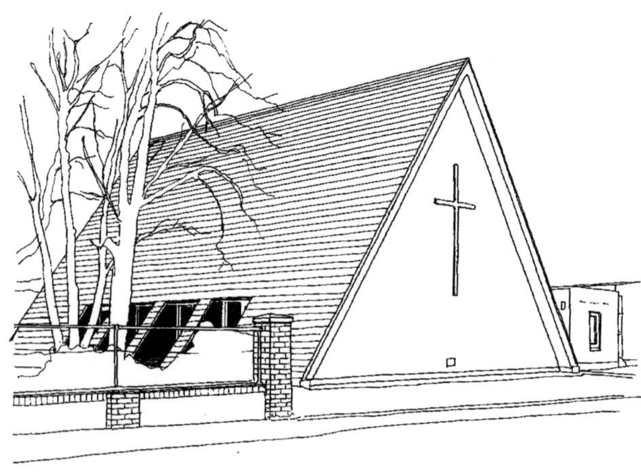

ROSYTH METHODIST CHURCH

421 ALL SAINTS', ST ANDREWS

NO 512 168

North Castle Street, St Andrews

Complex of church hall, rectory and club in Scottish vernacular with an Italian flavour. Orange pantiled roofs and lots of crowsteps. Slated chancel and bell-tower by John Douglas of Chester 1906-9; the rest is by Paul Waterhouse 1919-24. Woodwork of rood, chapel altarpiece and front canopy by Nathaniel Hitch, stone Madonna and Child by Hew Lorimer 1945, marble font and wrought iron screen by Farmer & Brindley. Three windows by Herbert Hendrie, Louis Davis and Douglas Strachan. Sunday Services: 8am, 10am and 6pm

ALL SAINTS', ST ANDREWS

Open daily 10am-4.30pm

SCOTTISH EPISCOPAL (Ladyhead book and coffee shop) **B**

422 PARISH CHURCH OF THE HOLY TRINITY, ST ANDREWS

NO 509 167

South Street, St Andrews

Tower and occasional pillars 1412, completely rebuilt on original ground-plan in 1909, architect McGregor Chalmers. South porch commemorates John Knox preaching here. Much fine stained glass by Strachan, Davis, Hendrie, Wilson and others: clerestory windows have badges of all Scottish regiments of First World War. Elaborate memorial pulpit of Iona marble, alabaster and onyx. Decorated font of Caen stone. Memorial tomb of Archbishop Sharp. Oak barrel roof. Hunter and Memorial Aisle has much fine wood-carving. Seventeenth-century sacramental silver. Harrison and Harrison organ. Twenty-seven-bell Taylor of Loughborough carillon. Sunday Services: 11am and 6pm

Open Tuesday and Saturday 10am-12noon, as advertised, or by arrangement, telephone Mr Armour 01334 474494

CHURCH OF SCOTLAND **A**

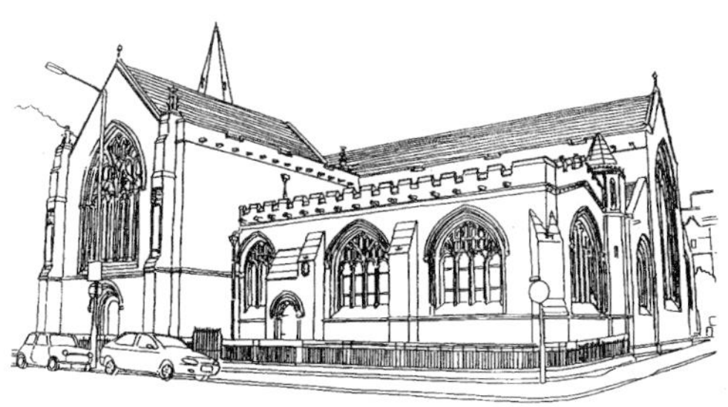

PARISH CHURCH OF THE HOLY TRINITY, ST ANDREWS

423 HOPE PARK CHURCH, ST ANDREWS

NO 505 167

St Mary's Place, St Andrews

Completed in 1865, Peddie & Kinnear. Unusual canopy pulpit. Stained glass. Pewter communion ware, pulpit falls. A91 St Andrews, turn right at first mini roundabout, 300 yards on left opposite bus station. Rail service to Leuchars. Sunday Services: 9.30am and 11am. Evening service as advertised in local press

Open Holy Week and Christmas week, Monday to Friday 10am-4pm, July to August, Wednesday 10am-4pm

CHURCH OF SCOTLAND A

HOPE PARK CHURCH, ST ANDREWS

424 MARTYRS CHURCH, ST ANDREWS

NO 510 168

North Street (opposite University Chapel)

Originally United Free Church, 1926-8 by Gillespie & Scott. Woodwork by Andrew Thom & Sons of St Andrews. Stained glass by Douglas Strachan, Herbert Hendrie, William Wilson, Sadie McLellan and Marjorie Kemp. Roll of Honour designed and painted by J D Macgregor. Sunday Service: 11.15am

Open most Wednesdays, September to April 2.00-3.30pm

CHURCH OF SCOTLAND (side door) (Wednesday afternoons) **B**

425 ST ANDREW'S CHURCH, ST ANDREWS

NO 509 164

Queen's Terrace, St Andrews

1869 by Sir R Rowand Anderson. Fine 19th-century stained glass in the east and west walls. Two bays of excellent modern stained glass work. A Biblical Garden developed by BBC television's Beechgrove Garden Hit Squad is part of the popular, well kept grounds for this vibrant and enthusiastic congregation. Sunday Services: Holy Communion 8am and 10am, Choral Evensong 5.30pm (not Sundays after Christmas, Easter, nor in July and August); Monday to Friday Morning Prayer 8.30am

SCOTTISH EPISCOPAL **B**

426 ST MONANS PARISH CHURCH

NO 523 014

Braehead, St Monans

Occupying a striking position close to the sea, the church was built by Sir William Dishington 1370, with alterations by William Burn 1828 and Ian G Lindsay 1961. Fourteenth-century sedilia, piscina and aumbry. Medieval consecration crosses. Early 19th-century votive model ship of the line, heraldic bosses. External angled buttresses and 'buckle' corbels. A917 to St Monans, signposted.
Sunday Service: 10.30am

Open April to October during daylight hours

CHURCH OF SCOTLAND A

ST MONANS PARISH CHURCH

427 SPRINGFIELD CHURCH

NO 342 119

Manse Road, Springfield near Cupar, Fife

Built in 1861 to a plain, rectangular design. It contains notable late Victorian stained glass windows. The building was refurbished in 1970. Linked with Ceres Church. Sunday Service: 9.45am

Open by arrangement, telephone the Minister 01334 828233

CHURCH OF SCOTLAND WC

SPRINGFIELD CHURCH

WEMYSS PARISH CHURCH

428 WEMYSS PARISH CHURCH

NT 340 968

Main Road, East Wemyss

Red sandstone church, 1937, Peter Sinclair. United with West Wemyss and Lower Wemyss in 1976, now known as Wemyss Parish Church. Light oak furnishings, pipe organ, memorial stained glass. Surrounded by gardens with lovely views. A915 Kirkcaldy–Leven. Sunday Service: 11am

Open by arrangement, telephone Mr Barker 01592 714874, or Miss Tod 01592 651495. Open in conjunction with Wemyss Environmental Centre Open Day. Second Sunday each summer month until September 2-4.30pm. Guided parties to famous caves, some with Pictish and Viking markings, and Macduff Castle

CHURCH OF SCOTLAND

429 THE CHURCH AT WEST WEMYSS

NT 328 949

Main Street, West Wemyss

Built in 1890, Alexander Tod, simple crow-stepped cruciform church of pink sandstone. Spiral tracery in the gable's big rose window. Repurchased from the Church of Scotland in 1972 by Captain Michael Wemyss, who agreed to maintain the building externally if the church continued to be used for worship. The congregation of Wemyss Parish Church is responsible for the interior and continuing worship. Beautiful mural by William McLaren on the inner wall of the transept which now accommodates halls, vestry and kitchen. New wall hangings 2001, sewn by members on the theme 'Jesus, Light of the World'. Old graveyard. Signed off A915 Kirkcaldy–Leven. Sunday Service: 9.30am

Open by arrangement, telephone A Tod, Corner Cottage, 40 South Row, Coaltown of Wemyss 01592 651498

CHURCH OF SCOTLAND **A**

WEMYSS PARISH CHURCH

430 ST KENNETH'S PARISH CHURCH, WINDYGATES

No 346 006

Originally the United Free Church built by James McIntosh in 1926.

Sunday Service: 9.45am

Church website: www.stkenneths.freeserve.co.uk

Open by arrangement with Kennoway Parish Church, telephone 01333 351372

CHURCH OF SCOTLAND WC

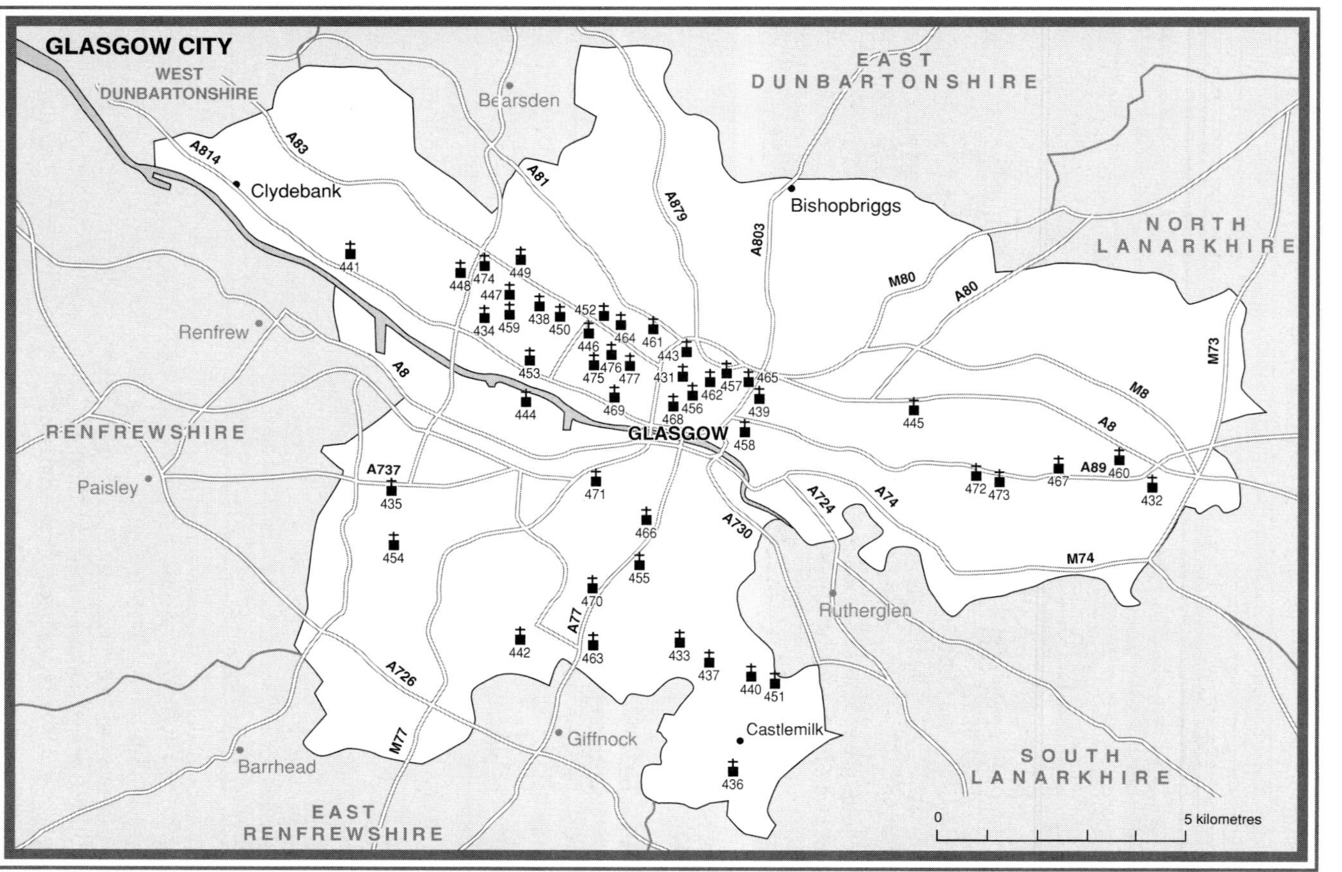
GLASGOW CITY
WEST DUNBARTONSHIRE
EAST DUNBARTONSHIRE
NORTH LANARKHIRE
SOUTH LANARKHIRE
RENFREWSHIRE
EAST RENFREWSHIRE
GLASGOW
Clydebank
Bearsden
Bishopbriggs
Renfrew
Paisley
Rutherglen
Giffnock
Castlemilk
Barrhead
A814
A83
A81
A879
A803
M80
A80
M73
M8
A8
A89
A74
A724
A730
M74
A737
A77
A726
M77
441
448
474
449
447
434
459
438
450
452
446
464
461
443
453
476
475
477
431
462
457
465
439
444
469
456
468
458
445
472
473
467
460
432
435
471
466
454
455
470
442
463
433
437
440
451
436
0
5 kilometres

GLASGOW

Local Representative: Mrs Jane Boyd, Manager, Renfield St Stephen's Church Centre, 260 Bath Street, Glasgow G2 4JP (*telephone:* 0141 332 4293)

ADELAIDE PLACE BAPTIST CHURCH

431 ADELAIDE PLACE BAPTIST CHURCH

NS 584 658

209 Bath Street, Glasgow (corner of Bath Street and Pitt Street)

Built 1877 T L Watson. Stunning redevelopment 1995 of decaying building creating a multi-functional centre including sanctuary, guest house, cafe and nursery. Westbound M8, junction 15 along Cathedral Street and Bath Street. Eastbound M8, junction 19, left into Pitt Street. Sunday Services: 11am; Monthly Evening Services

Church website: www.adelaides.co.uk

Open daily 8am–8pm. Takes part in Glasgow Doors Open Day. Also wide variety of concerts and other events, telephone 0141 248 4970 for details

BAPTIST ♿ 🦻 WC **B**

432 BAILLIESTON ST ANDREW'S CHURCH

NS 681 639

Church Street, Baillieston, Glasgow

Present church completed 1974 following the union of Baillieston Old and Rhinsdale Churches in 1966. Sexagonal design with slim spire, by James Houston & Sons of Kilbirnie. Allen organ installed. Sunday Services: 11am and 6.30pm

Open Monday, Wednesday and Friday 9.30am–12 noon

CHURCH OF SCOTLAND ♿ 🦻

BAILLIESTON ST ANDREW'S CHURCH

433 BATTLEFIELD EAST PARISH CHURCH

NS 586 613

1220 Cathcart Road

The first church on this site was by John Honeyman 1865 in Early English style. It became the hall in 1912 when the adjacent red sandstone church by John Galt was opened. Spacious interior with galleries supported on cast-iron columns and a fine timber wagon roof. Stained glass includes windows by Sadie McLellan (1971) and Susan Laidler (1980). Pipe organ by Ingram of Edinburgh. Near Mount Florida railway station. Sunday Service: 11am; and occasional Evening Service 6.30pm

Open Tuesdays to Fridays 9.30am–12 noon.

Ring bell on door of glass corridor for the Beadle

CHURCH OF SCOTLAND ♿ 👂 WC ☕ **B**

BATTLEFIELD EAST PARISH CHURCH

434 BROOMHILL CHURCH

NS 549 674

Randolph Road, Glasgow

Red sandstone church 1902, and hall 1899, designed by Stewart & Paterson. Stained glass by Guthrie & Wells, Glasgow, Abbey Studio, Edinburgh and Brian Hutchison. Pipe organ refurbished by Harrison and Harrison 1997. Located at corner of Randolph Road/Marlborough Avenue.

City buses: 6, 16, 44.

Sunday Services: 11am and 6.30pm

Open by arrangement, telephone Mr J Boyle 0141 339 2552

CHURCH OF SCOTLAND B

BROOMHILL CHURCH

435 CARDONALD PARISH CHURCH

NS 526 639

2155 Paisley Road West, Glasgow

Opened 1889 as a mission church. This is the first church designed by P MacGregor Chalmers. Early English Gothic of Ballochmyle red sandstone. Stained timber roofs open to the top. Chancel has alabaster and stone pulpit by Jackson Brown & Co and fine workmanship in its oak communion table, reading desk and elders' benches. North wall screen by Ross & Manson. Rich and varied collection of stained glass windows including three-light chancel window by J & W Guthrie, series of six windows by Sadie McLellan, Millennium window (2000) by Roland Mitton. Sunday Services: 11.15am, Communion Sundays 11.15am and 6.30pm

Open Tuesday mornings January to May, September to December 10am–11am. (Viewing by arrangement 11am–12noon) 0141 882 1051. Open daily Christmas week 10am–12noon

CHURCH OF SCOTLAND

WC B

CARDONALD PARISH CHURCH

CARMUNNOCK PARISH CHURCH, 'THE KIRK IN THE BRAES'

436 CARMUNNOCK PARISH CHURCH, 'THE KIRK IN THE BRAES'

NS 599 575

Kirk Road, Carmunnock

Rebuilt 1767 on pre-Reformation site and repaired in 1840. External stone staircases to three galleries. Laird's gallery. Stained glass by Norman Macleod MacDougall. Ancient graveyard has watch-house with original instructions for grave watchers 1828, and burial vault of Stirling-Stuart family, Lairds of Castlemilk. City bus 31. Sunday Service: 11am

Open April to October, Saturday 1.30-3pm. Other times by arrangement, telephone 0141 644 1578. Conducted tours, Sunday 2pm on Glasgow Doors Open Day

CHURCH OF SCOTLAND (in village) **B**

437 CATHCART OLD PARISH CHURCH

NS 587 606

119 Carmunnock Road

Original design 1923 by Clifford & Lunan, but completed 1928 by Watson, Salmon & Gray. The size is enhanced by the low porch and range of vestries. South transept contains a display of the Church's history over 800 years, the north transept was converted in 1962 to the McKellar Memorial Chapel. Tapestry of The Last Supper by Charles Marshall, stained glass by R Douglas McLundie. Organ by John R Miller 1890, restored and converted to electro-mechanical action 1994. Services: Sunday 11am, Thursday 10.45am

Open Monday to Friday 10am–2pm

CHURCH OF SCOTLAND WC **B**

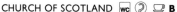

CATHCART OLD PARISH CHURCH

438 CATHEDRAL CHURCH OF ST LUKE

NS 563 675

27 Dundonald Road, Dowanhill, Glasgow

Formerly Belhaven United Presbyterian Church by James Sellars 1877, powerfully vertical Normandy Gothic. The congregation of St Luke's relocated here in 1960. The main front is inspired by Dunblane Cathedral. Marvellous display of stained glass, Stephen Adam 1877, richly stencilled roof timbers, and original light fittings and furniture. Modern iconostasis featuring icons, some of which were painted on Mount Athos in the traditional Byzantine style. Sunday Service: 10.30am-1pm

Open by arrangement, telephone Mr N Pitticas 0141 339 7368

GREEK ORTHODOX **B**

CATHEDRAL CHURCH OF ST LUKE

439 CATHEDRAL CHURCH OF ST MUNGO

NS 603 656

Castle Street, Glasgow

Dedicated in 1136, the largest and most complete of Scotland's medieval cathedrals still in use. Medieval stone screen. Crypt with shrine of St Mungo. Modern tapestry. Sunday Services: 11am and 6.30pm

Open daily, April to September, 9.30am-1pm, 2pm-6pm, Sunday 2-5pm; October to March, 9.30am-1pm, 2pm-4pm, Sunday 2pm-4pm. Light lunches, etc, in adjacent St Mungo's Museum

CHURCH OF SCOTLAND (May to September) **A**

440 CROFTFOOT PARISH CHURCH

NS 603 602

318 Croftpark Avenue, Glasgow

Keppie & Henderson 1936. A neat Byzantine design in red brick with ashlar facings. Carved patterns, symbolising scriptural themes, decorate the main door portico, nave and chancel columns and chancel furnishings. The bell is the Second World War memorial. Ten minute walk from Croftfoot railway station. Sunday Services: 11am and 6.30pm

Open Monday to Friday, 9am-noon, and 1.30pm-4pm, except public holidays.
Tours, telephone Mr W Yule 0141 637 7613

CHURCH OF SCOTLAND

CROFTFOOT PARISH CHURCH

441 DRUMRY ST MARY

NS 515 709

Drumry Road East, Drumchapel

Simple church (Ross, Doak & Whitelaw, 1955-7) with shallow-pitched roof, linked to hall by a vestibule with a bell turret. Contains a 120-year old marble font from Old Partick Parish Church. Main feature is the Garden of Remembrance for Bereaved Parents as designed by and featured in BBC's 'Beechgrove Garden'. Stones in the garden from the 'Peel of Drumry'. Sunday Service: 11am

Church open weeknights evenings; Garden open at all times (access via rear gate)

CHURCH OF SCOTLAND

442 EASTWOOD PARISH CHURCH

NS 558 607

5 Mansewood Road, Glasgow

Built 1863, in transitional Gothic, arranged on a cruciform plan. Designed by Charles Wilson, who died before its completion, assisted by David Thomson. Its stained glass windows include examples by the Königliche Glasmalerei-Anstalt, München (Royal Glass Painting Establishment, Munich) and by Gordon Webster. The family church of the Maxwells of Pollock. Sunday Service: 11.15am

Open by arrangement, telephone 0141 586 6684 or 0141 632 0724

CHURCH OF SCOTLAND **B**

EASTWOOD PARISH CHURCH

443 GARNETHILL SYNAGOGUE

NS 502 661

129 Hill Street, Glasgow

Opened in 1879, the first purpose-built synagogue in Scotland. It was designed by John McLeod of Glasgow in Romanesque-cum-Byzantine style. A round-arched portal with highly decorated orders leads to the body of the synagogue. Ladies' gallery is carried on octagonal piers with ornate Byzantine capitals. Stained glass by J B Bennet & Sons. Refurbished in 1996. From Sauchiehall Street walk up Garnet Street to Hill Street. Services: Saturday 10am, Jewish Festivals 9.30am

Open by arrangement, telephone the caretaker, Mr Gibson, 32 Minerva Street, Glasgow G3 8LD (0141 204 1236). Scottish Jewish Archives open by arrangement, telephone 0141 332 4911

JEWISH (three steps) **B**

GARNETHILL SYNAGOGUE

GOVAN OLD PARISH CHURCH (ST CONSTANTINE'S)

444 GOVAN OLD PARISH CHURCH (ST CONSTANTINE'S)

NS 554 659

866 Govan Road, Glasgow

Affectionately called 'the people's cathedral'. Set well back in a churchyard of great antiquity, the present building is the last in a long series of churches on this site. Completed in 1888, the design by Robert Rowand Anderson proved very influential for the next 50 years. Its style is Early English in the Scottish manner, with details based on Pluscarden Priory near Elgin. A set of twelve windows by Charles E Kempe. Good stained glass by Burlison & Grylls and Clayton & Bell in the Steven Chapel and by Shrigley & Hunt in the baptistry. Archaeological excavation has provided a fresh context for the large collection of early medieval sculpture including hogback stones, cross shafts, cross slabs and the richly ornamented and recently conserved Govan Sarcophagus. Fine pipe organ by Brindley and Foster. City buses and underground to Govan Station. Sunday Service: 11am; Daily Service: Monday to Friday 10am

Open first Wednesday in June to third Saturday in September, Wednesdays 10.30am-12.30pm, and Wednesdays, Thursdays and Saturdays 1-4pm.

Also open by arrangement, telephone 0141 445 1941

CHURCH OF SCOTLAND WC **A**

445 HIGH CARNTYNE PARISH CHURCH

NS 636 653

358 Carntynehall Road, Glasgow

First church extension charge of Church of Scotland. Congregation met in 'the hut' until building was completed by J Taylor Thomson 1932. Original single bell still in use. Extensive suite of halls built alongside the church in 1955. Buses 33, 41, 42, 51. Sunday Service: 11am; Wednesday 9.30am

Open daily 10am-12 noon

CHURCH OF SCOTLAND (by arrangement) WC **B**

HILLHEAD BAPTIST CHURCH

446 HILLHEAD BAPTIST CHURCH

NS 568 671

Cresswell Street, off Byres Road, Glasgow

Designed by T L Watson 1883, in Greek Revival style. The impressive harmony and richness of the original dark woodwork and pews gives an intimacy to this interior where sunlight is filtered through delicately coloured glass. Fine Lewis pipe organ. Near to Botanic Gardens. Sunday Services: 11am and 6.30pm

Open by arrangement, telephone 0141 339 3254

BAPTIST **B**

447 HYNDLAND PARISH CHURCH

NS 559 675

79 Hyndland Road, Glasgow

William Leiper 1887 in red Ballochmyle sandstone. Timber roof and columns with richly carved foliage capitals. Gleaming original terrazzo floor. Original furnishings, Henry Willis pipe organ, and fine stained glass, including windows by Douglas Strachan, Gordon Webster, William Wilson and Sax Shaw. Major refurbishment 1997 including lighting of timber roof. New community window. City buses 44, 59. Also by rail and underground. Sunday Service: 11am October to Easter; 10.30am Easter to October; 6.30pm October to Easter

Open easily by arrangement with church office, telephone 0141 338 6637

CHURCH OF SCOTLAND

 **A**

HYNDLAND PARISH CHURCH

448 JORDANHILL PARISH CHURCH

NS 544 682

28 Woodend Drive, Glasgow

JORDANHILL PARISH CHURCH

Church 1905 and hall, west aisle and gallery 1923 by James Miller in Perpendicular style. Battlemented and pinnacled tower. Mock hammerbeam roof spans the broad interior. Further extensions to hall 1971 and sanctuary refurbishment 1980 by Wylie Shanks. Organ by Lewis 1923. Woodend Drive is off Crow Road (A739 Clyde Tunnel to Bearsden). Sunday Services: 10.30am and 6.30pm (October to June); Wednesday: 10am (September to June)

Open Monday to Friday 8.30am–12.30pm and 1.30pm–5pm

CHURCH OF SCOTLAND WC **B**

449 ST JOHN'S RENFIELD, KELVINDALE

NS 558 683

Beaconsfield Road, Kelvindale, Glasgow

Bold and striking church in a commanding position. Topped by an openwork flèche, the stonework has the understated detail characteristic of its time, 1931 (architect James Taylor Thomson). Light and lofty interior, complete with original fitments, and stained glass by Douglas Strachan and Gordon Webster. Turn off Great Western Road to Kelvindale. Sunday Service: 11am all year; 8.30pm September to Easter, and first Sunday of month Easter to August

Open Wednesday, Thursday, Friday 9.30am–12.30pm

CHURCH OF SCOTLAND WC **B**

450 KELVINSIDE HILLHEAD PARISH CHURCH

NS 567 673

Saltoun Street, Observatory Road, Dowanhill, Glasgow

KELVINSIDE HILLHEAD PARISH CHURCH

1876 by James Sellars, the design is said to have been much influenced by William Leiper. A tall apsed church, the west front is full of carving. The interior was recast in 1921 by P MacGregor Chalmers. Communion table of Rochette marble. Good stained glass by Burne-Jones for William Morris & Co 1893 and Sadie McLellan 1958. Organ by H Willis & Son 1876, restored in 1930. At junction of Saltoun Street with Observatory Road. City buses and underground to Hillhead. Sunday Services: 11am; also October to May 6.30pm

Open Saturday 10.30am–12.30pm all year. Other times, telephone the Minister 0141 339 2865. Venue for many concerts

CHURCH OF SCOTLAND WC **A**

451 KING'S PARK PARISH CHURCH

NS 601 608

242 Castlemilk Road, Glasgow

KING'S PARK PARISH CHURCH

Red brick with stone dressings, Romanesque in style by Hutton & Taylor 1932, an innovation in church design specially evolved by the Presbytery of Glasgow. The commission was the result of an architectural competition. Notable collection of stained glass windows by Sadie McLellan, Gordon Webster, Douglas Hamilton and others. Set in a pleasant small garden. Ample parking. By rail to King's Park or Croftfoot, ten minute walk. First Bus number 7 to Castlemilk Road. Sunday Services: 11am, 6.30pm, (11am only July to August)

Open Monday to Friday 9.30am–12 noon, all year except public holidays. Tours, telephone Mr Ian Henderson 0141 589 5603

CHURCH OF SCOTLAND (on request) (Tues am) WC **A**

452 LANSDOWNE PARISH CHURCH

NS 576 669

416 Great Western Road, Glasgow

Built 1863 to a design by John Honeyman. Spire 218 feet, one of the slimmest in Europe, a powerful landmark on Great Western Road. Box pews. Beautiful stained glass by Alfred and Gordon Webster, and war memorial frieze by Evelyn Beale. Pipe organ 1911, Norman & Beard, said to have the finest tuba rank in Glasgow with some wonderful flutes. On corner with Park Road, opposite Kelvinbridge underground. City buses 20, 41, 59, 66, from city centre. Sunday Service: 11am (creche available)

Open by arrangement. Also Glasgow Doors Open Day, telephone the Minister 0141 339 2794, or Mr J Stuart 0141 339 2678

CHURCH OF SCOTLAND WC **A**

453 PARTICK METHODIST CHURCH

NS 553 666

524 Dumbarton Road

Church and halls by W F McGibbon, opened in 1881. Good stained glass by Abbot & Co 1957. Fine organ by Forster & Andrews, 1886. Organ recitals most Saturday afternoons (contact church to confirm times). Public transport by bus, underground and train. Sunday Service: 11.00am, occasional evening services

Open by arrangement, telephone 0141 334 1181

METHODIST WC

ST JAMES'S PARISH CHURCH, POLLOCK

454 ST JAMES'S PARISH CHURCH, POLLOK

NS 530 626

183 Meiklerig Crescent, Pollok, Glasgow

Church built 1895 as Pollokshields Titwood Church, and moved stone by stone from its original site four miles away by Thomson, McCrae & Sanders, and rededicated in 1953. Congregation worshipped in a school hall and then in a wooden hut until the building was completed. Good stained glass. Bus service 50 from Glasgow city centre. M8, Junction for Paisley Road West. Sunday Service: 11am

Open Saturdays 10am–12 noon. Close to Pollok House, the Burrell Collection, Crookston Castle and Ross Hall

CHURCH OF SCOTLAND WC **B**

455 QUEEN'S PARK BAPTIST CHURCH

NS 579 266

180 Queen's Drive and Balvicar Drive, Glasgow

'QP', an evangelical-charismatic church, is a changing church and recent years have seen significant growth which parallels spiritual renewal in the fellowship, preaching, ministry, outreach and worship. Since October 1995 the church occupies two nearby sites: a Romanesque building (Camphill), McKissack & Rowan 1887; and a French Gothic building (Queen's Drive), William Leiper 1876. The interiors of both buildings have been significantly modernised and renovated to make them relevant places for Christian worship and work in the 21st century. The Camphill building was fully stone cleaned and repaired during 1998–9. Queen's Drive/Pollokshaws Road, two minutes from Queen's Park Station. Sunday Services: 10.30am and 6.30pm

Open Sundays, and other times by arrangement, telephone Dr J Brooks 0141 423 3962

BAPTIST **A** (Camphill) **B** (Queen's Drive) WC

456 RENFIELD ST STEPHEN'S PARISH CHURCH AND CENTRE

NS 582 659

260 Bath Street, Glasgow

Designed as an Independent Chapel by London architect J T Emmett in 1852 in Decorated Gothic style. Built in beautiful polished Kenmure sandstone with tall clerestoried nave supported on clustered columns with finely moulded capitals and arches, each with carved musical angels. The main stained glass windows are by Norman Macdougall 1905 depicting the four evangelists, and representations of Christian vertues, flanking Christ in Glory. There is also a window by John Clark. A Church Centre with Side Chapel, offices, extensive halls and restaurant were added in the 1960s. Patio with fountain from Glasgow garden festival. Following the collapse of the steeple during a storm on St Stephens Day 1998, the church and basement have been sensitively restored and modernised by Hunter and Clark, architects CRGP. Sunday Service: 11am

Open daily 9am-10pm. Oasis Restaurant open 9am-4pm

CHURCH OF SCOTLAND

457 ST ALOYSIUS CHURCH

NS 586 660

25 Rose Street, Glasgow

Fine late-Renaissance style church, designed in 1910 by Belgian-born architect Charles Menart, with a 150ft campanile, domed crossing and ornate marble-lined interior. The church is in the care of the Jesuit Order, and Jesuit saints figure in the stained glass. The shrine of St John Ogilvie SJ is in the east transept, with mosaics depicting his martyrdom in Glasgow in 1615. Near Glasgow School of Art and Sauchiehall Street. Sunday Services: 9am, 10.30am, 12 noon (Sung), and 9pm

website: www.aloyius.glasgow.ukgateway.net

Open daily 7.30am to 6.30pm and on Sunday until 10pm. Full details of services on the website

ROMAN CATHOLIC **A**

ST ALOYSIUS CHURCH

458 ST ALPHONSUS CHURCH

NS 600 646

217 London Road, Glasgow

A late work by Peter Paul Pugin 1905. Rock-faced sandstone screen façade. The tracery in the gable window formalised into a saltire cross. Inside, the nave arcades have polished granite piers. One hundred and fiftieth anniversary commemorative window 1996 by Lorraine Lamond. Church is in the middle of the 'Barras', 500 metres east of Glasgow Cross. Services: Saturday 5pm (Vigil); Sundays 10am, 11am, 12 noon, 4.45pm

Church website: www.alphonsus.fsbusiness.co.uk/home.htm

Open Monday to Friday 12 noon-2pm, Saturday and Sunday 9am-6pm

ROMAN CATHOLIC **B**

459 ST BRIDE'S CHURCH, HYNDLAND

NS 559 676

69 Hyndland Road, Glasgow

Designed by G F Bodley, who built the chancel 1904, the nave 1907 and part of the north aisle. H O Tarbolton completed the church (1913-6) including rebuilding part of the nave, and adding two north aisles and the tower. The interior scheme is mainly Bodley's. Carved woodwork by Scott Morton & Co. Sculpture of Our Lady and Child by Eric Gill, 1915. Two-manual organ by Hill. Sunday Services: Sung Eucharist 10.30am; Daily Eucharist, times vary

Open by arrangement, telephone Mr Rae 0141 332 8430 and Rev R F Jones 0141 334 1401. Occasional Choral Evensong, usually with visiting choirs and concerts as advertised

SCOTTISH EPISCOPAL WC **B**

ST BRIDE'S CHURCH

460 ST BRIDGET'S CHURCH, BAILLIESTON

NS 680 642

15 Swinton Road, Baillieston, Glasgow

Built 1893 by Pugin & Pugin in light sandstone. Notable 'Creation' rose window above sanctuary area and carved 'Christ Triumphant' below. Mosaic work 'Suffer the Children', 'Nativity', 'Glories of Mary', 'Annunciation', and stained glass windows 'Christ with Saints' and 'Sacred Heart' 1945-9 by the John Hardman Studios. 'St Bridget' and 'St Colmcille' windows by Shona McInnes 1999. Located 200 yards west of Edinburgh Road/Coatbridge Road A8/A89. Sunday Services: 9am and 10.30am, 12 and 6pm; Daily Service 9.30am; Saturday 6.30pm.

Open for some hours each day. Otherwise contact Church House adjacent

ROMAN CATHOLIC

ST BRIDGET'S CHURCH, BAILLIESTON

461 ST COLUMBA'S CHURCH

NS 583 671

74 Hopehill Road, Glasgow

By Gillespie, Kidd & Coia, completed in 1941, the year of the Clydebank and Govan blitz, and the cost met by the families of the area, each of whom paid 6d per brick. Italian Romanesque style with an imposing west front. Sculpture of the Paschal Lamb over central door. Painted panels of the Stations of the Cross by Hugh Adam Crawford, from the Catholic Pavilion at the Glasgow Empire Exhibition 1938. In the sanctuary a marble reredos with a carved crucifix by Benno Schotz. North of St George's Cross, via Maryhill Road. Services: Saturday Vigil Mass 6pm; Sunday Mass 11am and 5pm

ST COLUMBA'S CHURCH

Open at any time, by contacting the Priest in the house adjacent

ROMAN CATHOLIC ♿ 🦻 A

462 ST GEORGE'S – TRON PARISH CHURCH

NS 590 655

165 Buchanan Street, Glasgow

Designed by William Stark and completed 1808. Originally St George's Parish Church and the eighth burgh church to be built in Glasgow in what was then the extreme west-end of the city. St George's united with Tron St Anne's in 1940. Baroque-style tower with five stages capped by a ribbed dome and obelisk. Plain, galleried interior with flat ceiling. The Christ-centred life and ministry of the Rev Tom Allan (1955-64) was instrumental in the awakening of the evangelical Christian church in Glasgow and beyond. Sunday Services: 11am and 7pm; Wednesday Prayer Meeting and Bible Study 7.30pm, except May, June and September when House Groups are held

Church website: www.thetron.com

Church open for prayer and meditation Tuesday, Wednesday and Thursday from 12 noon. Other times by arrangement, telephone Mr William Bradford 0141 332 0187

CHURCH OF SCOTLAND ♿ 🦻 A

ST GEORGE'S – TRON PARISH CHURCH

463 ST MARGARET'S, NEWLANDS

ST MARGARET'S, NEWLANDS

NS 569 610

Kilmarnock Road, Newlands, Glasgow

The church, a 'classic of the Romanesque Revival', was designed by Dr Peter MacGregor Chalmers and built in stages between 1910 and 1935. A basilica with double apse, it is splendid in size and simple beauty. The stained glass windows include examples by Morris & Co, the St Enoch Studio and Gordon Webster. Sunday Services: Said Eucharist 9am, Sung Eucharist 10.30am, Evensong 6.30pm; Tuesdays 10am; and Thursdays Said Eucharist 10.30am

Open 9-12noon, Monday to Friday. Other details from church office 0141 636 1131

SCOTTISH EPISCOPAL (Anglican) **B**

464 ST MARY'S CATHEDRAL

NS 578 668

300 Great Western Road, Glasgow

Fine Gothic revival church by Sir George Gilbert Scott with outstanding contemporary murals by Gwyneth Leech and newly restored Phoebe Traquair reredos. Three-manual pipe organ. Glasgow's only full peal of bells. Major restoration 2001. A82, three-quarters of a mile west of St George's Cross. Two minutes walk Kelvinbridge Underground. Sunday Services: Eucharist 8am, Sung Eucharist 10am, Eucharist 12 noon, Choral Evensong 6.30pm

Open daily, 9.30am-5pm

SCOTTISH EPISCOPAL **A**

ST MARY'S CATHEDRAL

465 ST MUNGO'S CHURCH

NS 600 659

Parson Street, Glasgow

Designed by the London architect George Goldie 1869 in French Gothic style. High altar by Gillespie, Kidd and Coia 1952. The church is in the care of the Passionist congregation. Five apsidal chapels include St Paul of the Cross – founder of the Passionists – St Margaret of Scotland, and Our Lady of Sorrows which has a Portuguese polychrome wood statue. Late 19th-century stained glass by Mayer of Munich. Gothic-style timber confessionals. Opposite Charles Rennie Mackintosh's Martyrs School, and five minutes walk from Glasgow Cathedral and the St Mungo Museum. Sunday Services: 10am, 12 noon and 7pm

Open Monday to Friday 9.30am-1pm, 5.30-6.30pm; Saturday 9.30am-1pm, 4.30-8pm; Sunday 9.30am-1pm, 6.30-8pm

ROMAN CATHOLIC **B**

ST MUNGO'S CHURCH

466 ST NINIAN'S CHURCH, POLLOKSHIELDS

NS 582 632

1 Albert Drive, Pollokshields, Glasgow

The foundation stone of St Ninian's was laid on 16 September 1872, and building commenced to a design by David Thomson. Completed in 1877, and extended west in 1887. The apse is decorated with frescoes painted by William Hole 1901, and the charming little sacristy designed by H D Wilson, a member of the congregation, in 1914. Good stained glass including windows by Heaton, Butler & Bayne. The windows in the chancel represent The Gospel Story, by Stephen Adam. Sunday Services: Holy Communion (Said) 8.30am, Sung Eucharist and Sermon 10.15am, Evening Prayer (Said) 6.30pm

Open by arrangement, telephone Mrs Y Grieve 0141 638 7254

SCOTTISH EPISCOPAL (from rear of church, notification needed) **B**

467 ST PAUL THE APOSTLE, SHETTLESTON

NS 653 641

1653 Shettleston Road

Basilican church by Jack Coia 1959. Exterior copper calvary and stations of the cross by Jack Mortimer. Spacious interior with much marble and slate, re-ordered for modern liturgy. Interesting baptistry and a rebuilt organ from Greenlaw Parish Church, Paisley. Services: Daily 9.30am, Saturday 6.30pm, Sunday 9.00am, 10.30am, Family Service 12 noon, Youth Mass 6.30pm

Church website: www16.brinkster.com/saintpauls/index.htm

Parish Feast Day Conversion of St Paul, 25 January.

Open 8am-7.30pm; access to Blessed Sacrament Chapel 8am-7.30pm

ROMAN CATHOLIC WC (adapted in Hall) WC **B**

468 ST VINCENT STREET – MILTON FREE CHURCH

NS 583 656

265 St Vincent Street, Glasgow

Alexander Thomson's masterpiece, distinctive Victorian Presbyterian church, designed in the classical style, and embellished by a unique Thomsonian combination of Egyptian, Indian and Assyrian influences 1859. Owned by Glasgow City Council. Sunday Services: 11am and 6.30pm

Open by appointment. Also Doors Open Day, telephone Mr Sieczowski 0141 649 1563

FREE CHURCH OF SCOTLAND ♿ WC **A**

ST VINCENT STREET – MILTON FREE CHURCH

469 SANDYFORD HENDERSON CHURCH

NS 570 659

13 Kelvinhaugh Street

Early Gothic style 1855 by J T Emmett, completed by John Honeyman. Fine stained glass aisle windows in geometric/floral patterns by Ballantine & Allan, Edinburgh, 1857, and three pictorial west windows by William Wailes, Newcastle, 1859-60. Three-manual 'Father' Willis organ 1866 moved into First World War memorial chancel, added in 1922. Exterior stonework restored in 2000. Sunday Services: 11am and 6.30pm; Wednesday: 7.30pm Prayer and Bible Study

Open by arrangement, telephone Professor A Nash 0141 886 5871

CHURCH OF SCOTLAND WC 👂 **B**

SANDYFORD HENDERSON CHURCH

SHAWLANDS UNITED REFORMED CHURCH, GLASGOW

470 SHAWLANDS UNITED REFORMED CHURCH, GLASGOW

NS 570 622

111 Moss-side Road, Shawlands, Glasgow

Formerly a Churches of Christ church, by Miller & Black 1908, in red sandstone. Open baptistry. From Shawlands Cross 300 yards. Sunday Service: 11am

Open Thursday 10.30-11.30am

UNITED REFORMED

471 SHERBROOKE ST GILBERT'S CHURCH, POLLOKSHIELDS

NS 561 636

240 Nithsdale Road, Pollokshields, Glasgow

The original building by William Forsyth McGibbon was ravaged by fire in 1994, its centenary year. Now the church is restored by James Cuthbertson, architect. The interior features the work of Scottish craftsmen: stained glass windows, inspired by the themes of creation, the Cross and rebirth, by Stained Glass Design Partnership, Kilmaurs; three-manual pipe organ by Lammermuir Pipe Organs; pulpit, tables and font by Bill Nimmo, East Lothian. Close to Dumbreck railway station, and on 59 bus route. Sunday Service: 10.30am

Open by arrangement, telephone the Church Officer 0141 427 1968

CHURCH OF SCOTLAND B

472 SHETTLESTON METHODIST CHURCH

NS 643 642

1104 Shettleston Road, Glasgow

Former Primitive Methodist Church of 1902 which replaced a tin tabernacle of 1889. The Church incorporates windows from the former Parkhead Methodist Church. Opposite Shettleston Police Station. Services: Sunday 11am; Tuesday 10.30am

Church website: zyworld.com/shettlestonmethodist

Open by arrangement, telephone the Church Office 0141 778 5063

METHODIST

SHETTLESTON METHODIST CHURCH

473 SHETTLESTON OLD PARISH CHURCH

NS 649 370

111 Killin Street, Shettleston, Glasgow

Church by W F McGibbon, opened in 1903. Fine collection of stained glass, including windows by Alfred Webster and Gordon Webster. Fine two-manual organ. Train to Shettleston. City buses 30, 61. Sunday Service: 11am

Open by arrangement, telephone the Church Officer 0141 778 2484

CHURCH OF SCOTLAND **B**

474 TEMPLE-ANNIESLAND CHURCH

NS 547 699

869 Crow Road, Glasgow

Red sandstone Gothic-style church built by Badenoch & Bruce 1905. Adjoining hall was original United Presbyterian church built in 1899 by Alexander Petrie. U-plan interior with red pine panelled gallery and pews. War memorial, from Temple Parish Church (united with Temple-Anniesland 1984 and now demolished) with unique clock designed and built 1921 by first minister, Rev J Carswell. Sunday Services: 11am and 6.30pm, July to August 11am only; Thursday: 11am

Open Thursdays 10am-12noon (not July)

CHURCH OF SCOTLAND **B**

TEMPLE-ANNIESLAND CHURCH

475 UNIVERSITY MEMORIAL CHAPEL

NS 568 666

The Square, Glasgow University, Glasgow

1923-27 by Sir J J Burnet in Scots Gothic and in harmony with the University buildings of Sir George Gilbert Scott. The structure is reinforced concrete, faced with stone. Tall interior with sculpture by Archibald Dawson. Ten of the stained glass windows are by Douglas Strachan in a cycle depicting the whole of human life as a spiritual enterprise. Other windows by Gordon Webster and Lawrence Lee. The chapel incorporates the Lion and Unicorn Stair salvaged from the Old College. Sunday Service: 11am; Monday to Friday: 8.45am during term time

Open 9am-5pm Monday to Friday, 9am-noon Saturday. Chapel Choir Service December. Tours available from visitors' centre

ECUMENICAL (all in visitors' centre) **A**

476 WELLINGTON CHURCH

NS 570 667

University Avenue, Glasgow

T L Watson's Roman Classical church with mighty Corinthian columned portico 1884. Renaissance style interior with fine plaster ceilings. Pipe organ Forster & Andrews. Refectory situated in crypt. City buses 44, 59. Underground to Hillhead or Kelvinbridge, ten minutes walk. Sunday Services: 11am and 7pm

Church website: www.wellingtonchurch.co.uk

Open July and August, Saturdays 12 noon-3.00pm. Crypt open, Monday to Friday, during University term. Also Glasgow Doors Open Day

CHURCH OF SCOTLAND (and lunch during term time) WC **A**

WELLINGTON CHURCH

477 WOODLANDS METHODIST CHURCH

NS 576 665

229 Woodlands Road, Glasgow

Built for Swedenborgians by David Barclay 1909 in use by Methodists since 1977. A wide stair leads to the church. Organ 1876 from Cathedral Street Swedenborgian Church, amalgamated with pipes from Willis organ at St John's, Sauchiehall Street. Windows by Guthrie & Wells and George Benson, and war memorial window from St John's. Nearest rail station Charing Cross. Services: Sunday 11am; Last Tuesday of the month 12.30pm

Open by arrangement, telephone the church office 0141 332 7779

METHODIST

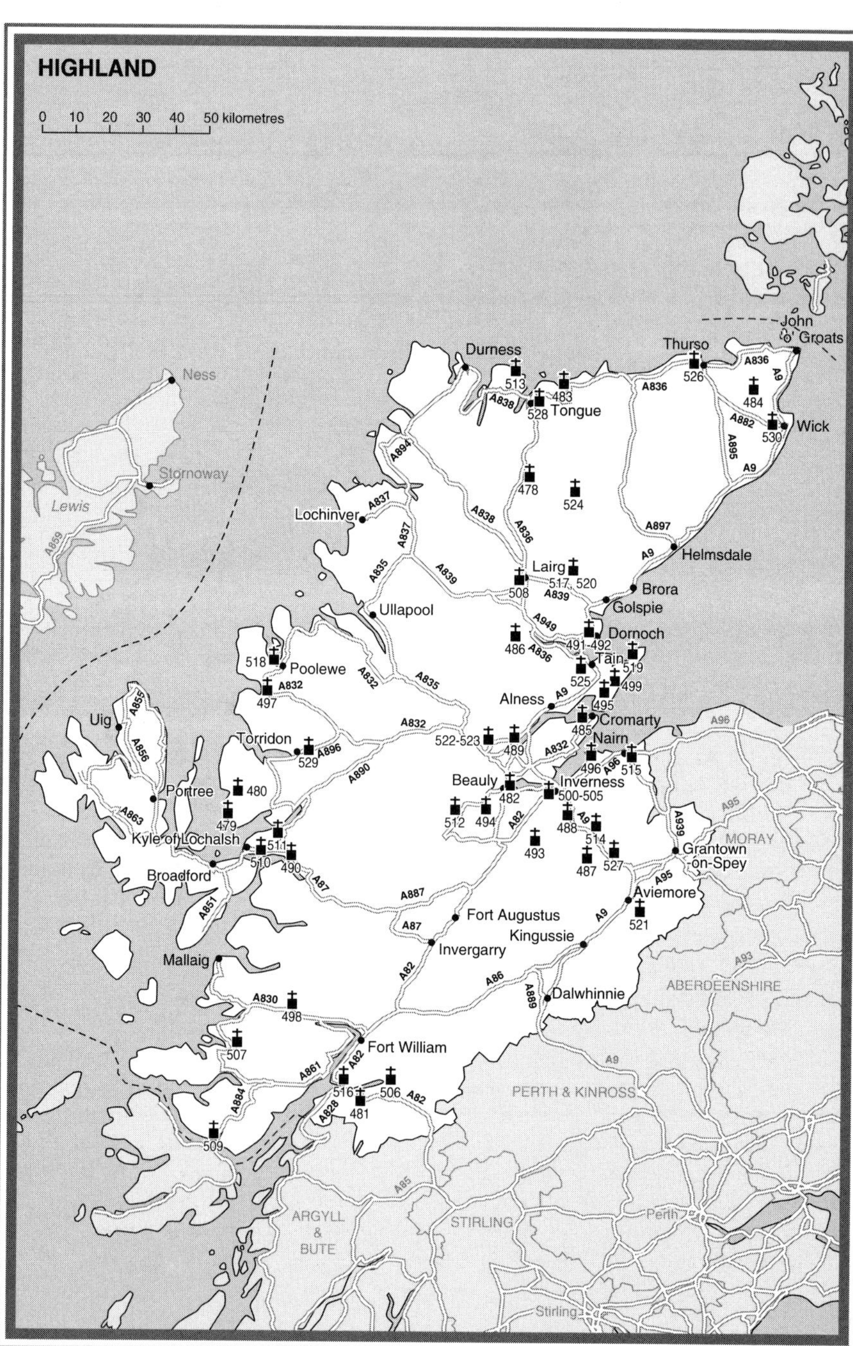

HIGHLAND
0 10 20 30 40 50 kilometres
Durness
513
483
528
Tongue
Thurso
526
John o' Groats
484
530
Wick
478
524
Lochinver
Lairg
508
517, 520
Helmsdale
Brora
Golspie
Ullapool
Dornoch
486
491-492
518
Poolewe
Tain
519
525
499
497
Alness
495
Cromarty
485
Uig
Torridon
529
522-523
489
Nairn
496
515
480
Portree
479
Beauly
482
Inverness
500-505
512
494
488
514
Kyle of Lochalsh
511
510
490
493
487
527
Grantown-on-Spey
Broadford
Aviemore
521
Fort Augustus
Kingussie
Invergarry
Mallaig
Dalwhinnie
498
507
Fort William
516
506
481
509
Ness
Stornoway
Lewis
MORAY
ABERDEENSHIRE
PERTH & KINROSS
ARGYLL & BUTE
STIRLING
Perth
Stirling
A836
A9
A882
A895
A838
A894
A837
A836
A897
A835
A839
A949
A832
A835
A855
A856
A896
A890
A863
A96
A95
A939
A82
A87
A887
A851
A830
A86
A889
A861
A884
A828
A93
A85
A859

HIGHLAND

Local Representatives: Atisha McGregor Auld, Tollie Farm, Poolewe, Ross-shire (*telephone* 01445 781280); and Lyndall Leet, 8 Burnside, Thurso, Caithness (*telephone* 01847 896989)

478 ALTNAHARRA PARISH CHURCH, CAITHNESS

ALTNAHARRA PARISH CHURCH, CAITHNESS

NC 568 355

Half-way between the school and the Telford bridge, the church was built 1854–7 by Hugh MacKay as a Free Church. Fine stonework and interior woodwork. Oil lamps now converted to electricity. Long communion tables between front pews for Communicants to sit at. Stained glass window in memory of Kathleen Joan Kimball. Sunday Service: 3pm on first and third Sundays of each month

Open at all times

CHURCH OF SCOTLAND

479 APPLECROSS CHURCH, ROSS-SHIRE

NG 711 417

Camusterrach, Applecross (two miles towards Toscaig from Post Office)

Plain harled church built 1855 for the Free Church. Became United Free Church in 1900 and Church of Scotland in 1929. Clachan Church (see below) at head of Applecross Bay is also open to visitors. Applecross has connections with 7th-century St Maelrubha. Sunday Services: 12 noon in hall, 6pm in church

Open by arrangement with the Minister, telephone 01520 744263

CHURCH OF SCOTLAND ♿ WC

480 CLACHAN CHURCH, APPLECROSS, ROSS-SHIRE

NG 712 459

Standing on the ancient site of St Maelrubha's church (AD 673), the present church was built in 1817. The beauty and tranquillity of the surroundings complement the quiet simplicity of the plain stone building. To the left of the gate stands a tall, plain slab with an incised Celtic cross, said to mark the grave of Ruairidh Mor MacAogan, abbot of Applecross, who died in AD 801. The remains of carved Celtic crosses, dating from eighth century, are in glass cases. The church is recommended for its simplicity and peace, a fitting heritor of the old Gaelic name of *'A'Chomraich'* - the Sanctuary. No regular services, but used for weddings, funerals and memorial services

Open daily

INTERDENOMINATIONAL **B**

481 ST MUN'S, BALLACHULISH, INVERNESS-SHIRE

NN 083 579

Built 1837 by Bishop Scott, Vicar-Apostolic for West of Scotland. Simple Highland church in good condition. Adjacent building was originally the Priest's house. Sunday Service: 11.00am, daily as announced

Open at all times

ROMAN CATHOLIC WC

ST MUN'S, BALLACHULISH, INVERNESS-SHIRE

482 ST MARY'S CHURCH, BEAULY, INVERNESS-SHIRE

NH 528 467

High Street, Beauly

Nave, chancel and north aisle, and adjoining house, built as a unit in red sandstone 1864, probably by Joseph A Hansom. Nearby the ruins of Beauly Priory, founded for Valliscaulian monks in 1230, maintained by Historic Scotland. Also serves St Mary's, Eskadale. Sunday Mass 11am

Open Easter to September. Other times, call at Priest's house adjoining

ROMAN CATHOLIC **B**

ST MARY'S CHURCH, BEAULY, INVERNESS-SHIRE

483 FARR PARISH CHURCH, BETTYHILL, CAITHNESS

NC 708 622

Built 1909 to a standard design used for United Free Churches in the Highlands. Nearby, at Clachan, stands the old Parish Church, built 1774, now a museum of the Clearances and Clan MacKay. Amongst the gravestones is the Farr Stone, a Christianised Pictish stone. Strathnaver Trail of 29 sites of archaeological, historical and natural heritage interest runs from the museum to Altnaharra. Sunday Service: 11.30am

Open at all times

CHURCH OF SCOTLAND WC

FARR PARISH CHURCH, BETTYHILL, CAITHNESS

484 BOWER PARISH CHURCH, CAITHNESS

ND 238 622

Midway between Thurso and Wick on B876

Built 1847, architect William Davidson. Re-casting and alterations, architect Donald Leed 1902. Finialled and panelled Gothic screen flanks pulpit. Unusual in that two long windows which formerly flanked the pulpit are in the north, not south, wall. Stained glass window dedicated to Sir John Sinclair, seventh Baronet of Dunbeath. Mural memorials to members of Henderson and Sinclair families and plaque in memory of Zachary Pont, minister 1605–13, and his wife Margaret, daughter of John Knox. Ongoing restoration work has uncovered bronze bell from pre-Reformation church. Sunday Service: 12.15pm

Open by arrangement, telephone Mrs McAdie 01955 661252

CHURCH OF SCOTLAND WC **B**

485 EAST CHURCH, CROMARTY, ROSS-SHIRE

NH 791 673

Church Street, Cromarty

Described by John Hume as 'unquestionably one of the finest 18th century parish churches in Scotland'. Starting as a simple east-west rectangle in the late 16th century, the north aisle was added 1739 to create a T-plan church. Further alterations in 1756 and 1798. The interior dates principally from the 18th century with galleries added to accommodate the growing congregation, the most elaborate being the Cromartie loft of 1756. Several fine monuments. Owned and maintained by the Scottish Redundant Churches Trust. Four services during summer months (telephone 01555 666023 for dates) plus occasional services by arrangement

Special events during 2002 to celebrate bi-centenery of the birth of Hugh Miller, telephone 01555 666023 for details. Open 8.30am–5pm (4pm in winter)

CHURCH OF SCOTLAND WC **A**

EAST CHURCH, CROMARTY, ROSS-SHIRE

486 CROICK CHURCH, ARDGAY, SUTHERLAND

NH 457 915

Ardgay, Strathcarron

Harled T-plan 'Parliamentary' Church built by James Smith 1827 from a Thomas Telford design. One of the few Parliamentary churches still in use in its original form. Furnishings virtually unchanged since first built; old-style long communion table and original pulpit. East window has messages scratched in 1845 by evicted inhabitants of Glencalvie. Pictish broch in church glebe. Ardgay is ten miles west of A9/A836 (signed). Sunday Services: second Sunday, May to September, 3pm; Communion second Sunday in July, 3pm

Open during daylight hours

CHURCH OF SCOTLAND **A**

CROICK CHURCH, ARDGAY, SUTHERLAND

487 DALAROSSIE CHURCH, INVERNESS-SHIRE

NH 767 242

3 miles from old A9

Dalarossie Church, on the River Findhorn, is an ancient place of worship dating back to the 8th century – St Fergus. The present building, set within the walled graveyard, dates from 1790 and features an ancient baptismal font as well as a 'covenant stone'. Services: April to October, first and third Sundays 10.30am; November to March, first Sunday 10.30am

Open by arrangement, telephone Rev Lilian M Bruce 01463 772242 or Mrs Vivian Roden 01808 511355

CHURCH OF SCOTLAND (by arrangement) **B**

DALAROSSIE CHURCH, INVERNESS-SHIRE

488 DAVIOT CHURCH, INVERNESS-SHIRE

NH 722 394

On A9, 6 miles south of Inverness

Built in 1826 and restored 1991. There has been a place of worship on the site since early times, long before its charter was granted in the 13th century. The surrounding graveyard tells of the changing history of this interesting parish. Sunday Service: 12noon

Open by arrangement, telephone Rev Lilian M Bruce 01463 772242

CHURCH OF SCOTLAND

(guides by arrangement) **B**

DAVIOT CHURCH, INVERNESS-SHIRE

489 ST JAMES THE GREAT CHURCH, DINGWALL, ROSS-SHIRE

NH 552 588

Castle Street, Dingwall

The building is on the site of an earlier chapel (1806) which was demolished in 1851 and the new building erected to a New Gothic design by J L Pearson. It was consecrated in 1854 but gutted by fire in 1871. Restoration, by Alexander Ross, Inverness, began immediately, following the original design. Sunday Services: 9.30am or 11.30am. Please check notice board

Open daily during daylight hours

SCOTTISH EPISCOPAL WC

ST JAMES THE GREAT CHURCH, DINGWALL, ROSS-SHIRE

490 ST DUTHAC'S CHURCH, DORNIE, ROSS-SHIRE

NG 884 268

Dornie, by Kyle of Lochalsh (beside Eilean Donan Castle)

The first Catholic church on the site was built in 1703. The present building dates from 1860, architect Joseph A Hansom. It is in simple Gothic style with nave and chancel. The stone reredos has polished granite shafts, while similar columns support the altar. The simplicity continues with the demi-octagonal stone pulpit and braced rafter roof. Sunday Service: 10.30am; Saturday Vigil 7.30pm

Open daily

ROMAN CATHOLIC **B**

491 DORNOCH CATHEDRAL, DORNOCH, SUTHERLAND

NH 797 897

High Street, Dornoch

Cathedral founded by Bishop Gilbert de Moravia in 13th century; the first service in the building was held in 1239. The medieval masonry of the chancel and the crossing piers remains mostly intact today. The nave was destroyed by fire in 1570, the transepts and choir were reroofed 1616, and the nave rebuilt 1837. In 1924 the interior stonework was exposed. Lavish display of stained glass, including several windows by James Ballantine, others by Percy Bacon, and the St Gilbert window by Crear McCartney 1989. Sunday Services: all year 11am, summer months 8.30pm

Open during daylight hours

CHURCH OF SCOTLAND **A**

492 ST FINNBARR'S, DORNOCH, SUTHERLAND

NH 799 898

Schoolhill, Dornoch

Simple but picturesque Gothic by Alexander Ross, 1912-3. Stained glass triple lancet east window by Percy Bacon. Of special note are the 70 tapestry kneelers with highland themes executed by 14 members of the congregation between 1981 and 1993. Sunday Services: Holy Eucharist 9.45am, first, third and fifth Sundays of month, 11.30am second and fourth

Open April to October 10am-4pm, at other times by arrangement with Vestry Secretary, telephone 01862 810877

SCOTTISH EPISCOPAL

493 DUNLICHITY CHURCH, DUNLICHITY, INVERNESS-SHIRE

NH 659 327

near Loch Duntelchaig

An ancient place of worship, much earlier than the present building which dates back in part to the 16th century. Many interesting features, including a 1702 handbell, and surrounded by a graveyard of much historical interest, with its own 1759 watch-house. Services: April to October first Sunday 7pm; November to March, first Sunday, 10.45am

Open by arrangement, telephone Rev Lilian M Bruce 01463 772242

CHURCH OF SCOTLAND (guides by arrangement) **B**

494 ST MARY'S CHURCH, ESKADALE, INVERNESS-SHIRE

NH 453 399

A spacious white harled church in a picturesque woodland setting. Built 1826 by the 14th Lord Lovat. Alterations and additions by Peter Paul Pugin 1881. Founder's tomb in the chancel. Lovat family graveyard to the west of the church. The contemporary stable to accomodate horses ridden by those attending Mass, 50m to the west of the church, is an unusual feature. On a minor road on the south east side of the River Beauly. Served by St Mary's, Beauly. Sunday Mass 9am alternate Sundays

Open by arrangement, telephone Mr James Christie 01463 741536

ROMAN CATHOLIC **B**

495 FEARN ABBEY, ROSS-SHIRE

NH 837 773

Hill of Fearn

Known as 'The Lamp of the North', it is one of the oldest pre-Reformation Scottish churches still in use for worship. Rebuilt 1772 by James Rich and restored by Ian G Lindsay & Partners 1972. Further restoration in summer 2001. Originally a monastery of Premonstratensian monks of the Order of St Augustine. Patrick Hamilton, burnt for heresy at St Andrews in 1528, was the Commendatory Abbot from 1517 to 1528. A9, Hill of Fearn Village. Sunday Service: 11.30am

Open daily Easter to September, 10am-4.30pm, or by appointment, telephone Mr J Maxwell 01862 871247

CHURCH OF SCOTLAND WC **A**

FEARN ABBEY, ROSS-SHIRE

496 FORT GEORGE CHAPEL, INVERNESS-SHIRE

NH 761 567

Fort George, Ardersier

The garrison chapel built in 1767, probably to a design by William Skinner. Interior, two-tiered arcade on three sides supported by Roman Doric columns. Eighteenth-century three-decker pulpit. Working garrison. Visitor displays, Historic Scotland. Off A96, north-east of Inverness

Open April to September, Monday to Saturday 9.30am-6.30pm, Sunday 9.30am-6.30pm; October to March, Monday to Saturday 9.30am-4.30pm, Sunday 2-4.30pm

NON-DENOMINATIONAL **A**

FORT GEORGE CHAPEL, INVERNESS-SHIRE

497 GAIRLOCH FREE CHURCH, GAIRLOCH, ROSS-SHIRE

NG 804 761

On a commanding site overlooking Loch Gairloch. Gothic in style, to a design by Matthews & Lawrie 1881. Simple interior with original fittings and Gothic panelled gallery across east end. Spandrels of roof trusses with cusped decoration. Fabric appeal. A832 to Gairloch. Sunday Services: 11am and 5pm. Gaelic Service: 12noon alternate Sunday

Open by arrangement, telephone the Minister 01445 712371

FREE CHURCH OF SCOTLAND [wheelchair] [book] [WC] **C**

498 ST MARY AND ST FINNAN CHURCH, GLENFINNAN, INVERNESS-SHIRE

NM 904 808

The church was consecrated in 1873. Designed by E Welby Pugin in the Gothic style, the church enjoys an elevated and commanding position overlooking Loch Shiel with a spectacular view of the loch and surrounding hills. The church is a memorial chapel to the MacDonalds of Glenaladale, the family with whom Bonnie Prince Charlie stayed prior to the raising of the Jacobite standard at Glenfinnan in August 1745. The church contains memorial stones to the Prince and to members of the MacDonald family. In the village, 15 miles west of Fort William on A830 to Mallaig. Sunday Mass 1pm

Open daily sunrise to sunset

ROMAN CATHOLIC **B**

ST MARY AND ST FINNAN CHURCH, GLENFINNAN, INVERNESS-SHIRE

499 INVER MEETING HOUSE, INVER, ROSS-SHIRE

NH 863 828

New Street, Inver

A meeting house in the style of cottages. Inver, largely in original form, originates as a settlement of persons displaced during clearances. Memorial, to north of village on the shore, marks common grave of cholera victims, a large proportion of the population. Sunday Service: 10am

Open by appointment, telephone Mr Skinner 01862 871522

CHURCH OF SCOTLAND

500 OLD HIGH CHURCH, INVERNESS

NH665 455

Church Street, Inverness

Present building completed 1772 to a plan by George Fraser of Edinburgh on site of medieval church. Traditionally thought to be the site where St Columba converted Brude, King of the Picts, to Christianity. Porches, apse and chancel arch date from 1891, to designs by Ross & Macbeth. Lowest portion of the west bell-tower is 15th or 16th century. The colours of the Queen's Own Cameron Highlanders are hung and the Regiment's Books of Remembrance are housed in the church. Two-manual organ by Henry Willis & Sons 1895, rebuilt by H Hilsdon 1923. Stained glass by, amongst others, Douglas Strachan 1925, Stephen Adam & Co 1893, and A Ballantine & Gardiner 1899. Sunday Service: 11.15am all year; mid-June to mid-September Fridays 1pm-1.15pm

Open June, July and August, Fridays noon-2pm. Guided tour at 12.30pm

CHURCH OF SCOTLAND A

OLD HIGH CHURCH, INVERNESS

501 ST ANDREW'S CATHEDRAL, INVERNESS

NH 664 450

Ardross Street, Inverness

One of the first new cathedrals completed in Great Britain after the Reformation 1869, by local architect Alexander Ross. Polished granite pillars, stained glass, fine furnishings. Angel font after Thorvaldsen. Founder's memorial, ikons presented by Tsar of Russia. Peal of bells. Fine choir. On west bank of River Ness, just above Ness Bridge, A862, close to town centre. Sunday Services: Eucharist 8.15am, Family Eucharist 9.30am, Sung Eucharist 11am, Choral Evensong 6.30pm; Matins, Eucharist and Evensong daily

Open daily 8.30am-6pm (later June to September)

SCOTTISH EPISCOPAL May to September WC A

502 ST MARY'S CHURCH, INVERNESS

NH 662 455

30 Huntly Street, Inverness

On the west bank of the River Ness, very close to the city centre. Built 1837 by William Robertson in Gothic Revival manner. Re-decorated recently and new stained-glass window installed to mark the Millennium and the Great Year of Jubilee. Sunday Services: Mass 10am and 6.30pm; Vigil Mass Saturday 7pm (June to September)

Open daily, summer 9am-6pm, winter 9am-3pm

ROMAN CATHOLIC ♿ 🦻 **A**

503 ST MICHAEL & ALL ANGELS, INVERNESS

NH 659 457

Abban Street/Lochalsh Road, Inverness

In 1877 Canon Edward Medley established a mission in the thatched cottage at Maggot Green, close to River Ness: a church was built in 1886 to a design by Alexander Ross. As the site proved liable to flooding, it was re-built in extended form in Abban Street in 1903-4, also by Ross. Many interior fittings, altar with gilded angels and tester, font with lofty steeple cover and archangel east window were designed by Sir Ninian Comper and installed between 1904-1928. Situated close to the town centre, by the riverside, to the north-west of Friar's Bridge. Sunday Services: Sunday Low Mass 8am, Parish Mass 11am, Low Mass daily

Open daily 9am-4pm. Other times, telephone Canon Black 01463 233797

SCOTTISH EPISCOPAL ♿ WC **B**

ST MICHAEL & ALL ANGELS, INVERNESS

504 ST STEPHEN'S, INVERNESS

NH 672 449

Southside Road, Inverness

By W L Carruthers 1897 in Arts and Crafts Gothic, the hall added later. The church consists of a nave, single north transept and an apsidal chancel. Square tower with a delicate needle spire. High open roof, pulpit of locally grown native oak. Noteworthy stained glass of 1897 and 1906 by A Ballantine & Son. Two-manual organ by Wadsworth Bros 1902. Substantially renovated in 2000 by Sandy Edmonstone. At junction of Old Edinburgh Road and Southside Road. Sunday Service: 10am; Evening Communion 8pm Easter Sunday, fourth Sunday of June and last Sunday of January and September

Open by arrangement, telephone the Minister 01463 237129

CHURCH OF SCOTLAND ♿ 🦻 WC **B**

ST STEPHEN'S, INVERNESS

505 TWEEDMOUTH MEMORIAL CHAPEL, INVERNESS

NM 663 445

Royal Northern Infirmary, Ness Walk, Inverness

Earliest example of purpose-built ecumencial worship space in Scotland, built in 1898, architect A Ross and R B MacBeth. Three sanctuary areas for Reformed, Roman Catholic and Episcopalian worship. Sunday Service: 2.30pm; Monday: 3.30pm

Keys available from Hospital Porters

INTERDENOMINATIONAL ♿ WC 🦻 **A**

TWEEDMOUTH MEMORIAL CHAPEL, INVERNESS

506 KINLOCHLEVEN PARISH CHURCH, INVERNESS-SHIRE

NS 187 621

Riverside Road, Kinlochleven

Built 1930 to a simple but elegant design by J Jeffrey Waddell with a high arch at the chancel end. Chancel area is a round bell-shape with stained glass windows depicting biblical scenes. Two stained glass windows in the south wall of the nave depicting St Andrew and St George. Linked with Nether Lochaber in 1981. A82 from Glencoe. Sunday Services: 10am and 6.30pm

Keys available from 15 Wades Road, Kinlochleven

CHURCH OF SCOTLAND

KINLOCHLEVEN PARISH CHURCH, INVERNESS-SHIRE

507 ST FINAN'S CHURCH, KINLOCHMOIDART, INVERNESS-SHIRE

NM 710 728

The church stands on a ledge of level ground in woodland above the mouth of the River Moidart and below an impressively steep hillside. It was built in 1857 to a design by Alexander Ross in simple Early English style, with crow stepped gables, a small belfry and a porch. There are two unusual stained glass windows by the Victorian artist Jemima Blackburn. Up a track leading off the A861, half-mile north of the bridge over the River Moidart. Services: Christmas, Easter and Sundays, May to September 5.30pm

Open daily

SCOTTISH EPISCOPAL **C**

508 LAIRG PARISH CHURCH, SUTHERLAND

NC 583 065

Church Hill Road, Lairg

A simple Gothic church, built of local granite 1847, designed by William Leslie. The graveyard, one and a half miles away, served the original church and contains some interesting monuments, including a large marble monument to Sir James Matheson of Achany. Linked with St Callan's, Rogart and Pitfure. Sunday Service: 10.45am; also 6.30pm on first Sunday of month

Open by arrangement, telephone Rev J Goskirk 01549 402373. Adjacent church hall (built 1998) has level access and adapted toilets

CHURCH OF SCOTLAND 

509 KIEL CHURCH, LOCHALINE, INVERNESS-SHIRE

NM 972 538

Lochaline, Morvern

The present church is the third on this site. Ruins of a medieval church are on the site of the original and much earlier building which, according to legend, was erected at the command of St Columba. Today's church was designed by P MacGregor Chalmers 1898. Interesting stained glass. Memorial plaque to the MacLeods, father and son, whose ministry here spanned more than a century. Fifteenth-century cross outside the front of the church. The nearby 18th-century Session House contains a collection of carved stones 8th to 16th centuries. One mile out of the village on the Drimnin road. Sunday Service: 11am

Open daily all year

CHURCH OF SCOTLAND C

510 ST DONNAN'S, LOCHALSH

NG 855 272

Nostie, by Lochalsh

Unassuming, simple church by Stevenson & Dunworth 1962-4. East wall inside is patterned with panels inset with stones from the Nostie Burn. The angels on the altar pedestal were carved by F R Stevenson. Sunday Service: 10.30am

If church is locked, key obtainable from Mrs C Dodds, Fernfield, Nostie (opposite the church)

SCOTTISH EPISCOPAL WC

511 LOCHCARRON PARISH CHURCH (WEST CHURCH), ROSS-SHIRE

NG 893 391

Former United Free Church designed by William Mackenzie 1910, sited in centre of Lochcarron. Crisply painted; standard UF layout. Also of interest the burial ground one mile east of the village with roofless former parish church (1751), superseded by neighbouring big, white-harled East Church (1834-6), James Smith, architect. Open during summer months. Services (West church only): every Sunday 11am, and second and fourth Sunday 6pm

Open during daylight hours

CHURCH OF SCOTLAND (after services) WC

OUR LADY AND ST BEAN, MARYDALE, CANNICH, INVERNESS-SHIRE

512 OUR LADY AND ST BEAN, MARYDALE, CANNICH, INVERNESS-SHIRE

NH 342 317

Simple stone church in Gothic style, with adjoining presbytery, walled garden, school and schoolhouse, built as a unit by Joseph A Hansom 1868. The church has nave and apse with a porch and circular bell-tower. St Bean is said to have been a monk of Iona, a cousin of St Columba, and the first to evangelise Strathglass. Sputan Bhain (NH 334 305) was the spring at which he baptised. On the other side of the road is Clachan Comair, a walled graveyard with the ruins of a small 17th-century church, on the site of an early 10th-century chapel dedicated to St Bean. In 1998 a new altar was installed made from solid 300 year old oak, designed by local artist Alistair MacPherson. The former presbytery is being developed as a monastic retreat, with an icon painting workshop. On the north side of the A831, between Cannich Bridge and Comar Bridge. Mass 5pm Saturdays (Vigil)

Church website: www.sanctiangeli.org

Open daily

ROMAN CATHOLIC WC **B**

513 MELNESS CHURCH, SUTHERLAND

NC 586 634

Near Talmine, 4 miles from junction with A838 (Tongue-Durness)

Built at the turn of the 20th century by local craftsmen to replace an earlier building at an adjacent site. Interior totally wood lined. Local feeling was that it should have been called the 'Kerr Memorial Church' as it was due to the Minister at the time, Rev Cathel Kerr, that the church was completed. Sunday Service: 12.30pm (Holy Communion held twice yearly)

Open at all times

CHURCH OF SCOTLAND WC

514 MOY CHURCH, INVERNESS-SHIRE

NH 772 342

On old A9, 13 miles south of Inverness

Built in 1765, on a previous site, and surrounded by an interesting graveyard with its own watch-house. Memorial stone to Donald Fraser, the hero of the 'Rout of Moy', just before the Battle of Culloden in 1746. Services: April to October fourth Sunday, 10.45am; November to March third and fifth Sunday, 10.45am

Open by arrangement, telephone Rev Lilian M Bruce 01463 772242 or Mrs Vivian Roden 01808 511355

CHURCH OF SCOTLAND

(by arrangement) **B**

MOY CHURCH, INVERNESS-SHIRE

515 NAIRN OLD PARISH CHURCH, NAIRN

NH 879 564

Academy Street/Inverness Road, Nairn

Considered the finest structure in the area, 1897 by John Starforth. Architecture of Early English Transition period, Gothic reminiscences are abundant. Transeptal in form but almost circular in shape. Square tower is almost 100ft high. Lovely light interior. Glorious stained glass. Sunday Service: 10.30am

Open weekdays 9.30am-12.30pm

CHURCH OF SCOTLAND WC **A**

516 NETHER LOCHABER PARISH CHURCH, ONICH, INVERNESS-SHIRE

NN 031 614

Onich, nr Fort William

Built in 1911 to replace original Telford church at Creag Mhor, using some of the original stone. Known as one of the finest rural churches in the Highlands. Most illustrious minister was Dr Alexander Stewart 1851-1901, known as 'Nether Lochaber' and renowned throughout the Celtic world for his wide-ranging learning and writing. Celtic cross, 20 ft, erected by the Stewart Society at Innis-na Bhirlin cemetery off A82 five miles north of Onich. Linked with Kinlochleven 1981. Church located on A82 in Onich village eleven miles south of Fort William. Sunday Service: 12 noon

Keys available from Tigh-na-Mara, Onich

CHURCH OF SCOTLAND

NETHER LOCHABER PARISH CHURCH, ONICH, INVERNESS-SHIRE

517 PITFURE CHURCH, ROGART, SUTHERLAND

NC 710 038

A simple, pleasant place to worship. Built by the United Free congregation in 1910, architect Robert J Macbeth, Inverness. Linked with Lairg and St Callan's Rogart. Sunday Service: first, third and fifth Sundays of month, October to May 12.15pm; June to September 11.30am. Second Sunday of month 6.30pm

Open by arrangement, telephone Rev J Goskirk 01549 402373

CHURCH OF SCOTLAND

518 ST MAELRUBHA'S, POOLEWE, ROSS-SHIRE

NG 857 807

St Maelrubha's Close, Poolewe

The first Episcopal church to be built on the NW coast of Scotland since the Jacobite rebellion of 1745, St Maelrubha's (a former cow byre) was dedicated in 1965. Tiny, simple and made of local stone, it houses a fragment of the Celtic cross erected as a monument to the Saint and brought from Applecross. Memorial to the Highland Fieldcraft Training Centre. Visiting clergy take Sunday Services: during the summer. Close to Inverewe Gardens (National Trust for Scotland). Sunday Service: 11am; Wednesday 10am

Open during daylight hours

SCOTTISH EPISCOPAL

519 PORTMAHOMACK CHURCH, ROSS-SHIRE

NH 917 846
Off Main Street
Simple rectangular former United Free Church building, architects Andrew Maitland & Sons 1908. Flower Festival during Gala Week (last in July). Tarbat Discovery Centre (former Tarbat Old Parish Church) has displays of church and archaeology, including Pictish stones, and place for private prayer in crypt. Adjacent archaeological dig ongoing.
Sunday Service: 11.30am
Please ask for key at Village Shop (50m), shop hours only
CHURCH OF SCOTLAND WC

PORTMAHOMACK PARISH CHURCH, ROSS-SHIRE

520 ST CALLAN'S CHURCH, ROGART, SUTHERLAND

NC 715 038
Rebuilt in 1777 on the site of a medieval church. The austere whitewashed exterior with its plain sash windows gives little hint of the warm, gleaming interior. A high canopied pulpit stands against the east wall. Long communion table and pews. Other pews are tiered from the entrance to the west end. Two small stained glass memorial windows on either side of the pulpit – Nativity and Penitence by Margaret Chilton and Marjorie Kemp 1929. Modern vestry wing built in 1984. From crossroads at Pittentrail, take Rhilochan/Balnacoil road. Church on right approximately two miles. Linked with Lairg and Pitfure.
Sunday Service: second and fourth Sundays of month, October to May 12.15pm; June to September 11.30am
Open by arrangement, telephone Rev J Goskirk 01549 402373
CHURCH OF SCOTLAND WC **B**

521 ST JOHN THE BAPTIST CHURCH, ROTHIEMURCHUS INVERNESS-SHIRE

NH 900 111
Church founded by John Peter Grant, 11th Laird of Rothiemurchus 1930. Architect, Sir Ninian Comper. A simple white interior with a groin vaulted ceiling and a rose damask baldacchino. Simple burial ground surrounds the church. Approximately one mile from the centre of Aviemore, 'the little white church on the ski road'. Sunday Service: Holy Eucharist 10.30am
Open by arrangement, contact the Rectory, Inverdruie 01479 811433
SCOTTISH EPISCOPAL **B**

ST JOHN THE BAPTIST CHURCH, ROTHIEMURCHUS, INVERNESS-SHIRE

522 FODDERTY & STRATHPEFFER PARISH CHURCH, ROSS-SHIRE

NH 482 480

Strathpeffer

Designed by William C Joass and built 1888–90 as part of the development of Strathpeffer as Britain's most northerly Spa town. A rectangular building with side aisles and balcony to the rear; the chancel extends from the nave under a low roof. Services: Sunday 11.00am; also last Sunday in the month April to October 8.00pm

Open by arrangement, telephone the Minister on 01997 421398

CHURCH OF SCOTLAND WC

FODDERTY & STRATHPEFFER PARISH CHURCH, ROSS-SHIRE

523 ST ANNE'S CHURCH, STRATHPEFFER, ROSS-SHIRE

NH 483 580

Designed by John Robertson as a memorial to Anne, Duchess of Sutherland and Countess of Cromartie, it was constructed between 1890 and 1892 with the chancel added in 1899. The pulpit is of Caen stone and alabaster, the altar and reredos of marble and alabaster showing carved reliefs. Stained glass windows are by J Powell & Sons 1891 and Heaton, Butler & Bayne 1892–c.1910. Sunday Service: 9.30am or 11am. Please check notice board

Open daily, Easter to September

SCOTTISH EPISCOPAL **B**

ST ANNE'S CHURCH, STRATHPEFFER, ROSS-SHIRE

524 STRATHNAVER PARISH CHURCH, SYRE, SUTHERLAND

NC 694 439

Junction of Kinbrace and Syre roads

Built 1901 as a mission station from Altnaharra. Neat and tiny corrugated iron church lined with wood. Plaque in memory of the Rev Robert Sloan, Minister 1969-74. Other Ministers are buried in the modern cemetery across the road. Nearby is the Rossal clearance village, maintained by the Forestry Commission, and Patrick Sellar's House. Sunday Service: on the second, fourth and fifth Sundays of each month 3pm

Open at all times

CHURCH OF SCOTLAND **C**

STRATHNAVER PARISH CHURCH, SYRE, SUTHERLAND

ST ANDREW'S CHURCH, TAIN, ROSS-SHIRE

525 ST ANDREW'S CHURCH, TAIN, ROSS-SHIRE

NH 777 822

Manse Street, Tain

Designed 1887 by Ross & Macbeth, replacing an earlier corrugated iron structure. The earliest stained glass, by Ballantyne and Gardner, was moved from the earlier church. Other glass by A L Ward 1910, and W Wilson 1955 and 1961. Fine organ by Hamilton & Muller, restored 1986. Forward altar designed and carved from American oak by Peter Bailey of Skye 1995. Services: Sunday Eucharist 11.15am; first Sunday of every month Matins 10am; Thursday Eucharist 6pm

Church website: www.moray.anglican.org

Open 10am-4 pm

SCOTTISH EPISCOPAL WC **B**

526 ST PETER'S & ST ANDREW'S CHURCH, THURSO, CAITHNESS

ND 115 684

Princes Street, Thurso

Built in 1832 to a design by William Burn, the church is the centre point of the town, fronted by town square garden and war memorial. U-plan gallery. Pipe organ, Norman & Beard 1914. Stained glass includes 'The Sower' by Oscar Paterson 1922. Sunday Services: 11am and 6.30pm

Open July to August daily, 2-4pm, 7-8pm

CHURCH OF SCOTLAND WC **B**

ST PETER'S & ST ANDREW'S CHURCH, THURSO, CAITHNESS

527 TOMATIN CHURCH, INVERNESS-SHIRE

NH 803 290

On east side of old A9 in village of Tomatin

A fine example of the 'tin churches' erected c.1910 by the United Free Church to serve as mission churches and halls in areas of new population. Services: April to October, second and fifth Sundays 10.30am; November to March, second and fourth Sundays 10.30am

Open by arrangement, telephone Rev Lilian M Bruce 01463 772242 or Mrs Vivian Roden 01808 511355

CHURCH OF SCOTLAND (by arrangement)

TOMATIN CHURCH, INVERNESS-SHIRE

ST ANDREW'S PARISH CHURCH, TONGUE, SUTHERLAND

528 ST ANDREW'S PARISH CHURCH, TONGUE, SUTHERLAND

NC 591 570

Tongue

Rebuilt by Donald Mackay, Master of Reay, in 1680 following the Reay family's conversion to Protestantism (c.1600). The site was that of the ancient Celtic and latterly Roman Catholic Church (St Peter's Chapel). During a renovation in 1729, a vault was built covering the graves of earlier members of the MacKay family. Information leaflets are available free in the church. The church is on the Durness road (A838) past Tongue Hotel. Sunday Service: 11.00am

Open all year, daylight hours

CHURCH OF SCOTLAND **A**

529 CORRY CHURCH, TORRIDON, ROSS-SHIRE

The architect for Corry Church was Alexander Ross. The church was built near the head of Loch Torridon, originally as a Free Church, in 1887 in the local red sandstone inside and out. Splendid views all around of the majestic Torridon mountains. Sunday Service: 12.15pm May to September

Open May to September. At other times,
contact Keyholder, telephone 01445 791323

CHURCH OF SCOTLAND

530 ST JOHN THE EVANGELIST, WICK, CAITHNESS

ND 363 505

Francis Street/Moray Street

Built 1870 to a design Alexander Ross of Inverness, St John's is especially attractive with a warm friendly atmosphere. Four-light windows known affectionately as the 'I am' windows ('I am the Good Shepherd, … the Resurrection and the Life, … the True Vine, … the Bread of Life'), by David Gulland, a former member of the vestry of St John's and a recognised expert in glass. Sunday Service: Sung Eucharist 11.30am

Open by arrangement with Peter MacDougall, telephone 01955 602914

SCOTTISH EPISCOPAL **B**

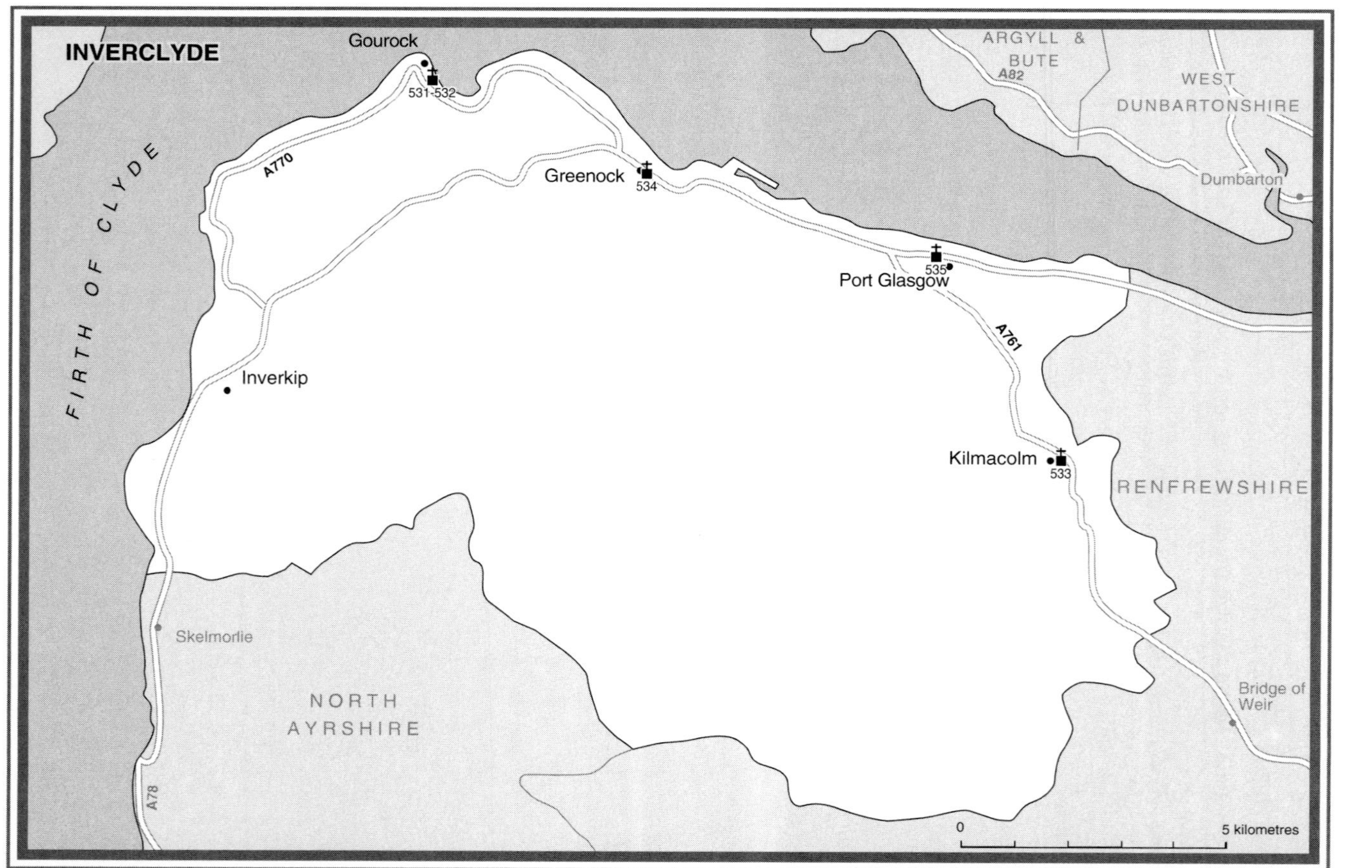

INVERCLYDE
Gourock
531-532
A770
Greenock
534
Port Glasgow
535
A761
Kilmacolm
533
Inverkip
FIRTH OF CLYDE
ARGYLL & BUTE
A82
WEST DUNBARTONSHIRE
Dumbarton
RENFREWSHIRE
Bridge of Weir
NORTH AYRSHIRE
Skelmorlie
A78
0
5 kilometres

INVERCLYDE

Local Representative: Mr Ian Milne, 5 Robertson Street, Greenock (*telephone* 01475 796331)

531 ST BARTHOLOMEW'S, GOUROCK

NS 239 777

Barrhill Road, Gourock

This beautiful little church sits on a cliff overlooking the River Clyde. Designed by J C Sharp of Gourock 1867. Chancel extension enhanced by a beautiful window depicting the Ascension designed by George Walton. Mural of the Nativity on the west wall. Memorial lectern and font. Plaque of Dutch tiles in remembrance of the hospitality given to Dutch soldiers, sailors and airmen during the Second World War. Sunday Service: Sung Eucharist 10.30am; Wednesday and Saints' Days Holy Eucharist 10.30am

Open by arrangement contact Mrs Boeker telephone 01475 521411

SCOTTISH EPISCOPAL WC B

ST BARTHOLOMEW'S, GOUROCK

532 ST NINIAN'S CHURCH, GOUROCK

NS 242 777

18 Royal Street, Gourock

Gourock formed part of the pre-Reformation parish of Inverkip, mentioned in Papal registers of 1216-27. In 1878 Archbishop Eyre of Glasgow arranged for the construction of a chapel-school to be dedicated to St Ninian. The foundation stone was laid in 1879. Extension carried out in 1982 for the visit to Scotland of Pope John Paul II. The altar contains marble from the papal altar at Bellahouston. Mosaics by Frank Tritschler, stained glass by Dom Ninian Sloan of Pluscarden Abbey, and a chasuble fashioned from an original Paisley shawl by Debbie Gonet. Small museum. Sunday Mass: 9.30am and 11.30am; Daily 10am and Vigil Mass Saturday 5.30pm

Church website: //website.lineone.net/~st.ninians

Open daily 9am-4pm. Information leaflets in French, Spanish, Italian and German – children's worksheets also available. For access to museum, telephone Parish Priest 01475 632078 or fax 01475 631984

ROMAN CATHOLIC WC

ST NINIAN'S CHURCH, GOUROCK

533 KILMACOLM OLD KIRK

NS 359 670

Built in 1830 James Dempster, Greenock, on the site of 13th and 16th-century churches. Thirteenth-century chancel is incorporated as the Murray Chapel. South aisle, J B Wilson, Glasgow, added 1903 contains stained glass window by C E Moira. Other stained glass by Norman Macdougall. Near centre of village, west of junction of B786 with A761. Sunday Service: 11am, July and August 10am

Open daily 10am–4pm

CHURCH OF SCOTLAND WC B

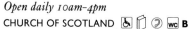

KILMACOLM OLD KIRK

534 THE OLD WEST KIRK, GREENOCK

NS 279 765

Esplanade, Greenock

Cruciform church first built 1591 at Westburn, but rebuilt here (1926-8) with a new tower designed by James Miller. The masonry, window tracery and balustraded forestair are all original. Also brought from the old site are the surrounding headstones and graveslabs, some bearing trade emblems or coats of arms. Inside the church are galleries originally intended to be occupied by the laird, the sailors and the farmers of the parish. Notable collection of stained glass including windows by Morris & Co and Daniel Cottier. Behind the octagonal pulpit is a mural panel by the local artist Ian Philips 1991. Sunday Service: 11am

Church website:www.greenockoldwestkirk.freeserve.co.uk

Open Wednesdays mid-May to mid-September from 10.30am-12noon. Second Saturday, September 10am-4pm (Inverclyde Doors Open Day). Other times by contacting Rev Ian Johnson 01475 888277

CHURCH OF SCOTLAND **B**

535 ST JOHN THE BAPTIST, PORT GLASGOW

NS 319 746

Shore Street, Port Glasgow

Built 1864 with pinnacles rising from the buttressed gable front. Refurbished 2000. Stained glass including 'The Risen Christ' above the main door by Edward Harkness. Fresco of St Thérèse above Sacristy door by George Duffy. Services: Sunday 9.30 and 11.00 am; Monday Mass 9.30 am; Tuesday Mass 6.30 pm; Wednesday to Friday Mass 9.30am; Saturday Mass 10.00am, Vigil Mass 6.00pm

Church website: www.portglasgow.com/stjohns

Open by arrangement with Housekeeper, telephone 01475 741139

ROMAN CATHOLIC

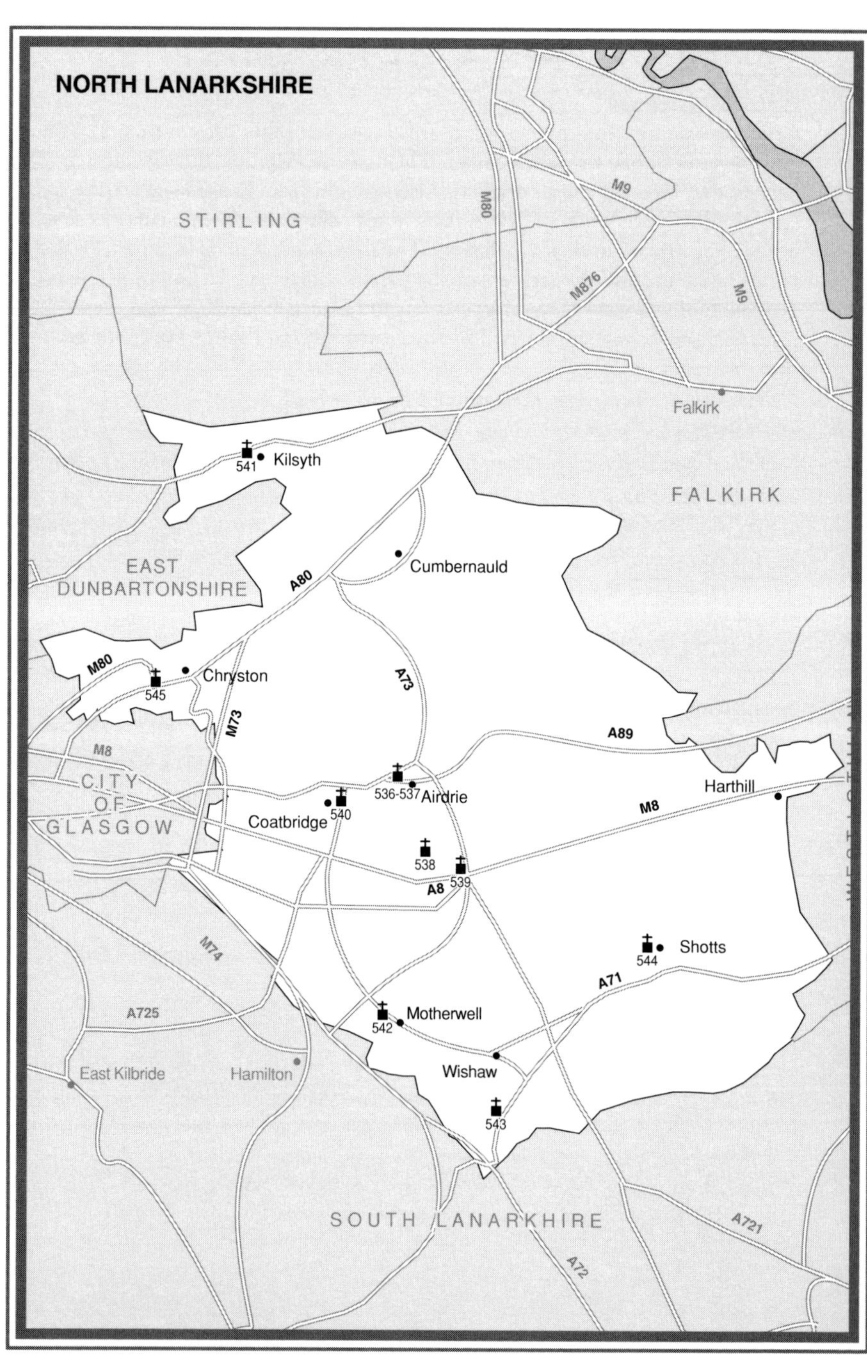
NORTH LANARKSHIRE
STIRLING
M80
M9
M876
M9
Falkirk
FALKIRK
541
Kilsyth
EAST
DUNBARTONSHIRE
A80
Cumbernauld
M80
545
Chryston
M73
A73
M8
A89
CITY
OF
GLASGOW
536-537
Airdrie
Coatbridge
540
Harthill
M8
538
539
A8
M74
544
Shotts
A71
A725
542
Motherwell
Wishaw
East Kilbride
Hamilton
543
SOUTH LANARKHIRE
A721
A72

NORTH LANARKSHIRE

Local Representatives: Sheriff and Mrs V Canavan, Flat 10, 9 Victoria Circus, Glasgow (*telephone* 0141 334 5462)

536 NEW MONKLAND PARISH CHURCH, AIRDRIE

NS 753 678

Condorrat Road, Glenmavis, Airdrie

A fine old Scots plain kirk which hides an attractive interior, Andrew Bell of Airdrie 1776. It holds a commanding position at the highest point in the village, and incorporates the bell-tower of an earlier church (1698) which housed a cell for minor offenders. The old church was replaced when it 'suffered so badly from overcrowding that youthful members of the congregation colonised the exposed joists to roost!' The apse was added in 1904 by John Arthur. Extensive restoration 1997. Simple watchhouse by the cemetery. Sunday Service: 10.30am

Open by arrangement, telephone Mr John Blades 01236 766511

CHURCH OF SCOTLAND WC **B**

537 ST MARGARET'S, AIRDRIE

NS 765 656

96 Hillcraig Street, Airdrie

Parish founded in 1836, this simple neo-classical church by Wilkie & Gray, 1839, has a square tower and spire rising above the pedimented front. Before it was built, adherents had to travel to Glasgow for services, many on foot. Services: Weekdays 10.00 am, Saturday 5.00pm Vigil, Sunday 10.00am, 12 noon and 4.00pm

Open during summer 9am-6pm, winter 9am-4pm, or by arrangement with Parish Priest telephone 01236 763370

ROMAN CATHOLIC WC

538 CORPUS CHRISTI, CALDERBANK

NS 768 630

In the middle of Calderbank village

The Parish was founded in 1948 and the church was opened in 1952. It has undergone several renovations inside to accommodate liturgical changes. Stained glass window of the Sacraments, 1985, designed by Shona McInnis. New church furnishings by J McNally, made by a local craftsman. Sunday Services: 9am, 11am; Weekdays: 10 am; Saturday: 8.45am and Vigil 6pm.

Open 8am-8pm (if main door closed, use right-hand side door)

ROMAN CATHOLIC 

ST ALOYSIUS, CHAPELHALL

539 ST ALOYSIUS, CHAPELHALL

NS 7829 6257

Main Street, Chapelhall

Opened in 1894, built to a design by Pugin and Pugin. Sanctuary completely renewed 1941-52. Marble reredos with gold mosaic panels depticting scenes from the life of St Aloysius. Stained glass installed in rose window, 1984, by Shonna McInnes of Orkney who also designed the remaining four windows in the Sanctuary installed in 1994 to celebrate the Church Centenary. Beautiful gardens behind the church with excellent presbytery house designed by McInally. Services: Saturday Vigil 6.30pm, Sunday 10.00am, 12 noon and 5.30pm

Open daily 9am-7.30pm

ROMAN CATHOLIC

540 ST PATRICK, COATBRIDGE

NS 733 651

Main Street, Coatbridge

Built for the many Irish labourers fleeing the potato famine and disposessed Highlanders. Designed by Pugin and Pugin, 1896, in elegant Gothic with a finely composed gable frontage. Services: Weekdays 10.00 am, Saturday Vigil 6.00pm, Sunday 10.00am, 12 noon and 6.00pm; Holidays 7.30pm Vigil, 10.00am, 1.00pm and 7.30pm

Open 10am-4.30pm

ROMAN CATHOLIC **B**

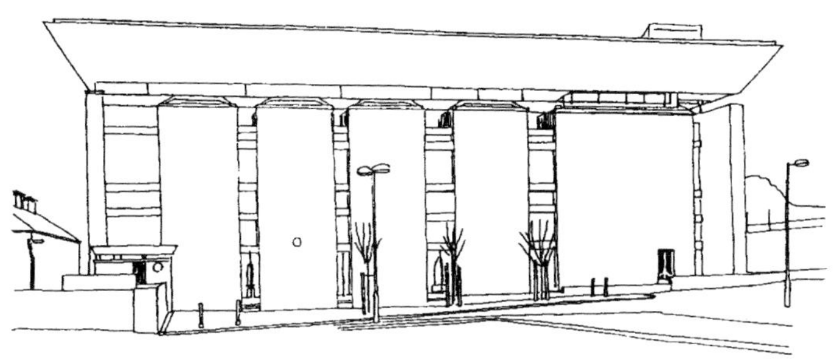

ST PATRICK'S, KILSYTH

541 ST PATRICK'S, KILSYTH

NS 720 777

30 Low Craigends, Kilsyth

Large-scale one box brick structure surmounted by a clerestory and unusual roof by Gillespie, Kidd & Coia 1965. One of only four Gillespie, Kidd & Coia churches with all its original features intact. Recent (2000) Historic Scotland and Heritage Lottery Funded restoration. Services: Saturday 6.30pm Vigil, Sunday 9.30am and 12 noon, Weekdays 10.00am

Open by arrangement with the Parish Priest, telephone 01236 822136

ROMAN CATHOLIC A

542 DALZIEL ST ANDREW'S, MOTHERWELL

NS 752 571

Motherwell Cross

Union of the former Dalziel and St Andrew's Church of Scotland congregations in 1996. The parish of Dalziel has a history stretching back to the 12th century, while St Andrew's was a daughter church of Dalziel. Erected in 1874, the building houses a Walker organ of 1900, recently restored. Worship is a sensitive mixture of traditional and modern with a warm welcome for all ages. Sunday Services: 11am in the Main Sanctuary; Evening worship 6.30pm in the Mission Hall, Jupiter Street (except July and August)

Open Saturday 10am–12noon, or by arrangement with the Church Officer 01698 266 284

CHURCH OF SCOTLAND

DALZIEL ST ANDREW'S, MOTHERWELL

543 OVERTOWN PARISH CHURCH

NS 801 527

Main Street, Overtown, by Wishaw

Village church built in 1876. Near picturesque Clyde Valley, Strathclyde Country Park and many other places of interest. A71, Edinburgh to Kilmarnock, 35 miles from Edinburgh

Open 13 and 20 May 2000 for sale of plants, with guided tours and cafe

CHURCH OF SCOTLAND WC

544 ST PATRICK, SHOTTS

NS 876 599

84 Station Road, Shotts

The church, designed by P P Pugin, is a classic example of his work. White Carrara marble altars and reredos added 1930s. Stained glass depicts Crucifixion and scenes of the local pits and iron works, as well as St Barbara (patron saint of miners), St Joseph, St Cecilia, St John Ogilvie and the Baptism of The Lord. Stations of the Cross are from Germany. The church has been adapted to changing liturgical practice while retaining its original character and quality. Services: Saturday Vigil 6.30pm; Sunday: 10.45am (Sung Mass with Choir), 6.00pm; Monday to Friday 10am; Saturday 9.30am

Church website: www.saintpatrick.org.uk

Open Monday to Thursday 9am–1pm, Friday 9am–6pm

ROMAN CATHOLIC WC

OVERTOWN PARISH CHURCH

545 STEPPS PARISH CHURCH

NS 657 686

17 Whitehill Avenue, Stepps

Fine example of the neo-Gothic style favoured by ecclesiastical architect P MacGregor Chalmers 1900. Designed to reflect scale and simplicity of a village church. Interesting stained glass including works by Stephen Adam (1900). Pipe organ, Joseph Brook 1884, rebuilt James MacKenzie 1976. On rail and bus routes Glasgow–Cumbernauld. Sunday Service: 10am mid-June to mid-August, 11am mid-August to mid-June

Open Tuesday, Thursday 10am–12 noon all year. Other times, telephone 0141 779 9556

CHURCH OF SCOTLAND

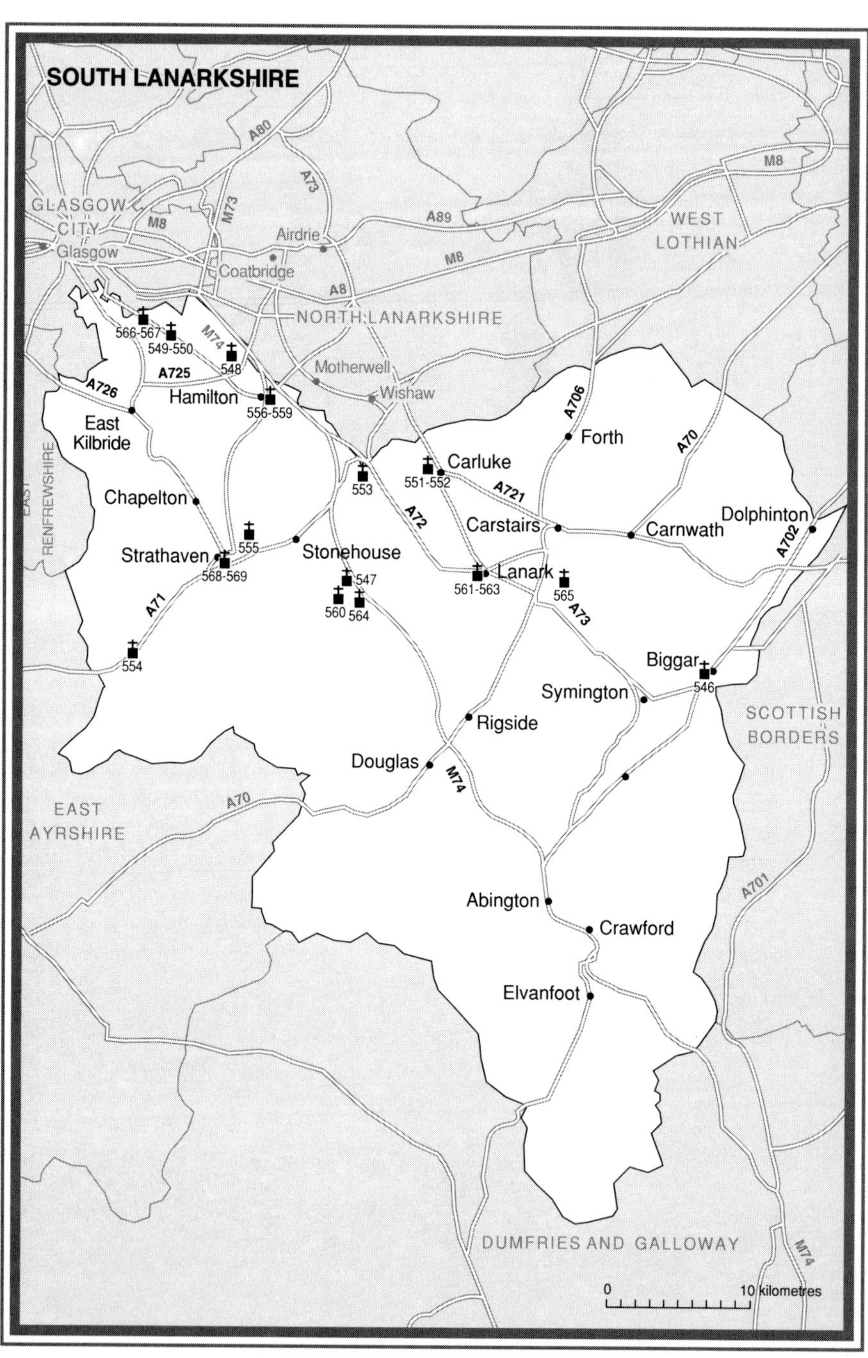
SOUTH LANARKSHIRE
GLASGOW CITY
Glasgow
M8
M73
A80
A73
Airdrie
Coatbridge
A89
M8
A8
WEST LOTHIAN
M8
NORTH LANARKSHIRE
566-567
549-550
M74
548
A725
A726
Motherwell
Wishaw
Hamilton
556-559
East Kilbride
EAST RENFREWSHIRE
A706
Forth
A70
Carluke
551-552
553
A721
Chapelton
A72
Carstairs
Carnwath
Dolphinton
555
Strathaven
568-569
Stonehouse
547
Lanark
561-563
565
A702
A71
560
564
A73
554
Biggar
546
Symington
Rigside
SCOTTISH BORDERS
Douglas
M74
EAST AYRSHIRE
A70
A701
Abington
Crawford
Elvanfoot
DUMFRIES AND GALLOWAY
M74
0
10 kilometres

SOUTH LANARKSHIRE

Local Representative: Mr Sandy Gilchrist, 11 Mercat Loan, Biggar (*telephone* 01899 221350)

BIGGAR KIRK

546 BIGGAR KIRK

NT 040 379

Kirkstyle, Biggar

Rebuilt 1546, the last collegiate church to be founded before the Reformation in Scotland. A cruciform building with fine stained glass, including work by William Wilson and Crear McCartney. In the kirkyard are memorials to the forebears of William Ewart Gladstone and also Thomas Blackwood Murray, the Scottish motor pioneer of 'Albion'. From M74, A702, twelve miles from Abington. Sunday Services: 11am; also 9.30am June, July and August

Open daily in summer 9am–5pm.

In winter, key from Moat Park Heritage Centre opposite

CHURCH OF SCOTLAND **B**

547 OUR LADY AND ST JOHN, BLACKWOOD

NS 790 439

Carlisle Road, Blackwood, Kirkmuirhill

Stone building in Gothic style, opened 1880. The grounds for the church were donated by the Hope-Vere family. The sanctuary extended in 1881 to accommodate the altar donated by Mrs Lancaster. Stained glass windows were also added at this time. The first two parish priests were Benedictines from Ampleforth. Services: Saturday 6pm; Sunday 10am and 6pm

Open by arrangement, telephone 01555 893459

ROMAN CATHOLIC

548 BOTHWELL PARISH CHURCH

NS 705 586

Main Street, Bothwell

Scotland's oldest collegiate church still in use for worship and dedicated to St Bride, occupies the site of a former 6th-century church. Medieval choir. Nave and tower 1833, David Hamilton, altered 1933. Monuments to the Earls of Douglas and the Duke of Hamilton. Stained glass by Gordon Webster, Douglas Strachan and Sir Edward Burne-Jones. Fascinating tales of an outstanding royal wedding and link with Bothwell Castle. Graveyard. Off A725 near Hamilton. Sunday Service: 10.30am

Open daily Easter to September.

Bus parties welcome by arrangement, telephone 01698 853189

CHURCH OF SCOTLAND WC **A**

549 CAMBUSLANG OLD PARISH CHURCH

NS 646 600

3 Cairns Road, Kirkhill, Cambuslang

St Cadoc is believed to have had a holy site here AD c.550, and early buildings have been recorded from 12th century. The present building is by David Cousin 1841. Steeple with clock and bell. The chancel is by P MacGregor Chalmers 1922. Stained glass and tapestries by Sadie McLellan 1957. Millennium wall-hanging in vestibule 2001. Heraldic shields of heritors decorate the ceiling. Interesting gravestones in churchyard including one to Rev William McCulloch, Minister at Scotland's largest ever revival 'The Cambuslang Wark' in 1742. Near Greenlees Road B759. Sunday Services: September to June 11am and 6.30pm; July and August 9.30am and 11am

Church website: www.cambuslang-old-parish-church.com

Open by arrangement, telephone Mrs F McQueen 0141 641 4845

CHURCH OF SCOTLAND WC **B**

CAMBUSLANG OLD PARISH CHURCH

550 ST BRIDE'S, CAMBUSLANG

NS 643 604

21 Greenlees Road, Cambuslang (opposite Police Station)

The church, which opened in 1960, has a Crucifixion window, an example of the early work of stained glass artist Gordon M Webster, and another free-standing window also by Webster. Services: Saturday Vigil 6pm; Sunday 8.30 and 10am, 12noon and 6pm

Open 8am–8pm every day

ROMAN CATHOLIC WC

551 ST ANDREW'S PARISH CHURCH, CARLUKE

NS 843 508

Mount Stewart Street, Carluke

The original church was replaced by the present building in 1799 following designs by Henry Bell (of the steamship 'Comet' fame). It incorporates an arch inside the porch and a window with slender fluted pillars in the front of tower from the old church. The tower of the old church has been retained as a monument in its original site in the old graveyard at the bottom of the town. Within the church are an organ made by H Willis and Sons and installed in 1903, stained glass windows including one made by Gordon McWhirter Webster (1932) and a pulpit fall and companion communion table runner by Marilyn E W McGregor DA (1999). Memorial garden 'Garden of Hope' (2001). Sunday Service: 11.00am

ST ANDREW'S PARISH CHURCH, CARLUKE

Open by arrangement, telephone Mrs Jennifer Johnstone 01555 750155

CHURCH OF SCOTLAND **B**

552 ST ATHANASIUS, CARLUKE

NS 844 508

21 Mount Stewart Street, Carluke

The present church was erected in 1857, but a larger building was required by the 1980s when the building was extended as far as the grounds allowed. The marriage of old and new buildings in 1984 has given a modern and attractive church while still retaining much of the original character. The architects were Cullen, Lochhead and Brown. Services: Saturday Vigil 6pm; Sunday 9am and 11.15am; Weekdays 10am

Open 9am–4pm daily

ROMAN CATHOLIC

553 DALSERF PARISH CHURCH

NS 800 507

Built 1655, centre transept added 1892. Oblong building with pulpit on long side. Outside stairs to three galleries. Belfry. Two large Memorial windows on either side of pulpit by Douglas Hogg. The graveyard contains a pre-Norman hogback stone and an outstanding Covenanting memorial, 1753, to Rev John MacMillan, founder of the Reformed Presbyterian Church. Off A72 between Garrion Bridge and Rosebank. Sunday Service: 12 noon

Open by arrangement, telephone Church Officer, Mr W Knox 01698 883770

CHURCH OF SCOTLAND **A**

DALSERF PARISH CHURCH

554 DRUMCLOG MEMORIAL KIRK

NS 640 389

J McLellan Fairley 1912. The church has strong associations with the covenanters. A71, five miles west on Darvel road. Part of Avendale Old Church. Sunday Service: 9.30am. All-age communion on the third Sunday of each month, except July and August. There is also an open-air Conventicle Service at the Battle of Drumclog Monument on the first Sunday of June. Details of special services to be found on church website

Church website: www.garrion.co.uk/avendale

Open by arrangement, telephone Mr J Spence 01357 521939

CHURCH OF SCOTLAND

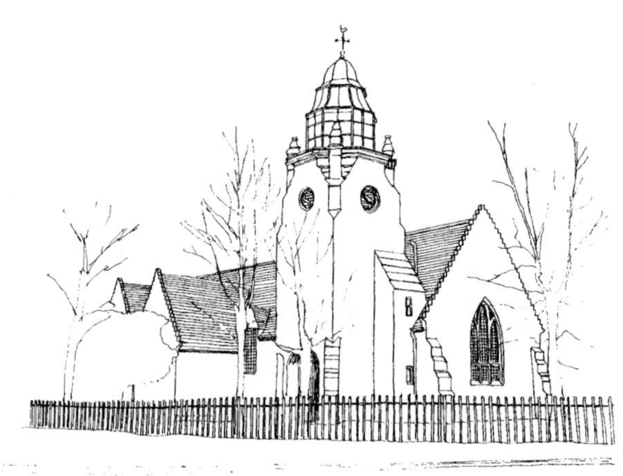

DRUMCLOG MEMORIAL KIRK

555 GLASFORD PARISH CHURCH, GLASSFORD

NS 726 470

Jackson Street, Glassford

Built 1820. Memorial stained glass windows to Rev Gavin Lang, grandfather of Cosmo Lang, Archbishop of Canterbury. Ruins of 1633 church and Covenanter's stone. Off A71 Stonehouse–Strathaven or A723 Hamilton–Strathaven. Linked with Strathaven East. Sunday Service: 10am

Open by arrangement. Also Doors Open Day, telephone Rev W Stewart 01357 521138

CHURCH OF SCOTLAND WC **B**

556 HAMILTON OLD PARISH CHURCH

NS 723 555

Strathmore Road, Hamilton

The present building is a Georgian gem. The only church designed and built by William Adam, 1734. Samples from the roof timbers found to be full of lead shot – Adam used wood from an old man-of-war! Chancel furnishings include embroidery by Hannah Frew Paterson. Exceptionally detailed engraved glass windows by Anita Pate depict the history of the church back to the 6th century. Memorial stained glass window of African animals to John Stevenson Hamilton, founder of Kruger National Park. Eleventh-century Netherton Cross and Covenanting memorials in graveyard. In centre of town. Sunday Service: 10.45am, July and August 10am

Church website: www.hopc.fsnet.co.uk

Open Monday to Friday, 10.30am–3.30pm. Or by arrangement, telephone 01698 281905, Monday to Friday 9am–2pm. Easter Sunday, Church decorated with thousands of daffodils

CHURCH OF SCOTLAND (by arrangement on weekdays) WC **A**

HAMILTON OLD PARISH CHURCH

557 HAMILTON WEST PARISH CHURCH

NS 712 558

Peacock Cross, Burnbank Road, Hamilton

The church was originally founded in 1874 as the 'Burnbank Mission Station' of St John's Free Church. Having been raised to full status in 1875, the church was rebuilt in 1880 and the Glasgow architect John Hutchison was commissioned. The result is the present building, whose design exhibits many features in the 13th-century Gothic style. The interior has one of the best examples in Scotland of a wooden hammerbeam roof. The organ was built by Hill & Son of London 1902 and is still in use today. The exterior is floodlit, highlighting the stonework which was restored in 1988. Sunday Service: 10.45am, except July 10.00am

HAMILTON WEST PARISH CHURCH

Open by arrangement, telephone Mr James Murdie 01698 425237

CHURCH OF SCOTLAND WC **B**

558 ST JOHN'S CHURCH, HAMILTON

NS 724 523

Duke Street, Hamilton

Idiosyncratic classical building (originally a chapel of ease) 1835. The interior was renovated in 1971 by Cullen Lochead & Brown who also completed the St John's Centre, opened 1970, and incorporating the former St John's Grammar School of 1836 and the Centenary Hall of 1934. In October 2000 the firm Cullen Lochhead and Brown also completed a Millenniium Project which involved the re-fashioning of most of the existing suite of halls and the erection of an extension. In the St John's Centre Chapel, stained glass ('Wings') by Susan Bradbury. Located at the 'Top Cross' opposite Marks & Spencer. Sunday Services: 10.45am and 6.30pm (summer 10am and 9pm)

St John's Centre open to the public Monday to Friday 10am–12 noon and 2pm–4pm, and on Saturday from 10am–4pm

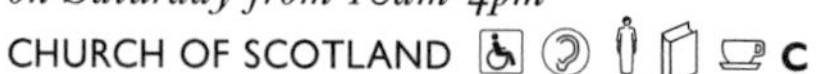

CHURCH OF SCOTLAND **C**

ST JOHN'S CHURCH, HAMILTON

559 ST MARY THE VIRGIN, HAMILTON

NS 721 567

Auchingramont Road, Hamilton

ST MARY THE VIRGIN, HAMILTON

The building designed by John Henderson was opened for worship in 1847 and is Early English in style. Chancel ceiling panels were painted by Mabel Royds (1874-1941). There are fine stained glass commemorative windows with several memorials in marble and stone reflecting the links with the town's military history. Sunday Services: 8.30 and 10am, first and third Sunday 6pm; Wednesday 10am

Open daily during March to September (key at Rectory)

SCOTTISH EPISCOPAL B

560 KIRKMUIRHILL PARISH CHURCH

NS 799 429

Carlisle Road, Kirkmuirhill

KIRKMUIRHILL PARISH CHURCH

Built in 1868 by the United Presyterian Church, Architect Robert Baldie. Early English Gothic Revival style, the most prominent feature being the spire which dominates the surroundings. Four stained glass windows by Robert Paterson (1941), Douglas Hamilton (1954) and Linda Fraser (1986). Embroidered pew and chair cushions designed by Pat Hodgson of Hawksland Lesmahagow and worked by members of the congregation. Sunday Services: 11am and 6.30pm

Open by arrangement with Session Clerk, telephone 01555 892305

CHURCH OF SCOTLAND

561 GREYFRIARS PARISH CHURCH, LANARK

NS 880 437

Bloomgate, Lanark

William Leiper designed this, his smallest church, in 1875 for the Bloomgate United Presbyterian Congregation. Its simple gothic interior is enlivenend by a slender bellcote inspired by Andrew Heiton's Findlater Church in Dublin. Leiper designed a star-spangled ceiling to be one of the glories of the interior. Two-manual pipe organ by Ingram, recently fully refurbished. Pulpit fall and welcome banner by local artist Myra Gibson.

Sunday Service: 11am

Church website: www.webartz.com/greyfriars

Open on Doors Open Day and by arrangement with the Minister, telephone 01555 663363

CHURCH OF SCOTLAND B

562 ST MARY'S, LANARK

NS 886 435

70 Bannatyne Street, Lanark

Gothic revival cruciform church by Dublin architects Ashlin & Coleman 1908. Graceful 144-feet spire. Remarkable interior decoration including imposing reredos of Caen stone and marble, statues of St Mungo, St Margaret and St Columba and fine stained glass. Services: Weekdays 9.30am, Saturday Vigil 6.30pm, Sunday 9.30am, 11am and 6.30pm

Open during daylight hours

ROMAN CATHOLIC WC WC A

563 ST NICHOLAS PARISH CHURCH, LANARK

NS 881 437

The Cross, Lanark

By John Reid of Nemphlar 1774. Stained glass, baptismal font in Caen stone. Fine pipe organ. On A73, 30 miles south of Glasgow, follow signs for New Lanark. Sunday Service: 11am; Wednesday 10.15am

Open during Doors Open Day and by arrangement, telephone Rev J Thomson 01555 662600.

CHURCH OF SCOTLAND WC B

ST NICHOLAS PARISH CHURCH, LANARK

564 LESMAHAGOW OLD PARISH CHURCH

NS 814 399

David I granted a church and lands to the Tironensian monks in 1144. He also granted the right of sanctuary, violated in 1335 when the church was burned, with villagers inside, by John Eltham, brother of Edward I. The present church was built in 1803 and the apse added in the 1890s. Pipe organ 1889. Several stained glass windows including one whose central panel, 'The Descent from the Cross', is a copy of that in Antwerp Cathedral. The bell is dated 1625. Display in the Chapter House. Lesmahagow on M74, 23 miles south of Glasgow. A conservation village. Sunday Service: 10am

Church website: www.lopc.org.uk

Open by arrangement, telephone Rev Sheila Mitchell 01555 892425 or Church Officer Mr Alex McInnes 01555 892697

CHURCH OF SCOTLAND WC

LESMAHAGOW OLD PARISH CHURCH

565 PETTINAIN CHURCH

NS 955 429

7 miles east of Lanark, between A73 and A70

Fine example of a rural parish kirk, with outstanding views across open countryside. The site has been a place of worship since the early 12th century when David I established the chapel of 'Pedynane'. The present church dates principally from the 18th century with an earlier belfry of 1692 and an incised cross slab re-used as a relieving lintel. Interesting walled burial ground. Acquired by the Scottish Redundant Churches Trust in 2000 with the generous support of local people. Occasional services, plus weddings and funerals by arrangement

Open July and August, Sundays, 1pm-4pm or by arrangement with the SRCT, telephone 01555 666023

FORMER CHURCH OF SCOTLAND B

566 RUTHERGLEN OLD PARISH CHURCH

NS 613 617

Main Street x Queen Street, Rutherglen

The present church was designed by the architect J J Burnet 1902 in Gothic style, the fourth on this site since the original foundation in the 6th century. The gable end of an 11th-century church still stands in the graveyard supporting St Mary's steeple (15th century). It contains the church bell 1635. Stained glass including a First World War memorial. Communion cups dated 1665 are still in use. The churchyard occupies an ancient site, at its gateway two stone offertory shelters, and a sundial set above its entrance dated 1679. Sunday Service: 11am

Church website:www.rutherglen.clara.co.uk/index.htm

Centenerary celebrations; Flower Festival, 1 and 2 June 2002. Open second Saturday of every month, 10am-12 noon

CHURCH OF SCOTLAND WC B

567 ST COLUMBKILLE'S CHURCH, RUTHERGLEN

NS 614 616

Main Street, Rutherglen

Magnificent church, Coia 1940, replacing original church founded in 1851. Modern adaptation of an Italian basilica. Between A724 and A731. Trains and city buses. Sunday Masses 9am, 10.30am, 12 noon and 7pm; Vigil Mass Saturday 5.30pm

Open Monday to Thursday 9am-5pm, Friday 9am-2pm

ROMAN CATHOLIC WC

ST COLUMBKILLE'S CHURCH, RUTHERGLEN

568 AVENDALE OLD PARISH CHURCH, STRATHAVEN

NS 701 443

59a Kirk Street, Strathaven

Records show a church in Strathaven in 1288. This church was built in 1772 and the interior renovated 1879. The centre section of the south gallery was reserved for the family and tenants of the Duke of Hamilton and is known as 'The Duke's Gallery'. Stained glass window of the Last Supper, Crear McCartney 1996. In town centre A71. Sunday Service: 11am. All-age communion is celebrated at the 11am service on the third Sunday of each month, except July and August. Details of evening services to be found on church website

Church website: www.garrion.co.uk/avendale

Open Monday to Friday 9am–12 noon (not school holidays). Other times, telephone Session Clerk 01357 521939

CHURCH OF SCOTLAND

WC **B**

AVENDALE OLD PARISH CHURCH, STRATHAVEN

STRATHAVEN EAST PARISH CHURCH

569 STRATHAVEN EAST PARISH CHURCH

NS 702 446

Green Street, Strathaven

The white painted exterior is a local landmark. Built 1777 with clock tower added 1843. Major rebuilding 1877. Prominent pulpit and memorial windows. Linked with Glasford Church. Sunday Service: 11.30am

Open by arrangement, telephone Rev W Stewart 01357 521138

CHURCH OF SCOTLAND (hearing loop) WC **A** (tower) **B** (church)

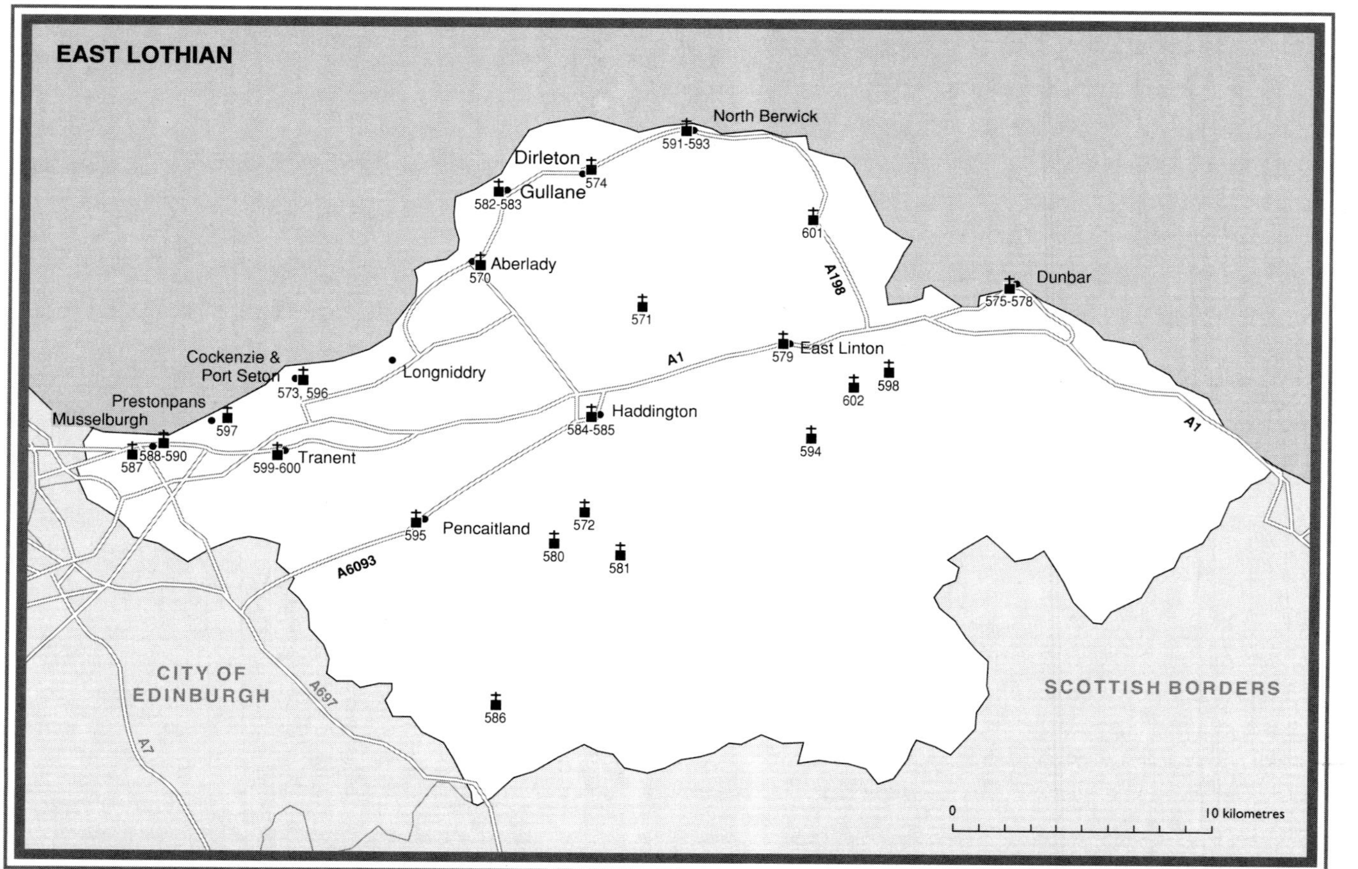
EAST LOTHIAN
North Berwick
591-593
Dirleton
574
Gullane
582-583
601
A198
Aberlady
570
571
Dunbar
575-578
East Linton
579
A1
Cockenzie &
Port Seton
573, 596
Longniddry
602
598
Prestonpans
597
Haddington
584-585
Musselburgh
588-590
587
Tranent
599-600
594
A1
Pencaitland
595
572
580
581
A6093
CITY OF
EDINBURGH
A697
A7
586
SCOTTISH BORDERS
0
10 kilometres

EAST LOTHIAN

Local Representative: Mrs Margaret Beveridge, St Andrews, Duns Road, Gifford EH41 4QW (*telephone* 01620 810694)

570 ABERLADY PARISH CHURCH

NT 462 799

Main Street, Aberlady

Fifteenth-century tower, the body of the church recast in 1886 by William Young. Stained glass by Edward Frampton, London 1889. Eighth-century cross. Marble monument attributed to Canova. Tour guide boards in English, French, German, Spanish, Swedish. A198 Edinburgh–North Berwick. Sunday Service: 11.15am

Open 1 May to 30 September, 8am-dusk. Other times, telephone B White 01875 853137, or F Burnett, 14 Rig Street, Aberlady 01875 870237

CHURCH OF SCOTLAND **A**

571 ATHELSTANEFORD PARISH CHURCH

NT 533 774

The original church 'Ecclesia de Elstaneford' on this site is said to have been founded in 1176 by the Countess Ada, mother of William the Lion. The present church dates from 1780. Cruciform design with central aisle, transepts and semi-octagonal chancel. Bellcote on the west gable. Three stained glass windows by C E Kempe. Doocot 1583. Church has historic link with the Scottish Saltire: commemorative plaque and Saltire floodlit. Heritage Centre to rear of church opened in 1997 with audio visual display (entry free). From A1, B1347. Sunday Service: 10am

Open daily, dawn to dusk

CHURCH OF SCOTLAND WC **B**

ATHELSTANEFORD PARISH CHURCH

572 BOLTON PARISH CHURCH

NT 507 701

There has been a church on this site since before 1244. The present building dates from 1809 and remains structurally unchanged since that time. The architect was probably Archibald Elliot. The interior is plain and unspoiled, complete with carpenter's Gothic pulpit, and gallery on clustered iron posts. Robert Burns's mother, brother and sisters are buried in the churchyard. Graveguard and other items dating from the time of the 'Resurrection Men' displayed in the porch. Linked with Saltoun, Humbie and Yester. B6368 from Haddington. Sunday Service: 10am, alternating with Saltoun

Church website: www.lbes.demon.co.uk

Open daily

CHURCH OF SCOTLAND **B**

BOLTON PARISH CHURCH

573 COCKENZIE METHODIST CHURCH

NT 398 756

28 Edinburgh Road, Cockenzie

The third of East Lothian's three Primitive Methodist Chapels, 1878. Simple and attractive. Original interior. South side of main road at west end of village. Sunday Service: 2.30pm

Open by arrangement, telephone Christine Thomson 01875 811137

METHODIST

COCKENZIE METHODIST CHURCH

DIRLETON KIRK

574 DIRLETON KIRK

NT 513 842

Attractive stone building erected in 1612 to replace 12th-century kirk in Gullane which was 'continewallie overblawin with sand'. Archerfield Aisle added 1650, first example of neo-classical design in Scotland. Tower crowned with Gothic pinnacles 1836. Stained glass window depicting St Francis and the Animals, Margaret Chilton 1936. Sunday Service: 11.45am, 9.30pm July and August

Open daily 10am to dusk. Light lunches, snacks in adjacent Dirleton Gallery

CHURCH OF SCOTLAND WC **A**

575 CHURCH OF OUR LADY OF THE WAVES, DUNBAR

NT 678 791

Westgate, Dunbar

Built in 1877, the church has stained glass behind the altar and wood carvings showing the Way of the Cross.

Open by arrangement, telephone 01368 862701

ROMAN CATHOLIC

CHURCH OF OUR LADY OF THE WAVES, DUNBAR

576 DUNBAR METHODIST CHURCH

NT 679 791

10 Victoria Street, Dunbar

Scotland's oldest Methodist Church, built in 1764. John and Charles Wesley were trustees and John often preached here. Enlarged 1857, renovated 1890. Fine interior, unexpected from plain exterior. Oak pulpit. Stained glass windows from St Giles, Edinburgh. South side of road leading from High Street to Harbour. Sunday Service: 11am

Open by arrangement 01875 610388

METHODIST A

DUNBAR METHODIST CHURCH

577 DUNBAR PARISH CHURCH

NT 682 786

Queen's Road, Dunbar

The building, designed by Gillespie Graham in 1821, has been beautifully reconstructed by Campbell & Arnott 1990 following a devastating fire in 1987. The colourful and modern interior includes the early 17th-century monument to the Earl of Dunbar and some fine stained glass by Shona McInnes and Douglas Hogg 1990. Two hundred yards south of High Street south end. Intercity trains to Dunbar. Sunday Service: 11am

Open daily 11am–4pm. Sunday 2pm–4pm, June to September. Various exhibitions during season

CHURCH OF SCOTLAND WC A

578 ST ANNE'S CHURCH, DUNBAR

NT 678 791

Westgate, Dunbar

The church is by H M Wardrop and Sir R Rowand Anderson 1890. Built in the Gothic revival style and decorated with some Scots detail. Carved oak furnishings, Henry Willis organ, stained glass by Ballantine & Gardiner, Heaton, Butler & Bayne, and the Abbey Studio. North end of Dunbar High Street. Sunday Service: 11am

Open Saturday 19 June, 10am–4pm.

Other times, telephone Rev P Allen 01368 865711

SCOTTISH EPISCOPAL WC (open day only) B

ST ANNE'S CHURCH, DUNBAR

579 PARISH OF TRAPRAIN, PRESTONKIRK, EAST LINTON

NT 592 778

Preston Road, East Linton

Dedicated to St Baldred, the church possesses in its former chancel the best fragment of 13th-century church architecture in East Lothian. The tower dates from 1631, the main building from 1770, enlarged 1824, redesigned internally 1892 by James Jerdan. Organ by Vincent of Sutherland. St Baldred window 1959 and two Second World War memorial windows by William Wilson. Among the gravestones are those of Andrew Meikle, inventor of the threshing machine, and George Rennie, agriculturalist and brother of John Rennie, the civil engineer. Off A1, follow signs to Preston Mill. Sunday Service: 11.30am; 24 December 11.30am, 25 December 10am. Please note times of services may be changed

Open by arrangement, telephone 01620 860598

CHURCH OF SCOTLAND

♿ (by arrangement) WC (in Church Hall) **A**

PARISH OF TRAPRAIN, PRESTONKIRK, EAST LINTON

580 SALTOUN PARISH CHURCH, EAST SALTOUN

NT 474 678

There has been a church on this site since before 1244. The present building is a T-plan Gothic kirk of 1805 which John Fletcher Campbell built 'as a monument to the virtues of his ancestors'. The actual designer is most likely to have been Robert Burn. The interior was recast in 1885, the architect was John Lessels. Beneath the church lies the Fletcher Vault, containing the remains of Andrew Fletcher 'The Patriot' and members of his family. Linked with Bolton, Humbie and Yester. Sunday Service: 10am, alternating with Bolton

Church website: www.lbes.demon.co.uk

Open daily

CHURCH OF SCOTLAND A

SALTOUN PARISH CHURCH, EAST SALTOUN

581 YESTER PARISH CHURCH, GIFFORD

NT 535 681

Main Street, Gifford

By James Smith, finished 1710. A white harled T-plan church with square staged tower and slated spire. Weather vane in the form of a heron, William Brown, Edinburgh 1709. Church bell from the old Church of Bothans 1492. Pulpit 17th-century with bracket for baptismal basin. Memorial in village wall opposite to Rev John Witherspoon, son of the Manse, who signed the American Declaration of Independence 1784. B6369 from Haddington. Hourly bus service. Sunday Service: 11.30am

Open daily, April to October, 9am to sunset. Village gala day June. Flower show August

CHURCH OF SCOTLAND WC A

YESTER PARISH CHURCH, GIFFORD

582 GULLANE PARISH CHURCH (ST ANDREW'S)

NT 480 827

East Links Road, Gullane

The church, designed by Glasgow architect John Honeyman and completed in 1888, replaced an earlier 12th-century building vacated in 1612 when the congregation was rehoused in a new kirk at Dirleton. The Kirk Session of Dirleton decided to build the present parish church for the benefit of 'the large number of summer visitors annually residing in the village'. Simple Norman style with east apse. The zig-zagged chancel arch is derived from the old parish church, as is the south doorway whose tympanum has a low relief of St Andrew. A198 to North Berwick. Sunday Service: 9.45am

Open daily all year. Coffee on Tuesdays 10-11.30am

CHURCH OF SCOTLAND **A**

583 ST ADRIAN'S CHURCH, GULLANE

NT 480 838

Sandy Loan, Gullane

A simple aisleless church in Arts and Crafts style by Reginald Fairlie 1926. Built of stone from the Rattlebag quarry with a low tower and slated pyramidal spire. Three-light chancel window by Douglas Strachan 1934. Sandy Loan is the beach road at the west end of the village. Sunday Services: Sung Eucharist 9.30; Said Eucharist first and third Sundays 8am

Open 10am-5pm, April to September

SCOTTISH EPISCOPAL **B**

ST ADRIAN'S CHURCH, GULLANE

584 HOLY TRINITY CHURCH, HADDINGTON

NT 518 739

Church Street, Haddington

Built 1770 on site of original 'Lamp of Lothian'. Chancel added 1930. Stations of the Cross, Bowman. Christ Crucified, Sutherland. Medieval walls of former priory and town defences. Sunday Services: 8.30am, Eucharist 10am, Evensong 6pm (except July and August); Wednesday Eucharist 10am

Open Wednesday 10am-4pm, and in summer Saturday 10am-4pm. Other times, contact the Rectory adjacent

SCOTTISH EPISCOPAL WC **B**

HOLY TRINITY CHURCH, HADDINGTON

585 ST MARY'S COLLEGIATE CHURCH, HADDINGTON

NT 519 736

Sidegate, Haddington

Dating back to the 14th century, one of the three great pre-Reformation churches of the Lothians, known as 'The Lamp of Lothian', largest parish church in Scotland with fascinating history. Nave repaired for John Knox and the reformers after Siege of Haddington 1548 and used as the parish church for almost 400 years. Transepts and choir restored, Ian G Lindsay & Partners 1973. Lauderdale Aisle, now The Chapel of the Three Kings, in regular ecumenical use. Fine stone carvings, especially west door. Notable stained glass by Sir Edward Burne-Jones and Sax Shaw. Modern tapestries. Fine pipe organ by Lammermuir Pipe Organs 1990. A peal of eight bells installed in the tower (and dedicated by the Moderator) in 1999. Sunday Services: 9.30am Family Circle and 11am Parish Worship

Church website: www.kylemore.btinternet.co.uk/stmarys.htm

Open Good Friday to 30 September, daily, 11am-4pm, Sunday 2-4.30pm.

Annual ecumenical Whitekirk/Haddington Pilgrimage Saturday 11 May 2002.

Brass Rubbing Centre open Saturday throughout season 11am-1pm, except weddings.

Regular concerts and recitals of international repute

CHURCH OF SCOTLAND

 A

ST MARY'S COLLEGIATE CHURCH, HADDINGTON

586 HUMBIE KIRK

NT 461 637

On the site of a pre-Reformation church, set in an ox-bow of Humbie Burn, a T-plan Gothic church by James Tod dated 1800. Vestry added 1846, and alterations by David Bryce 1866. The chancel added 1930, probably W J Walker Todd. Open scissor-braced timber roof. Stained glass. Organ by David Hamilton c.1840 with decorative Gothic dark wood case, from the Norwegian Seamen's Chapel at Granton. Fine gravestones with classical detail dating from earlier church. Broun Aisle, 1864 Bryce, sited at west gate, erected by Archibald Broun of Johnstonburn 'in lieu of the burial place of his family within the church, which in deference to the feelings of the parishioners, he has now closed'! Linked with Bolton, Saltoun and Yester. Sunday Service: 10am

Open daily

CHURCH OF SCOTLAND **B**

587 PARISH CHURCH OF ST MICHAEL'S, INVERESK

NT 344 721

Musselburgh

There has been a church on the site since the 6th century. The present church was built in 1805 to the design of Robert Nisbet, the steeple by William Sibbald. The interior was reorientated and remodelled in 1893 by J MacIntyre Henry. Known as the 'visible Kirk' because of its prominent position, it stands on the site of a Roman praetorium and replaces a medieval church. Fine Adam-style ceiling and some excellent stained glass. Magnificent pipe organ enlarged 1897 by Lewis & Co. of London. Surrounded by a fine graveyard with many interesting old stones. Sunday Service: 11.15am

Open by arrangement, telephone Mr G Burnet 0131 665 2689.

Open when village gardens open under Scotland's Gardens Scheme

CHURCH OF SCOTLAND (two steps to door) WC **A**

588 MUSSELBURGH CONGREGATIONAL CHURCH

NT 341 729

6 Links Street, Musselburgh

Simple but charming Georgian building completed in 1801, built with stone carried by fishermen and sailors from the shores of the Forth at Fisherrow. Oldest church in Musselburgh and one of first Congregational churches in Scotland. Pipe organ, fine example of the work of George Holdich built 1860 for St Michael's, Appleby. Rebuilt for Musselburgh Congregational church 1977. Church sits behind Brunton Hall. Sunday Service: 11am

Open by arrangement, telephone Mr J Brown, 11 Links Street 0131 665 3768

CONGREGATIONAL WC **C**

MUSSELBURGH CONGREGATIONAL CHURCH

589 OUR LADY OF LORETTO AND ST MICHAEL, MUSSELBURGH

NT 346 753

17 Newbigging, Musselburgh

Stone building opened in 1905. Sanctuary recently modernised. All windows are of stained glass and the walls of the sanctuary are covered in fine art work, in gold leaf, depicting the events in the life of our Lord, corresponding to the Joyful Mysteries of the Rosary. Sunday Services: 9 and 11.30 am; Saturday Vigil 6pm

Open daily

ROMAN CATHOLIC **B**

OUR LADY OF LORETTO AND ST MICHAEL, MUSSELBURGH

590 ST PETER'S EPISCOPAL, MUSSELBURGH

NT 348 723

High Street, Musselburgh

Anglican church, near the site of the Battle of Pinkie (1547), in a traditional French Gothic style by Paterson & Shiells, 1865. Narrow chancel and semi-circular apse and steeply pitched roof. Fine, older stained glass windows and 17th-century character wooden panelling in St Michael's Chapel. Services follow traditional biblical exposition according to the Lectionary. Services: Sunday 11.15am; Monday 7.00pm

Open by arrangement with Mr Alan Stevens, telephone 0131 665 6697

SCOTTISH EPISCOPAL WC **B**

ABBEY CHURCH, NORTH BERWICK

591 ABBEY CHURCH, NORTH BERWICK

NT 551 853

High Street, North Berwick

Built 1868 as United Presbyterian by Robert R Raeburn in Early English style. A complete early 20th-century scheme of stained glass with, superimposed on one window, an arrangement of suspended planes representing an ascent of doves, by Sax Shaw 1972. Sunday Services: 10.15am and 6pm

Open 9am–6pm, Mondays to Fridays, July and August

CHURCH OF SCOTLAND

592 CHURCH OF OUR LADY STAR OF THE SEA, NORTH BERWICK

NT 553 850

Law Road, North Berwick

Built in 1879, it is a simple Victorian church by Dunn & Hansom with seating for 200 people. The chancel was added by Basil Champreys in 1889 and the Lady Chapel by Sir Robert Lorimer in 1901. The interior contains a number of pictures after Benozzo Gozzoli and Botticelli and a Della Robbia (probably a copy). Services: daily 10am; Saturday Vigil 6pm; Sunday 10am

Open daily, 8am–8pm

ROMAN CATHOLIC **B**

593 ST BALDRED'S CHURCH, NORTH BERWICK

NT 556 853

Dirleton Avenue, North Berwick

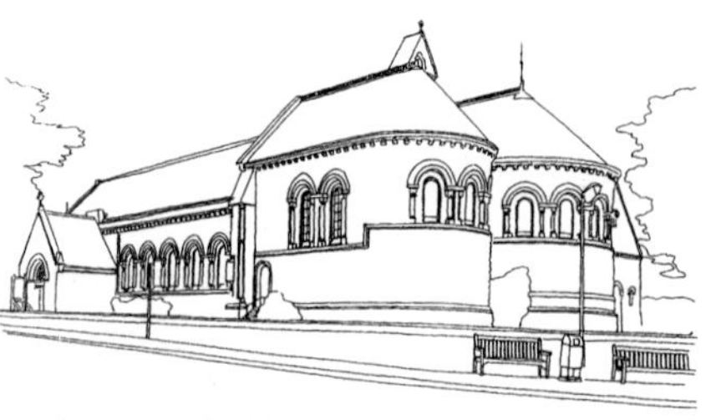

ST BALDRED'S CHURCH, NORTH BERWICK

The original Norman-style church by John Henderson 1861 was cleverly extended in 1863 incorporating the old masonry by Seymour & Kinross, who also designed the altar. The porch with its magnificent carved doors was added by Robert Lorimer in 1916. Choir stalls by H O Tarbolton, porch doors by Mrs Meredith-Williams. Stained glass by Ballantine & Son. Convenient for North Berwick railway station. Sunday Services: Sung Eucharist 11am; second and fourth Sunday, Said Eucharist 8am

Open all year, 10am-4pm

SCOTTISH EPISCOPAL **B**

594 NUNRAW ABBEY

NT 593 700

Garvald, by Haddington

Modern Monastery of Cistercian Monks built 1952-70 (but unfinished), architect Peter Whiston. Nunraw House is a historic building and functions as the Abbey guest house where people may stay for a few days of retreat in the monastic atmosphere. Sunday Services: Mass 11am, Vespers 4pm, Compline 7.30pm; Weekday Services: Lauds and Mass 6.45pm, Vespers 6pm, Compline 7.30pm

Reception area and church open at all times

ROMAN CATHOLIC WC

595 PENCAITLAND PARISH CHURCH

NT 443 690

Consecrated in 1242, the earliest part of the church dates from the 12th century. The present building consists of nave, with a gallery at the west end, and two aisles on the north side, the older called the Winton Aisle and the other the Saltoun Aisle. Churchyard with many interesting gravestones, offering houses, renovated carriage house, stables, harness room and cottage. Coffee shop on Thursdays from 2-4pm in Carriage House, except the first Thursday of the month. A1 from Edinburgh to Tranent, B6355 to Pencaitland. Bus 113 from Edinburgh. Sunday Service: 10am; Sunday evening Service 6.30pm, every fortnight

Open July and August, Sunday 2-5pm; September to June, Saturday 9.30am-1pm. Other times, telephone Rev Mark Malcolm 01875 340208

CHURCH OF SCOTLAND WC **A**

PENCAITLAND PARISH CHURCH

596 CHALMERS MEMORIAL CHURCH, PORT SETON

NT 403 757

Edinburgh Road, Port Seton

Built to a design by Sydney Mitchell for the United Free Church, the foundation stone was laid in 1904. It has a very elegant spire and bell-tower and unique stencilled interior. Stained glass windows by Margaret Chilton and Marjorie Kemp 1924-50. Sunday Services: 11.15am and 6.15 all year

The Church is open to visitors and for coffee at the end of both services every Sunday. Visitors are also welcome every third Wednesday of every month 2pm-4pm

CHURCH OF SCOTLAND  A

CHALMERS MEMORIAL CHURCH, PORT SETON

597 ST ANDREW'S EPISCOPAL, PRESTONPANS

NT 392 749

West Loan, Prestonpans

Stone-built simple hall church, built as a Free Kirk in 1843, with slender cast-iron columns supporting the roof. Light spacious interior. Former gallery now enclosed to form upper room over kitchen and toilets. Fine stained glass including a recent window by Sax Shaw. Sunday Service: 9.30am Sung Eucharist

Open by arrangement with Mr John Busby, telephone 01875 340512

SCOTTISH EPISCOPAL

598 STENTON PARISH CHURCH

NT 641 753

Main Street, Stenton

By William Burn 1829, a T-plan kirk with a splendid east tower. Redesigned internally by James Jerdan in 1892. Stained glass by E C Kempe and Ballantine & Gardiner. In the graveyard is a fragment of the 16th-century kirk and a fine selection of monuments. Rood well in village. Follow signs to Stenton off A1. Sunday Service: 10am. Please note time of service may be changed

Open daily dawn to dusk

CHURCH OF SCOTLAND

(only available at services) **B**

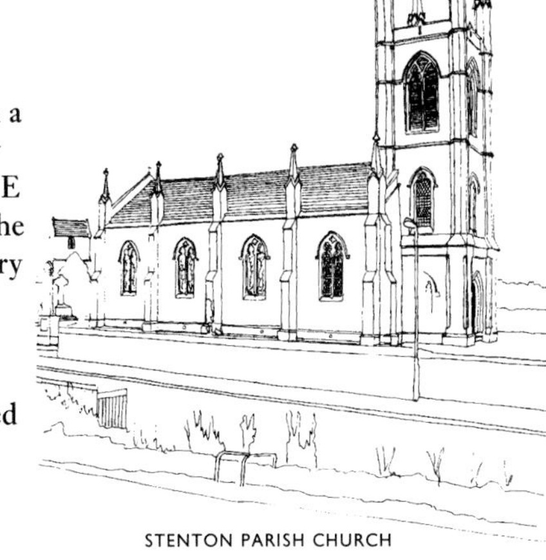

STENTON PARISH CHURCH

TRANENT METHODIST CHURCH

599 TRANENT METHODIST CHURCH

NT 403 729

63 Bridge Street, Tranent

Built 1870, second of East Lothian's three Primitive Methodist Chapels. Subdivided 1958 to create church hall. Simple interior. Monument to Barnabas Wild, minister 1890s. North side of main road at west end of town. Sunday Service: 11am

Open first Saturday of month for coffee morning

METHODIST **A**

600 ST MARTIN OF TOURS, TRANENT

NT 410 727

East end of High Street (opposite Co-op supermarket)

This is the third church building on the site in one hundred years and was built in 1969 in an octagonal shape using the Scandinavian compressed timber girder design. Contains two rough stained glass windows and an early 20th-century Italian crucifix above the altar. Irish limestone statue of classical design of St Martin as a Roman soldier. Sunday Service: 10.30am; weekdays 9am; Saturday: 10am and Vigil 6pm

Open by arrangement, telephone 01875 610232

ROMAN CATHOLIC

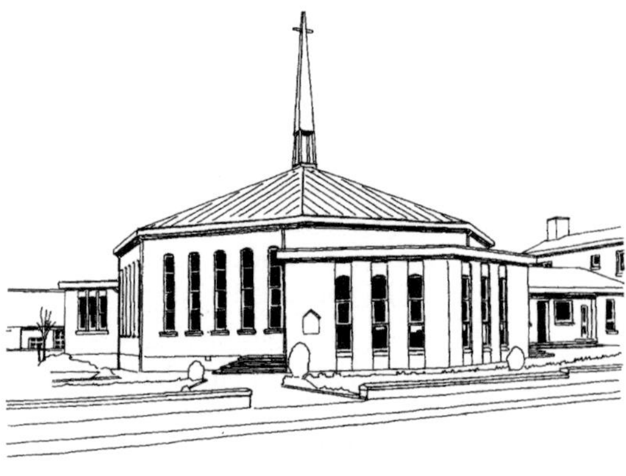

ST MARTIN OF TOURS, TRANENT

ST MARY'S PARISH CHURCH, WHITEKIRK

601 ST MARY'S PARISH CHURCH, WHITEKIRK

NT 596 815

Dating from 12th century, the original building was reconstructed during the 15th century starting with the vaulted stone choir, built in 1439 by Adam Hepburn of Hailes. In medieval times Whitekirk was an important place of pilgrimage. The church was set on fire in 1914 by suffragettes. Restored by Robert Lorimer. Ceiled wagon roof over nave and transepts, communion table, pulpit, lectern and font all by Lorimer. Stained glass by C E Kempe 1889 and Karl Parsons 1916. Tithe barn and historic graveyard. On A198. Sunday Service: 11.30am

Open daily dawn to dusk

CHURCH OF SCOTLAND WC **A**

602 WHITTINGEHAME PARISH CHURCH

NT 603 737

Main Street

Spiky battlemented Gothic T-plan church built 1722, and added to by Barclay and Lamb in 1820 for James Balfour, grandfather of A J Balfour, Prime Minister 1902-5. Eighteenth-century burial enclosure of Buchan Sydserfs of Ruchlaw and good late 17th-century headstones show that there was an earlier church on the site. Follow signs to Whittingehame off A1. No regular Church Services

Open daily dawn to dusk

CHURCH OF SCOTLAND **B**

WHITTINGEHAME PARISH CHURCH

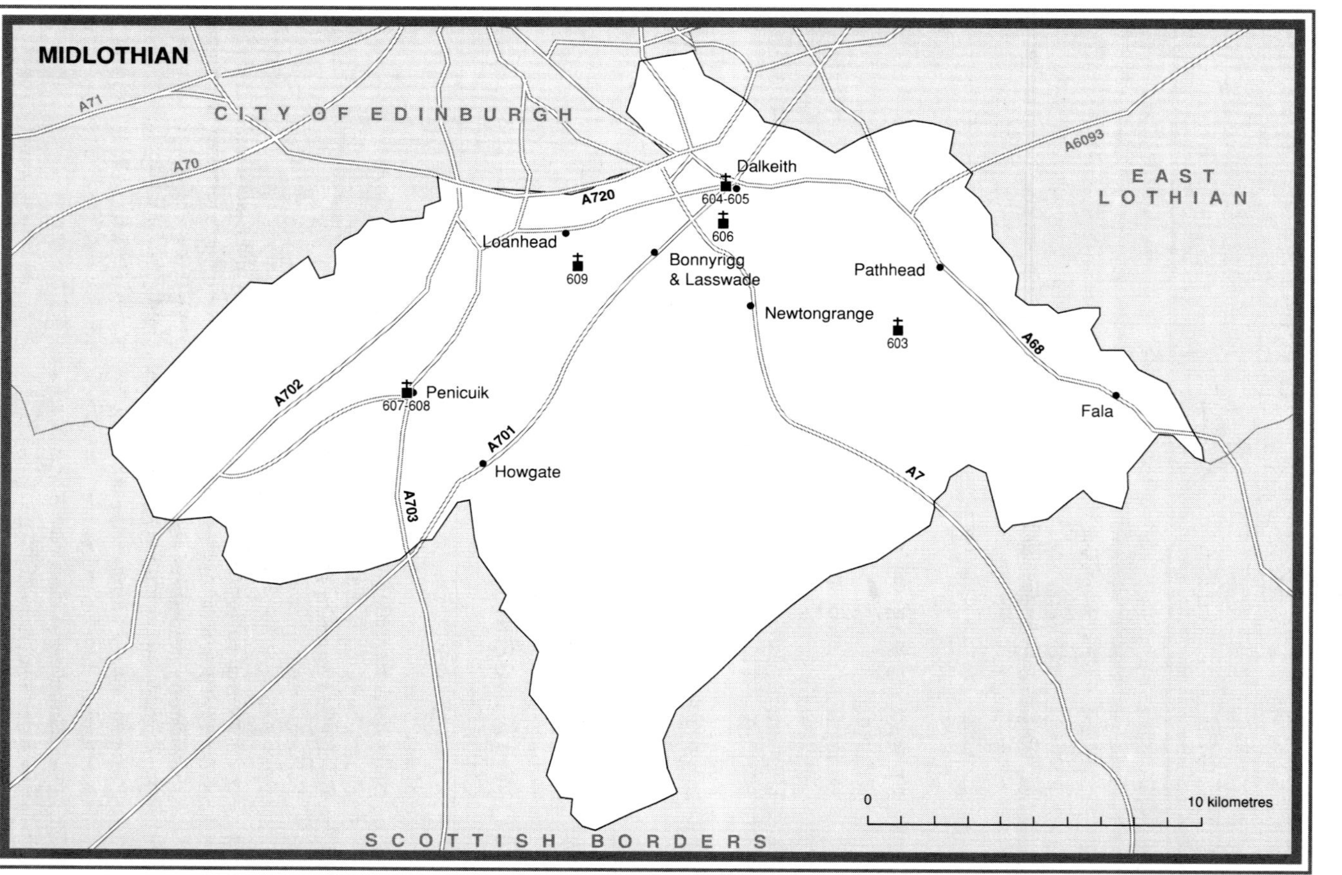
MIDLOTHIAN
CITY OF EDINBURGH
EAST LOTHIAN
SCOTTISH BORDERS
A71
A70
A720
A6093
A702
A701
A703
A68
A7
Dalkeith
604-605
606
Loanhead
609
Bonnyrigg & Lasswade
Pathhead
Newtongrange
603
Penicuik
607-608
Howgate
Fala
0
10 kilometres

MIDLOTHIAN

603 CRICHTON COLLEGIATE CHURCH

NT 381 616

Crichton, Pathhead

Collegiate church rebuilt in 1449 by William Crichton, Lord Chancellor of Scotland. Restored by Hardy & White 1898 and Benjamin Tindall 1998. Fine pointed barrel vaults over choir and transepts and splendid square tower over crossing. Organ by Joseph Brook & Co. Magnificent position at head of Tyne valley close to Crichton Castle. Signed road B6367 from A68 at Pathhead. Programme available of occasional services and concerts in summer months

Open May to September, Sunday 2-5pm. Or by appointment, telephone Mrs Tindall 01875 320341. Crichton Castle open 1 April to 30 September

NON-DENOMINATIONAL **A**

CRICHTON COLLEGIATE CHURCH

604 ST MARY'S CHURCH, DALKEITH

NT 335 677

Dalkeith Country Park, Dalkeith

Built as the chapel for Dalkeith Palace in 1843 by William Burn and David Bryce. Early English style with splendid features: double hammerbeam roof, stained glass windows, heraldic floor tiles by Minton, and the only working water-powered Hamilton organ in Scotland. Sunday Service: 9.45am

Open on Sunday 2-4pm from May to August; on Midlothian Doors Open Day in September, and at other times by arrangement, telephone Mr Fiddes 0131 663 3359. Summer concerts. Charity fun day in September

SCOTTISH EPISCOPAL **A**

605 ST NICHOLAS BUCCLEUCH PARISH CHURCH, DALKEITH

NT 333 674

High Street, Dalkeith

Medieval church, became collegiate in 1406. Nave and transepts 1854 by David Bryce. James, first Earl of Morton and his wife Princess Joanna (the profoundly deaf third daughter of James I) are buried within the choir, c.1498. Memorial monument with their effigies mark the burial site. Two hundred yards east of A68/A6094 junction. Sunday Services: Family Worship 9.30am, Parish Worship 11am

Open Easter Sunday to 30 September, weekdays, 10am–12 noon and 2–4pm, Sunday 10–11am. Or contact Mr A Brown, telephone 0131 663 0799

CHURCH OF SCOTLAND **A**

ST NICHOLAS BUCCLEUCH PARISH CHURCH, DALKEITH

606 NEWBATTLE CHURCH

NT 331 661

Newbattle Road, Newbattle

Harled, T-plan church with belfry by Alexander McGill 1727. Two galleries added 1851. A remarkable number of the original fittings survive including the upper part of the 17th-century pulpit and the pilastered wooden frame of the Lothian Loft. Good 17th-century gravestones including the amazing, ornamented Welsh family monument. Sunday Service: 10am

Open by arrangement, telephone Mr Iain McCarter 0131 663 3896

CHURCH OF SCOTLAND WC **B**

NEWBATTLE CHURCH

607 PENICUIK SOUTH CHURCH

NT 236 595

Peebles Road, Penicuik

Designed in 1863 by Frederick T Pilkington. Open timber roof. Stained glass. Fully restored 1991. Short history available, models of church on sale. Sunday Services: 11.15am and 7pm

Open Saturday all year, 10am-12 noon

CHURCH OF SCOTLAND B

PENICUIK SOUTH CHURCH

608 ST JAMES SCOTTISH EPISCOPAL CHURCH, PENICUIK

NT 232 597

Broomhill Road, Penicuik

The original church which now forms the nave was designed by H Seymour of Seymour & Kinross 1882. The chancel, vestries, tower and bell were added by H O Tarbolton, 1899. An excellent lot of stained glass, including one light by Shrigley & Hunt of Lancaster and four magnificent lights by C E Kempe. Rood screen designed by Tarbolton and carved by T Good; communion rails also designed by Tarbolton and carved by Scott Morton & Co. Reredos designed and executed by Mrs Meredith-Williams, 1921. Sunday Services: 8am and 10.15am; first Sundays Choral Evensong 6.30pm

Open by arrangement, telephone the Rector 01968 672862

SCOTTISH EPISCOPAL B

609 ROSSLYN CHAPEL (ST MATTHEW'S)

NT 275 631

Chapel Loan, Roslin

Built 1450 as the church of a college established by William Sinclair, 3rd Earl of Orkney. Intended to be cruciform but only the choir was completed. Famous for its decorative stone carving that covers almost every part of the building. The 'Prentice Pillar' has spectacular decoration. Sunday Services: 10.30am and 3.30pm in winter, 5.30pm summer

Open all year, Monday to Saturday 10am-5pm, Sunday 12 noon-4.45pm

SCOTTISH EPISCOPAL A

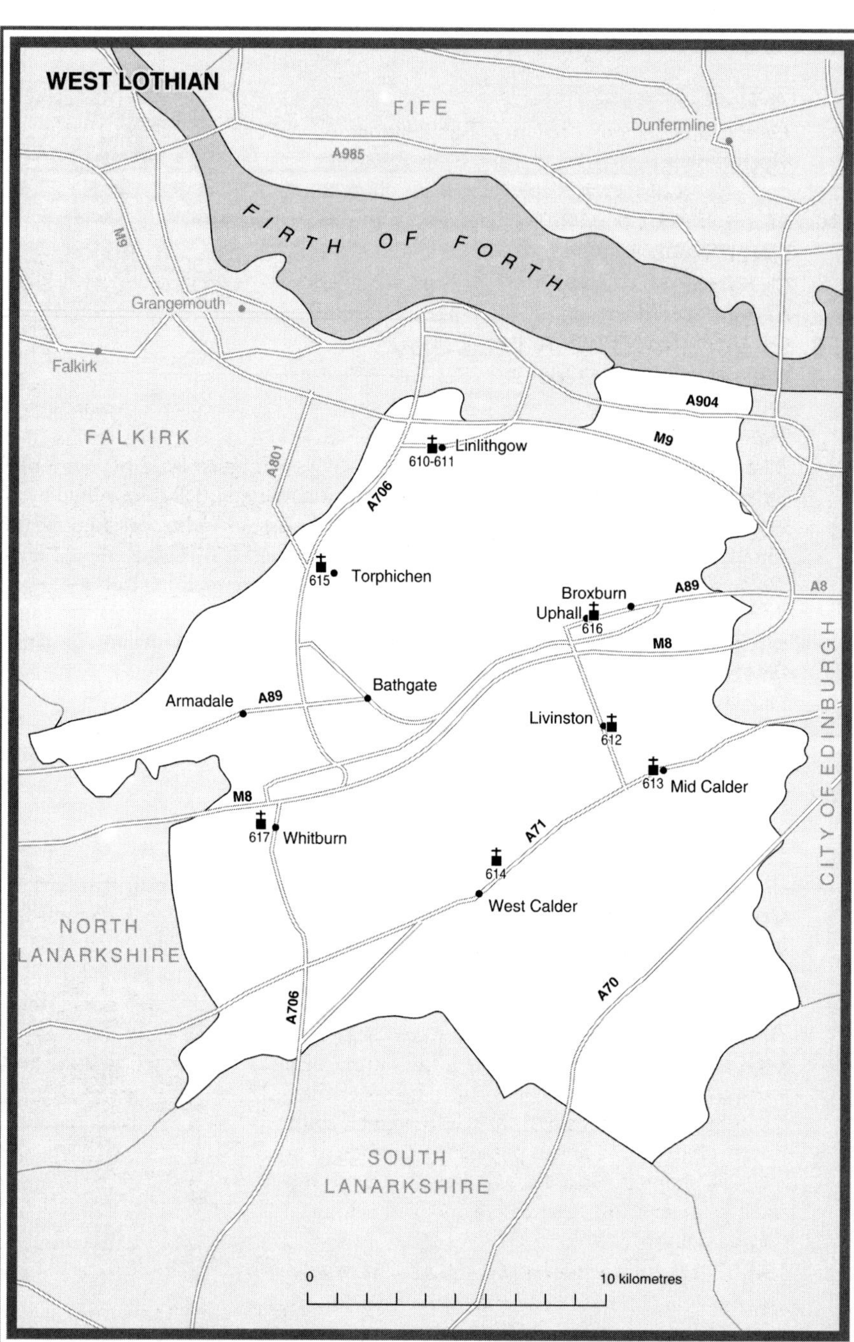
WEST LOTHIAN
FIFE
Dunfermline
A985
FIRTH OF FORTH
M9
Grangemouth
Falkirk
FALKIRK
A904
M9
Linlithgow
610-611
A801
A706
Torphichen
615
Broxburn
A89
A8
Uphall
616
M8
Bathgate
Armadale
A89
Livinston
612
613
Mid Calder
M8
617
Whitburn
A71
614
West Calder
CITY OF EDINBURGH
NORTH
LANARKSHIRE
A706
A70
SOUTH
LANARKSHIRE
0
10 kilometres

WEST LOTHIAN

Local Representative: Mr Alan Naylor, Candiehill, Candie, Avonbridge, Falkirk (*telephone* 01324 861583)

610 ST MICHAEL'S PARISH CHURCH, LINLITHGOW

NT 002 773

Kirkgate, Linlithgow

One of the finest examples of a large medieval burgh church. Consecrated in 1242 on the site of an earlier church, most of the present building dates from the 15th century with some 19th and 20th-century restoration. Situated beside Linlithgow Palace, its history is intertwined with that of the royal house of Stewart. The modern aluminium crown 1964 symbolises the Church's continuing witness to Christ's Kingship. Window commemorating 750th anniversary of the church, 1992, by Crear McCartney. The Peel, Linlithgow Palace and Loch adjacent. Sunday Services: 9.30am and 11am

ST MICHAEL'S PARISH CHURCH, LINLITHGOW

Church website: www.stmichaels-parish.org.uk

Open all year, May to September, Monday to Saturday 10am-4pm; Sunday 12.30pm-4pm. October to April, Monday to Friday 10am-3pm

CHURCH OF SCOTLAND (on request) **A**

611 ST PETER'S EPISCOPAL CHURCH, LINLITHGOW

NS 000 770

High Street, Linlithgow

Built in 1928 as a memorial to George Walpole, Bishop of Edinburgh and his wife Mildred with assistance from missions in England and USA. Design by J Walker Todd of Dick Peddie & Todd is a Byzantine basilica with a 'cross in the square' plan form, a high central dome and half dome over the sanctuary apse. It is a small church located on south side of High Street, and is popular as a refuge from the main shopping area. Sunday Services: 9.30am and 8.30am on fourth Sunday of month (to 1929 prayer book)

Open Tuesday and Saturday, from May to September 2-4pm, or telephone Rev Stuart Bonney 01506 842384

SCOTTISH EPISCOPAL WC

ST PETER'S EPISCOPAL CHURCH, LINLITHGOW

LIVINGSTON VILLAGE KIRK

612 LIVINGSTON VILLAGE KIRK

NT 037 669

Kirk Lane, Livingston

There has been a church on the site since 12th century. The present building was rebuilt 1732. Late 18th-century pews and pulpit with Gothic sounding board and a pretty stair. Pewter communion vessels and old collecting shovels on display. Plaque in entrance commemorates Covenanters from village drowned off Orkney. Kirkyard has some fine monuments from 17th and 18th centuries, including some lively headstones featuring phoenixes and leafy cartouches. Close to Heritage Centre. Sunday Service: 10am. Other services as advertised on notice board

Open by arrangement, telephone the Minister 01506 420227

CHURCH OF SCOTLAND **B**

613 KIRK OF CALDER, MID CALDER

NT 074 673

Main Street, Mid Calder

This 16th-century parish church, recently restored, won the West Lothian Award for Conservation in 1992. John Knox, James 'Paraffin' Young, David Livingston and Frederick Chopin have already visited here – we look forward to meeting you too! Admission free, donations welcome. Restoration of stained glass windows 1995. Off A71 on B7015 in village of Mid Calder. Sunday Service: 10.30am

Church website: www.kirkofcalder.com

Open May to September, Sunday 2-4pm. Near to Almondell Country Park, open all year

CHURCH OF SCOTLAND **A**

Scottish Tourist Board COMMENDED

KIRK OF CALDER, MID CALDER

614 POLBETH HARWOOD PARISH CHURCH

NT 017 628

Chapelton Drive, Polbeth, West Calder

The congregation was formed in 1795 and the church completed in 1796 as Burgher Kirk. Congregation translated from West Calder to Polbeth in 1962. A71 between Livingston New Town and West Calder. Fifteen minutes walk from West Calder station. Sunday Service: 11am

Open Monday and Wednesday during school term time, 10am-12 noon; Thursday 6-8pm during summer

CHURCH OF SCOTLAND

POLBETH HARWOOD PARISH CHURCH

615 TORPHICHEN KIRK

NS 969 725

The Bowyett, Torphichen

Built in 1756 on the site of the nave of the 12th-century preceptory, it is a T-shaped building with three galleries including a laird's loft. Two centre pews can be tipped back to form extended communion tables. Sanctuary stone in the graveyard. Preceptory church adjoining in the care of Historic Scotland. Sunday Service: 11.15am

Open parish church and preceptory Easter to end October, Saturday 11am-5pm, Sunday 2-5pm. Exhibition. Charge for entry to preceptory. Groups welcome for guided tours of both buildings, telephone Mrs Mary Wilson 01506 653475

CHURCH OF SCOTLAND WC **A**

616 ST NICHOLAS, UPHALL

NT 060 722

Ecclesmachan Road, Uphall

Tower and nave with Romanesque doorway of 1187, Buchan stairs of the 17th century, aisles added 1590 and 1878. A picture shows the balconies that existed before the restoration of 1938. Buried in the tower are Erskines, Earls of Buchan and sons. Mixture of old and modern stained glass windows. The bell, one of the oldest in West Lothian, is inscribed '*in onore sancte nicolae campana ecclegie de strabork anno dni mviii*'. 'Judas' Bible of 1613. Sunday Service: 11.30am

Open by arrangement, telephone the Minister 01506 852550

CHURCH OF SCOTLAND WC **B**

WHITBURN SOUTH PARISH CHURCH

617 WHITBURN SOUTH PARISH CHURCH

NS 947 646

Manse Road, Whitburn

In its present form dating from 1729, the walls house a modern interior of the 1950s, the result of a fire. Cruciform and typically Georgian, though some earlier architectural features are evident. The graveyard is host to several local notables and is the last resting place of Robert Burns' eldest daughter, Elizabeth Paton (dear 'Bought' Bess) who married John Bishop, the overseer at Polkemmet Estate. Sunday Service: 11am all year; first Sunday September to May 6pm; first Sunday in June 3pm; Christmas Day 10am, Maundy Thursday 7pm

Open by arrangement, telephone the Church Officer, Mr John Tennant, 01501 741627

CHURCH OF SCOTLAND **B**

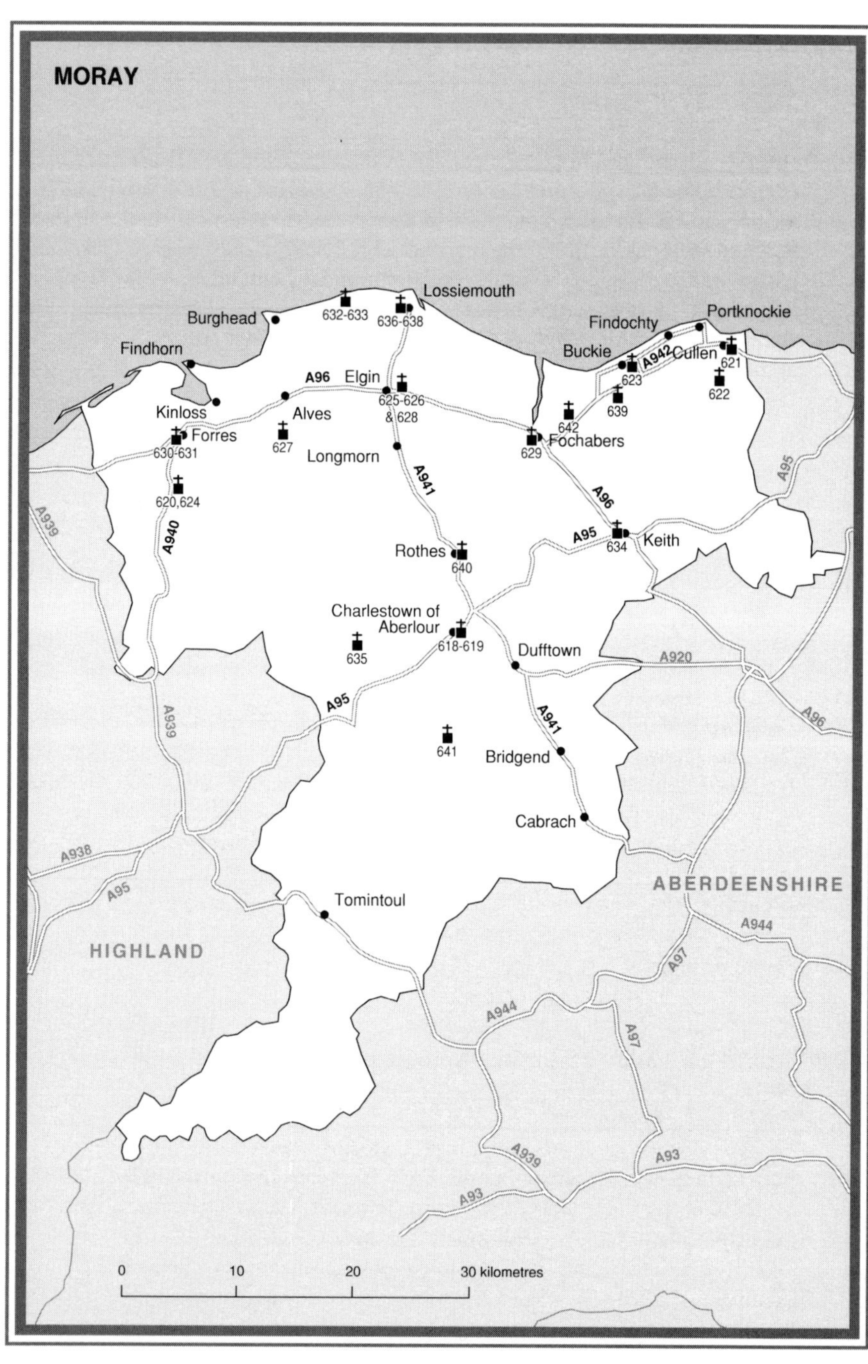
MORAY
Lossiemouth
Burghead
632-633
636-638
Findochty
Portknockie
Findhorn
Buckie
A942
Cullen
621
A96
Elgin
623
622
Kinloss
Alves
625-626
& 628
639
642
Forres
630-631
627
Longmorn
629
Fochabers
A941
620,624
A95
A96
A939
A940
A95
634
Keith
Rothes
640
Charlestown of
Aberlour
618-619
635
Dufftown
A920
A95
A939
A941
641
Bridgend
A96
Cabrach
A938
A95
ABERDEENSHIRE
Tomintoul
A944
HIGHLAND
A97
A944
A97
A939
A93
A93
0
10
20
30 kilometres

MORAY

Local Representative: Mrs Elizabeth Beaton, Keam Schoolhouse, Hopeman, Moray (*telephone* 01343 830301)

ABERLOUR PARISH CHURCH

618 ABERLOUR PARISH CHURCH

NJ 264 428

The Square, Aberlour

Originally dedicated to St Drostan, the church was built in 1812. The Norman tower 1840 was the sole survivor of a disastrous fire in 1861. George Petrie, architect, rebuilt the church in neo-Norman style. Choir added 1933 by J Wittet in memory of Sir James Ritchie Findlay. First organ by Brindlay & Foster 1900, rebuilt by Arnest Lawson 1932, and present organ rebuilt by Sandy Edmonstone, 1991. Sunday Service: 11.00am

Open 10am–5pm

CHURCH OF SCOTLAND **B**

619 ST MARGARET OF SCOTLAND, ABERLOUR

NJ 272 431

High Street, Aberlour

Designed by Alexander Ross and consecrated in 1879, the tall Gothic church retains its splendid original interior. Built for the orphanage 120 years ago, the feet of hundreds of children have worn down the Victorian tiled floor. Lovely carvings of flowers, birds and squirrels on pillar capitals and screen arch. Sunday Services: 11am, first Sunday in the month; 9.15am other Sundays

Key from Aberlour Hotel (must be signed for)

SCOTTISH EPISCOPAL **A**

620 EDINKILLIE PARISH CHURCH

NJ 020 466

Edinkillie, Dunphail, nr Forres

Small church built 1741 in traditional 18th-century style. Central pulpit and galleries on three sides. Fine pipe organ. Beautifully situated on the banks of the River Divie, nine miles south of Forres on the A940 from Forres to Grantown-on-Spey. Linked with Dyke. Sunday Service: 12 noon

Open by arrangement, telephone Mr C J Falconer (Beadle) 01309 611220, or Mr W Reid 01309 611279

CHURCH OF SCOTLAND ♿ WC

ST MARGARET OF SCOTLAND, ABERLOUR

621 OLD KIRK OF CULLEN

NJ 507 664

Cullen

This 13th-century church was originally dedicated to St Mary the Virgin and is the burial place of the 'interior parts' of Queen Elizabeth de Burgh 1327. A chaplaincy was endowed here by Robert I in 1327 and the church acquired collegiate status in 1543. Later additions include the St Anne's Aisle of 1539, while there is a fine example of a laird's loft 1602. Other features include a pre-Reformation aumbry or sacrament house, tombs and monuments including one to James, first Earl of Seafield, Chancellor of Scotland at the Treaty of Union of 1707, and 17th-century box pews. The churchyard has many interesting and imposing tombs, monuments and gravestones. The Church is at Old Cullen, three-quarters of a mile south-west of the town centre. Sunday Service: 10.30am

Open summer 2-4pm Tuesday and Friday, and by arrangement, telephone the Minister 01542 841851

CHURCH OF SCOTLAND

♿ WC **A**

OLD KIRK OF CULLEN

622 ST JOHN'S CHURCH, DESKFORD

NJ 509 617

Built in 1871 in the Victorian Gothic style, architect John Miller (architect and master of works to Seafield Estates, Cullen). It has unusual tracery detail in the transept window. Inside there is stencil work on the walls. The Old St John's Church (ruined) at Kirkton of Deskford incorporates a fine aumbry 1551 with inscriptions in English and Latin and carvings of angels supporting monstrance. B9018, three miles south of Cullen. Sunday Service: second and fourth of every month, 12 noon

Open by arrangement, telephone the Minister 01542 841851

CHURCH OF SCOTLAND ♿ **B**

623 ST PETER'S CHURCH, BUCKIE

NJ 419 653

St Andrew's Square, Buckie

To plans donated by Bishop Kyle and supervised by A and W Reid of Elgin. Dedicated on a site donated by Sir William Gordon. Rose window. Recent art work includes six murals of excellent quality in church hall and two canvases of David and Saul and of the 'Death of St Joseph' in the church, by local artist Lynn Thain. High altar of Italian marble surrounded by murals depicting 'The Calming of the Storm' and 'The Walking on the Water'. Reredos and baptistry, C J Menart 1907. Statue of Our Lady of Aberdeen, copy of original in Brussels. Services: Saturday Vigil Mass 6.30pm; Sunday 10am; Weekdays 9.30am

Open daily, 9am–6pm

ROMAN CATHOLIC **A**

ST PETER'S CHURCH, BUCKIE

624 DYKE PARISH CHURCH

NH 990 584

Dyke, nr Forres, Moray

Built 1781 in centre of village. Interesting crypt and triple pulpit (one of the only two in Scotland). Follow road to Brodie Castle, turning right to village before castle entrance. Linked with Edinkillie. Sunday Service: 10.30am

Open by arrangement, key in village, telephone Minister 01309 641239

CHURCH OF SCOTLAND **A**

625 GREYFRIARS CONVENT OF MERCY, ELGIN

NJ 219 628

Abbey Street, Elgin

Beautiful and careful restoration, 1891-1908, by architect John Kinross for the 3rd Marquess of Bute, of a 15th-century Franciscan friary. Magnificently carved oak screen divides the choir from the nave and a splendid barrel-vaulted ceiling stretches unbroken to the stained glass window above the altar. Fine cloister with original medieval well. Services: Masses Tuesday 10am and Fridays 7pm

Open by arrangement with the Sisters of Mercy, telephone 01343 547806.

Rose garden open May to September (entrance in Institution Road)

ROMAN CATHOLIC WC **A**

626 HOLY TRINITY, ELGIN

NJ 214 630

Trinity Place, Elgin

Gothic style on a Greek cross ground-plan to a design by William Robertson 1826. The crenellated and pinacled south entrance gable intended as an architectural feature visible from the High Street is now blocked by the ring-road. Chancel added 1852 and interior recast; nave lengthened 1879. Plain dignified interior with late 19th-century stained glass. Services: Sunday Holy Communion 8am, Family Eucharist 11am, Evensong 6.30pm, Holy Communion Tuesday 7pm, Wednesday 8am, Friday 11am, Saturday 9am

Open 9am-5pm

SCOTTISH EPISCOPAL WC **B**

627 PLUSCARDEN ABBEY, ELGIN

NJ 143 576

Pluscarden, near Elgin

Founded in 1230 by Alexander II for Valiscaulian monks, it became Benedictine in 1454. Following the Reformation it was the property of various local families, culminating in the Dukes of Fife from whom it was bought by the Marquess of Bute, and whose son, Lord Colum, gave it to the monks in 1943. The buildings were eventually re-occupied in 1948. There are a number of interesting works by prominent artists and architects following the restoration. Abbey is signposted from A96 and B1090. Member of Moray Church trail. The Abbey

PLUSCARDEN ABBEY, ELGIN

offers retreat accommodation for men and women. Full details of this, together with Services and opening times, may be obtained by telephoning 01343 890257 (fax 01343 890258)

Church website: www.pluscardenabbey.org

Annual Pluscarden Pentecost lectures: Tuesday, Wednesday and Thursday after Pentecost. Open daily 4.45am–8.45pm

ROMAN CATHOLIC **A**

628 ST SYLVESTER'S, ELGIN

NJ 219 626

Institution Road, Elgin

The church and presbytery were designed and completed in 1844, architect Thomas Mackenzie of Elgin. Dedication in recognition of the financial support by the younger brother of Sir William Drummond of Grantully who took the name Sylvester on converting to Catholicism. Lady Altar 1915, by R B Pratt. Sanctuary altered 1968 in keeping with the new liturgy. Major alterations to church and adjoining school 2000 to form sacristy and meeting rooms by Ashley Bartlam Partnership. Large cross by the monks of Pluscarden. Services: Saturday 6.00pm Vigil; Sunday 11.15am

Open 9am–8pm daily except Tuesdays

ROMAN CATHOLIC **B**

GORDON CHAPEL, FOCHABERS

629 GORDON CHAPEL, FOCHABERS

NJ 346 589

Castle Street, Fochabers

Built in 1834 to a design by Archibald Simpson, restored in 1874. Stained glass designed by Sir Edward Burne-Jones. A fine Hill's organ. The church is upstairs with the rectory (originally a school) below. Sunday Services: Said Eucharist 8am; Family Service 10.30am weekly; first Sunday of month Choral Evensong 6.30pm

Open daily during daylight hours.

SCOTTISH EPISCOPAL WC **A**

630 ST LAURENCE PARISH CHURCH, FORRES

NJ 035 588

High Street, Forres

Built on a site of Christian worship dating from mid 13th century, today's neo-Gothic building – designed by John Robertson and dedicated in 1906 – is a fine example of the stonemason's craft. The pitch-pine ceiling and the stained glass windows by Douglas Strachan and Percy Bacon help to create the special atmosphere of peace and beauty. Font replica of one in Dryburgh Abbey. Information leaflets in English, French, German, Spanish and Italian are free. Welcomers on duty. Sunday Service: 10am

Open May to September, Monday to Friday 10am-12 noon, 2-4pm.

Other times by arrangement, telephone 01309 672260

CHURCH OF SCOTLAND WC **B**

ST JOHN'S CHURCH, FORRES

631 ST JOHN'S CHURCH, FORRES

NJ 041 592

Victoria Road, Forres

Built in 1841, to a design by Patrick Wilson, remodelled in Italianate manner by Thomas Mackenzie, Elgin. The building has been beautified over the years including the laying of mosaic tiles throughout the chancel and aisles. The frontage is adorned with a wheel window, the entrance sheltered by an arcaded logia and flanked by a campanile. A large canvas in the apse 1906 and mural behind the font 1911 are the work of William Hole RSA. Sunday Services: 8am, 10am and 6pm

Open daylight hours (or key at Rectory)

SCOTTISH EPISCOPAL ♿ 👂 📖 **A**

632 THE MICHAEL KIRK, GORDONSTOUN

NJ 193 689

Duffus, by Elgin

Reached along a hushed, enchanted avenue from Gordonstoun, this dignified little church was built in 1705 as a mausoleum chapel for 'the Wizard Laird', Sir Robert Gordon, on the site of the ancient Kirk of Ogstoun. Roofed, furnished and fitted by John Kinross in 1900 for Lady Gordon-Cumming. In style it is pure 15th-century Gothic with remarkable window tracery enhanced by flower carvings. Services: Holy Communion 08.40am most Sundays during the academic year; candlelit Compline 9pm, Thursdays during winter term

Church website: www.gordonstoun.org.uk

Key by the door, or contact the Chaplain at Gordonstoun School reception, telephone 01343 835804

INTERDENOMINATIONAL 📖 (school shop) **A**

633 ST CHRISTOPHER'S, GORDONSTOUN

NJ 184 690

Duffus, by Elgin

Gordonstoun School was founded in 1934 by Kurt Hahn, with the aim of encouraging self-reliance and independence. St Christopher's is the main school chapel, built 1965-6 to designs by former pupil Patrick Huggins, to complement the Michael Kirk (see above). Seating is 'gathered about the lectern pulpit and the Communion Table' whose positions emphasise the equal importance of Word and Sacrament, while giving space for orchestral or dramatic performances. Main school service: Sunday 10.45am during term time

Church website: www.gordonstoun.org.uk

Report to Gordonstoun School reception

INTER-DENOMINATIONAL (school shop)

634 ST THOMAS' CHURCH, KEITH

NJ 430 502

Chapel Street, Keith

ST THOMAS' CHURCH, KEITH

Built 1831, architect William Robertson, Elgin. Successor to 1785 chapel and cottage at Kempcairn, following planning and fundraising by Father Lovi. Roman Doric pilastered exterior and 'plain' interior with nave and sanctuary. Enlarged with copper-clad dome, altar, communion rails, pulpit and oak pews 1915. Altar piece painting 'The Incredulity of St Thomas', commissioned by Charles X of France 1828. Fine stained glass windows 1970s. St John Ogilvie Chapel commemorating saint born nearby. Extensive restoration 1996

Open daily, dawn to dusk

ROMAN CATHOLIC **A**

635 KNOCKANDO PARISH CHURCH

NJ 186 429

Award-winning design for new church by the Law & Dunbar-Nasmith Partnership 1993 on the site of an earlier building destroyed by fire in 1990. Sympathetic with the building which it has replaced. The Creation is symbolised in a new stained glass window by Andrew Lawson-Johnson. From A95 Aviemore–Elgin or A941 Dufftown–Elgin, take B9102 Archiestown Knockando. At Cardhu turn right. Church is signposted. Linked with Rothes. Sunday Service: 10.30am

Open Wednesday only, 2pm–4pm July and August

CHURCH OF SCOTLAND

KNOCKANDO PARISH CHURCH

636 ST COLUMBA'S, LOSSIEMOUTH

NJ 232 711

Union Street, Lossiemouth

Small church in the shape of a Latin Cross, designed by Arthur Harrison of Stockton-on-Tees and paid for by the Bute family. The building materials were all shipped from Teesside. The sanctuary lamp is in the form of a ship's lamp. Stained glass window by Fr Ninian Sloan of 'Our Lady Star of the Sea' dedicted to the memory of the Royal and Allied navies stationed at Lossiemouth 1946-72 and donated by them. Sunday Mass: 6.30pm

Open by arrangement with Mrs Margaret Kinnaird, telephone 01343 813539

ROMAN CATHOLIC

637 ST GERARDINE'S HIGH, LOSSIEMOUTH

NJ 233 706

St Gerardine's Road, Lossiemouth

The foundation stone was laid in 1898 and the building is of Norman Romanesque design by Sir J J Burnet. The plainness of the Norman Tower, white harled walls and red roof belie the magnificent interior. The features include many items of stained glass depicting various Biblical themes. Sunday Service: 11am and 6pm

Open by arrangement, telephone the Minister 01343 813146, or Mr James Cumming 01343 812194

CHURCH OF SCOTLAND B

ST GERARDINE'S HIGH, LOSSIEMOUTH

638 ST MARGARET OF SCOTLAND, LOSSIEMOUTH

NJ 227 706

Stotfield Road, Lossiemouth

Small church of 1922 with Gothic detailing built to a design by Alexander Ross of Inverness, responsible for Episcopal churches great and small throughout the north, including Inverness Cathedral. Simple interior with open timber vaulted ceiling. Sunday Service: Parish Eucharist 9.30am; Thursday Eucharist 10am and Eventide Prayer 5pm

Open May to September, Fridays 2pm–5pm

SCOTTISH EPISCOPAL

639 ST GREGORY'S CHURCH, PRESHOME

NJ 409 615

Preshome, Clochan

Built in 1790, James Byres, architect. A wide rectangular church with harled walls and freestone dressing. The church is adorned with urn finials; its west end is a charming product of 18th-century taste, in which Italian Baroque has been skilfully naturalised to a Banffshire setting. Copy of a painting of St Gregory the Great by Annibale Caracci. Two holy water stoups of Portsoy marble. Services: Sunday Mass occasionally at 6pm

Open by arrangement, telephone Mr G Gordon, St Gregory's Chapel House

ROMAN CATHOLIC **A**

640 ROTHES PARISH CHURCH

NJ 278 492

High Street/Seafield Square, Rothes

Built in 1781 with a steeple added in 1870. A traditional Scottish design of the Reformed tradition with the pulpit on the long wall, a three-sided gallery and apse. Pipe organ 1901 has recently been restored. Linked with Knockando. Sunday Service: 12 noon

Open July to August, Tuesday to Friday 2–4.30pm

CHURCH OF SCOTLAND

ROTHES PARISH CHURCH

641 OLD SEMINARY, SCALAN

NJ 246 195

Braes of Glenlivet, Ballindalloch, Banffshire

Scalan (Gaelic for a turf-roofed shelter) is a plain 18th-century house, the most significant relic of 'penal days'. Built in 1717 as a seminary for the training of priests. 1995 award of The Association for the Protection of Rural Scotland. Turn off B9008 Tomintoul–Dufftown at Pole Inn (signposted). Services: Annual Mass, first Sunday July 4pm

Open all year

ROMAN CATHOLIC **A**

OLD SEMINARY, SCALAN

642 ST NINIAN'S, TYNET

NJ 379 613

Mill of Tynet, Fochabers

The oldest post-Reformation Catholic church still in use in Scotland. At the request of the Duke of Gordon 1755, built to resemble a sheep-cot in days when it was still an offence to celebrate Mass. Renovated 1957, Ian Lindsay, architect, the long low whitewashed building is still 'a church in disguise'. Sunday Service: 8.30am; Saturday: Vigil Mass 5.30pm

Open by arrangement, telephone Mr P Cromar, 'Golar', Newlands of Tynet (opposite church)

ROMAN CATHOLIC **A**

ST NINIAN'S, TYNET

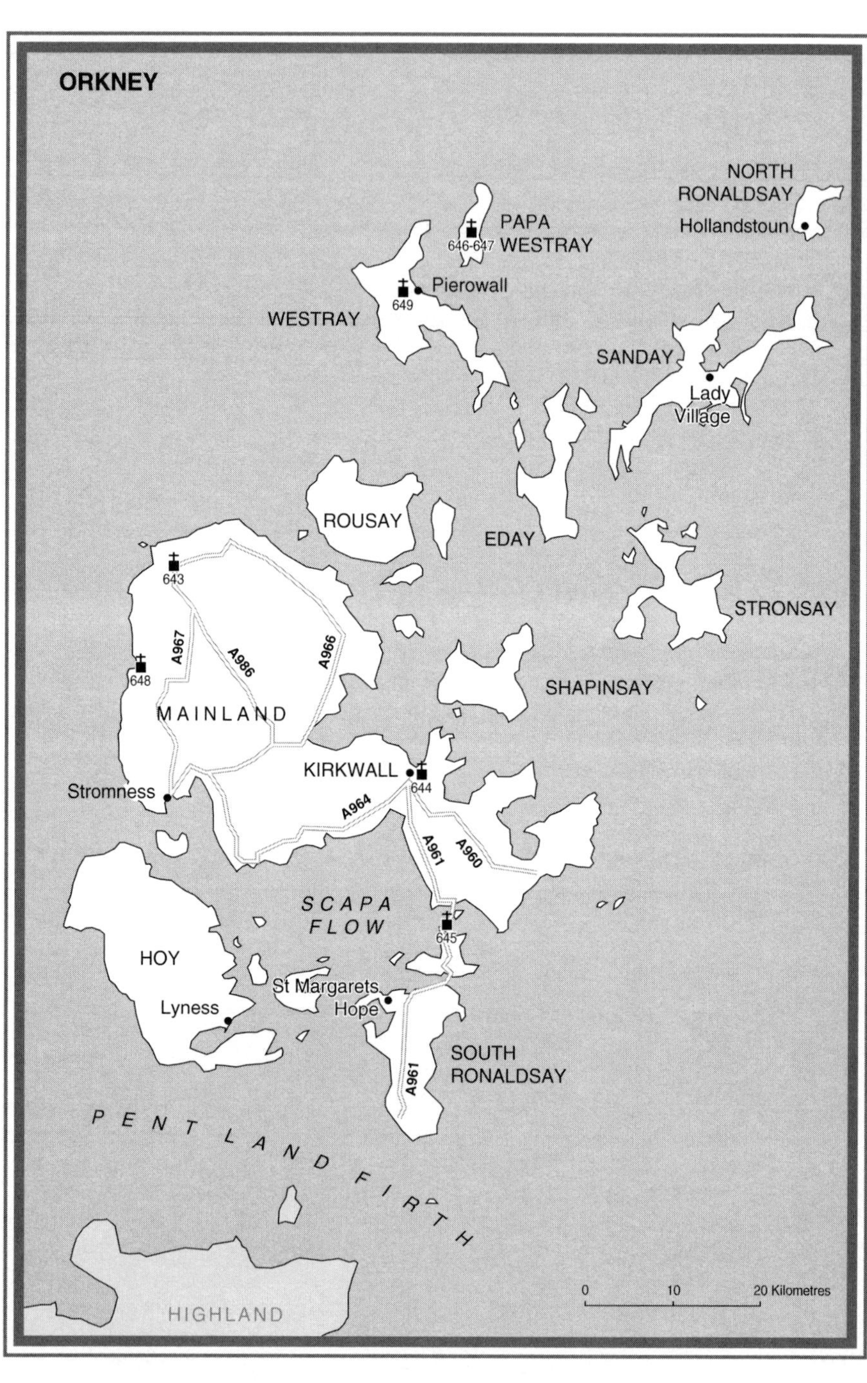

ORKNEY
NORTH RONALDSAY
Hollandstoun
PAPA WESTRAY
646-647
WESTRAY
649
Pierowall
SANDAY
Lady Village
ROUSAY
EDAY
STRONSAY
SHAPINSAY
643
648
A967
A986
A966
MAINLAND
KIRKWALL
644
Stromness
A964
A961
A960
SCAPA FLOW
645
HOY
St Margarets Hope
Lyness
SOUTH RONALDSAY
A961
PENTLAND FIRTH
HIGHLAND
0
10
20 Kilometres

ORKNEY

Local Representative: Mr R L B Cormack, Westness House, Rousay, Orkney (*telephone* 01856 821286)

643 ST MAGNUS CHURCH, BIRSAY

HY 248 277

The original church was built by Earl Thorfinn c.1060 and has been altered and restored several times, most recently in 1986. Stained glass window by Douglas Strachan showing scenes from the life of St Magnus. Inside the church are two 16th and 17th-century tombstones. Seventeenth-century belfry. The Mons Bellus stone is probably from the nearby Bishop's Palace. The church is now maintained by the St Magnus Church Birsay Trust. Twenty miles from Kirkwall, across the road from the Earl's Palace. Occasional Services: details locally

Open daily, April to September. Key available all year from village shop. St Magnus Day Service of Praise on 16 April; Jazz Festival Praise Service at end of April

NON-DENOMINATIONAL (nearby) **B**

644 ST MAGNUS CATHEDRAL, KIRKWALL

HY 449 108

Broad Street, Kirkwall

The Cathedral Church of St Magnus the Martyr was founded in 1137 by Earl Rognval Kolson and dedicated to his uncle, Earl Magnus Erlendson. Completed c.1500. It contains many items of interest and ranks as one of the finest cathedrals in Scotland. Although it is owned and maintained by Orkney Islands Council, the Society of Friends of St Magnus was formed in 1958 to help raise funds for its preservation. Custodian on duty. St Magnus Centre in Palace Road open Monday to Saturday 8.30am-6.30pm. Sunday 1.30-6.30pm (reduced hours in winter); heritage centre, study library, refreshments and souvenirs; free entry, disabled access/toilets. Sunday Service: 11.15am

Open April to September, Monday to Saturday 9am-6pm, Sunday 2-6pm; October to March, Monday to Saturday 9am-1pm and 2-5pm. Closed public holidays and Christmas festive season, except for Church Services

CHURCH OF SCOTLAND

(side entrance) (public nearby)

(braille and audio tape versions of guidebook available) **A**

ST MAGNUS CATHEDRAL, KIRKWALL

THE ITALIAN CHAPEL

645 THE ITALIAN CHAPEL

HY 488 006

Lambholm, Orkney

All that remains of the Italian Prisoner of War Camp 60, the famous Italian Chapel was created from two Nissen huts in 1943, using material from sunken blockships in Scapa Flow. Wonderful testimony to the artistic skills of Domenico Chiocchetti and his fellow prisoners who came to Orkney to work on the construction of the Churchill Barriers. Beautifully designed chancel, altar, altar-rail and Holy water stoup. Painted glass windows depicting St Francis of Assisi and St Catherine of Siena. Restored 1960. A Preservation Committee is dedicated to the upkeep of the Chapel. Service: on first Sunday of summer months 3pm

Open daily

ROMAN CATHOLIC **B**

646 ST ANN'S, PAPA WESTRAY

HY 496 516

Next to school in centre of island

Built in 1842, this was the first kirk in Scotland to be given to the Free Church by the proprietor. Rectangular building with rubble masonry walls and harled exterior. Restoration 2001 by Orkney Islands Council, Health Board and congregation, St Ann's is now home to the Island's surgery, a small flat and community facilities. Several beautiful locally made felt hangings. Sunday Service: 2.30pm

Open at all times

CHURCH OF SCOTLAND **C**

647 ST BONIFACE, PAPA WESTRAY

HY 488 527

Kirkhouse, Papa Westray

Founded in the 8th century, St Boniface was an important church in the early Middle Ages, possibly the seat of Orkney's first Bishopric. The present building is 12th century, enlarged early 1700s and furnished with box pews, gallery and high pulpit. Restored 1993. Viking age hog-backed tombstone in the kirkyard, Pictish cross-slab now in the Orkney Museum, Kirkwall. Services: Wednesdays 8 pm mid-June to end-August; also Christmas, Holy Week and occasional services in winter

Open at all times

NON-DENOMINATIONAL

648 ST PETER'S, SANDWICK

HY 235 199

Two miles north of Skara Brae, Mainland

A rare survival of a quite exceptional unaltered Scots Parish Kirk of 1836. Situated on a rugged and exposed site, commanding views over the Bay of Skaill with Skara Brae in the distance. Dominated by a towering pulpit reaching to gallery height, the austere interior powerfully evokes the experience of Presbyterian worship in the 19th century when over 500 packed the building - each allowed a mere 18 inches of pew. Acquired by the Scottish Redundant Churches Trust in 1998 and restored in 2001

For opening and service arrangements, telephone the SRCT 01555 666023

FORMER CHURCH OF SCOTLAND **A**

649 WESTRAY PARISH KIRK

HY 457 462

Kirkbrae, Westray

Oblong barn-style building, built 1834, with part-piended roof of local flagstone slates. Original pulpit with canopy, topped by a dove. Whole building is due to undergo major renovations in 2001/2. Pipe organ by Solway Organs 1967. Sunday Service: 11.30am; Evening Services in rotation with Baptist and United Free Kirks (see local notices)

Open by arrangement, telephone the Minister 01857 677357

CHURCH OF SCOTLAND WC **C**

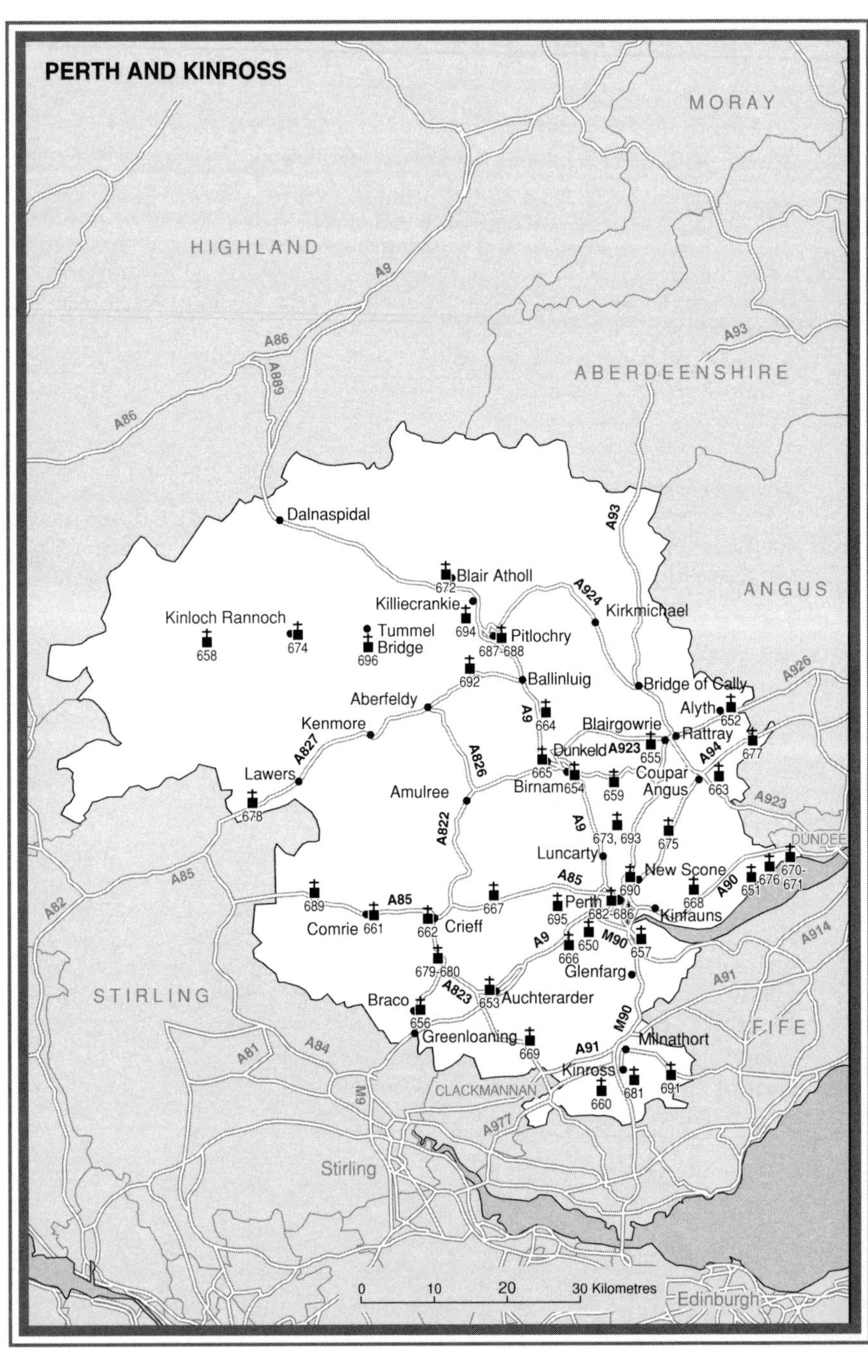
PERTH AND KINROSS
MORAY
HIGHLAND
ABERDEENSHIRE
ANGUS
STIRLING
FIFE
CLACKMANNAN
DUNDEE
A9
A86
A889
A93
A924
A926
A827
A826
A822
A85
A82
A923
A94
A90
A914
A91
M90
A823
A81
A84
M9
A977
Dalnaspidal
Blair Atholl
672
Killiecrankie
694
Kirkmichael
Kinloch Rannoch
658
674
Tummel Bridge
696
Pitlochry
687-688
692
Ballinluig
Bridge of Cally
Alyth
652
Aberfeldy
664
Kenmore
Blairgowrie
Rattray
677
Dunkeld
655
Lawers
665
Birnam
654
659
Coupar Angus
663
678
Amulree
673, 693
675
Luncarty
New Scone
690
668
651
676
670-671
689
667
Perth
682-686
Kinfauns
Comrie
661
662
Crieff
695
650
666
657
679-680
Glenfarg
Braco
656
653
Auchterarder
Greenloaning
669
Milnathort
Kinross
660
681
691
Stirling
0
10
20
30 Kilometres
Edinburgh

PERTH & KINROSS

Local Representative: The Rev Malcolm Trew, 155 Park Road West, Rosyth
e-mail: malcolm.trew@virgin.net

650 ABERDALGIE AND DUPPLIN CHURCH

NO 064 194

Aberdalgie

Nestling in the Earn Valley on a site of enduring worship for centuries, the present church was built by the Earl of Kinnoull in 1773. A T-plan church of local sandstone features a fine laird's loft and Georgian retiring room. Fourteenth-century Tournai marble Oliphant monument. Sir Robert Lorimer remodelled the interior in 1929. Extensive use of Austrian oak gives the church a sense of peace and simple dignity. Renovations 1994. Signed off B9112, south of Aberdalgie village. One of the four churches of the Stewartry of Strathearn. Sunday Service: 11.15am

Open by arrangement, telephone Rev Colin Williamson 01738 625854

CHURCH OF SCOTLAND WC **B**

651 ABERNYTE PARISH CHURCH

NO 267 311

Abernyte, by Inchture

The present church was built in 1736 to replace a building of pre-1400, although there may have been a Celtic church here much earlier. Major renovations in 1837 when the present cruciform shape was established. Intricate beams, stained glass and a modern wall hanging of 1992. Signposted from village. Linked with Longforgan and Inchture with Kinnaird. Sunday Service: 11am

Open during daylight hours

CHURCH OF SCOTLAND **B**

ABERNYTE PARISH CHURCH

652 ALYTH PARISH CHURCH

NO 243 488

Kirk Brae, Alyth

In a prominent position overlooking the town, Alyth Parish Church was completed in 1839 to a design by Thomas Hamilton. Gothic, with Romanesque influences, and an unusually high spire. Eighth or 9th century Pictish stone stands four feet high in the vestibule. All windows are stained glass and include work by Holliday, Adam and Webster. Large funeral escutcheon marks the death of Sir George Ramsay in a duel in 1790. Three-manual organ by Harrison & Harrison 1890. Sunday Service: 11am

Open July and August, Saturday 10am-12noon, Sunday 2pm-4pm

CHURCH OF SCOTLAND WC **B**

653 ST KESSOG'S CHURCH, AUCHTERARDER

NN 942 128

High Street, Auchterarder

Built 1897, architect Alexander Ross of Inverness. Beautiful altar and reredos of Caen stone, both richly decorated with Florentine mosaic. Rood screen of white stone. East and west windows by Kempe of London. In quiet grounds and garden 50 yards off High Street. Linked with St James, Muthill. Sunday Service: January to June 9.30am, July to December 11am

Open July and August, Monday to Friday 2-4pm, or by arrangement, telephone The Very Rev Randal MacAlister 01764 662525

SCOTTISH EPISCOPAL WC **C**

654 ST MARY'S CHURCH,BIRNAM

NO 032 418

Perth Road, Birnam

The main church and clock tower to a design by William Slater 1858, with north aisle by Norman & Beddoe 1883. Slater font and cover, Kempe east window, William Morris windows to Burne-Jones designs, three-bell chime, clock by James Ramsay of Dundee 1882. Beautifully kept churchyard. On old A9 in centre of village. Sunday Service: 9.45am; Wednesday 9.30am

Open by arrangement, telephone 01350 727329

SCOTTISH EPISCOPAL (via Rectory) WC **B**

655 ST ANDREW'S, BLAIRGOWRIE

NO 177 454

James Street, Blairgowrie

The present building was completed in 1904 in Early English Gothic style with transepts, aisles, apse and a small back gallery. Five stained glass windows in the apse depict scenes from the life of Moses. Norman & Beard organ 1907, rebuilt 1989 by Mr A F Edmondstone. The first Free Church of Blaigowrie 1843 is now the hall and back vestibule. Sunday Service: 11.15am.

Open June to August, Thursday and Saturday 2-4pm

CHURCH OF SCOTLAND WC

656 ARDOCH PARISH CHURCH, BRACO

NO 839 098

Feddal Road, Braco

Officially opened for worship in 1781 as a chapel of ease, the church was originally a rectangular building. The bellcote was added in 1836 and a chancel built on the east end by William Simpson of Stirling in 1890. The most recent addition is the church hall, built 1985. Ardoch Church sits close by the famous Roman camp. Directions: A9 north of Dunblane, take A822 to Braco, turn onto B8033 to Kinbuck and church is on right. Sunday Service: 10am in 2001; 11.30am in 2002

Open by arrangement, telephone 01786 880589

CHURCH OF SCOTLAND C

657 DUNBARNEY PARISH CHURCH, BRIDGE OF EARN

NO 130 185

Manse Road, Bridge of Earn

Built 1787. Pedimented bellcote added, interior recast and other alterations 1880. Rectangular plan with bow-ended west porch. Off the main street of Bridge of Earn. Sunday Service: 9.30am

Open June to August by arrangement, telephone 01738 812463. Annual Flower Festival, last weekend in September (Friday, Saturday and Sunday)

CHURCH OF SCOTLAND C

658 BRAES OF RANNOCH PARISH CHURCH, BRIDGE OF GAUR

NN 507 566

South Loch Road, Bridge of Gaur

Built in 1907, Peter MacGregor Chalmers. The bellcote is from an earlier building of 1776 and also borne by a church built in 1855 on this site. Granite-walled interior, unusual chancel and lovely woodwork give a special atmosphere of peace and beauty. Rothwell pipe organ from Urquhart Church, Elgin rebuilt 1991, David Loosley. This was the only charge of Rev Archibald Eneas Robertson (1907-20), first ascender of all 'Munros' in Scotland (283 peaks over 3000ft). B846 Aberfeldy to Bridge of Gaur, and south Loch Rannoch road to Finnart. Sunday Service: 9.45am

Open daily

CHURCH OF SCOTLAND B

BRAES OF RANNOCH PARISH CHURCH, BRIDGE OF GAUR

659 CAPUTH PARISH CHURCH

NO 088 401

Caputh, near Dunkeld

Now into its 3rd century, Caputh Church was built in 1798. There has been a church in Caputh since the 9th century, the present one being a fine stone building. The interior has oak furnishings, stained glass windows and a fairly rare pipe organ. On A984, four miles east of Dunkeld, Perthshire. Sunday Service: 11.15am

Open by arrangement, telephone Mrs Easton 01738 710389

CHURCH OF SCOTLAND WC

CAPUTH PARISH CHURCH

660 CLEISH CHURCH

NT 095 981

Built on 13th-century site in 1832 with additions 1897. Organ and lights from St Giles, Edinburgh. The hymn 'Jesus, tender Shepherd, hear me' was written by former minister's wife in the manse. Interesting wall chart and graveyard. Exit 5 M90, Cleish two miles. Sunday Service: 11.15am

Open daily, 10am-5pm

CHURCH OF SCOTLAND **B**

CLEISH CHURCH

661 COMRIE PARISH CHURCH

NN 770 221

Burrell Street, Comrie

Designed and built in 1881 by George T Ewing on a site surrounded by attractive grounds overlooking the River Earn. Organ built 1910 for the London Exhibition. A85. Regular bus service from Perth. Linked with Dundurn. Sunday Service: 10am June to September; 10.30am October to May

Open daily

CHURCH OF SCOTLAND WC **C**

COMRIE PARISH CHURCH

662 ST NINIAN'S, CRIEFF

NN 862 219

Comrie Road, Crieff

Placed on the Burrell Street axis, the rectangular church has a broad gabled façade with a centre tower with a gabled and pinnacled parapet. The old West Church has been refurbished to become a modern conference centre. Alterations carried out in 1970. Sunday Service: 9.30am

Open all year during daylight hours (except Christmas Day)

CHURCH OF SCOTLAND WC **B**

663 KETTINS PARISH CHURCH

NO 238 390

Kettins, by Coupar Angus

On the site of one of six chapels established by a nearby Columban monastery, the present church dates from 1768, with the north wing added in 1870 and the tower in 1891. Sixteen stained glass windows dating from 1878 onwards. Belgian bell of 1519 now rests, complete with belfry, close to the west gable it once surmounted. Celtic stone. Off A923, Dundee–Coupar Angus, one and a quarter miles south-east of Coupar. Linked with Meigle. Sunday Service: 11.30am

Open by arrangement, telephone 01828 640278

CHURCH OF SCOTLAND **B**

664 ST ANNE'S, DOWALLY

NO 001 480

Built in 1818 on the site of a 16th-century building, St Anne's is a small country church with a bright interior. The designer was probably John Stewart, although the church has been much altered since. Dates on the bell (which is still in use) and belfry suggest that they came from the earlier church. The chancel has carved screens which were originally in Dunkeld Cathedral. One of the memorials is to John Robb, a minister of the parish who perished in the shipwreck in which Grace Darling became a national heroine. The Church is situated on the right hand side of the A9, three and a half miles north of Dunkeld. Sunday Service: 2pm, second, fourth and fifth Sundays of the month

Open by arrangement, telephone Mrs Jim Kirk 01796 482407

CHURCH OF SCOTLAND WC **B**

665 DUNKELD CATHEDRAL

NO 024 426

Cathedral Street, Dunkeld

The Cathedral lies in a superb setting on the banks of the Tay. The restored choir, now used as the parish church, was completed in 1350. Chapter house 1469 adjacent to choir, contains a small museum. The tower, ruined nave and south porch are in the care of Historic Scotland. Just off A9, at west end of Dunkeld. Sunday Service: Easter to Remembrance Sunday, 11am

Open daily, summer 9.30am–7pm, winter 9.30am–4pm

CHURCH OF SCOTLAND WC **A**

666 FORTEVIOT CHURCH (ST ANDREW'S), FORTEVIOT

NO 050 174

In an area of historical importance – in the 9th century Kenneth MacAlpin had his palace here, and a basilica existed from the first half of the 8th century – this church, the third, was erected in 1778. It was remodelled in the mid-19th century. Celtic bell dated AD 900, one of five Scottish bronze bells. Medieval carved stones. The font is from the pre-Reformation church of Muckersie united with Forteviot in 1618. Organ by Hamilton of Edinburgh. Extensively renovated 1994. One of the four churches of the Stewartry of Strathearn.

FORTEVIOT CHURCH (ST ANDREW'S), FORTEVIOT

Sunday Service: 10am

Open by arrangement, telephone Rev C Williamson 01738 625854

CHURCH OF SCOTLAND **C**

667 FOWLIS WESTER PARISH CHURCH

NN 928 241

The church is a 13th-century building renovated in 1927 by Jeffrey Waddell of Glasgow with much Celtic ornament. It retains many of the original features including a 'lepers' squint'. The Pictish cross under the north wall is evidence of over 1000 years of Christian worship in the area. Turn off A85, five miles from Crieff to Fowlis Wester (signed). Sunday Service: 10am for 2001 and 2002

Open by arrangement, telephone Mrs McColl 01764 683205

CHURCH OF SCOTLAND **B**

FOWLIS WESTER PARISH CHURCH

668 ST MADOES AND KINFAUNS CHURCH, GLENCARSE

NO 167 223

Glencarse, nr Perth

Built 1799 on the site of earlier churches and refurbished in 1923. T-plan church with laird's gallery. New vestry and entrance hall by David Murdoch of Methven 1996. Interesting historic graveyard with 18th-century gravestones of sculptural merit. Pictish St Madoes Stone now on display in Perth Museum and Art Gallery. Contemporary embroidered pulpit falls. Sunday Service: September to May 11am; June to August 10am

Open first Sunday of month, June to September 1-4pm

CHURCH OF SCOTLAND WC **B**

ST MADOES AND KINFAUNS CHURCH, GLENCARSE

669 GLENDEVON PARISH CHURCH

NN 979 051

West side of A823, one mile north of Tormaukin Hotel

Seventeenth-century church with large stained glass window by Webster of Glasgow 1913 and small stained glass window in memory of Rev Alexander Taylor 1872-1949. Various memorial plaques. Pulpit and Communion table and chair carved by Mr Philips of Tormaukin. Large gravestone to Jane Rutherford. Sunday Service: 11.15am

Open at all times

CHURCH OF SCOTLAND WC **B**

GLENDEVON PARISH CHURCH

670 ALL SOULS' CHURCH, INVERGOWRIE

NO 347 303

59 Main Street, Invergowrie

Red sandstone church with 140-ft spire, designed by Hippolyte Blanc 1890. High altar has beautiful Italian marble reredos and crucifix. Lady Chapel contains altar from Rossie Priory Chapel. Sculptured Stations of the Cross. Embroidered wall-hanging to celebrate centenary of consecration 1996. Church hall used for community activities. Services: Sunday 10am Sung Eucharist; Wednesday Said Eucharist 10.15am

Open weekdays during school terms, 9am–4pm

SCOTTISH EPISCOPAL WC (only availble if Hall is in use) **A**

671 INVERGOWRIE PARISH CHURCH

NO 346 304

Main Street, Invergowrie

Building opened 1909. Architect John Robertson. Early Gothic with square tower and fine open timber roof. Pulpit and Communion Table of Austrian oak with carvings by local branch of YWCA. War memorial bell 1924. Stained glass window depicting Disruption minister Rev R S Walker conducting open-air Communion. Sunday Service: 11am

Church website: www.invergowrie.f9.co.uk

Open July and August, Wednesday 2–4pm. Keyholder Mr W Smith 01382 562759

CHURCH OF SCOTLAND WC **B**

672 KILMAVEONAIG CHURCH

NN 874 658

Kilmaveonaig, Blair Atholl

An Episcopal Chapel rebuilt in 1794 by John Stewart on the site of the old parish church of Kilmaveonaig 1591, and having belonged to the Episcopal Communion without a break since the Revolution. Enlarged 1899. Lorimer reredos added 1912. Old bell 1629, from Little Dunkeld church. Off A9 to Blair Atholl, opposite Tilt Hotel. Sunday Service: 10am

Open by arrangement. Key available from Tilt Hotel

SCOTTISH EPISCOPAL **B**

KILMAVEONAIG CHURCH

673 KINCLAVEN PARISH CHURCH

NO 151 385

By Stanley, near Perth

Built 1848 on site of previous church. Mixed Romanesque and Tudor with a narthex at the west end and bellcote at the east end. Churchyard contains the war memorial lychgate 1919 by Reginald Fairlie, and some table tombs of the 17th century and later. Built into the churchyard wall is the monument to Alexander Cabel (Campbell), Bishop of Brechin 1608. Sunday Service: 9.45am

Open by arrangement, telephone Mr Gordon 01738 710548,

CHURCH OF SCOTLAND WC WC **B**

674 THE OLD CHURCH OF RANNOCH, KINLOCH RANNOCH

NN 663 585

South Loch Road, Kinloch Rannoch

A Thomas Telford church of 1829, extensively altered and enlarged 1893. Wooden beamed roof, stained glass window, hour-glass by pulpit. B846 from Aberfeldy, B8019 from Pitlochry. Sunday Service: 11.30am

Open daily 10am - dusk. Other times, key from Mrs D MacDonald, Bridgend Cottage, telephone 01882 632359

CHURCH OF SCOTLAND WC **C**

675 COLLACE PARISH CHURCH, KINROSSIE

NO 197 320

Kinrossie, by Perth

Early 19th century on site of an earlier church dedicated in 1242. Stained glass window 1919. Remains of medieval building. Important 17th and 18th-century gravestones. A94 from Perth, signposted from village smithy.

Sunday Service: 11.15am

Open Sunday 16 June 2002, 2-4pm

CHURCH OF SCOTLAND WC **B**

COLLACE PARISH CHURCH, KINROSSIE

676 LONGFORGAN PARISH CHURCH

NO 309 300

Main Street, Longforgan

Church of 1795 in traditional Scottish box shape. Tower 1690 with eight-sided steeple and unusual clock. Apse added 1900. Several stained glass windows. Wood carving by Sir Robert Lorimer and remains of medieval font. Unique pipe organ. Interesting tombstones preserved. Graveyard with lychgate.

LONGFORGAN PARISH CHURCH

Adjacent to A90, 16 miles from Perth and 7 miles from Dundee.
Sunday Service: summer months 9.15am, winter 11.30am

Open Wednesdays 2-4pm, April to September. Or by arrangement, telephone Mrs Hulbert 01382 360294

CHURCH OF SCOTLAND B

677 MEIGLE PARISH CHURCH

NO 287 446

The Square, Meigle

Re-built in 1870 by John Carver after fire destroyed the pre-Reformation stone church of 1431. Stands on the ancient site of a turf church erected by Columban missionaries around AD 606. Fine stone font. Interesting graveyard. Pictish stones in adjacent museum (Historic Scotland). Linked with Kettins.
Sunday Service: 10am

Open by arrangement, telephone 01828 640278

CHURCH OF SCOTLAND B

MEIGLE PARISH CHURCH

678 MORENISH CHAPEL

NO 607 356

By Killin

Built in 1902 by Aline White Todd in memory of her daughter Elvira who died in childbirth. The central piece of the chapel is the magnificent east window by Tiffany in heavily leaded tracery, and sumptuous stained glass showing Moses receiving the ten commandments on Mount Sinai. On A827 Killin–Kenmore. Served by Killin and Ardeonaig. Sunday Service: 3pm, first Sunday of month during the summer

CHURCH OF SCOTLAND

679 MUTHILL PARISH CHURCH

NN 868 171

Station Road, Muthill, by Crieff

Replacing the 12th-century church (still existing). Built in 1826 in Gothic style to a design by Gillespie Graham, nicknamed 'Pinnacle' Graham by those less enthusiastic for the sprockets of 19th-century Gothic. Pulpit canopy similarly sprocketed. A822, three miles south of Crieff. Buses from Stirling to Crieff. Sunday Service: 11.30am (coffee 11am), except August and September 10am

Open Sunday 1st August. Coincides with opening of nearby Drummond Castle Gardens (Scotland's Gardens Scheme)

CHURCH OF SCOTLAND B

680 ST JAMES CHURCH, MUTHILL

NN 869 170

Station Road, Muthill

Built 1836, designed by R & R Dickson of Edinburgh. Oldest Episcopal church in the area. Numerous family crests of historic interest and memorial tablets. Fifty yards from village centre opposite primary school. Linked with St Kessog's, Auchterarder. Sunday Service: 11am January to June, 9.30am July to December

Open by arrangement, telephone The Very Rev Randal MacAlister 01764 662525

SCOTTISH EPISCOPAL B

ST JAMES CHURCH, MUTHILL

681 ORWELL PARISH CHURCH

NO 121 051

Church constructed 1729 using stone from the Old Kirk of Orwell on the banks of Loch Leven. The roof was raised and the present windows, floor and seating installed and galleries added in 1769. The interior is enhanced by embroidered banners and kneelers crafted by members of the Church. Number of interesting gravestones in the graveyard. Sunday Services: 11.30am, 9.00am July and August; 7.00pm on third Sunday January to June and September to November

Open by arrangement with keyholder, Mr Foley, telephone 01577 863397

CHURCH OF SCOTLAND WC B

682 NORTH CHURCH, PERTH

NO 116 237

Mill Street, Perth

A pleasant city centre church built in 1880 by T L Watson of Glasgow in Italian Romanesque style. Sunday Services: 9.30am, 11am and 6.30pm; Thursday lunchtime 1pm

Open by arrangement, telephone Mr G Weaks 01738 444033

CHURCH OF SCOTLAND **B**

683 ST LEONARD'S-IN-THE-FIELD & TRINITY, PERTH

NO 117 232

Marshall Place, Perth

Fine example of the late Gothic revival by John L Stevenson of London, opened in 1885. Outstanding architectural features are the crown tower and the heavy buttresses. The organ, which came from North Morningside Church in Edinburgh, was installed in the centenary year 1985. Sunday Services: 11am

Open on Doors Open Day (September)

CHURCH OF SCOTLAND **A**

684 ST JOHN'S EPISCOPAL, PERTH

NO 119 233

Princes Street, Perth

The present site has been used for worship since 1800. Present building designed by John Hay of Liverpool 1850-1. Many stained glass windows, sculptures by Miss Mary Grant, chancel arch carved by Heiton. Fine Harrison & Harrison organ 1971. Services: Sunday: Holy Communion 8am, Sung Eucharist 10.30am; Thursday: Holy Communion 11am

Open by arrangement, telephone Mr T Mason 01738 627870

SCOTTISH EPISCOPAL

ST JOHN'S EPISCOPAL, PERTH

685 ST JOHN'S KIRK OF PERTH

NO 119 235

St John Place, Perth

Burgh Church of Perth dedicated to John the Baptist and consecrated in 1242 on site of earlier church. Divided into three churches after the Reformation and restored 1923-6 by Sir Robert Lorimer. Good examples of modern stained glass including window of Knox Chapel by Douglas Strachan. Statue of John the Baptist by Indian sculptor Fanindra Bose and tapestry opposite Shrine (part of the 1926 restoration) by Archie Brennan of Dovecote Studios Edinburgh. Nave with barrel vaulting has carvings of events in the life of Christ. Glass screen at west door installed 1988. Sunday Services: 9.30 and 11am

Open May to September, 10am-4pm weekdays, 12-2pm Sundays; October to April, when Church Officer is present, usually Wednesday to Saturday from 10am. Guided tours by arrangement, telephone Mrs M Howat 01738 626520

CHURCH OF SCOTLAND **A**

686 ST NINIAN'S CATHEDRAL, PERTH

NO 116 237

North Methven Street

ST NINIAN'S CATHEDRAL, PERTH

First Cathedral to be built after the Reformation, being consecrated in 1850. The architect was William Butterfield. Baldachino in Cornish granite, fine wooden statue of the Risen Christ and interesting stained glass. Founder's window, the font and one of the banners by Sir Ninian Comper. Services: Sunday: Holy Communion 8 am, Sung Eucharist 11am; Monday to Friday: Morning Prayer 9am; Wednesday: Holy Communion 11am; Thursday: Holy Communion 9am

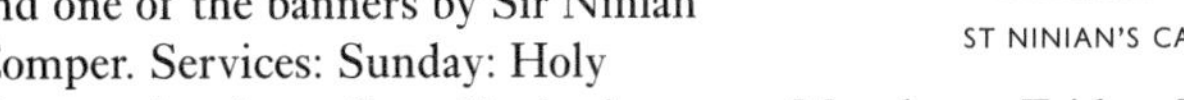

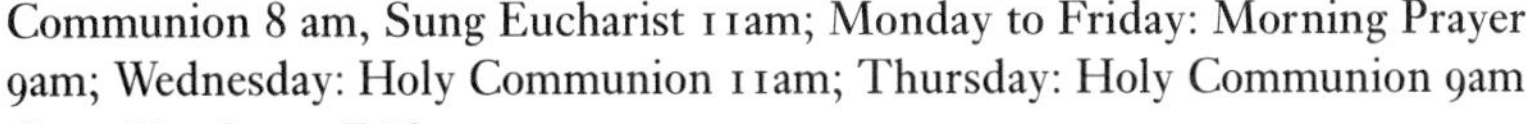

Open Monday to Friday 9am-5pm

SCOTTISH EPISCOPAL **B**

687 PITLOCHRY CHURCH

NO 942 581

Church Road, Pitlochry

Built in 1884 by C & L Ower, Dundee. The porch was added in 1995, built of stone from Pitlochry East Church, the East and West congregations having united in 1992. Seating arranged in a part circle around the communion table. Monument to Alexander Duff, 19th-century missionary. Identifiable as 'the church with the clock' 100 yards from main street. Sunday Services: 9.30am All Age Worship, and 11am Traditional form of service

Open mid-June to mid-September, Monday to Friday 10am-12 noon

CHURCH OF SCOTLAND **B**

PITLOCHRY CHURCH

688 PITLOCHRY BAPTIST CHURCH

NO 942 580

Atholl Road, next to Tourist Information Centre

Founded 1878 and originally meeting in a joiner's shop, the Pitlochry Fellowship built this church in 1884 to a design by Crombie of Edinburgh. Today's congregation welcomes visitors from across the world all year round. Annual Atholl Festival in July. Sunday Services: 11am and 6.30pm

Open by arrangement with Atholl Centre, a Christian holiday and conference centre, situated behind church, telephone 01796 473044

BAPTIST (Shop with Christian books and fair trade goods in adjoining Atholl Centre)

689 DUNDURN PARISH CHURCH, ST FILLANS

NN 697 241

Built 1878. Of particular interest is the medieval stone font. Oak panelling, pulpit and communion table with Celtic knotwork. Set in grounds with striking view across Loch Earn. Linked with Comrie Parish Church. Sunday Service: 11.30am June to September; 12 noon October to May

Open daily, Easter to October

CHURCH OF SCOTLAND

DUNDURN PARISH CHURCH, ST FILLANS

690 SCONE OLD PARISH CHURCH

NO 134 256

Burnside, Scone

Church built in 1286 near to Scone Palace. Moved to present site in 1806 using stone from original building. Mansfield pew presented by Queen Anne of Denmark 1615. Memorial to David Douglas, botanist, in graveyard. A94 from Perth. Number 7 bus from Perth. Sunday Service: 11am

Open Saturdays 8 March, 17 May, 16 August and 18 October 2002, 10am–12 noon

CHURCH OF SCOTLAND WC **B**

691 PORTMOAK PARISH CHURCH, SCOTLANDWELL

NO 183 019

One mile west of Scotlandwell

The present building, dated 1832, is the third on the site. The bell is dated 1642 and the Celtic crosses are of the 10th or 11th centuries. Memorial stone in the graveyard to Michael Bruce (1746-67) author of several of the scripture paraphrases used in Church of Scotland worship. Annual commemorative service in evening of first Sunday in July. Sunday Service: 10.00am

Open by arrangement with Mrs Crighton, telephone 01592 840550

CHURCH OF SCOTLAND **B**

692 ST ANDREW'S CHURCH, STRATHTAY

NN 910 534

The chancel was built in 1888 and the nave added in 1919. A vestibule and hall were added in 1982. Heavily carved woodwork on pulpit, lectern and priest's prayer desk. Lovely stained glass. A free-standing belfry was provided in 1995. In village, over River Tay from Grandtully on A827 between Ballinluig and Aberfeldy. Linked with St Mary's, Birnam. Sunday Service: 11.30am

Open by arrangement. Key from village shop

SCOTTISH EPISCOPAL WC **A**

693 STANLEY PARISH CHURCH

NO 108 330

Built in 1828 by local mill owners the Buchanan family for mill workers, the church seated 1000. It was adapted in 1962 and incorporated a new pew arrangement. The halls which are below the sanctuary were re-furbished in 1997. The vestibule houses the war memorial. The site is floodlit by night and the extensive church grounds hold an annual outdoor fête on the first Saturday of September.

Sunday Service: at 11.30am

CHURCH OF SCOTLAND  **B**

STANLEY PARISH CHURCH

694 TENANDRY CHURCH

NN 911 615

Tenandry, Pitlochry

Small country church built in 1836 of stone and slate and of traditional design. Fine view of the Pass of Killiecrankie from the road above the church. Turn north from B8019 at Garry Bridge two miles north of Pitlochry (signed).

Sunday Service: 11am

Open daily

CHURCH OF SCOTLAND WC **B**

695 TIBBERMORE CHURCH

NO 052 234

Quarter mile south of Tibbermore crossroads

The present church dates from 1632, though the site has been a place of worship from the Middle Ages onwards. The church was remodelled and enlarged in 1789 to designs by James Scobie, made T-plan in 1808 and the interior refurnished in 1874. The present interior is little altered since that date. The graveyard contains many monuments of interest, in particular the exceptional memorial to James Ritchie, displaying his curling equipment and the recumbent figure of his bull. Transferred to the ownership of the Scottish Redundant Churches Trust, 2001

For opening and service arrangements, contact the SRCT, telephone 01555 666023

FORMER CHURCH OF SCOTLAND ♿ **B**

696 FOSS KIRK, TUMMEL BRIDGE

NN 790 581

South Loch Tummel Road, Foss

Founded AD 625 by St Chad and used until the Reformation. Fell into disrepair 1580, restored 1821. Perth bell 1824. Ancient graveyard behind the church with view of Loch Tummel. Linked with Braes of Rannoch and Rannoch. B8019 from Pitlochry to Tummel Bridge, then B846 to Foss or B846 from Aberfeldy to Foss. Sunday Services: May to September, first and third Sundays 7pm; October to April, first Sunday 2.30pm

Open daily

CHURCH OF SCOTLAND **C**

FOSS KIRK, TUMMEL BRIDGE

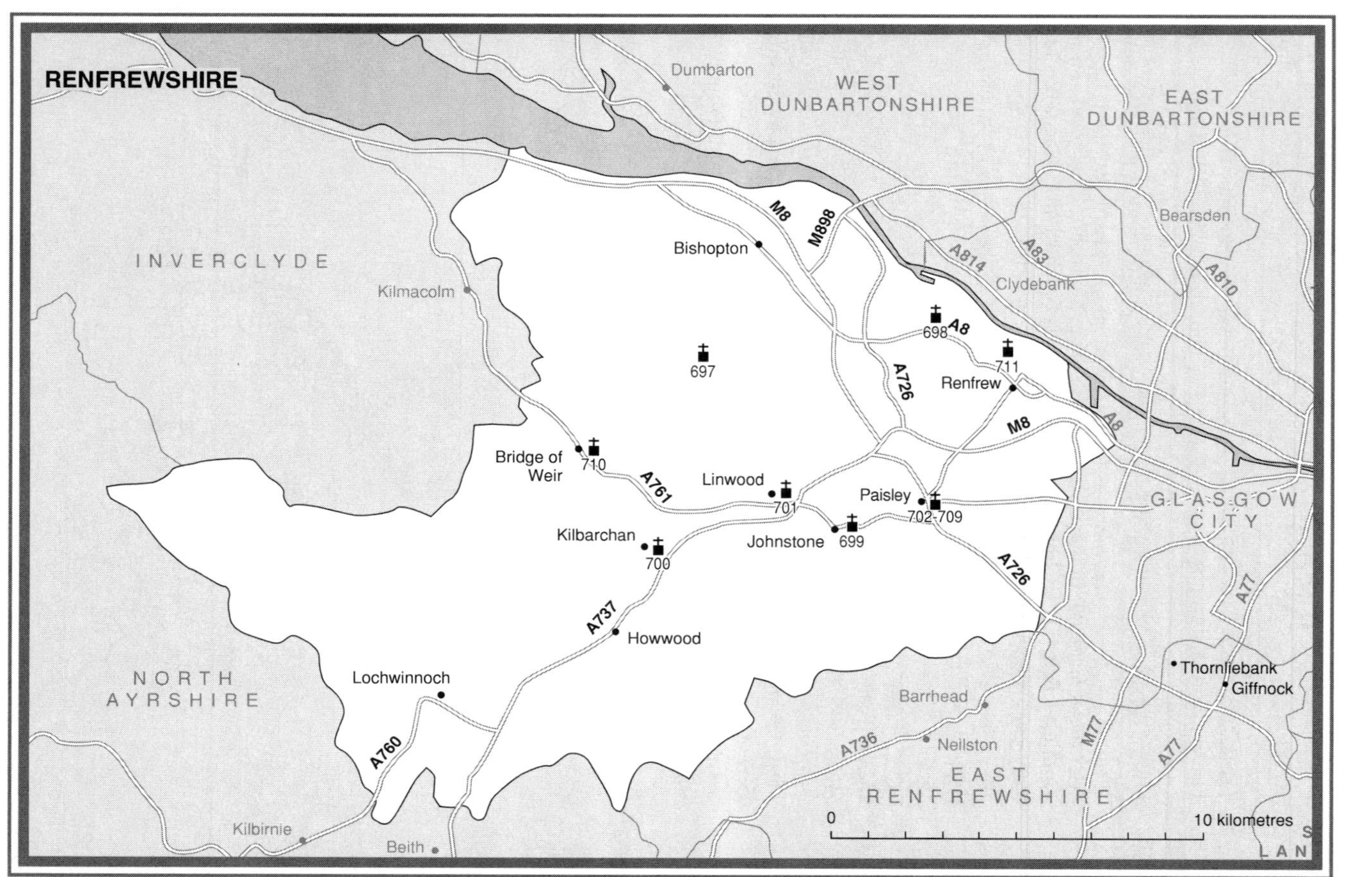
RENFREWSHIRE
Dumbarton
WEST DUNBARTONSHIRE
EAST DUNBARTONSHIRE
Bearsden
INVERCLYDE
Kilmacolm
M8
M898
Bishopton
A814
A83
A810
Clydebank
697
698
A8
711
A726
Renfrew
M8
A8
Bridge of Weir
710
A761
Linwood
701
Paisley
702-709
GLASGOW CITY
Kilbarchan
700
Johnstone
699
A726
A77
A737
Howwood
Lochwinnoch
NORTH AYRSHIRE
Thornliebank
Giffnock
Barrhead
A760
A736
Neilston
M77
A77
EAST RENFREWSHIRE
0
10 kilometres
Kilbirnie
Beith

RENFREWSHIRE

Local Representative: Mr Norman MacGilvray, 15 Carriagehill Drive, Paisley PA2 6JG (*telephone* 0141 887 7481)

697 HOUSTON & KILLELLAN PARISH CHURCH

NS 410 671

Kirk Road, Houston

Gothic, 1874 by David Thomson, this building is the third on this ancient site. Very good stained glass. Interesting organ. Between Bridge of Weir and Inchinnan. Sunday Service: 11am

Open Sundays 11am–1pm

CHURCH OF SCOTLAND **B**

698 INCHINNAN PARISH CHURCH (ST CONVAL'S KIRK)

NS 490 680

Old Greenock Road, Inchinnan

Sir R Rowand Anderson's Church of 1904 was razed to make way for Glasgow Airport, and the present building by Miller and Black, consecrated in 1968, incorporates much of interest and beauty from the earlier church. Foundation by St Conval in 597. King David I gave patronage of first stone church to Knights Templar, succeeded by Knights of St John. Celtic and medieval stones. Two miles west of Renfrew on A8. Sunday Service: 10.45am

Open Thursday during term time, noon–1.30pm. Light lunches available

CHURCH OF SCOTLAND WC

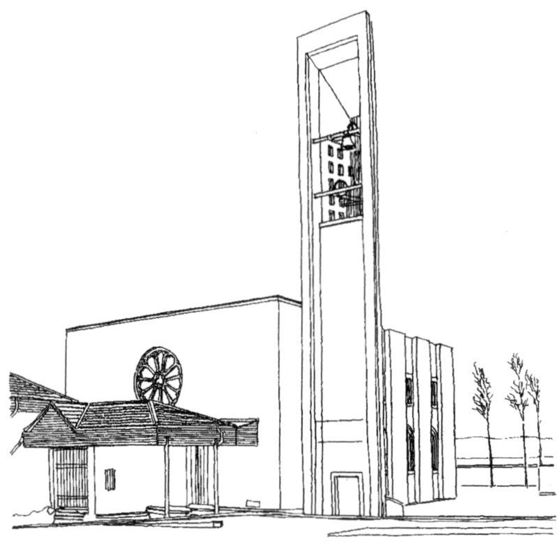

INCHINNAN PARISH CHURCH (ST CONVAL'S KIRK)

699 JOHNSTONE HIGH PARISH CHURCH

NS 426 630

Quarry Street, Johnstone

An octagonal building of grey sandstone built in 1792. Clock tower with spire. Stained glass. Historic graveyard. Town centre. Trains from Glasgow every 20 minutes. Sunday Service: 11am; Songs of Praise first Sunday 6.30pm

Open Thursday to Saturday 10am–12 noon, all year. Tours by arrangement at church hall coffee shop

CHURCH OF SCOTLAND WC B

JOHNSTONE HIGH PARISH CHURCH

700 KILBARCHAN WEST CHURCH

NS 401 632

Church Street, Kilbarchan

Hall built as the church in 1724 on the site of an earlier church. Present church completed 1901, architect W H Howie. Some fine stained glass resited from old church and glass from early 20th century. Three-manual organ built 1904 by William Hill & Sons. On A737 next to Weaver's Cottage. Sunday Services: 11am; Wednesdays: 10.30am, October to May

Open by arrangement 01505 342930

CHURCH OF SCOTLAND WC B

701 LINWOOD PARISH CHURCH

NS 432 645

Blackwood Avenue, Linwood

A spacious red brick building dating from 1965. An earlier church of 1860 existed on another site, demolished in 1976. The furniture and communion silver are from the earlier church. Contemporary art work includes a large aluminium cross presented by the former Rootes Vehicle Plant. Fine pipe organ 1957. Sunday Services: 9.30am and 11am

Open Friday 11.30am–1.30pm during school term, and by arrangement, telephone Mrs F Dooley 01505 331 065

CHURCH OF SCOTLAND

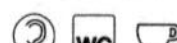

LINWOOD PARISH CHURCH

702 PAISLEY ABBEY

NS 4864

Founded in 1163. Early 20th-century restoration of the choir by P MacGregor Chalmers and Lorimer. Medieval architecture, royal tombs of Marjory Bruce and Robert III, the 10th-century Barochan Cross. Exceptionally fine woodwork by Lorimer, stained glass by Burne-Jones and others. M8, junction 27, follow signs to Paisley town centre. By train to Paisley, Gilmour Street. Sunday Services: 11am, 12.15pm Holy Communion, 6.30pm

Open daily, Monday to Saturday 10am–3.30pm. Other details from Abbey Office, telephone 0141 889 7654

CHURCH OF SCOTLAND **A**

PAISLEY ABBEY

703 CASTLEHEAD PARISH CHURCH, PAISLEY

NS 486 640

Main Road, Castlehead, Paisley

Built 1781 as the first Relief church in Paisley. Interior renovated 1881. Bishop organ 1898. Graveyard has graves of Robert Tannahill (local poet), past ministers, merchants and the mass graves of the cholera epidemic. At west end of town, at junction of Castlehead Main Road and Canal Street. Sunday Service: 11am

Open May to September, Monday, Wednesday and Friday 2–4pm

CHURCH OF SCOTLAND **B**

704 GLASGOW INTERNATIONAL AIRPORT CHAPEL, PAISLEY

NS 478 663

Second Floor, Terminal Building, Glasgow Airport

A recent addition to Glasgow Airport, open to passengers and staff of all faiths and creeds. Christian Services are announced 30 minutes in advance by public address.

Open at all times

NON-DENOMINATIONAL

705 MARTYRS' CHURCH, PAISLEY

NS 474 639

Broomlands Street, Paisley

The church is named after the Paisley martyrs who were executed in 1685. Built 1847 with additions and alterations, including tower and south front in neo-Norman style 1905, T G Abercrombie, architect. Inside are galleries on three sides on cast-iron colonnettes. The pulpit, 18-ft long, has been likened to the bridge of a ship. On A737 west of Paisley centre. Sunday Service: 11am

Open Friday 10am–1pm

CHURCH OF SCOTLAND **B**

MARTYRS' CHURCH, PAISLEY

706 NEW JERUSALEM CHURCH, PAISLEY

NS 481 637

17 George Street, Paisley

Built for Wesleyan Methodists in 1810, and in use by Swedenborgians since 1860, this is an unusual building with halls on the ground floor and the church upstairs. Three striking stained glass windows by W & J J Keir, including one designed by Sir Noel Paton. Fine pulpit, communion table, and ceiling rose. Nearest railway stations Paisley Canal and Paisley Gilmour Street. Sunday Service: 11am

Open by arrangement, and on Doors Open Day, September 11am–4pm, telephone Rev Robert Gill 0141 887 4119

SWEDENBORGIAN WC

NEW JERUSALEM CHURCH, PAISLEY

707 ST JAMES'S CHURCH, PAISLEY

NS 477 644

Underwood Road, Paisley

Early French Gothic style to a design by Hippolyte Blanc, largely gifted by Sir Peter Coats 1884. Spire 200ft. Full peal of bells, rung every Sunday. Father Willis pipe organ, rebuilt J Walker 1967. Stained glass windows 1904. Landscaped grounds. M8, junction 29, St James interchange. Sunday Service: 11am

Open Monday, Wednesday and Friday, 10am-4pm. Also Doors Open Day, September 10am-4pm. Contact day centre at rear of church for access

CHURCH OF SCOTLAND WC **B**

708 THOMAS COATS MEMORIAL BAPTIST CHURCH, PAISLEY

NS 478 640

High Street, Paisley

Built by the Coats Family as a memorial to Thomas Coats. Hippolyte Blanc Gothic, opened May 1894. Beautiful interior, 'by far the grandest of the Paisley churches' (Groome's Gazetteer) with carved marble and alabaster. Famous Hill four-manual pipe organ. On main street going west from Paisley Cross. Sunday Service: 11am

Church website: www.tenet.co.uk/coats

Open May to September, Monday, Wednesday, Friday 2-4pm.

Or by arrangement, telephone Church Secretary 0141 889 6690

BAPTIST WC **A**

THOMAS COATS MEMORIAL BAPTIST CHURCH, PAISLEY

709 WALLNEUK NORTH CHURCH, PAISLEY

NS 486 643

Abercorn Street, Paisley

Built 1915. Pipe organ by Abbott & Smith 1931, dedicated to Peter Coats, donor of this church. Its fine oak case was designed by Abercrombie & Maitland, Glasgow and carved and built by Wylie & Lochead, Glasgow. Near town centre. Sunday Service: 11am; also first Sunday in Mossvale Hall 6.30pm; Wednesday: 12.30pm

Open during Doors Open Day, September

CHURCH OF SCOTLAND A

710 ST MACHAR'S, RANFURLY

NS 386 653

Kilbarchan Road, Ranfurly, Bridge of Weir

Early Gothic 1878 by Lewis Shanks, brother of one of the local millowners. The chancel was added in 1910 by Alexander Hislop. Stained glass by J S Melville & J Stewart 1900, Herbert Hendrie 1931, William Wilson 1946, Gordon Webster 1956. Descriptive booklet by Maurice L Gaine 1996. A761 at east end of village. Sunday Service: 11am (10.30am July and August)

Open Fridays 10am–12noon. Bridge of Weir Gala Week in June

CHURCH OF SCOTLAND WC

ST MACHAR'S, RANFURLY

711 RENFREW OLD PARISH CHURCH

NS 509 676

26 High Street, Renfrew

The Church of Renfrew was bestowed by King David on the Cathedral Church of Glasgow in 1136. Within the present lancet Gothic 1862 sanctuary are two late medieval monuments, a hooded vault with recumbent effigies and an altar tomb. In Renfrew town centre. Regular bus services from Glasgow and Paisley.

Sunday Services: 11.15am and 6.30pm

Open during Doors Open Day, September

CHURCH OF SCOTLAND WC **B**

RENFREW OLD PARISH CHURCH

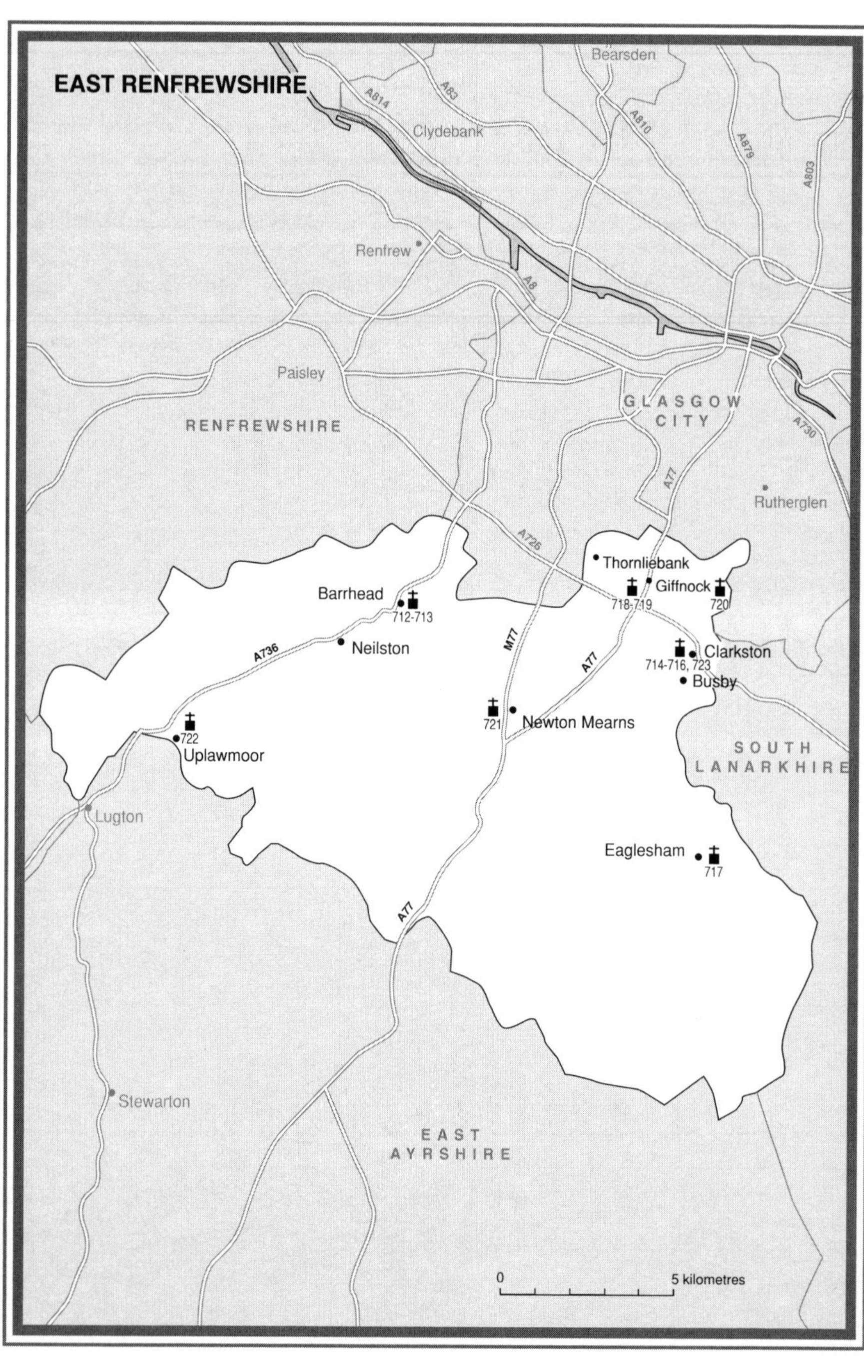

EAST RENFREWSHIRE
Bearsden
A814
A83
A810
A879
A803
Clydebank
Renfrew
A8
Paisley
GLASGOW CITY
RENFREWSHIRE
A730
A77
Rutherglen
A726
Thornliebank
Giffnock
Barrhead
718-719
720
712-713
Neilston
M77
Clarkston
A736
A77
714-716, 723
Busby
722
721
Newton Mearns
Uplawmoor
SOUTH LANARKHIRE
Lugton
Eaglesham
717
A77
Stewarton
EAST AYRSHIRE
0
5 kilometres

EAST RENFREWSHIRE

712 ARTHURLIE PARISH CHURCH, BARRHEAD

NS 501 588

Ralston Road/Main Street, Barrhead

Built 1967 to replace the 1796 'whitewashed kirk'. Designed by Honeyman, Jack and Roberton of Glasgow. High roof and long aisles. The open pews, constructed from the same light hardwood (ramin) as the cross, font, lectern and choirstalls, create an understated unity. Stained glass by Gordon Webster in the style 'Dalles de Verre'. The grounds, laid out by Bessie McWhirter, are open to all. Services: Sunday 11.00am; Wednesday 10.45am

Open by arrangement with Church Officer, telephone 0141 881 1792

CHURCH OF SCOTLAND (side entrance) WC

GREENBANK CHURCH, CLARKSTON

713 ST JOHN'S, BARRHEAD

NS 508 592

Aurs Road, Barrhead

Built in 1961, architect Thomas S Cordiner, after the old building was burnt down in 1941, before its centenary Mass. Note the prevalence of Greek iconography over Latin and the recurrence of the motif of St John. Tabernacle door designed by Hew Lorimer and presidential chair by John McLachlan. Rushworth and Dreaper organ. Services: Saturday Vigil 6.30pm; Sunday 10.00am, 12 noon and 6.30pm

Open by arrangement with Presbyery House, telephone 0141 876 1553

ROMAN CATHOLIC (side door) WC

714 GREENBANK CHURCH, CLARKSTON

NS 574 568

Eaglesham Road, Clarkston

The Church designed by McKissack & Rowan was opened in 1884. The Chancel, furnishings and stained glass windows were added in 1937. A mural by Alistair Gray in the transept was completed in 1979. The Centenary Chapel was opened in 1984. Sunday Services: 9.30am and 11.00am

Church website: www.ldallan.demon.co.uk/greenbank

Open by arrangement, telephone Church Officer 0141 644 2839

CHURCH OF SCOTLAND WC

715 ST AIDAN'S, CLARKSTON

NS 573 574

Mearns Road, Clarkston

Hall Church built 1924 and present church 1951, architects Noad & Wallace. Building has a steel frame and brick interior. Red sandstone facing matches Hall. Stained glass including a pair of windows by Susan Bradbury 1998. Sunday Services: 8am Holy Communion, 10am Sung Eucharist, 6.30 Evensong/Evening Prayer

Church website: www.staidans.freeserve.co.uk

Open Wednesdays 9–11.30am

SCOTTISH EPISCOPAL

716 STAMPERLAND CHURCH, CLARKSTON

NS 576 581

Stamperland Gardens, Clarkston

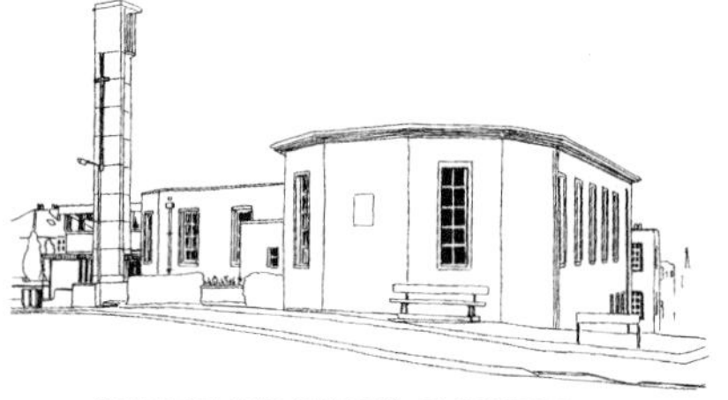

STAMPERLAND CHURCH, CLARKSTON

Congregation's first service held in an air raid shelter of a local garage in 1940. Thereafter a local shop was occupied at 38 Stamperland Crescent before a hall church was built in 1941 (now hall of Church). Present modern building erected 1964, architect J Thompson King & Partners. Concrete bell-tower. Three stained glass windows by Gordon Webster, previously in Woodside Parish Church. Pipe organ 1897 by Lewis & Co of Brixton and earlier in Regent Place UP Church, Dennistoun, Glasgow. Furnishings include items from 1938 Glasgow Empire Exhibition Church. Bas-relief of mythical pelican on outside wall. Sunday Services: 10am and 11am

Open by arrangement, telephone Samuel Esler 0141 571 8451

CHURCH OF SCOTLAND

717 EAGLESHAM PARISH CHURCH

NS 572 518

Montgomery Street, Eaglesham

The present attractive church with clock steeple was designed by Robert McLachlane and completed in 1790. It replaced churches on this site since early times. Former United Free Church is now the Church Halls and Carswell United Presbyterian Church refurbished as 'The Carswell Halls' (both located on Montgomery Street). 'Father Willis' organ and fine embroidered pulpit falls by Kathleen Whyte and Fiona Hamilton. Covenanter graves in churchyard. Sunday Services: 9.30am and 11am, except June to August 10.30am

Church website: www.eaglesham-parish-church.com

Open during Doors Open Day, September, and by arrangement, telephone the Beadle 01355 303411

CHURCH OF SCOTLAND WC **B**

EAGLESHAM PARISH CHURCH, EAGLESHAM

718 GIFFNOCK SOUTH PARISH CHURCH

NS 559 582

Greenhill Avenue, Giffnock

A 'hall church' (now Eglinton Hall) was opened in 1914. The present church was begun in 1921 and dedicated in 1929. It is by Stewart & Paterson in late Gothic style with blonde sandstone. There is a fine collection of stained glass windows, including six by Gordon Webster. There are three recent windows, one by Sadie McLellan and two by Brian Hutchison. Sunday Service: 11.15am.

CHURCH OF SCOTLAND **B**

GIFFNOCK SOUTH PARISH CHURCH

719 ORCHARDHILL PARISH CHURCH, GIFFNOCK

NS 563 587

Church Road, Giffnock

Church and hall built in Gothic Revival style, H E Clifford 1900. Of local stone with a red tiled roof, squat tower with spiral wooden stair and roof turret. Extensions carried out in 1910 and 1935. Stained glass 1936-86 by Webster, McLellan, Wilson and Clark. Wood panelling 1900-35. Two-manual pipe organ, Hill, Norman & Beard. Embroidered pulpit falls 1993. On east side of Fenwick Road, north of Eastwood Toll. Buses from Glasgow Buchanan and trains from Glasgow Central. Sunday Services: 10am, 11.15am and 6.30pm (part year only)

ORCHARDHILL PARISH CHURCH, GIFFNOCK

Open by arrangement, telephone Church Officer 0141 589 4353 or Secretary 0141 638 3604

CHURCH OF SCOTLAND **B**

720 NETHERLEE PARISH CHURCH

NS 557 590

Ormonde Avenue, Netherlee

Built in neo-Gothic style of red Dumfriesshire sandstone by Stewart & Paterson 1934. Oak panelling and furnishings beautifully carved. Lovely stained glass. City buses via Clarkston Road. Sunday Services: September to May, 11am and some at 6.30pm; June to August 9.30am and 11am

Open by arrangement, telephone Mr McVey 0141 637 6853

CHURCH OF SCOTLAND

WC **B**

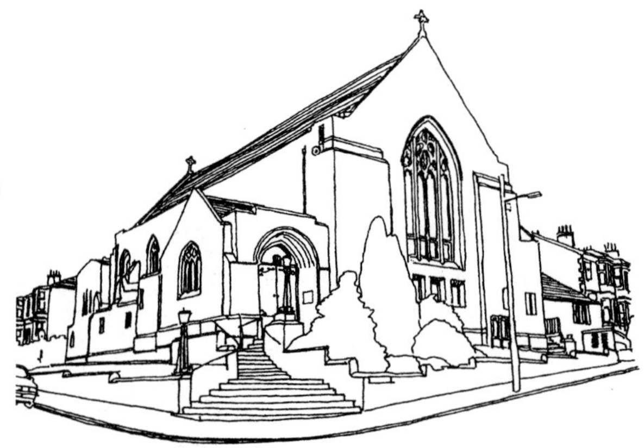

NETHERLEE PARISH CHURCH

721 MEARNS PARISH CHURCH, NEWTON MEARNS

NS 551 556

Junction of Eaglesham Road and Mearns Road

Religious settlement and site since AD 800, the present church dates from 1813 and was extensively renovated in 1932. Organ originally from Glasgow City Hall. Stained glass windows by Gordon Webster and James McPhie. South wall tapestry donated by the late Lord Goold. A phosphor-bronze weathercock weighing two and a half cwts atop the bell-tower was erected in the late 1940s. Gate posts in the form of sentry boxes date from the era of the 'Resurrectionists'. Sunday Services: 9.30 and 11am

Open by arrangement, telephone the Minister 0141 616 2410

CHURCH OF SCOTLAND B

MEARNS PARISH CHURCH, NEWTON MEARNS

722 CALDWELL PARISH CHURCH, UPLAWMOOR

NS 435 552

Neilston Road, Uplawmoor

Simple country church built 1889 William Ingram. Memorial glass sculpture depicting the Trinity by Ralph Cowan 1989. Garden of Remembrance dedicated 1997. Off B736 Barrhead–Irvine. On main street opposite village shop. Sunday Service: 11am; Wednesday brief act of worship 12 noon

Open daily 11am–3pm. Soup lunch in hall adjacent October to March, Friday 12 noon–1.30pm

CHURCH OF SCOTLAND

723 WILLIAMWOOD PARISH CHURCH

NS 567 576

Seres Road, Williamwood

Built in 1937 as a church extension charge, the church is a fine example of mid-1930s church architecture. Original and somewhat austere interior upgraded and enriched. Historical and other information available. By rail from Glasgow Central to Williamwood or Clarkston, 10 minutes walk from both stations. Bus services from Glasgow to Eaglesham, alight at Clarkston. Sunday Service: 11am

Open February to June and September to December, weekdays, 9.45am–12 noon. Other information, telephone 0141 638 2091

CHURCH OF SCOTLAND

WILLIAMWOOD PARISH CHURCH

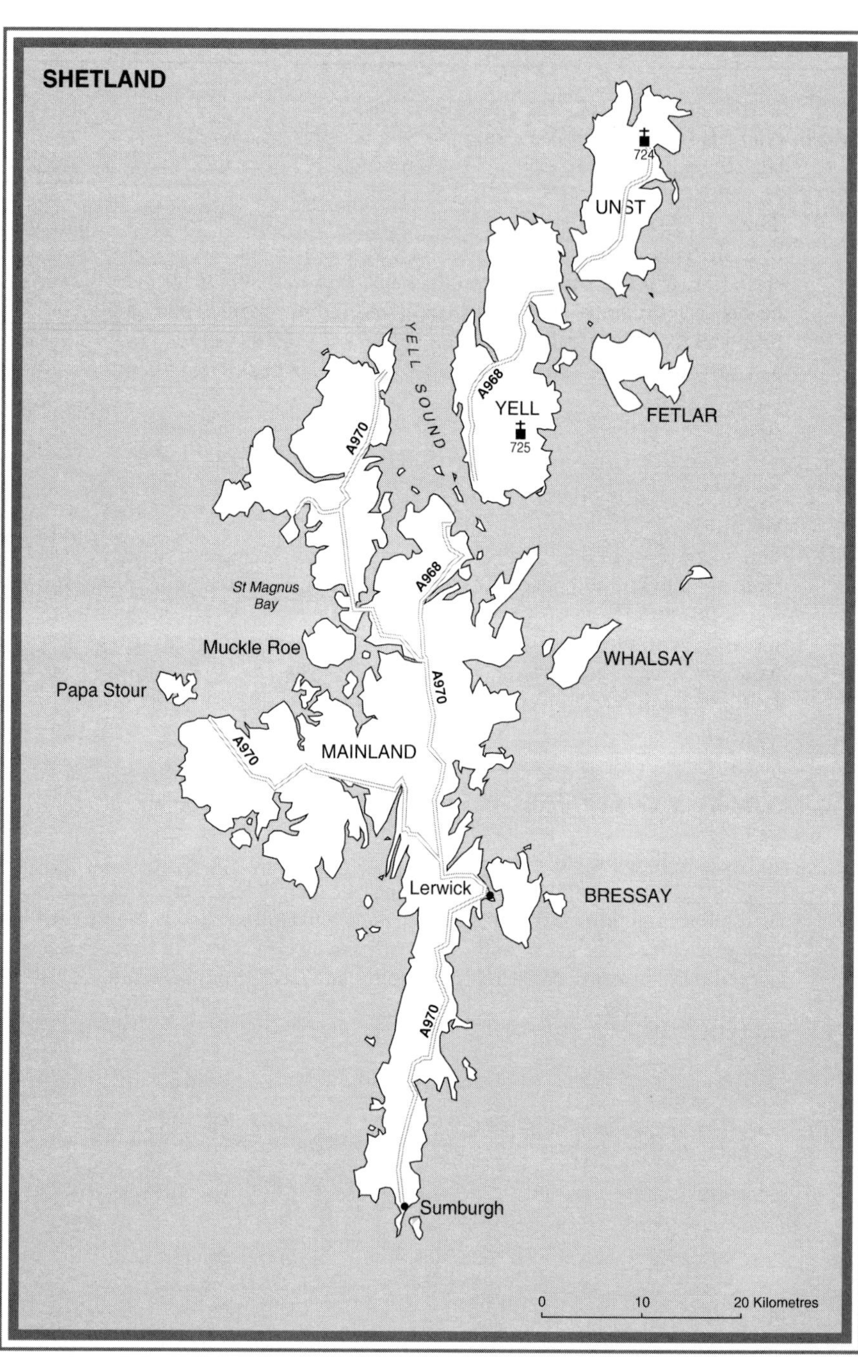
SHETLAND
724
UNST
YELL SOUND
A968
YELL
725
FETLAR
A970
A968
St Magnus
Bay
Muckle Roe
WHALSAY
Papa Stour
A970
A970
MAINLAND
Lerwick
BRESSAY
A970
Sumburgh
0
10
20 Kilometres

SHETLAND

724 HAROLDSWICK METHODIST CHURCH, UNST

HP 646 134

Haroldswick, Unst

The most northerly church in Britain. The present building 1993 was designed by a Shetland architect, based on a simplified form of a Norwegian wooden stave kirk. Most of the work was done by local voluntary labour. The interior beams and panelling are Scandinavian pine and the lightness, warmth and proportion of the worship area are striking. New bell turret for the 1867 bell has just been completed. Sunday Service: 11am or 6.00pm (alternate Sundays)

Open all the time

METHODIST

725 EAST YELL METHODIST CHURCH, YELL

HP 517 855

Otterswick, East Yell

Built 1892 to serve the needs of the local community, this lovely Chapel in the Valley is noted for its simple beauty, warmth of its welcome and ecumenical nature of its congregation. The chapel has been described as a 'little gem'. Much admired unique pulpit fall, designed and crafted locally, depicting the Lamb of God. Sunday Services: 10.45am or 2.45pm (alternate Sundays)

Open all the time

METHODIST

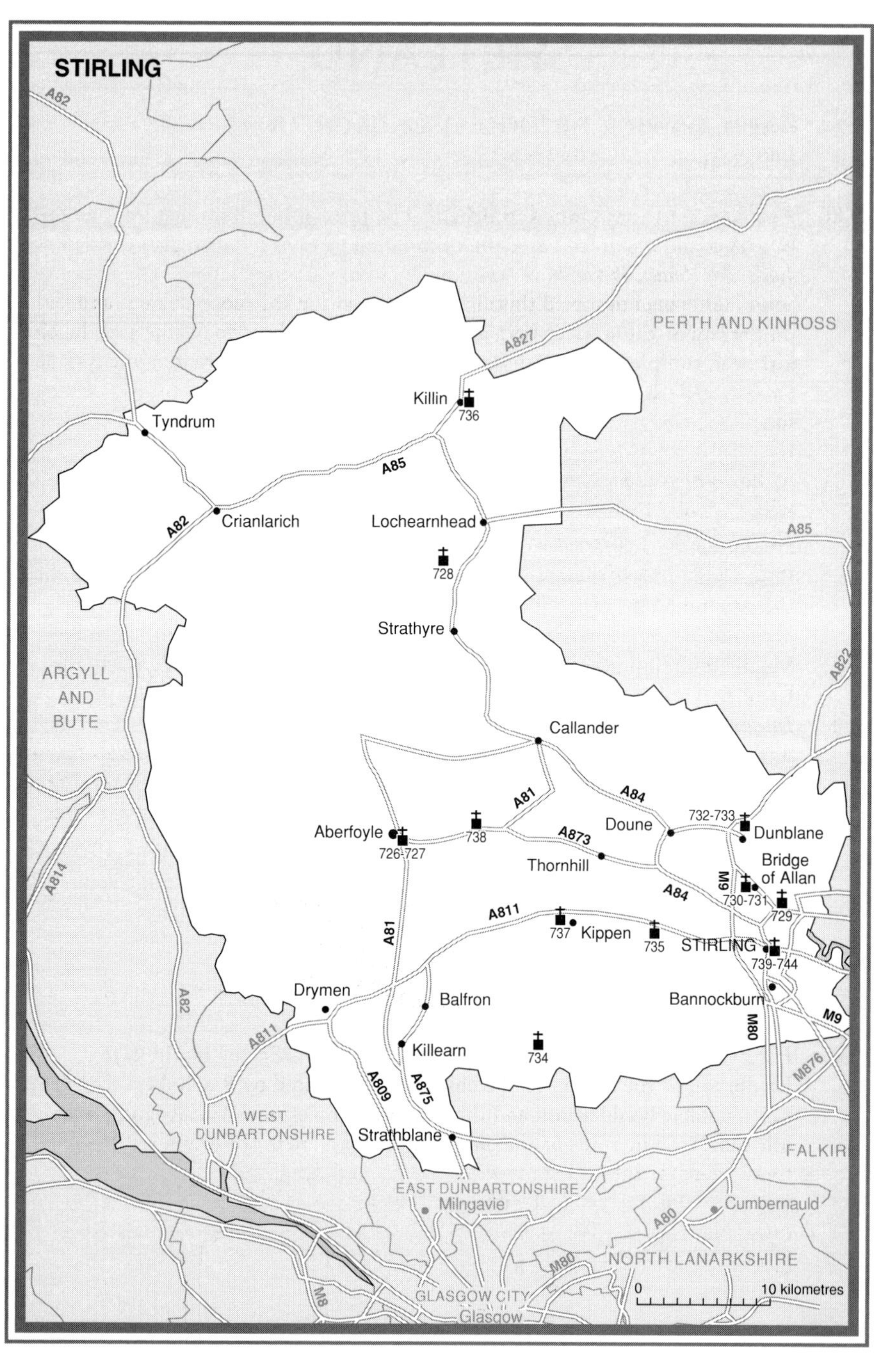
STIRLING
PERTH AND KINROSS
ARGYLL AND BUTE
WEST DUNBARTONSHIRE
EAST DUNBARTONSHIRE
NORTH LANARKSHIRE
FALKIRK
GLASGOW CITY
Glasgow
Milngavie
Cumbernauld
Tyndrum
Killin
736
Crianlarich
Lochearnhead
728
Strathyre
Callander
Aberfoyle
726-727
738
Doune
732-733
Dunblane
Thornhill
Bridge of Allan
730-731
729
737
Kippen
735
STIRLING
739-744
Bannockburn
Drymen
Balfron
Killearn
734
Strathblane
A82
A827
A85
A81
A84
A873
A811
A809
A875
A814
A822
M9
M80
M876
A80
M8
0
10 kilometres

STIRLING

Local Representative: Mr Louis Stott, Browsers' Bookshop, 25 High Street, Dunblane FK15 OEE (*telephone* 01786 824738)

726 ABERFOYLE PARISH CHURCH

NN 518 005

Loch Ard Road, Aberfoyle

John Honeyman designed this church which sits at the foot of Craigmore and on the banks of the River Forth. In early-Gothic style 1870, it replaced the old kirk of Aberfoil on the south bank of the river reached by crossing the hump-backed bridge. The new church was enlarged in 1884 to include transepts. The interior is elegant with the minimum of ornamentation. Magnificent roof timbers. Stained glass, including a window by Gordon Webster 1974. Two-manual pipe organ 1887 by Bryceson Brothers, London. On the B829. Linked with Port of Menteith. Sunday Service: 11.15am

Open Saturday afternoon in August for church sale. Other times, telephone Mr I Nicholson 01877 382337

CHURCH OF SCOTLAND WC **B**

727 ST MARY'S, ABERFOYLE

NN 524 010

Main Street, Aberfoyle

The church was deigned by James Miller, who also designed Gleneagles Hotel. It was built 1892-3 by workers from the local slate quarry. The stone came from Aisla Craig by railway (free of charge) to test the weight capacity of the new branch railway. Oak panelled reredos. Organ by Henry Willis. Sunday Services: Sung Eucharist 9.30am, first Sunday; 11.00am other Sundays

Open by arrangement with Mrs M Johnson, telephone 01877 382611

SCOTTISH EPISCOPAL WC

728 BALQUHIDDER PARISH CHURCH

NN 536 209

Handsome parish church in dressed stone, built in 1853 by David Bryce. Exhibition of the history of the church. Bell donated by Rev Robert Kirk (1644-92), a notable boulder font and the supposed gravestone of St Angus, possibly 9th-century. The ruins of the old parish church are in the graveyard where there are many intriguing carved stones, including that of Rob Roy MacGregor. A84 at Kinghouse. Linked with Killin. Sunday Service: 12 noon

Open daily. Summer Music Sunday evenings during summer months

CHURCH OF SCOTLAND WC **B**

BALQUHIDDER PARISH CHURCH

729 LOGIE KIRK, BY BLAIRLOGIE, STIRLING

NS 829 968

The tower, square and pedimented and surmounted by an octagonal belfry, was designed by William Stirling of Dunblane 1805. The remainder of the church, an elegant whinstone box, by McLuckie & Walter of Stirling 1901. Stained glass windows include one by C E Kempe and two modern windows by John Blyth. Fourteen oak panels depicting scenes from the Bible enclose the chancel and pulpit. The ruined Old Kirk of Logie, with its good selection of 17th and 18th-century gravestones, is nearby. In idyllic rural setting at foot of Dumyat and in the shadow of the Wallace Monument. A91, four miles north-east of Stirling. Sunday Service: telephone 01786 475414

Open Sundays, August 2-5pm

CHURCH OF SCOTLAND WC **B**

LOGIE KIRK, BY BLAIRLOGIE, STIRLING

730 HOLY TRINITY PARISH CHURCH, BRIDGE OF ALLAN

NS 791 974

Keir Street, Bridge of Allan

Built in 1860 and enlarged later, the church contains chancel furnishings designed in 1904 by the eminent Scottish architect, Charles Rennie Mackintosh. The church has an attractive timber roof and excellent stained glass windows. On corner with Fountain Road, opposite Somerfield car park. Bus service from Stirling to Royal Hotel, one block. Rail service to Bridge of Allan Station, 10 minutes walk. Sunday Service: 11am

HOLY TRINITY CHURCH, BRIDGE OF ALLAN

Open June to September, Saturdays 10am-4pm

CHURCH OF SCOTLAND B

731 ST SAVIOUR'S CHURCH, BRIDGE OF ALLAN

NS 792 973

Keir Street, Bridge of Allan

Built in 1857, and later enlarged, St Saviour's forms part of a group of Gothic revival buildings comprising church, hall and rectory by Alexander Ross. West window Stephen Adam. Pipe organ, Forster & Andrews 1872. By road, bus and rail services from Stirling. On corner with Fountain Road. Sunday Services: 8am Said Eucharist, 10am Sung Eucharist and Sermon; occasional Matins, as announced

ST SAVIOUR'S CHURCH, BRIDGE OF ALLAN

Open generally 10am-5pm

SCOTTISH EPISCOPAL B

732 SCOTTISH CHURCHES HOUSE CHAPEL, DUNBLANE

NN 783 014

Kirk Street, opposite Cathedral

Uncovered in 1961 during restoration of buildings which became Scottish Churches House. Medieval in origin, possibly a chapel of one of several ecclesiastical residences which then surrounded the Cathedral. Fine barrel-vaulted roof. Restored for use as the chapel of Scottish Churches House, an ecumenical Conference House and Retreat Centre. House Prayers: 9am daily

Church website: www.scottishchurcheshouse.org

Open at all times

ECUMENICAL WC B

ST BLANE'S CHURCH, DUNBLANE

733 ST BLANE'S CHURCH, DUNBLANE

NN 783 014

High Street/Sinclairs Street Lane, Dunblane

Open 1854 as Free Church which through unions became East United Free Church and East Church of Scotland. United with former Leighton Church in 1952 to become St Blane's Church. Stained glass includes windows from Leighton Church, other windows by Roland Mitton. Interesting tapestries in vestibule including a reproduction of 'The Light of the World' by Holman Hunt. Pipe organ 1860 by Peter Conacher, perhaps the earliest example of his work in Scotland. Sunday Services: 11.15am (10.15am June to August), and 6.30pm

Open by arrangement, telephone the Minister 01786 822268, or Dr Duncan 01786 822657 or Mr Cattan 01786 822142

CHURCH OF SCOTLAND **B**

734 FINTRY KIRK

NS 627 862

Fintry Village

The present church, built in 1823, was constructed around the original kirk of 1642, and the congregation continued to worship in the old sanctuary while building went on around them! On completion, the inner church was demolished. The bell was transferred from old to new and is still in use today. Early 20th-century stained glass, including a First World War memorial window. Session House in the kirkyard added 1992. Linked with Balfron. Sunday Service: 10am

Open Easter Saturday, and first Saturday May to September, Saturday 2-4pm

CHURCH OF SCOTLAND **B**

GARGUNNOCK PARISH CHURCH

735 GARGUNNOCK PARISH CHURCH

NS 707 943

Manse Brae, Gargunnock

Situated in very beautiful rural location. Village church 1650 on pre-Reformation foundation, renovated 1774 and 1891. Three individual outside stairs to three separate lairds' lofts. Two good 20th-century stained glass windows. War memorial by Lorimer. Mountain indicator. Graveyard. Five miles west of Stirling, off A811. Sunday Service: 11.30am

Open by arrangement, telephone Mr Calder 01786 860542

CHURCH OF SCOTLAND B

736 KILLIN AND ARDEONAIG PARISH CHURCH, KILLIN

NN 571 330

Main Street, Killin

Distinctive white-harled octagonal classical church built in 1744 by the mason Thomas Clark to a design by John Douglas of Edinburgh. Inside it has been altered from a 'wide' church to a 'long' church. The Fillan Room, a small chapel for prayer in the tower, was created in 1990. In front of the church is a monument to Rev James Stewart (1701-96), minister of Killin, who first translated the New Testament into Scots Gaelic (published 1763). At the eastern end of the village. Serves Morenish Chapel (see Perth & Kinross); linked with Balquhidder. Information about Services in Morenish Chapel from Tourist Information by Falls of Dochart in village. Sunday Service: 10am

Open May to October during daylight hours

CHURCH OF SCOTLAND WC B

KIPPEN PARISH CHURCH

737 KIPPEN PARISH CHURCH

NS 652 849

Fore Road, Kippen

Built 1827 by William Stirling, extensively redesigned 1924-6 by Reginald Fairlie and Eric Bell. Exceptionally graceful, Latinate in style, and incorporating a splendid and perfectly combined display of (mainly) 20th-century Christian art, including works by Sir Alfred Gilbert, Alfred Hardiman, James Woodford and Henry Wilson, as well as local craftsmen. Stained glass by Herbert Hendrie. Sunday Service: 11.30am

Open 9am-4.30pm (dusk in winter) (presently under review)

CHURCH OF SCOTLAND (ramp available for wheel chairs) WC **B**

738 PORT OF MENTEITH CHURCH

NS 583 011

On the shore of the Lake of Menteith, a church built in 1878 to designs by John Honeyman on a site of earlier churches with medieval connections. Simple rectangular plan, Gothic style, with square tower containing carillon of eight bells. Victorian pipe organ, probably by Brook. Surrounded by a graveyard and a few minutes walk from the ferry to Inchmahome where the ruined 13th-century Augustinian Priory may be visited. On B8034 beside the Lake Hotel. Linked with Aberfoyle. Sunday Service: 10am

Open by arrangement, telephone Mr G Ellis 01877 385201

CHURCH OF SCOTLAND WC **B**

ALLAN PARK SOUTH CHURCH, STIRLING

739 ALLAN PARK SOUTH CHURCH, STIRLING

NS 755 933

Dumbarton Road, Stirling

Peddie & Kinnear 1886 with the interior modernised for the centenary in 1986 by Esmie Gordon. Radical change under consideration to bring interior and grounds to the requirements of the 21st century. Two large circular and three smaller stained glass windows to commemorate the fallen in the two World Wars, the ministry of the Rev Alan Johnston and members of the Kinross family. Sunday Service: 10am January to June, 11.30am July to December

Open by arrangement, telephone Church Secretary 01786 471998.

Office hours Tuesday, Wednesday and Friday 11.30am–2.30pm

CHURCH OF SCOTLAND WC **B**

740 THE CHAPEL ROYAL, STIRLING CASTLE

NS 790 941

There has been a Chapel in the Castle since at least 1117. It became the Chapel Royal of Scotland in the time of James IV in about 1500. The present building was built in 1594 by James VI for the baptism of Prince Henry. It was redecorated in 1629 in advance of the visit in 1633 of Charles I. After being sub-divided to serve military uses, there was a first phase of restoration in the 1930s, and the latest phase of work was completed in 1996. A large rectangular building with Renaissance windows and a central entrance framed by a triumphal arch along its south front. Notable features include decorative paintings of 1629 by Valentine Jenkin, a modern wagon ceiling reflecting the profile of the original, and modern furnishings including a communion table cover designed by Malcolm Lochead. Services by arrangement

Open April to October 9.30am–6pm; November to March 9.30am–5pm

NON-DENOMINATIONAL (Castle Restaurant) **A**

THE CHAPEL ROYAL, STIRLING CASTLE

741 CHURCH OF THE HOLY RUDE, STIRLING

NS 792 937

St John Street, Stirling

The original parish kirk of Stirling, used for the coronation in 1567 of James VI, at which John Knox preached. Largely built in 15th and 16th centuries. Medieval open-timbered oak roof in nave. Choir and apse added in 1555, the work of John Coutts, one of the greatest master masons of the later Middle Ages. Notable stained glass. Fine pipe organ, recently restored. Oak choir stalls and canopies 1965. Historic graveyard. Near to Stirling Castle. On Historic Stirling (open top) bus route. Sunday Service: 11.30am January to June, 10.00am July to December

Church website: www.stir.ac.uk/town/facilities/holyrude/index.html

Open May to September, 10am–5pm. Venue for many concerts

CHURCH OF SCOTLAND ♿ WC **A**

742 HOLY TRINITY CHURCH, STIRLING

NS 793 934

Albert Place, Dumbarton Road, Stirling

One of Sir R Rowand Anderson's most distinctive churches 1878, close to Stirling Castle, old town and shops. Very close to town centre, on Historic Stirling (open top) bus route. Sunday Services: Eucharists 8.30 and 10.30am; Evening Prayer 6.30pm

Open mornings daily

SCOTTISH EPISCOPAL ♿ **B**

HOLY TRINITY CHURCH, STIRLING

743 ST NINIAN'S OLD, STIRLING

NS 797 917

Kirk Wynd, St Ninian's. Stirling

Only the tower and bell of 1734 survive following desecration of the nave by Cromwellian troops and an explosion of munitions stored in the 13th-century church by Jacobites. Present building is of 1751 with remodelling 1937 by A A McMichael. Major restoration programme will enhance exterior and interior. Sunday Services: 10.30am and 6.30pm (second Sunday in March, June, September and December)

ST NINIAN'S OLD, STIRLING

Open by arrangement with Mr Robert Simpson, telephone 01786 813335

CHURCH OF SCOTLAND wc **A** (Steeple) **C** (Hall)

744 VIEWFIELD PARISH CHURCH, STIRLING

NS 795 938

Irvine Place, Stirling

The present building, seating 600, was erected in 1860 to replace the 1752 meeting house. The congregations have been part of the Secession of 1733, going through United Presbyterian and United Free Churches until joining the Church of Scotland in 1929. Interior largely as constructed, though the window of the creation story behind the pubpit is a modern intervention by Christian Shaw. Sunday Service: 11.00am

Open by arrangement with keyholder, Mr Monteith, telephone 01786 461350

CHURCH OF SCOTLAND (from Irvine Place) wc

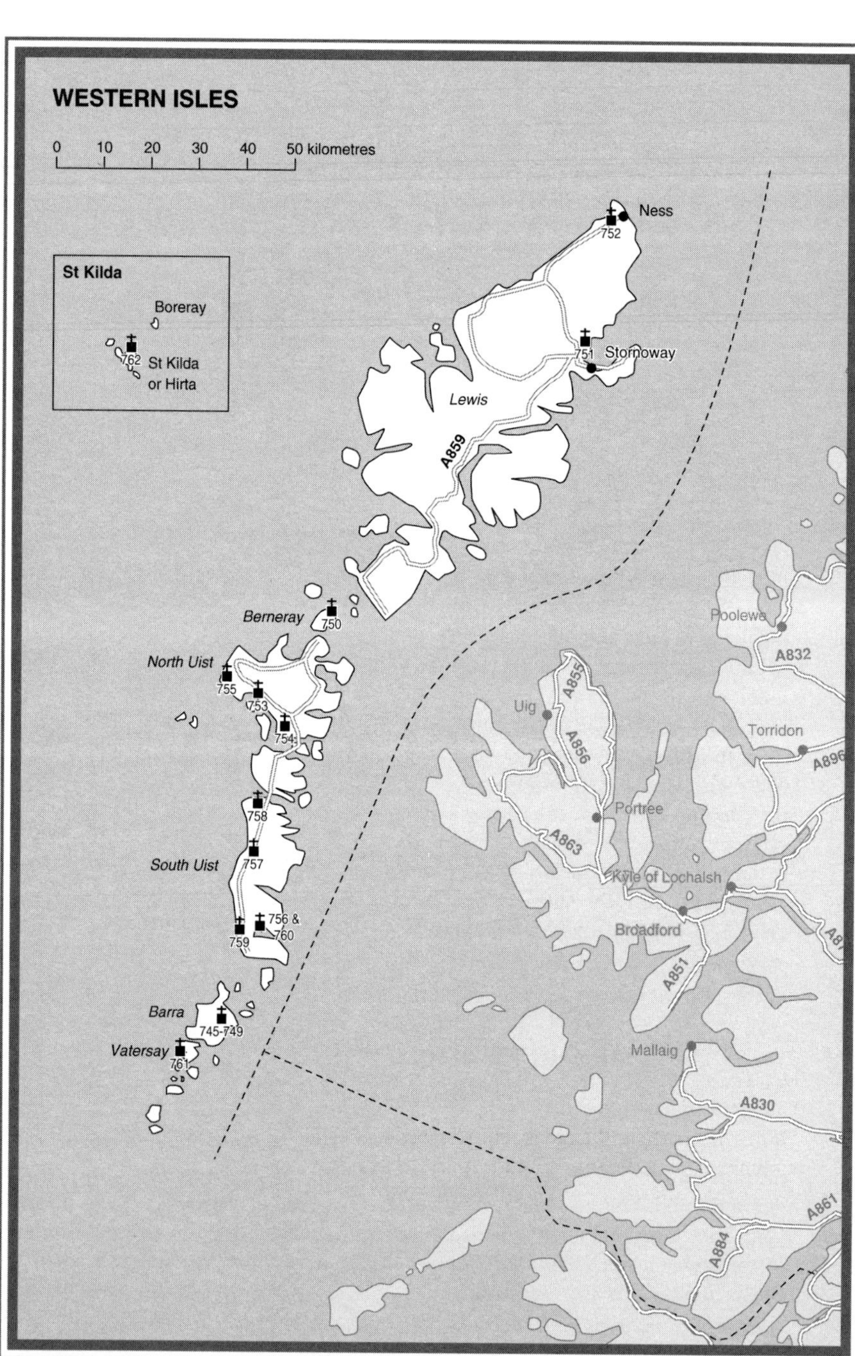

WESTERN ISLES
0 10 20 30 40 50 kilometres
St Kilda
Boreray
762
St Kilda
or Hirta
Ness
752
751
Stornoway
Lewis
A859
Berneray
750
North Uist
755
753
754
758
757
South Uist
759
756 &
760
Barra
745-749
Vatersay
761
Poolewe
A832
Uig
A855
A856
Torridon
A896
Portree
A863
Kyle of Lochalsh
Broadford
A851
Mallaig
A830
A861
A884

WESTERN ISLES

Local Representative: Atisha McGregor Auld, Ruisgarry, Isle of Berneray, by Loutmaddy, North Uist H56 5BQ

OUR LADY STAR OF THE SEA, CASTLEBAY, BARRA

745 OUR LADY STAR OF THE SEA, CASTLEBAY, BARRA

NL 667 983

Castlebay, Barra

Opened Christmas 1886, architect Woulfe Brenan of Oban. Statue by Dupon of Bruges of Our Lady Star of the Sea. Stained glass of crucifixion in Sanctuary, and of Our Lady Star of the Sea installed as War Memorial in early 1950s. Bell in tower; the clock chimes the hour during day and night. Sunday Service: 11am

Open at all times

ROMAN CATHOLIC ♿ (ramp access available) 👂 **B**

746 ST BRENDAN, CRAIGSTON, BARRA

NF 657 018

Craigston, Barra

Dating from 1805, the oldest church in the Isles of Barra. Restored 1858. Two etchings (scraperboard white on black) of St Brendan and St Barr, by Fr Calum MacNeill, retired priest of the diocese. Service: Saturday Vigil 7pm

Open at all times

ROMAN CATHOLIC ♿

747 ST VINCENT DE PAUL, EOLIGARRY, BARRA

NF 703 076

Built in 1964, the church has a tall roof with swept eaves. Small cemetary at Cille Bharra, burial place of MacNeil chieftans.

Sunday: Mass 11am

Open at all times

ROMAN CATHOLIC

ST VINCENT DE PAUL, EOLIGARRY, BARRA

748 NORTH CHAPEL, CILLE BHARRA, EOLIGARRY, BARRA

NF 705 074

Twelfth-century church built on site of 7th century foundation dedicated to St Finbarr of Cork, Eire. Re-roofed with help from the Scottish Development Department. Contains notable 12th-century runic stone (original now in the Royal Museum, Edinburgh) and 16th-century grave-slabs with carvings of animals and foliage. Mass on the feasts of the Celtic saints

Open at all times

ROMAN CATHOLIC

749 ST BARR'S, NORTHBAY, BARRA

NF 707 031

A simple lancet-windowed building by G Woulfe Brenan 1906, with porch and vestry added 1919. Small bellcote on porch. Services daily: Mass 7.30pm; Sunday 11am

Open at all times

ROMAN CATHOLIC

750 BERNERAY CHURCH, ISLE OF BERNERAY

NL 552 801

Opposite War Memorial

Built 1887, architect Thomas Binnie of Glasgow, for the United Free Church. By uniting with the Established Church, now in ruins, it became the Church of Scotland and still flourishes as such. HRH the Prince of Wales worshipped here on a private visit in 1991. Berneray is now accessible by a causeway across Sound of Harris. Sunday Services: 12 noon in English, 6pm in Gaelic

Open by arrangement with Mr MacLean, telephone 01876 540249

CHURCH OF SCOTLAND WC

751 ST MOLUAG'S COMMUNITY CHURCH, TONG, LEWIS

NB 448 366

Opposite Tong School, on B895

In 1999 the building, which had formerly been a village shop and Post Office, was converted into a church, opened and dedicated 2000. Sunday Service: Sung Eucharist 11am (except first Sunday of month from May to September and Easter Day – Service at Eoropaidh)

Open by arrangement with Rector, telephone 1851 820559

SCOTTISH EPISCOPAL (at Service)

752 ST MOLUAG, EOROPAIDH, NESS, LEWIS

NB 519 651

The building probably dates from the 12th century, but the site is believed to have been consecrated in the 6th century and is probably the place where Christianity was first preached to the people of Lewis. The church was restored in 1912 by Norman Forbes of Stornoway, under the guidance of the architect J S Richardson; the altars date from this restoration. The side chapel is connected to the main church only through a squint. The church has no heating, electricity or water; lighting is by candles and oil lamps. Two hundred yards from B8013 (signed Eoropaidh from A857). Services: 11am Easter Day, and on first Sunday of May to September

Open during daylight hours, Easter to last weekend in October. Vehicular access impossible. In wet weather, path to church can be muddy

SCOTTISH EPISCOPAL **A**

753 CARINISH CHURCH, NORTH UIST

NF 820 604

Clachan an Luib, North Uist

The original Church of Scotland for North Uist. The main feature is that the communion pews run down the length of the church so that those taking communion would sit side-on to the pulpit. Sunday Service: 6pm, Gaelic once a month

Open by arrangement, telephone 01875 580219

CHURCH OF SCOTLAND WC **B**

754 CLACHAN CHURCH, NORTH UIST

NF 874 760

Built 1889 for the United Free Church, architect Thomas Bennie of Glasgow. Considerable difficulty was experienced procuring the site from Sir William Powlet Campbell Orde, Bart. After lengthy negotiations he reluctantly gave the present site at an annual rental of £3.9*s*. Sunday Service: 12 noon in English

Open by arrangement, telephone 01875 580219

CHURCH OF SCOTLAND WC

CLACHAN CHURCH, NORTH UIST

755 KILMUIR CHURCH, NORTH UIST

NF 708 706

West side of North Uist, close to Balranald RSPB Reserve

Originally North Uist Parish Church. Gothic T-plan by Alexander Sharp 1892-4. In the south-west inner angle is a two-stage tower, its battlemented parapet enclosing a slated pyramidal spire. Inside, a wealth of pitch-pine. One of the few remaining Gaelic-essential charges; during the morning Gaelic service one can hear, and participate in, the precenting of Gaelic psalms. Sunday Services: 10am in Gaelic, 6pm in English.

Open by arrangement, telephone Mr Macbain 01876 510241

CHURCH OF SCOTLAND WC

KILMUIR CHURCH, NORTH UIST

756 DALIBURGH/DALABROG, SOUTH UIST

NF 754 214

Built originally as South Uist Free Church in 1862-3, now Church of Scotland. Manse completed 1880 and vestry/hall behind low wall added later. All harled. Church rectangular in plan with three bays with round-headed openings and a single window in either gable. Door and apex belfry to south gable. Pulpit with panelled front. Communion table and War Memorial based on design of that at Howmore by Archibald Scott. Sunday Service: 11.00am

Open at all times

CHURCH OF SCOTLAND WC B

757 HOWMORE CHURCH, SOUTH UIST

NF 758 364

Simple austere building by John McDearmid 1858, set in open land overlooking the Atlantic. Acts as landmark for west coast fishermen. One of few churches in Scotland with central Communion table. Nearby are remains of 13th-century church. Sunday Service: 12.30pm

Open at all times

CHURCH OF SCOTLAND WC B

HOWMORE CHURCH, SOUTH UIST

758 IOCHDAR CHURCH, EOCHAR, SOUTH UIST

Built 1889 as a Mission House by David MacIntosh, a small, compact church with traditional pews and central pulpit. The church particularly lends itself to be a place for quiet prayer and meditation. Sunday Service: 6pm first Sunday of the month

Open by arrangement, telephone Mrs Stephenson 01870 610401

CHURCH OF SCOTLAND

759 OUR LADY OF SORROWS, SOUTH UIST

NP758 165

Garrynamonie

Built 1965, Architect Richard J McCarson, with a monopitch roof. Above Blessed Sacrement altar is a ceramic on the theme of the Sacred Heart by David Harding of Edinburgh who was also responsibile for original mural of Our Lady of Sorrows at the entrance. This was replaced in 1994 by the present mural reflecting the sorrows of the contemporary world by Michael Gilfeddar, commissioned by Canon Galbraith. Sunday Service: 10am

Open throughout each day

ROMAN CATHOLIC ♿ WC

760 ST PETER'S, SOUTH UIST

NF 745 211

Daliburgh

Big harled church of 1868 with a birdcage bellcote on the south gable and a tall concrete hoop bellcote on the 1960s porch. North sanctuary added 1907. Services: Saturday Vigil 8pm; Sunday 11.30am

Open throughout each day

ROMAN CATHOLIC WC **C**

761 OUR LADY OF THE WAVES & ST JOHN, VATERSAY

NL 646 961

Uidh, Vatersay

Small functional church for celebration of Mass and other church services. reached by causeway from Barra. Sunday Service: 3.30pm

Open at all times

ROMAN CATHOLIC WC

762 CHRIST CHURCH, ST KILDA

NF 100 994

Village Bay, St Kilda

The stimulus for the kirk, designed by Robert Stevenson, came from the Rev Dr John Macdonald who visited St Kilda several times in the early 19th century. The church fell into disrepair after evacuation in 1930. Renovated over a period of 20 years since coming into the care of the National Trust for Scotland in 1957. Services by arrangement. St Kilda is Scotland's first World Heritage Site.

Open by arrangement, contact The National Trust for Scotland, telephone 01631 570000

INTER-DENOMINATIONAL

CHURCHES WITH A HISTORIC SCOTTISH CONNECTION

763 THE CHURCH OF SCOTLAND IN CARLISLE

NY 3956

Chapel Street, Carlisle

Built 1834, altered 1979 and extended 1994. A city centre church, the interior is arranged over two floors with halls and kitchen on the ground floor and sanctuary on the first floor. The extension provides three floors housing ecumenical One World Centre, coffee lounge and Fair Trade shop. Two minutes from main 'Lanes' shopping area and civic centre; five minutes from the cathedral, castle and parks; ten minutes from Tullie House Museum. Two minutes from bus station in Lowther Street. Sunday Service: 11am; also 6.30pm first Sunday (except January, July and August)

Open Monday to Friday 10am-2pm.

Coffee lounge and Fair Trade shop, open Monday to Friday 10am-2pm

CHURCH OF SCOTLAND **A**

764 CROWN COURT, COVENT GARDEN, LONDON

Adjacent to Fortune Theatre, Russell Street

Historic London church in the heart of Theatreland. The 'Kirk of the Crown of Scotland' dates from 1909, replacing an earlier church of 1711. Longest established Presbyterian Church in England. Royal arms of George I above communion table. Baptismal font of Iona marble. Superb stained glass. Sunday Services: 11.15 and 6.30pm; Thursdays 1.10-1.30pm

Church website: www.crowncourtchurch.org.uk

Open July and August, 11.30-2.30pm Tuesday, Wednesday and Thursday. At other times, telephone the Church Secretary on 020 7836 5643

CHURCH OF SCOTLAND

765 ST COLUMBA'S, LONDON

Pont Street, London

The present building, re-dedicated in 1955, replaced the original building destroyed by incendiary bombs in 1941. The architect was Sir Edward Maufe. Fine rose window, 'The Creative Spirit of God' by Moira Forsyth. The London Scottish Chapel contains the Rolls of Honour of the London Scottish Regiment. The arms of the Scottish Counties, painted in heraldic colours, are carved at the base of the tall windows all round the church. Services: Sundays 11am and 6.30pm; Wednesdays 1pm

Church website: www.stcolumbas.org.uk

Open 9.30am-5pm, Monday to Friday

CHURCH OF SCOTLAND **Grade II**

SCOTLAND'S CHURCHES SCHEME

ENCOURAGES CHURCHES TO:

- Open their doors with a welcoming presence
- Tell the story of the building, its purpose and the faith which inspired it
- Care for visitors in a sensitive and enriching way
- Work together with others to make the Church the focus of its community

SUPPORTS CHURCHES WITH:

- The publication of its comprehensive guidebook – *Churches to Visit in Scotland*
- Free advice on all aspects of visitor welcome, publicity, interpretation and exhibitions
- A network of local representatives in direct contact with headquarters
- Effective national publicity

SCOTLAND'S CHURCHES SCHEME GRATEFULLY ACKNOWLEDGES SUPPORT FROM:

BANK OF SCOTLAND
THE CRUDEN FOUNDATION
THE EAST-WEST TRUST
THE INCHCAPE FOUNDATION
THE INCHES CARR TRUST
THE MANIFOLD TRUST
THE OPEN CHURCHES TRUST
THE P F CHARITABLE TRUST
THE ROBERTSON TRUST
THE ROYAL BANK OF SCOTLAND
THE RUSSELL TRUST
SCOTTISH & NEWCASTLE PLC
THE WEBSTER CHARITABLE TRUST
AND SEVERAL ANONYMOUS PRIVATE BENEFACTORS

DONATIONS

Please consider making a donation to Scotland's Churches Scheme, either in an individual or corporate capacity, so that this guide may become an indispensable part of the Scottish calendar, and the permanent financial future of the Scheme is secured.

Options, including Gift Aid which generates additional monies through the reclaim of tax already paid by donors, are:

[a] Gift Aid

[b] Gifts through the Charities Aid Foundation

[c] Give As You Earn schemes operated by employers, and

[d] Bequests in a Will, which are exempt from Inheritance Tax

Information and forms for [a] and [b] may be obtained from:

Scotland's Churches Scheme
Dunedin, Holehouse Road
Eaglesham
Glasgow G76 0JF

Telephone: 01355 302416
Fax: 01355 303181
E-mail: fraser@dunedin67.freeserve.co.uk
Website: http://churchnet.ucsm.ac.uk/scotchurch/

Donation Form

I enclose £ as a donation to Scotland's Churches Scheme

Name

Address

Postcode

CHURCHES TO VISIT IN SCOTLAND

To:
The Director, Scotland's Churches Scheme,
Dunedin, Holehouse Road, Eaglesham, Glasgow
Telephone: 01355 302416
Fax: 01355 303181 *E-mail:* fraser@dunedin67.freeserve.co.uk
Website: http://churchnet.ucsm.ac.uk/scotchurch/

Please send me details and an application form for entry in the next Guidebook

Name

Address

Postcode

Name of Church

Address of Church

Postcode

SCOTLAND'S GARDENS SCHEME

2001 has been a difficult year for the Scheme due to the foot and mouth epidemic and sadly many of our beautiful gardens had to cancel for this reason. But when such unexpected disasters happen, we have to then find other ways to raise funds for our beneficiaries. Several large plant sales have taken place and lectures by well known horticulturists have attracted good audiences. We have also tried to encourage gardens and churches which were close together to open on the same day, and although this has had a slow start we are hoping many more will join in next year. Why not try having a plant display or sale in your area and then contact us at the number below so that we can help to find a garden to join in. If you can arrange a date before the end of November we will print the details in our annual handbook each year.

Our first gardens always open in February, weather permitting, and generally feature a magnificent display of snowdrops. Gardens then continue to open throughout Scotland until October, so you need to buy your copy of *Gardens of Scotland* early to find out where you can go and plan your visit. Remember that every time you go to one of our gardens on the opening day, you are supporting several different charities and also one or more recommended by the garden owner. The name of this charity is shown under the garden details in the handbook.

Watch your local press for details of your local openings, and remember that the owners will be on hand to offer advice as to what you can grow in your own garden and suggest which plants you should buy.

Ring us now on the number below to order your copy of *Gardens of Scotland* which costs £4 or £5 to include postage. We welcome your support and look forward to meeting you in one of our lovely gardens.

Scotland's Gardens Scheme
22 Rutland Square
Edinburgh EH1 2BB

Telephone: 0131 229 1870
Fax: 0131 229 0443

Email: sgsoffice@aol.com
website: www.ngs.org.uk

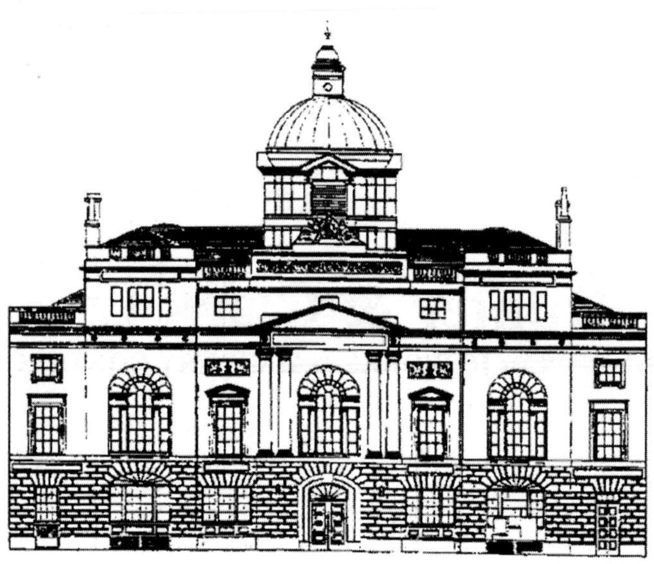

SPONSOR A WINDOW OPPORTUNITY

The refurbishment of the Trades Hall is now about to enter its final phase.

The Heritage Lottery Fund has awarded a grant of £632,000 towards that and further support is indicated from Glasgow City Council, Historic Scotland and Scottish Enterprise Glasgow from whom it is confidently anticipated we will receive approximately £167,000.

The Trust already has £240,000 paid or pledged, making a total Refurbishment Fund of £1,039,000 toward the estimated costs of £1,200,000.

An important and highly visible part of the work will be the reinstatement of the beautiful fan windows on the first floor of the facade.

This is 'A WINDOW OF OPPORTUNITY'

to be a visible part of this triumphant restoration. Over 30 principal panes of glass are involved in the construction of each window – each representing a potential sponsor. A brass plaque in the shape of the windows will be commissioned with the name of every major sponsor of a complete window. Each window will cost £25,000. An individual pane of glass will cost £200 and the donor's name listed in the engraving and donations book.

GET YOUR NAME IN THE FRAME NOW !!

If you are interested in sponsoring a pane or a whole window please get in touch with Mr William N Stevenson or Mrs Carole Nelson at the Trust's Office, 310 St Vincent Street, Glasgow G2 5QR. Tel/Fax 0141 248 5566

ST COLUMBA'S CHURCH OF SCOTLAND, PONT STREET, LONDON

INDEX OF ARTISTS

Number refers to church entry, not page

INDEX OF CHURCHES

Number refers to church entry, not page